Spinning the Semantic Web

Spinning the Semantic Web

Bringing the World Wide Web to Its Full Potential

Edited by Dieter Fensel, James Hendler, Henry Lieberman, and
Wolfgang Wahlster

The MIT Press
Cambridge, Massachusetts
London, England

First MIT Press paperback edition, 2005

© 2003 Massachusetts Institute of Technology

This book was set in Stone Sans and Stone Serif on 3B2 by Asco Typesetters, Hong Kong. Printed and bound in the United States of America.

Library of Congress Cataloging-in-Publication Data

Spinning the semantic web : bringing the World Wide Web to its full potential / edited by Dieter Fensel . . . [et al.].
     p.   cm.
  Includes bibliographical references and index.
  ISBN 0-262-06232-1 (hc. : alk. paper), 0-262-56212-X (pb.)
  1. World Wide Web. I. Fensel, Dieter.
  TK5105.888 .S693   2003
  004.67'8—dc21   2002016503

  10 9 8 7 6 5 4 3 2

Contents

3   DAML-ONT: An Ontology Language for the Semantic Web   65

Deborah L. McGuinness, Richard Fikes, Lynn Andrea Stein, and
James Hendler

4   Ontologies and Schema Languages on the Web   95

Michel Klein, Jeen Broekstra, Dieter Fensel, Frank van Harmelen, and
Ian Horrocks

5   UPML: The Language and Tool Support for Making the Semantic Web Alive   141

Borys Omelayenko, Monica Crubézy, Dieter Fensel, Richard Benjamins,
Bob Wielinga, Enrico Motta, Mark Musen, and Ying Ding

6   **Ontologies Come of Age**   *171*

Deborah L. McGuinness

II   **Knowledge Support**

7   **Sesame: An Architecture for Storing and Querying RDF Data and Schema Information**   *197*

Jeen Broekstra, Arjohn Kampman, and Frank van Harmelen

8   **Enabling Task-Centered Knowledge Support through Semantic Markup**   *223*

Rob Jasper and Mike Uschold

III   Dynamic Aspect

12   Semantic Gadgets: Ubiquitous Computing Meets the Semantic Web   363

Ora Lassila and Mark Adler

13   Static and Dynamic Semantics of the Web   377

Christopher Fry, Mike Plusch, and Henry Lieberman

14   Semantic Annotation for Web Content Adaptation   403

Masahiro Hori

15   Task-Achieving Agents on the World Wide Web   431

Austin Tate, Jeff Dalton, John Levine, and Alex Nixon

Foreword

Tim Berners-Lee

The Semantic Web is the realization of an aspect of the Web that was part of the original hopes and dreams of 1989, but whose development has, until now, taken a back seat to the Web of multimedia human-readable material. Even though at the first WWW conference, in 1994, I ended my talk with a few slides about the Semantic Web, the steps along the way were slow for many years.

However, now at the end of 2002 things are different. Different layers of the diagram (on next page) are in different states but progressing rapidly.

Progress is measured on a scale that starts with the conception of an idea, which works through its acceptance as a common technology and becomes an interoperable standard, and ends with a global market based on it.

The Semantic Web is specifically a web of machine-readable information whose meaning is well-defined by standards: it absolutely needs the interoperable infrastructure that only global standard protocols can provide.

The basic layer of data representation is standardized as the Resource Description Framework (RDF), which became a W3C Recommendation in 1999. RDF is based on existing standards of XML (another W3C Recommendation, dating back to 1998), URIs (which date back to the invention of the Web, in 1989) and Unicode. Built on top of RDF, the Ontology layer—in the form of the OWL language—is being developed by the W3C's Web Ontology Working Group, part of the W3C's Semantic Web Activity.

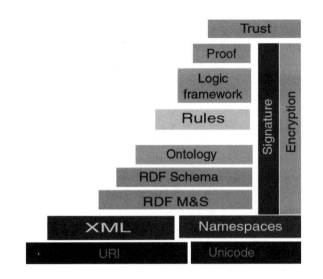

Layers above RDF, such as rules languages and logic interchange, are the subject of many prototype systems that will soon make their way into the standards process; in the experimental phase the questions are fundamental ones, about what is possible, while in the standards phase, they become more arbitrary questions, such as what name to use for a new tag.

So this scene is changing very quickly, and although this book provides a background, be aware that checking the W3C Web site ⟨http://www.w3.org/⟩ and the Semantic Web Activity home page ⟨http://www.w3.org/2001/sw/⟩ is essential for an understanding of the state of new developments.

This book was prepared from talks given at a conference in 1999. The rest of this foreword was written as an article in 1997. Rather than attempt to update it, I leave it as it stands, advising the reader that things change fast on the Internet, and one should take the following article in context of 1997.

December 2002

1   *The Original Dream*

The Web was designed to be a universal space of information, so when you make a bookmark or a hypertext link, you should be able to make that link to absolutely any piece of information that can be accessed using networks. This universality is essential to the Web: it loses its power if there are certain types of things to which you can't link.

There are a lot of sides to that universality. You should be able to make links to a hastily jotted crazy idea and to link to a beautifully produced work of art. You should be able to link to a very personal page and to something available to the whole planet. There will be information on the Web that has a clearly defined meaning and can be analyzed and traced by computer programs; there will be information, such as poetry and art, that requires the full human intellect for an understanding that will always be subjective.

And what was the purpose of all this universality? The first goal was to enable people to work together better. Although the use of the Web across all scales is essential to the development of the Web, the original driving force of the Web was collaboration at home and at work. The idea was that by building a hypertext Web, a group of whatever size would force itself to use a common vocabulary, to overcome its misunderstandings, and at any time to have a running model—in the Web—of its plans and reasons.

For me, the forerunner to the Web was a program called Enquire, which I made for my own purposes. I wrote it in 1980, when I was working at the European Particle Physics Lab (CERN), to keep track of the complex web of relationships among people, programs, machines, and ideas. In 1989, when I proposed the Web, it was as an extension of that personal tool to a common information space.

When we make decisions in meetings, how often are the reasons for those decisions (which we have so carefully elaborated in the meeting) then just typed up, filed as minutes, and essentially lost? How often do we pay for this, in time spent passing on half understandings verbally, duplicating effort through ignorance, and reversing good decisions from misunderstanding? How much lack of cooperation can be traced to an inability to understand where another party is "coming from"? The Web was designed as an instrument to prevent misunderstandings.

For the Web to work, it has not only to be easy to browse, but also to make it easy to express oneself. In a world of people and information, the people and information should be in some kind of equilibrium. Anything in the

Web can be quickly accessed, and any information someone determines is missing from the Web can be quickly added. The Web should be a medium for communication between people: communication through shared knowledge. For the Web to work, the computers, networks, operating systems, and commands have to become invisible, leaving us with an intuitive interface as directly as possible with the information.

2   Re-enter Machines

There was a second goal for the Web, which was dependent on the first: if one could imagine a project (company, whatever) that used the Web in its work, then there would be a map, in cyberspace, of all the dependencies and relationships that defined how the project was going. This raises the exciting possibility of letting programs run over this material and help us analyze and manage what we are doing. The computer renders the scene visibly as a software agent, doing anything it can to help us deal with the bulk of data, to take over the tedium of anything that can be reduced to a rational process, and to manage the scale of our human systems.

3   Where Are We Now?

The Web you see as a glorified television channel today is just one part of the original plan. Although the Web was driven initially by the group work need, it is not surprising that the most rapid Web growth has been outside of the work environment, in public information. Web publishing, in which a few write and many read, has profited most from the snowball effect of exponentially rising numbers of readers and writers. Now, with the invention of the concept of "intranets," Web use is returning to organizations and to the original goal of facilitating workplace collaboration. (In fact, it never left. There have always been, since 1991, many internal servers, but as they were generally invisible from outside the companies' firewalls, they didn't get much press.) The intuitive editing interfaces that would make authoring a natural part of daily life, however, are still maturing. In 1991 I thought that in 12 months we would have generally available intuitive hypertext editors. (I am still saying the same thing today!)

It is not just the lack of simple editors that has hindered use of the Web as a collaborative medium. For a group of people to use the Web in practice, they need reliable access control, so that they know their ideas will be seen only by those they trust. They also need access control and archival tools that, like browsing, don't require one to get into the details of computer operating systems.

There is also a limit to what we can do by ourselves with information without the help of machines. A familiar complaint of newcomers to the Web who have not learned to follow only links from reliable sources is about the mass of junk available on the Web. Search engines flounder amid the mass of undifferentiated documents accessible via the Web that cover a vast range in terms of quality, timeliness, and relevance. We need information about information—"metadata"—to help us organize it.

As it turns out, many of these long-term needs will, we hope, be met by technology that for one reason or another is being developed by the technical community, and agreed upon by groups such as the World Wide Web Consortium (W3C), in response to various medium-term demands.

4   *The World Wide Web Consortium*

The World Wide Web Consortium (W3C) exists as a place for those companies for which the Web is essential to meet and agree on the common standards that will allow everyone to go forward. The consortium currently has over 230 member organizations.

Whether developing software, hardware, networks, or information for sale or using the Web as a crucial part of their business lives, these companies are driven by emerging areas such as Web publishing, intranet use, electronic commerce, and Web-based education and training. From these fields medium-term needs arise and, where appropriate, the consortium starts an activity to help the members reach a consensus on computer protocols for the area involved. Protocols, in this context, are the rules that allow computers to talk together about a given topic. When the computer industry agrees on protocols for a particular area of computing, then a new standard can spread across the world, and new programs developed incorporating the protocol can all work together as they all speak the same language. This is key to the development of the Web.

5   Where Is the Web Going Next?

5.1   Avoiding the World Wide Wait

You've heard about the chronically lengthening response time on the Web; you may have even experienced it. But can anything be done about it?

One reason for the slow response you may get from a dial-up Internet account simply follows from the "all you can eat" pricing policy most Internet service providers have. The only thing that keeps the number of Internet users down in the face of such pricing policies is unacceptable response times, so if we were to suddenly make the Web faster, there would almost immediately be more users until it again reached a point of congestion and was slow again. I've seen it happen: when an overloaded server was speeded up by a factor of five, it quickly rose again to 100% utilization as the number of users increased by a factor of five.

Eventually, there will be differential pricing for different levels of quality in Internet access. But even in the face of today's unlimited access pricing, there are some things we can do to make better utilization of the bandwidth we have, such as using compression and enabling many overlapping asynchronous requests. The ability exists for guessing what a user may want next, so that the user does not have to request it and then wait for it. Taken to one extreme, this becomes subscription-based distribution, which works like e-mail or newsgroups.

One crazy aspect of the current Web use setup is that the user who wishes to publish something has to decide whether to use mailing lists, newsgroups, or the Web. The best choice in a particular case depends on the anticipated demand and likely readership pattern. A mistake can be costly. It is not always easy for a person to anticipate the demand for a particular Web page. For example, the pictures taken on a mountaintop of the Schoemaker-Levy comet hitting Jupiter and the decision Judge Hiller Zobel put onto the Web—both of these generated so much demand that the servers on which they had been placed were swamped, and in fact, both would have been better delivered as messages via newsgroups. Publishing on the Web would be more efficient if the "system"—the collaborating servers and clients together—could adapt to differing demands and use preemptive or reactive retrieval as necessary.

5.2   Data about Data: Metadata

It is clear that there should be a common format for expressing information about information (called metadata) for a dozen or so fields that need it, including privacy information, endorsement labels, library catalogs, tools for structuring and organizing Web data, distribution terms, and annotation. The Consortium's Resource Description Framework (RDF) is designed to allow data from all these fields to be written in the same form and therefore carried together and mixed.

That by itself will be quite exciting, once implemented. Proxy caches, which make the Web more efficient, will be able to check that they are really acting in accordance with the publisher's wishes in respect to redistributing material. Browsers will be able to get an assurance, before imparting personal information in a Web form, on how that information will be used. Users will be able, if the technology is matched by suitable tools, to endorse Web pages that they perceive to be of value. Search engines will be able to take such endorsements into account and give results that are perceived to be of much higher quality than those currently available. So a common format for information about information will make the Web a whole lot better.

5.3   The Web of Trust

In cases in which a high level of trust is needed for metadata, digitally signed metadata will allow the Web to include a "Web of trust." The Web of trust will be a set of documents on the Web that are digitally signed with certain keys and contain statements about those keys and about other documents. Like the Web itself, the Web of trust will not need to have a specific structure, such as a tree or a matrix. Statements of trust can be added in such a way as to reflect actual trust exactly. People learn to trust through experience and though recommendation. We change our minds about who we trust and for what purposes. The Web of trust must allow us to express this.

Hypertext is suitable for a global information system because it has the proper flexibility needed in the Web of trust: the power to represent any structure of the real world or a created, imagined one. Systems that force users to express information in trees or matrices are fine so long as they are used for describing trees or matrices. The moment users try to employ one to hold information that does not fit the mold, they end up twisting the information to fit and so misrepresenting the situation. Similarly, the W3C's role in creating the Web of trust will be to help the community have a common language for expressing trust. The W3C will not seek a central or controlling role in the content of the Web.

5.4 "Oh, Yeah?"

So, signed metadata is the next step in the development of the semantic Web. When we have this, we will be able to ask the computer not just for information, but why we should believe it. Imagine an "Oh, yeah?" button on your browser. There you are looking at a fantastic deal that can be yours just for the entry of a credit card number and the click of a button. "Oh, yeah?" you think. You press the "Oh, yeah?" button, asking your browser whether you should believe it. It, in turn, can challenge the server to provide some credentials: perhaps, a signature for the document or a list of signed documents that expresses what that encription key is good for. Your browser rummages through those documents with the server, looking for a way to convince you that the page is trustworthy for a purchase. Maybe it comes up with an endorsement from a magazine, which in turn has been endorsed by one of your friends. Maybe it finds an endorsement by the seller's bank, which in turn has an endorsement from your bank. On the other hand, maybe it won't find any reason at all for you to actually believe what you are reading.

5.5 Data about Things

All the information mentioned above is information about information. Perhaps the most important aspect of it is that it is machine-understandable data and that it may introduce a new phase of the Web in which much more data in general can be handled by computer programs in a meaningful way. The ideas presented above are just as relevant to information about the real world: about cars and people and stocks and shares and flights and food and rivers.

The Enquire program I wrote assumed that every Web page was about something. When the user created a new page, it made her say what sort of thing it was: a person, a piece of machinery, a group, a program, a concept, etc. Not only that, when the user created a link between two nodes, it would prompt her to fill in the relationship between the two things or people the nodes represented. For example, the relationships were defined as "A is part of B" or "A made B." The idea was that if Enquire were to be used heavily, it could then automatically trace the dependencies within an organization.

Unfortunately these dependencies were lost as the Web grew. Although in the original specifications, the Web had relationship types, it has evolved into a Web that does not make assertions about things or people. Can we still build a Web of well-defined information?

My initial attempts to suggest this fell on stony ground, and not surprisingly. Hypertext Markup Language (HTML) is a language for communicating a document for human consumption. The Standard Generalized Markup Language (SGML) (and now the Extensible Markup Language, or XML) gives structure, but not semantics. Neither the application, nor the language, called for it.

The apparatus we are constructing in RDF for describing the properties of documents has all the qualities we need to describe metadata and can be used equally well for describing anything else.

5.6   A Crying Need for RDF

Is there a real need for this metadata, and is there a market in the medium term that will lead companies to develop the metadata in this direction? In the medium term, we see the drivers of such development already: Web publishing, education and training, electronic commerce, and intranets.

I have mentioned the vicious circle that caused the Web to take off initially. The increasing amount of information on the Web was an incentive for people to get browsers, and the increasing number of browsers created more incentive for people to put up more Web sites. This process had to start somewhere, and it was bootstrapped by making "virtual hypertext" servers. These servers typically had access to large databases, such as telephone books, library catalogs, and existing documentation management systems. They had simple programs that would generate Web pages "on the fly" corresponding to various views and queries on the server database. This technique served as a very powerful bootstrap, as there is now a healthy market for tools to allow one to map one's data from their existing database form onto the Web.

Curiously, there is now so much data available on Web pages that there is a market for tools that "reverse engineer" that process. These are tools that read pages, and with a bit of human advice, re-create the original record from the database. Even though it takes human effort to analyze the way different Web sites are offering their data, it is worth it, as having a common, well-defined representation language for all the data, so that you can program on top of it, is a powerful tool. So the need for a well-defined interface to Web data in the short term is undeniable.

The intention is that when a program goes out to a server looking for data, say a database record, the data should be available in RDF, with the rows and columns all labeled in some well-defined way. That way it may be possible to look up the equivalence between field names at one Web site and at another and so merge information intelligently from many sources. This demonstrates a clear need for metadata, as evidenced, for example, by looking at the trouble libraries have had with the number of very similar, but slightly different, ways of making up a catalog card for the same book.

5.7 Interactive Creativity

I want the Web to be much more creative than it is at the moment. I have even had to coin a new word to describe this new level of creativity: "intercreativity," which means building things together on the Web. I have found that people think that the Web already is "interactive," because users get to click with a mouse and fill in forms! I have mentioned that more intuitive interfaces will be needed to support this intercreativity, but I don't think they will be sufficient without better security.

It would be wrong to assume that digital signature will be important only for electronic commerce, as if security were important only where money is concerned. One of my key themes is the importance of the Web's being used on all levels from the personal, through groups of all sizes, to the global population.

Those working in a group do things they would not do outside the group. They share half-baked ideas, reveal sensitive information. They use a vernacular that will be understood; they can cut corners in language and formality. Workers in groups do these things because they trust the people in the group and that outsiders won't suddenly have access to the group. To date, on the Web, it has been difficult to manage such groups or to allow them to control access to information in an intuitive way.

5.8 Letting Go

So where will this universal understanding get us? The Web is filled with documents, each of which has pointers to help a computer understand it and relate it to terms it knows. Software agents acting on our behalf can reason about these data. They can ask for and validate proofs of the credibility of the data. They can negotiate as to who will have what access to what and ensure that our personal wishes concerning privacy level will be met.

The world is a world of human beings, as it was before, but the power of our actions is again increased by the Web. It already increases the power of our writings, making them accessible to huge numbers of people and allowing us to draw on any part of the global information base by a simple hypertext link. Now we can imagine the world of people with active machines forming part of the infrastructure. We have only to express a request for bids, or make a bid, and machines will turn a small profit matching the two. Search engines, from looking for pages containing interesting words, will start indexes of assertions that might be useful for answering questions or finding justifications.

I think this will take a long time. I say this deliberately, because in the past I have underestimated how long something would take to become available (e.g., good editors in 12 months).

Now we will have to find how best to integrate our warm, fuzzy, right-brained selves into this clearly defined left-brained world. It is easy to know whom we trust, but it might be difficult to explain that to a computer. After seeding the semantic Web with specific applications, we must be sure to generalize it cleanly, leaving it uncluttered and simple, so that the next generation can learn the Web's logical concepts along with the alphabet.

If we can make of the Web something decentralized and of great simplicity, we must be prepared to be astonished at whatever might grow out of that new medium.

5.9 *It's Up to Us*

One thing is certain. The Web will have a profound effect on the markets and the cultures around the world: intelligent agents will either stabilize or destabilize markets; the demise of distance will either homogenize or polarize cultures; the ability to access the Web will be either a great divider or a great equalizer; the path will lead either to jealousy and hatred or to peace and understanding.

The technology we are creating may influence some of these choices, but mostly it will leave them to us. It may expose the questions in a starker form than before and force us to state clearly where we stand.

We are forming cells within a global brain, and we are excited that we might start to think collectively. What becomes of us still hangs crucially on how we think individually.

Acknowledgments

This foreword is based on a talk presented at the W3C meeting, London, December 3, 1997.

1 *Introduction*

Dieter Fensel, Jim Hendler, Henry Lieberman, and Wolfgang Wahlster

The World Wide Web (WWW) has drastically changed the availability of electronically accessible information. Currently there are around three billion static documents in the WWW that are used by more than 200 million users internationally, and this number is growing astronomically. In 1990, the WWW began with a small number of documents as an in-house solution for around a thousand users at CERN. By 2002, W3C (http://www.w3c.org) expects around a billion Web users and an even higher number of available documents. This success and exponential growth makes it increasingly difficult, however, to find, to access, to present, and to maintain information of use to a wide variety of users. Currently, pages on the Web must use representation means rooted in format languages such as HTML or SGML and employ protocols that allow browsers to present information to human readers. The information content, however, is mainly presented via natural language. Thus, there is a wide gap between the information available for tools to use in creating and maintaining Web pages and the information kept in human readable form on those pages, a gap that causes serious problems in accessing and processing the available information:

▪ *Searching for information.* Already, finding the right piece of information on the Web is often a nightmare. In searching the Web for specific information, one gets lost in huge amounts of irrelevant material and may often miss the relevant matter. Searches are imprecise, often returning pointers to many thousands of pages (and this situation worsens as the Web grows). In addition, a user must read through the retrieved documents to extract the desired information—so even once a truly relevant Web page is found, the search may be difficult or the information obscured. Thus, the same piece of knowledge must often be presented in different contexts on the same Web page and adapted to different users' needs and queries. However, the Web lacks automated translation tools to allow this information to be transformed automatically among different representation formats and contexts.

- *Presenting information.* A related problem is that the maintenance of Web sources has become very difficult. Keeping redundant information consistent and keeping information correct is hardly supported by current Web tools, and thus the burden on a Webmaster to maintain consistency is often overwhelming. This leads to a plethora of sites with inconsistent and/or contradictory information.

- *Electronic commerce.* Automatization of electronic commerce is seriously hampered by the way information is currently presented. Shopping agents use wrappers and heuristics to extract product information from weakly structured textual information. However, the development and maintenance costs involved are high and the services provided are limited. Business-to-business marketplaces offer new possibilities for electronic commerce; however, they are hampered by the large and increasing mapping costs required to integrate heterogeneous product descriptions.

There is an emerging awareness that providing solutions to these problems requires that there be a machine-understandable semantics for some or all of the information presented in the WWW. Achieving such a *Semantic Web* (Berners-Lee 1999) requires

- developing languages for expressing machine-understandable meta-information for documents and developing terminologies (i.e., namespaces or ontologies) using these languages and making them available on the Web.

- developing tools and new architectures that use such languages and terminologies to provide support in finding, accessing, presenting, and maintaining information sources.

▪ realizing applications that provide a new level of service to the human users of the semantic Web.

Developing such languages, ontologies, and tools is a wide-ranging problem that touches on the research areas of a broad variety of research communities. Therefore the development of this book brought together colleagues from these different research communities, including those in the areas of databases, intelligent information integration, knowledge representation, knowledge engineering, information agents, knowledge management, information retrieval, natural-language processing, metadata, and Web standards, as well as others. The book is based on a seminar held in Dagstuhl, Germany, in March 2000. The contents of the book are organized as follows. First, a number of arising Web standards are discussed that should improve the representation of machine-processible semantics of information. Second, ontologies are introduced for representation of semantics (in the sense of formal and real-world semantics) in these formalisms. Third, as these semantic annotations allow automatization in information access and task achievement, we discuss intelligent information access based on them. Finally, a number of applications of these new techniques are presented.

The purpose of this chapter is to provide an overall motivation for the book's subject. First, in section 1.1, we discuss in further depth the need for a Semantic Web, mainly as motivated by the shortcomings of the current state of the WWW. We show which kind of new services the Semantic Web will enable, and in section 1.2 we explain how they can be developed.

1.1   Why Is There a Need for the Semantic Web and What Will It Provide?

The Web has brought exciting new possibilities for information access and electronic commerce. It is the Web's simplicity that has fueled its quick uptake and exponential growth, but this same simplicity also seriously hampers its further growth. Here we discuss these bottlenecks with respect to knowledge management and electronic commerce (see Fensel 2001 for more further details).

1.1.1   Knowledge Management

Knowledge management is concerned with acquiring, maintaining, and accessing the knowledge of an organization. It aims to exploit an organization's intellectual assets for greater productivity, new value, and increased competitiveness. Because of globalization and the universal availability of the Internet, many organizations are increasingly geographically dispersed and organized around virtual teams. With the large number of documents made available online by organizations, several document management systems have entered the market. However, these systems have severe weaknesses:

- *Searching information.* Existing keyword-based search retrieves irrelevant information that uses the keyword in a context other than the one in which the searcher is interested or may miss relevant information that employs words other than the keyword in discussing the desired content.

- *Extracting information.* Human browsing and reading is currently required to extract relevant information from information sources, as automatic agents lack the commonsense knowledge required to extract such information from textual representations and fail to integrate information spread over different sources.

- *Maintenance.* Maintaining weakly structured text sources is a difficult and time-consuming activity when such sources become large. Keeping such collections consistent, correct, and up to date requires a mechanized representation of semantics and constraints that help to detect anomalies.

- *Automatic document generation.* Adaptive Web sites that enable a dynamic reconfiguration of information according to user profiles or other relevant aspects would be very useful. The generation of semistructured information presentations from semistructured data would require a machine-accessible representation of the semantics of these information sources, and such a representation currently does not exist.

Semantic Web technology will enable structural and semantic definitions of documents providing completely new possibilities: intelligent search instead of keyword matching, query answering instead of information retrieval, document exchange among departments via ontology mappings, and definition of customized views on documents.

1.1.2 Web Commerce

Electronic commerce (B2C) is an important and growing business area for two reasons. First, it is extending existing business models. It reduces costs and extends existing distribution channels and may even introduce new distribution possibilities. One example of such a business field extension is online stores. Second, it enables completely new business models or gives them a much greater importance than they had before. What has up to now been a peripheral aspect of a business field may suddenly receive its own important revenue flow. Examples of new business fields generated by electronic commerce are shopping agents, online marketplaces, and auction houses, which make comparison shopping or meditation of shopping processes into a business with its own significant revenue flow. The advantages of online stores and the success many have experienced has led to a large increase in the number of such shopping pages. The task for the new Web customer is now to find a shop that sells the product he is looking for, get it in the desired quality and quantity and at the desired time, and pay as little as possible for it. Achieving these goals via browsing requires significant time and even with a sizeable time investment, a customer will cover only a small share of the actual Web offerings. Very early on in B2C development, shopbots were developed that visit several stores, extract product information, and present to the customer an instant market overview. Their functionality is provided via wrappers written for each online store. Such wrappers use a keyword search, together with assumptions on regularities in the presentation format of stores' Web sites and text extraction heuristics, to find information about the requested product and return it to the customer. However, this technology has two severe limitations:

- *Effort.* Writing a wrapper for each online store is a time-consuming activity, and changes in the layout of stores result in high levels of required maintenance to keep the wrappers up to date.

▪ *Quality.* The product information extracted by shopbots using such technology is limited (mostly price information), error prone, and incomplete. For example, a wrapper may extract the direct price of a product but miss indirect costs such as shipping.

These problems are caused by the fact that most product information on Web sites is provided in natural language, and automatic text recognition is still a research area with significant unsolved problems. What is required is a machine-processible semantics for the information provided. The situation will drastically change when standard representation formalisms for the structure and semantics of data are available. Software agents can then be built that can "understand" the product information the Web sites provide. Meta-online stores can then be constructed with little effort, and this technique will also enable complete market transparency in various dimensions of diverse product properties. The low-level programming of wrappers based on text extraction and format heuristics will be replaced by semantic mappings that translate different formats used to represent products and can be used to navigate and search automatically for the required information.

1.1.3 Electronic Business

Electronic commerce in the business-to-business field (B2B) is not a new phenomenon. Initiatives to support electronic data exchange in business processes among different companies existed already even as long ago as the 1960s. To exchange information about business transactions, sender and receiver have to agree on a common standard (a protocol for transmitting the content and a language for describing the content). A number of standards arose for this purpose; one is the United Nations initiative Electronic Data Interchange for Administration, Commerce, and Transport (EDIFACT). In general, the automatization of business transactions has not lived up to the expectations of its propagandists. This can be explained by the serious shortcomings of an existing approach like EDIFACT: it is a rather procedural and cumbersome standard, making the programming of business transactions expensive, error prone, and hard to maintain. It assumes that business data are exchanged via special networks (extranets), which are not integrated with other document exchange processes, that is, EDIFACT is an isolated standard. Using the infrastructure of the Internet for business exchange significantly improved this situation. Standard browsers can be used to render specifications for business transactions, and these transactions can be transparently integrated into other document exchange processes in intranet and Internet environments. However, data exchange is currently hampered by the fact that HTML does not provide a means for presenting rich syntax and semantics of data. XML, which is designed to close this gap in current Internet technology, is already changing the situation. B2B communication and data exchange can then be modeled with the same means that are available for other data exchange processes, transaction specifications can easily be rendered by standard browsers, and maintenance will be cheap. XML provides a standard serialized syntax for defining the structure and semantics of data. Therefore, it provides means to represent the semantics of information as part of defining its structure. However, XML does *not* provide standard data structures and terminologies to describe business processes and exchanged products. Therefore, new Semantic Web technology will have to play important roles in XML-enabled electronic commerce:

▪ First, languages with a defined data model and rich modeling primitives will have to be defined that provide support in defining, mapping, and exchanging product data.

▪ Second, standard ontologies will have to be developed covering various business areas. Examples are Common Business Library (CBL), Commerce XML (cXML), ecl@ss, Open Applications Group Integration Specification (OAGIS), RosettaNet, and UN/SPSC. However, these "ontologies" are quite specific and provide only partial coverage of the domains, with quite limited semantics.

▪ Third, efficient translation services will be required in areas for which standard ontologies do not exist[1] or in which a particular client wants to use his own terminology and needs his terminology translated into the standard.

This translation service will have to cover structural and semantical as well as language differences.

Such support will significantly extend the degree to which data exchange is automated and will create complete new business models in the participating market segments.

The Semantic Web deals with important application areas such as knowledge management and electronic commerce (both B2C and B2B). It may help to overcome many of the current bottlenecks in these areas. The next section will explain how it can help do this.

1.2   How the Semantic Web Will Be Possible

In the preceding section we described new services provided by the Semantic Web. In this section we will discuss how such a new level of functionality can be achieved. First, we describe new languages that allow semantics to be added to the Web. Second, we describe important tools for adding semantics to the Web, and finally, we illustrate by some applications the potential utility of the Semantic Web.

1.2.1   Languages

Languages for the Semantic Web must include two aspects. First, they need to provide formal syntax and formal semantics to enable automated processing of their content. Second, they need to provide standardized vocabulary referring to real-world semantics enabling automatic and human agents to share information and knowledge. The latter is provided by ontologies.

1.2.1.1   Formal Languages

Originally, the Web grew mainly around HTML, which provide a standard for structuring documents that was translated by browsers in a canonical way to render documents. On the one hand, as noted above, it was the simplicity of HTML that enabled the fast growth of the WWW. On the other hand,

Languages for the Semantic Web

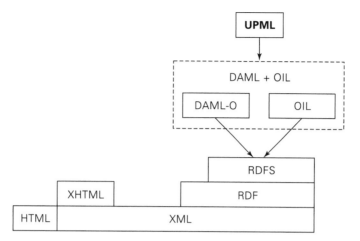

Figure 1.1
Layer language model for the WWW.

HTML's simplicity has seriously hampered more advanced Web application in many domains and for many tasks. This was the reason for defining another language, XML (see figure 1.1), which allows arbitrary domain- and task-specific extensions to be defined (as the figure shows, even HTML got redefined as an XML application, XHTML). Therefore, it is just a logical consequence to define the semantic Web as an XML application. The first step in this direction is taken by RDF, which defines a syntactical convention and a simple data model for representing machine-processible semantics of data. A second step is taken by the RDF Schema (RDFS), which defines basic ontological modeling primitives on top of RDF. A full-blown ontology modeling language as extension of RDFS is defined by the Ontology Inference Layer (OIL) and DARPA Agent Markup Language–Ontology (DAML-ONT), which conclude our discussion on Semantic Web languages.

RDF is a standard for Web metadata developed by W3C (Lassila 1998). Expanding from the traditional notion of document metadata (such as something like library catalog information), RDF is suitable for describing any Web resources, and as such provides interoperability among applications that exchange machine-understandable information on the Web. RDF is an XML application and adds a simple data model on top of XML. This data model provides three elements: objects, properties, and values of properties applied to a certain object.

The RDFS candidate recommendation (see Brickley and Guha 2000) defines additional modeling primitives on top of RDF. It allows the definition of classes (i.e., concepts), inheritance hierarchies for classes and properties, and domain and range restrictions for properties. OIL (http://www.ontoknowledge.org/oil) (see Fensel et al. 2001) takes RDFS as a starting point and extends it to a full-fledged ontology language. An ontology language must fulfill three important requirements:

- It must be highly intuitive to the human user. Given the current success of the frame-based and object-oriented modeling paradigm, it should have a framelike look and feel.

- It must have a well-defined formal semantics with established reasoning properties in terms of completeness, correctness, and efficiency.[2]

- It must have a proper link with existing Web languages like XML and RDF, ensuring interoperability.

In this respect, many of the existing ontology languages like CycL (Lenat and Guha 1990), the Knowledge Interchange Format (KIF) (Genesereth 1991), Ontolingua (Farquhar, Fikes, and Rice 1997), and Simple HTML Ontology Extensions (SHOE) (Luke, Spector, and Rager 1996) fail to satisfy these requirements. However, OIL fulfills all three criteria mentioned above. OIL unifies three important aspects provided by different communities: epistemologically rich modeling primitives as provided by the frame community, formal semantics and efficient reasoning support as provided by description logics, and a standard proposal for syntactical exchange notations as provided by the Web community.

Another candidate for such a Web-based ontology modeling language is DAML-ONT (http://www.daml.org) funded by the U.S. Defense Advanced

Research Projects Agency (DARPA). However, this language is still in an early stage of development and lacks a formal definition of its semantics.

1.2.1.2 Ontologies

Ontologies were developed in artificial intelligence to facilitate knowledge sharing and reuse. Since the beginning of the 1990s, ontologies have become a popular topic for investigation in artificial intelligence research communities, including knowledge engineering, natural-language processing, and knowledge representation. More recently, the notion of ontology has also become widespread in fields such as intelligent information integration, cooperative information systems, information retrieval, electronic commerce, and knowledge management. The reason ontologies are becoming so popular has to do in large part with what they promise: a shared and common understanding of some domain that can be communicated among people and application systems. Because ontologies aim at consensual domain knowledge, their development is often a cooperative process involving different people, possibly at different locations. People who agree to accept an ontology are said to "commit" themselves to that ontology.

Many definitions of ontologies have been offered in the last decade, but the one that, in our opinion, best characterizes the essence of an ontology is based on the related definitions by Gruber (1993): An ontology is a formal, explicit specification of a shared conceptualization. A "conceptualization" refers to an abstract model of some phenomenon in the world that identifies the relevant concepts of that phenomenon. "Explicit" means that the type of concepts used and the constraints on their use are explicitly defined. "Formal" refers to the fact that the ontology should be machine understandable. Different degrees of formality are possible. Large ontologies like WordNet (http://www.cogsci.princeton.edu/~wn) provide a thesaurus for over 100,000 terms explained in natural language. On the other end of the spectrum is CYC (http://www.cyc.com), which provides formal axiomating theories for many aspects of commonsense knowledge. "Shared" reflects the notion that an ontology captures consensual knowledge, that is, it is not restricted to some individual but accepted by a group.

1.2.2   Tools

Effective and efficient work with the semantic Web must be supported by advanced tools enabling the full power of this technology. In particular, it requires the following elements:

- Formal languages to express and represent ontologies (We already discussed some of these in the last section)

- Editors and semiautomatic construction to build new ontologies

- Reusing and merging ontologies (ontology environments that help to create new ontologies by reusing existing ones)

- Reasoning services (instance and schema inferences that enable advanced query answering service, support ontology creation, and help map between different terminologies)

- Annotation tools to link unstructured and semistructured information sources with metadata

- Tools for information access and navigation that enable intelligent information access for human users

- Translation and integration services between different ontologies that enable multistandard data interchange and multiple view definitions (especially for B2B electronic commerce).

In the following sections, we will briefly describe examples of these technologies.

1.2.2.1   *Editors and Semiautomatic Construction*

Ontology editors help human knowledge engineers build ontologies. They support the definition of concept hierarchies, the definition attributes for concepts, and the definition of axioms and constraints. They enable the inspection, browsing, codifying, and modification of ontologies and in this way support the ontology development and maintenance task. To be useful in this context, they must provide graphical interfaces and must conform to existing standards in Web-based software development. One example of an ontology editor that fulfills all of these criteria is Protégé (Grosso et al. 1999), developed at Stanford University, which allows domain experts to build knowledge-based systems by creating and modifying reusable ontologies and problem-solving methods. Protégé generates domain-specific knowledge acquisition tools and applications from ontologies. It has been used in more than 30 countries. It is an ontology editor that can be used to define classes and class hierarchies, slots and slot value restrictions, relationships between classes, and properties of these relationships (see figure 1.2). Protégé's in-

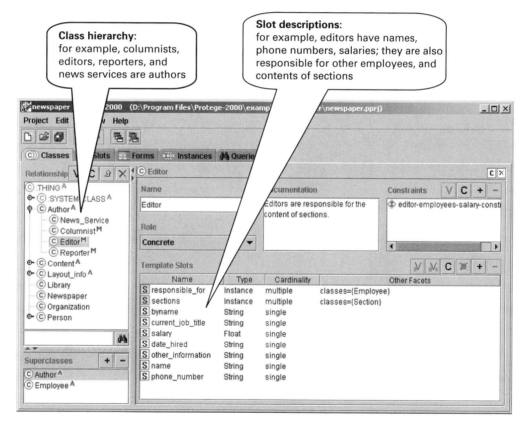

Figure 1.2
Protégé editor.

stances tab is a knowledge acquisition tool that can be used to acquire instances of the classes defined in the ontology.

Manually building ontologies is a time-consuming task. It is very difficult and cumbersome to manually derive ontologies from data. This appears to be true regardless of the type of data under consideration. Natural-language texts exhibit morphological, syntactic, semantic, pragmatic, and conceptual constraints that interact to convey a particular meaning to the reader. Thus, such texts transport information to the reader, and the reader embeds this information into his background knowledge. Through the understanding of the text, data are associated with conceptual structures and new conceptual structures are learned from the interacting constraints given through language. Tools that learn ontologies from natural language exploit the interacting constraints on the various language levels (from morphology to pragmatics and background knowledge) in order to discover new concepts and stipulate relationships among concepts. Therefore, in addition to editor support, such semiautomated tools in ontology development help improve the overall productivity. These tools combine machine learning, information extraction, and linguistic techniques. Their main tasks are extracting relevant concepts, building is-a hierarchies, and determining relationships among concepts.

An example of such a semiautomated ontology development tool is Text-To-Onto (figure 1.3) (Mädche and Staab 2000), developed by the Knowledge Management Group of the Institute AIFB at the University of Karlsruhe. The Text-To-Onto system provides an integrated environment for the task of learning ontologies from text. The system's text management module enables the selection of a relevant corpus of domain texts. These texts may be both natural-language texts and HTML-formatted texts. A meaningful text analysis requires that textual preprocessing be performed. The text management module serves as an interface with the system's information extraction server. If a domain lexicon already exists, the information extraction server performs domain-specific parsing. The results of the parsing process are stored in XML or feature value structures. Text-To-Onto's management module offers all existing learning components to the user. Typically these components are parameterizable. Existing knowledge structures (for example, a

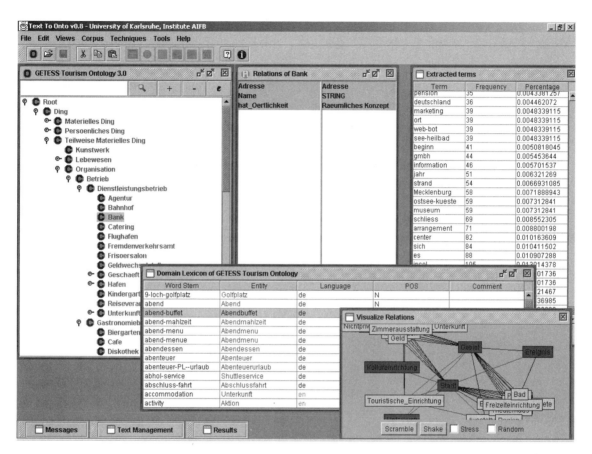

Figure 1.3
Text-To-Onto.

taxonomy of concepts) are incorporated as background knowledge. The system's learning component discovers, on the basis of the domain texts it processes, new knowledge structures, which are then captured in the ontology modeling module to expand the existing ontology.

1.2.2.2   Ontology Environments

Assuming that the world is full of well-designed modular ontologies, constructing a new ontology is a matter of assembling existing ones. Instead of building ontologies from scratch, one wants to reuse existing ontologies to save time and labor. Tools that support this approach must allow adaptation and merging of existing ontologies to make them fit for new tasks and domains. Operations necessary for combining ontologies are ontology inclusion, ontology restriction, and polymorphic refinement of ontology. For example, when one ontology is included in another, the composed ontology consists of the union of the two ontologies (their classes, relations, and axioms). The knowledge engineer needs a number of different kinds of support in merging multiple ontologies together and diagnosing ontologies, particularly in such tasks as using ontologies in differing formats, reorganizing taxonomies, resolving name conflicts, browsing ontologies, and editing terms. One such ontology environment tool is Chimaera (figure 1.4), developed at Stanford University, which provides support for two important tasks: merging multiple ontologies and diagnosing (and evolving) ontologies (McGuinness et al. 2000).

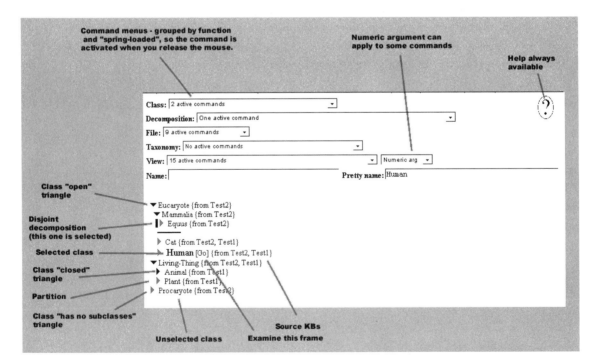

Figure 1.4
Chimaera.

1.2.2.3   Reasoning Services

Inference engines for ontologies can be used to reason over instances of an ontology or over ontology schemes.

▪ Reasoning over instances of an ontology involves deriving a certain value for an attribute applied to an object. Inference services of this type can be used to answer queries about the explicit and implicit knowledge specified by an ontology. The powerful support it provides in formulating rules and constraints and in answering queries over schema information is far beyond that available in existing database technology. These inference services are the equivalent of SQL query engines for databases, however, they provide stronger support (for example, recursive rules) than such query engines. An example of a system for reasoning over instances of an ontology is Onto-broker (Fensel, Angele, et al. 2000), available commercially through the company Ontoprise (http://www.ontoprise.de).

▪ Reasoning over concepts of an ontology automatically derives the right position for a new concept in a given concept hierarchy. One system with such a capacity, FaCT (Fast Classification of Terminologies) (Horrocks and Patel-Schneider 1999), developed at the University of Manchester and available in a commercial version can be used to derive concept hierarchies automatically. It is a description logic (DL) classifier that makes use of the well-defined semantics of OIL. FaCT can be accessed via a Corba interface. It has been developed at the University of Manchester and currently an internet start up may go for implementing a commercial version. It is one of the most, if not *the* most, efficient reasoner for the kinds of tasks it handles.

Both types of reasoners help to build ontologies and to use them for advanced information access and navigation, as we discuss below.

1.2.2.4   Annotation Tools

Ontologies can be used to describe a large number of instances. Annotation tools help the knowledge engineer to establish such links via:

▪ linking an ontology with a database schema or deriving a database schema from an ontology (in cases of structured data)

▪ deriving an XML DTD, an XML schema, and an RDF schema from an ontology (in cases of semistructured data)

▪ Manually or semiautomatically adding ontological annotation to unstructured data

More details can be found in Erdmann and Studer 2001 and Klein et al. 2000.

1.2.2.5   Tools for Information Access and Navigation

The Web is currently navigated at a very low level: clicking on links and using keyword searches is the main (if not the only) navigation technique. It is comparable programming with assembler and go-to instructions instead of higher-level programming languages. This low-level interface may significantly hamper the growth of the Web in the future for a number of reasons:

▪ Keyword-based search retrieves irrelevant information that uses a particular word in a different meaning from the one intended, and it may miss relevant links in which different words than the keyword are used to describe the content for which the user is searching. Navigation is supported only by predefined links; current navigation technology does not support clustering and linking of pages based on semantic similarity.

▪ Query responses require human browsing and reading to extract the relevant information from the information sources returned. This burdens Web users with an additional loss of time and seriously limits information retrieval by automatic agents, which lack all commonsense knowledge required to extract such information from textual representations.

▪ Keyword-based document retrieval fails to integrate information spread over different sources.

▪ Current retrieval services can retrieve only information that is directly represented on the WWW. No further inference service is provided for deriving implicit information that must be derived from the explicit text.

Ontologies help to overcome these bottlenecks in information access. They support information retrieval based on the actual content of a page.

They help the user navigate the information space based on semantic, rather than lexical, concepts. They enable advanced query answering and information extraction services, integrating heterogeneous and distributed information sources enriched by inferred background knowledge. This provides two main improvements over current methods:

▪ Semantic information visualization, which groups information not on location but on contents, providing semantic-based navigation support. Examples are the hyperbolic browsing interface of Ontoprise (see figure 1.5) and the page content visualization tool of Aidministrator (http://www.aidministrator.nl) (see figure 1.6).

▪ Direct query answering services based on semistructured information sources.

1.2.2.6   *Translation and Integration Services*

Around 80% of the Web's electronic business will be in the B2B area, in which all experts expect exponential growth. Many studies estimate that around 10,000 B2B marketplaces will be set up during the next few years. However, there is one serious obstacle to the projected growth: the heterogeneity of product descriptions on Web sites and the exponentially increasing effort that must be devoted to mapping these heterogeneous descriptions as the number of Web sites increases. Therefore, effective and efficient content management of heterogeneous product catalogues is the critical point for B2B success. Traditional B2B did not change the business model of the companies involved: it only helped reduce the transaction costs associated with the existing model. It required one mapping from one supplier to one customer or N mappings from one supplier to N customers. The new business model of B2B marketplaces, in contrast, changes the business model, bringing electronic commerce to its full economical potential: individual product search, corporative product search, market transparency, easy access, and negotiation.[3]

An Internet-based marketplace can help significantly to bring the sides of a business interaction together. It will provide instant market overview and

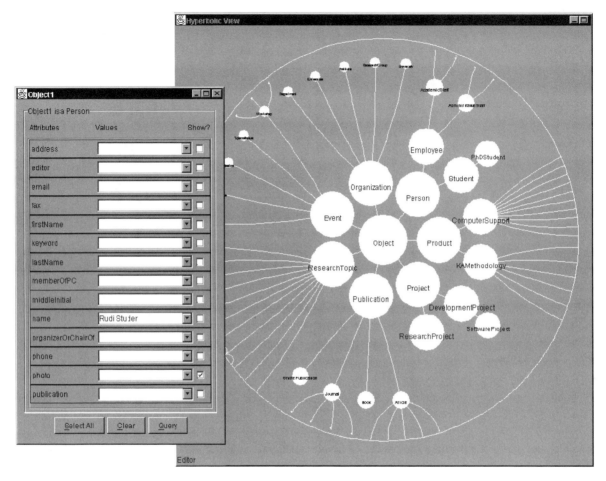

Figure 1.5
Hyperbolic browsing interface.

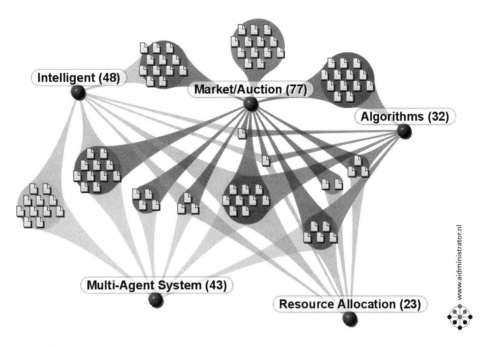

Figure 1.6
Automatically generated semantic structure maps.

offers comparison shopping. Such a marketplace will significantly change the business model of this market segment where it operates. Basically, it will replace or at least compete with traditional mediation agents, like wholesale traders. However, the number of required mappings will explode in comparison to that required in traditional B2B. In an Internet-based marketplace, M companies will exchange business transactions electronically with N companies in a fragmented market. In consequence one will need $M * N$ mappings. These mappings will arise at two levels:

▪ Different representations of product catalogs must be merged, as different vendors may use different representation of their catalog data. For example:
• A product catalog in EXPRESS must be merged with a product catalog in XML.

• A product catalogue in XML with DTD1 must be merged with a product catalogue in XML with DTD2.

▪ Different vocabularies used to describe products must be merged. Differences may appear in

• the languages used to describe products (English, Spanish, French, German, etc.)

• the concepts used to define products

• the attributes used to define products

• the values and value types used to define products

• the overall structure used to define products.

We need intermediate architectures that reduce drastically the inherent complexity of the process for each mapping and that reduce the number of mappings itself. Given the urgent need for flexible tools for mapping between ontologies, not many actual tools have been developed. A promising approach based on a metalevel architecture is descried in Bowers and Delcambre 2000.

1.2.3 Applications

At the beginning of the chapter we sketched three application areas for Semantic Web technologies: knowledge management, B2C Web commerce, and B2B electronic business. This section provide some prototypical examples for such applications. It is not meant as a representative survey of the field, which would require much more space and would be a chapter (if not a book) all its own.

On-To-Knowledge[4] (Fensel, van Harmelen, et al. 2000) builds an environment for knowledge management in large intranets and Web sites. Unstructured and semistructured data are automatically annotated, and agent-based user interface techniques and visualization tools help the user navigate and query the information space. On-To-Knowledge continues a line of research that was initiated with SHOE (Luke, Spector, and Rager, 1996) and Ontobroker (Fensel et al. 1998): using ontologies to model and annotate the semantics of information resources in a machine-processible manner. The developers of On-To-Knowledge are carrying out three industrial case studies—with SwissLife (http://www.swisslife.ch), British Telecom (http://www.bt.com/innovations), and Enersearch[5]—to evaluate the tool environment for ontology-based knowledge management. In this context, CognIT (http://www.cognit.no) extended its information extraction tool Corporum to generate ontologies from semistructured or unstructured natural-language documents. Important concepts and their relationships are extracted from these documents and used to build up initial ontologies. Figure 1.6 shows an automatically generated semantic structure map of the EnerSearch Web site using Aidministrator technology (http://www.aidministrator.nl).

An application of the Semantic Web technology in the B2C area has been developed by Semantic Edge (http://www.semanticedge.com) that offers front-end voice-based and natural-language access to distributed and heterogeneous product information. The technology will enable the human user, instead of manually browsing large volumes of product information, to ask simple questions like "Where can I get a cheap color printer for my Mac?"

Finally, the B2B area may become the most important application area of Semantic Web technology in terms of the market volume. Companies like VerticalNet (http://www.verticalnet.com) which builds many vertical marketplaces, or ContentEurope (http://www.contenteurope.com) which provides content management solutions for B2B electronic commerce, all face the same problem: integrating heterogeneous and distributed product information. Naturally such companies make use of ontology-based integration techniques to reduce the level of effort required to provide integrated solutions for B2B marketplaces.

Notes

1. Given the current situation, there will be many "standards" requiring interchange.

2. Note that we are speaking here about the *Semantic* Web.

3. Fixed prices turned up at the beginning of the 20th century, lowering transaction costs. However, negotiations and auctions (like those available on some Web sites) help allocate

resources more optimally. Still, the effort required for negotiation may outweigh the advantages in resource allocation and lead to unreasonably high demands on time (and transaction costs). Automated negotiation agents and auction houses reduce these high transaction costs and allow optimized resource allocation.

4. On-To-Knowledge is a European IST project (http://www.ontoknowledge.org).

5. See further http://www.enersearch.se. Enersearch research affiliates and shareholders are spread over many countries: its shareholding companies include IBM (United States), Sydkraft (Sweden), ABB (Sweden/Switzerland), PreussenElektra (Germany), Iberdrola (Spain), ECN (Netherlands), and Electricidade do Portugal.

References

Bowers, S., and L. Delcambre. 2000. Representing and Transforming Model-Based Information. In Electronic Proceedings of the ECDL 2000 Workshop on the Semantic Web at the Fourth European Conference on Research and Advanced Technology for Digital Libraries (ECDL-2000), Lisbon, Portugal, September 21, 2000. Available from http://www.ics.forth.gr/proj/isst/SemWeb/program.html.

Berners-Lee, T. 1999. *Weaving the Web.* London: Orion Business.

Brickley, D., and R. Guha. 2000. Resource Description Framework (RDF) Schema Specification 1.0 (candidate recommendation). World Wide Web Consortium. Available from http://www.w3.org/TR/2000/CR-rdf-schema-20000327.

Erdmann, M., and R. Studer. 2001. How to Structure and Access XML Documents with Ontologies. *Data and Knowledge Engineering* 36:317–335.

Farquhar, A., R. Fikes, and J. Rice. 1997. The Ontolingua Server: A Tool for Collaborative Ontology Construction. *International Journal of Human-Computer Studies* 46:707–728.

Fensel, D. 2001. *Ontologies: Silver Bullet for Knowledge Management and Electronic Commerce.* Berlin: Springer-Verlag.

Fensel, D., J. Angele, S. Decker, M. Erdmann, H.-P. Schnurr, R. Studer, and, A. Witt. 2000. Lessons Learned from Applying AI to the Web. *Journal of Cooperative Information Systems* 9(4):361–382.

Fensel, D., S. Decker, M. Erdmann, and R. Studer. 1998. Ontobroker: The Very High Idea. In *Proceedings of the 11th International Flairs Conference (FLAIRS-98), Sanibel Island, Florida, USA, May,* ed. D. J. Cook (pp. 131–135). Menlo Park, CA: AAAI.

Fensel, D., I. Horrocks, F. Van Harmelen, D. McGuiness, and P. Patel-Schneider. 2001. OIL: Ontology Infrastructure to Enable the Semantic Web. *IEEE Intelligent Systems* (March/April):38–45.

Fensel, D., F. van Harmelen, M. Klein, H. Akkermans, J. Broekstra, C. Fluit, J. van der Meer, H.-P. Schnurr, R. Studer, J. Hughes, U. Krohn, J. Davies, R. Engels, B. Bremdal, F. Ygge, U. Reimer, and I. Horrocks. 2000. On-To-Knowledge: Ontology-based Tools for Knowledge Management. In *Proceedings of the eBusiness and eWork (EMMSEC-2000) Conference, Madrid, Spain, October*. Available from http://www.ebew.net/.

Genesereth, M. R. 1991. Knowledge Interchange Format. In *Proceedings of the Second International Conference on the Principles of Knowledge Representation and Reasoning (KR-91)*, ed. J. Allen et al. San Francisco: Morgan Kaufman.

Grosso, W. E., H. Eriksson, R. W. Fergerson, J. H. Gennari, S. W. Tu, and M. A. Musen. Knowledge Modeling at the Millennium (The Design and Evolution of Protege-2000). In *Proceedings of the Twelfth Workshop on Knowledge Acquisition, Modeling and Management (KAW-1999), Banff, Alberta, Canada, October 16–21, 1999*. Available from http://smi-web.stanford.edu/pubs/SMI_Abstracts/SMI-1999-0801.html.

Gruber, T. R. 1993. A Translation Approach to Portable Ontology Specifications. *Knowledge Acquisition* 5:199–220.

Horrocks, I., and P. F. Patel-Schneider. 1999. Optimizing Description Logic Subsumption. *Journal of Logic and Computation* 9(3):267–293.

Klein, M., D. Fensel, F. van Harmelen, and I. Horrocks. 2000. The Relation between Ontologies and Schema-Languages: Translating OIL-Specifications to XML-Schema In *Proceedings of the Workshop on Applications of Ontologies and Problem-Solving Methods, 14th European Conference on Artificial Intelligence ECAI-2000, Berlin, Germany, August 20–25, 2000*, ed. V. R. Benjamins et al. Available from http://www.cs.vu.nl/~mcaklein/papers/.

Lassila, O. 1998. Web Metadata: A Matter of Semantics. *IEEE Internet Computing*, 2(4):30–37.

Lenat, D. B., and R. V. Guha. 1990. *Building Large Knowledge-Based Systems: Representation and Inference in the Cyc Project*. Reading, MA.: Addison-Wesley.

Luke, S., L. Spector, and D. Rager. 1996. Ontology-Based Knowledge Discovery on the World Wide Web. In *Working Notes of the Workshop on Internet-Based Information Systems at the 13th National Conference on Artificial Intelligence (AAAI96)*. Available from http://www.csl.sony.co.jp/person/amf/iis96.html.

Mädche, A., and S. Staab. 2000. Mining Ontologies from Text. In *Knowledge Acquisition, Modeling, and Management: Proceedings of the European Knowledge Acquisition Conference (EKAW-2000)*, ed. R. Dieng et al. Lecture Notes in Artificial Intelligence (LNAI). Berlin: Springer-Verlag.

McGuinness, D. L., R. Fikes, J. Rice, and S. Wilder. 2000. An Environment for Merging and Testing Large Ontologies. In *Proceedings of the Seventh International Conference on Principles of Knowledge Representation and Reasoning (KR-2000), Breckenridge, Colorado, April 12–15* (pp. 483–493). San Francisco: Morgan Kaufmann.

I   *Languages and Ontologies*

2 SHOE: A Blueprint for the Semantic Web

Jeff Heflin, James Hendler, and Sean Luke

2.1   Introduction

The World Wide Web is a vast repository of information, but its utility is restricted by limited facilities for searching and integrating this information. The problem of making sense of the Web has engaged the minds of numerous researchers from fields such as databases, artificial intelligence, and library science, and these researchers have applied numerous approaches in an attempt to solve it. Tim Berners-Lee, inventor of the Web, has coined the term "Semantic Web" to describe a vision of the future in which the "web of links" is replaced with a "web of meaning." In this chapter, we examine the thesis that the "the Semantic Web can be achieved if we describe web resources in a language that makes their meaning explicit."

Any language for the Semantic Web must take into account the nature of the Web. Let's consider some of the issues that arise:

1. The Web is distributed. One of the driving factors in the proliferation of the Web is the freedom from a centralized authority. However, since the Web is the product of many individuals, the lack of central control presents many challenges for reasoning with the information it presents. First, different communities will use different vocabularies, resulting in problems of synonymy (when two different words have the same meaning) and polysemy (when the same word is used with different meanings). Second, the

lack of editorial review or quality control means that each Web page's reliability must be questioned. An intelligent Web agent simply cannot assume that all of the information it gathers is correct and consistent. There have been quite a number of well-known "Web hoaxes" in which information was published on the Web with the intent to amuse or mislead. Furthermore, since there can be no global enforcement of integrity constraints on the Web, information from different sources may be in conflict. Some of these conflicts may be due to philosophical disagreement; different political groups, religious groups, or nationalities may have fundamental differences in opinion that will never be resolved. Any attempt to prevent such inconsistencies must favor one opinion, but the correctness of the opinion is very much in the eye of the beholder.

2. The Web is dynamic. The Web changes at an incredible pace, much faster than a user or even a softbot Web agent can keep up with. While new pages are being added, the content of existing pages is changing. Some pages are fairly static, others change on a regular basis, and still others change at unpredictable intervals. These changes may vary in significance: although the addition of punctuation, correction of spelling errors, or reordering of a paragraph does not affect the semantic content of a document, other changes may completely alter meaning or even remove large amounts of information. A Web agent must assume that the Web's data can be, and often will be, out of date.

The rapid pace of information change on the Internet poses an additional challenge to any attempt to create standard vocabularies and provide formal semantics. As understanding of a given domain changes, both the vocabulary may change and the semantics may be refined. It is important that such changes do not adversely alter the meaning of existing content.

3. The Web is massive. Recent estimates place the number of indexable Web pages at over two billion, and this number is expected to double within a year. Even if each page contained only a *single* piece of agent-gatherable knowledge, the cumulative database would be large enough to bring most reasoning systems to their knees. To scale to the size of the ever-growing

Web, we must either restrict the expressivity of the language of knowledge representation on the Web or use incomplete reasoning algorithms.

4. The Web is an open world. A Web agent cannot legitimately assume it has gathered all available knowledge after conducting a search; in fact, in most cases an agent should assume it has gathered rather little available knowledge. Even the largest search engines have only crawled about 25% of the available pages. However, in order to deduce more facts, many reasoning systems make the closed-world assumption. That is, they assume that anything not entailed in the knowledge base is not true. Yet it is clear that the size and evolving nature of the Web make it unlikely that any knowledge base attempting to describe it could ever be complete.

In an attempt to deal with these issues, we have designed a language, SHOE, that is one of the first languages that allows ontologies to be designed and used directly on the World Wide Web (Luke et al. 1997). In this chapter we describe work that influenced SHOE, present an overview of the language, describe its syntax and semantics, and discuss how SHOE addresses the issues posed in this introduction. We then discuss the problem of implementing a system that uses SHOE, describe some tools that enhance the language's usability, and discuss the application of these tools to two different domains. Finally, we provide an overview of related work and some concluding remarks.

2.2   Background

The success of the Web was made possible by HTML. With HTML, people can easily author sharable documents and link to related documents that might exist on different systems. However, HTML is mostly concerned with presentation (i.e., how a document is displayed in a Web browser), and it is difficult to extract content automatically from an HTML document.

In 1998, the World Wide Web Consortium officially released XML (Bray, Paoli, and Sperberg-McQueen 1998), a simplified version of SGML (ISO 1986) for the Web. XML allows special codes, called *tags*, to be embedded in a text data stream in order to provide additional information about the text, such as indicating that a certain word should be emphasized. Usually, each tag (referred to as a start-tag) has a corresponding end-tag, with arbitrary text or other tags contained between them. The combination of a start-tag, an end-tag, and the data between is called an *element*. Some tags have additional properties, called *attributes*.

Unlike HTML, which precisely defines the structure and usage of a specific set of elements, XML allows users to define their own elements and attributes. Thus, users can create a document using content-specific as opposed to presentation-specific tags. If a document conforms to basic rules of XML, then it is said to be well-formed. If a document conforms to a common grammar, as specified by a document type definition (DTD), then is said to be valid. A DTD specifies valid elements, the contents of these elements, and which attributes may modify an element. Thus a DTD provides a syntax for an XML document, but the semantics of a DTD are implicit. That is, the meaning of an element in a DTD is inferred by a human from the name assigned to it, is described in a natural-language comment within the DTD, or is described in a document separate from the DTD. Humans can then build these semantics into tools that are used to interpret or translate the XML documents, but software tools cannot acquire these semantics independently. Thus, an exchange of XML documents works well if the parties involved have agreed to a DTD beforehand but becomes problematic when one wants to search across the entire set of DTDs or to spontaneously integrate information from multiple sources (Heflin and Hendler 2000c).

A number of approaches, including information retrieval, wrappers, semistructured databases, machine learning, and natural-language processing, have been applied to the problem of querying and understanding HTML and/or XML Web pages. However, the lack of semantics in the sources and the lack of common human knowledge in the tools greatly limits the quality of the available techniques for such querying and understanding. We support an alternative approach: that authors should explicitly associate semantics with the content they provide.

In order to provide meaning for data, the knowledge must be represented in some way. Knowledge representation is a subfield of artificial intelligence concerned with such matters. The goal of knowledge representation is to provide structures that allow information to be stored, modified, and reasoned with, all in an efficient manner. Over time, numerous knowledge representation languages with different properties have evolved, from early languages such as KL-ONE (Brachman and Schmolze 1985) and KRL (Bobrow and Winograd 1977) to more recent languages such as LOOM (MacGregor 1991), Classic (Brachman et al. 1991), and Cyc-L (Lenat and Guha 1990).

One of the oldest knowledge representation formalisms is semantic networks. A semantic network represents knowledge as a set of nodes connected by labeled links. In such a representation, meaning is implied by the way a concept is connected to other concepts. Frame systems are another representation that is isomorphic to semantic networks. In the terminology of such systems, a frame is a named data object that has a set of slots, with each slot representing a property or attribute of the object. Slots can have one or more values; these values may be pointers to other frames.

Advanced semantic networks and frame systems typically include the notion of abstraction, which is represented using *is-a* and *instance-of* links. An is-a link indicates that one class is included within another, whereas an instance-of link indicates that a concept is a member of a class. These links have correlations in basic set theory: is-a is like the subset relation and instance-of is like the element-of relation. The collection of is-a links specifies a partial order on classes; this order is often called a taxonomy or categorization hierarchy. The taxonomy can be used to generalize a concept to a more abstract class or to specialize a class to its more specific concepts. As demonstrated by the popularity of Yahoo and the Open Directory, taxonomies clearly aid users in locating relevant information on the Web.

Many researchers in knowledge representation have become interested in the use of ontologies (Gruber 1993). The term "ontology," which is borrowed from philosophy, is defined as "a particular theory about being or reality" (Gruber 1993). As such, an ontology provides a particular perspective on the world or some part there of. Whereas a knowledge representation system specifies how to represent concepts, an ontology specifies what concepts to represent and how they are interrelated. Most researchers agree that an ontology must include a vocabulary and corresponding definitions, but it is difficult to achieve consensus on a more detailed characterization. Typically, the vocabulary includes terms for classes and relations, whereas the definitions of these terms may be informal text or may be specified using a formal language like predicate logic. The advantage of formal definitions is that they allow a machine to perform much deeper reasoning; the disadvantage is that these definitions are much more difficult to construct.

Numerous ontologies have been constructed, with varying scopes, levels of detail, and viewpoints. Noy and Hafner (1997) provide a good overview and comparison of some of these ontology construction projects. One of the more prominent themes in ontology research is the construction of reusable components. The potential advantages of such components are that large ontologies can be quickly constructed by assembling and refining existing components and that integration of ontologies is easier when the ontologies share components. One of the most common ways to achieve ontology reusability is to allow the specification of an inclusion relation that states that one or more ontologies are included in the new theory (Farquhar, Fikes, and Rice 1997; Lenat and Guha 1990). If these relations are acyclic and treat all elements of the included ontology as if they were defined locally, then an ontology can be said to "extend" its included ontologies.

One attempt to apply ideas from knowledge representation to the Web is the Resource Description Framework (RDF) (Lassila 1998). The RDF data model is essentially a semantic network without inheritance: it consists of nodes connected by labeled arcs, where the nodes represent Web resources and the arcs represent attributes of these resources. RDF can be embedded in Web documents using an XML serialization syntax, although its designers emphasize this is only one of many possible representations of the RDF model.

To allow for the creation of controlled, shareable, extensible vocabularies (i.e., ontologies), the RDF working group has developed the RDF Schema Specification (Brickley and Guha 1999). This specification defines a number of properties that have specific semantics. RDF Schema defines properties that are equivalent to the instance-of and is-a links commonly used in knowledge representation. It also provides properties for describing properties, including the specification of a property's domain and range, as well as any properties of which it is a subproperty.

Although RDF is an improvement over HTML and XML, it is insufficient for a Semantic Web language (Heflin and Hendler 2000c). In particular, it provides a very small set of semantic primitives and has relatively weak mechanisms for managing schema evolution. It is desirable that a Semantic Web language provide semantics that allow inferences beyond what is capable in RDF, but it is also important that the reasoning procedures for the language can scale to the volumes of data available on the Internet.

The field of deductive databases deals with combining inferential capabilities with the scalability of database systems. The datalog model (Ullmann 1998) is commonly used as the basis for describing deductive databases. Datalog is similar to Prolog in that it consists entirely of Horn clauses, but it differs from Prolog in that it does not allow function symbols and is a strictly declarative language.[1] Datalog is based on the relational model but defines two types of relations: *extensional database* (EDB) relations are those predicates that are physically stored in the database, whereas *intensional database* (IDB) relations are those that can be computed from a set of logical rules.

Datalog restricts its Horn clauses to being *safe*, meaning that all of its variables are *limited*. Datalog defines "limited" as follows: variables are limited if they appear in an ordinary predicate of the rule's body, appear in an "=" comparison with a constant, or appear in an "=" comparison with another limited variable. Datalog's Horn clauses may depend on each other recursively. Datalog allows negation in a limited form called *stratified negation*, which we will not discuss here.

Datalog is relevant to the design of a Semantic Web language because it allows important classes of rules to be expressed and because its inference algorithms, such as *magic sets*, which combine the best features of forward and backward chaining, provide efficient reasoning. Additionally, it seems reasonable to expect that the Web will eventually consist of a large EDB and a comparatively small IDB, which is an ideal situation for a deductive database system.

2.3   The SHOE Language

SHOE combines features of markup languages, knowledge representation, datalog, and ontologies in an attempt to address the unique problems of semantics on the Web. It supports knowledge acquisition on the Web by augmenting it with tags that provide semantic meaning. The basic structure consists of *ontologies*, which define rules that guide what kinds of assertions may be made and what kinds of inferences may be drawn on ground assertions, and *instances* that make assertions based on those rules. As a knowledge representation language, SHOE borrows characteristics from both predicate logics and frame systems.

SHOE can be embedded directly in HTML documents or used in XML documents. There are a number of advantages to using an XML syntax for SHOE. First, although more standard knowledge representation syntaxes than XML, such as first-order logic or S-expressions, could be embedded between a pair of delimiting tags, Web authors are comfortable with XML-like, tag-based languages. Second, the XML syntax permits SHOE information to be analyzed and processed using the Document Object Model (DOM), allowing software that is XML-aware, but not SHOE-aware, to use the information in more limited but nevertheless powerful ways. For example, some Web browsers are able to display the DOM of a document graphically as a tree, and future browsers will allow users to issue queries that will match structures contained within the tree. Third, SHOE documents can use the XSLT stylesheet standard (Clark 1999) to render SHOE information for human consumption. This is perhaps the most important reason for an XML syntax, because it can eliminate the redundancy of having a separate set of tags for human-readable and machine-readable knowledge.

In this section, we provide a brief description of the syntax of the SHOE language, followed by a formal model and a discussion of SHOE's key features. The interested reader can find a detailed description of SHOE's syntax in the SHOE Specification (Luke and Heflin 2000).

2.3.1 SHOE Ontologies

SHOE uses ontologies to define the valid elements that may be used in describing entities. Each ontology can reuse other ontologies by extending them. An ontology is stored in an HTML or XML file and is made available to document authors and SHOE agents by placing it on a Web server. This file includes tags that identify the ontology, state which ontologies (if any) are extended, and define the various elements of the ontology. Figure 2.1 shows an example of a SHOE ontology.

In SHOE syntax, an ontology appears between the tags $\langle$ONTOLOGY ID=*id* VERSION=*version*$\rangle$ and $\langle \backslash$ONTOLOGY$\rangle$ and is identified by the combination of the *id* and *version*. An ontology can define categories, relations, and other components by including special tags for these purposes.

The tag $\langle$DEF-CATEGORY$\rangle$ can be used to make *category definitions* that specify the categories under which various instances may be classified. Categories may be grouped as subcategories under one or more supercategories, essentially specifying the is-a relation that is commonly used in semantic networks and frame systems. The use of categories allows taxonomies to be built from the top down by subdividing known classes into smaller sets. The example ontology defines many categories, including Chair, which is a subcategory of Faculty.

The tag $\langle$DEF-RELATION$\rangle$ (which is closed by a $\langle \backslash$DEF-RELATION$\rangle$ tag) can be used to make *relational definitions* that specify the format of *n*-ary relational claims that may be made by instances regarding instances and other data. One of the relationships defined by the example ontology is advises, which is between an instance of category Faculty and an instance of category Student. A relation argument can also be one of four basic types (string, number, date, or boolean value), as is the case with the second argument of the relationship, hasGPA.

```
<!-- Declare an ontology called university-ont". -->
<ONTOLOGY ID="university-ont" VERSION="1.0">

<!-- Borrow some elements from an existing ontology, prefixed with a "g." -->
   <USE-ONTOLOGY ID="general-ont" VERSION="1.0" PREFIX="g"
                 URL="http://www.ontology.org/general1.0.html">

<!-- Create local aliases for some terms -->
   <DEF-RENAME FROM-"g.Person" TO="Person">
   <DEF-RENAME FROM-"g.Organization" TO="Organization">
   <DEF-RENAME FROM-"g.name" TO="name">

<!-- Define some categories and subcategory relationships -->
   <DEF-CATEGORY NAME="Faculty" ISA="Person">
   <DEF-CATEGORY NAME="Student" ISA="Person">
   <DEF-CATEGORY NAME="Chair" ISA="Faculty">
   <DEF-CATEGORY NAME="Department" ISA="Organization">

<!-- Define some relations; these examples are binary, but relations can be n-ary too -->
   <DEF-RELATION NAME="advises">
      <DEF-ARG POS="1" TYPE="Faculty">
      <DEF-ARG POS="2" TYPE="Student">
   </DEF-RELATION>

   <DEF-RELATION "hasGPA">
      <DEF-ARG POS="1" TYPE="Student">
      <DEF-ARG POS="2" TYPE=".NUMBER">
   </DEF-RELATION>

<!-- Define a rule that states that the head of a Department is a Chair -->
   <DEF-INFERENCE>
      <INF-IF>
         <RELATION NAME="g.headOf">
            <ARG POS="1" VALUE="x" USAGE="VAR">
            <ARG POS="2" VALUE="y" USAGE="VAR">
         </RELATION>
         <CATEGORY NAME="Department" FOR="y" USAGE="VAR">
      </INF-IF>
      <INF-THEN>
         <CATEGORY NAME="Chair" FOR="x" USAGE="VAR">
      </INF-THEN>
   </DEF-INFERENCE>

</ONTOLOGY>
```

Figure 2.1
Example SHOE ontology.

SHOE uses inference rules, indicated by the ⟨DEF-INFERENCE⟩ tag, to supply additional axioms. A SHOE inference rule consists of a set of antecedents (one or more subclauses describing claims that entities might make) and a set of consequents (consisting of one or more subclauses describing a claim that may be inferred if all claims in the body are made). The ⟨INF-IF⟩ and ⟨INF-THEN⟩ tags indicate the antecedents and consequents of the inference, respectively. There are three types of inference subclauses: category, relation, and comparison. The arguments of any subclause may be a constant or a variable, where variables are indicated by the keyword VAR. Constants must be matched exactly, and variables of the same name must bind to the same value. The ontology in the example includes a rule stating that the head of a department is a chair.

As is common in many ontology efforts, such as Ontolingua and Cyc, SHOE ontologies build on or extend other ontologies, forming a lattice with the most general ontologies at the top and the more specific ones at the bottom. Ontology extension is expressed in SHOE with the ⟨USE-ONTOLOGY⟩ tag, which indicates the ID and version number of an ontology that is extended. An optional URL attribute allows systems to locate the ontology if needed and a PREFIX attribute is used to establish a short local identifier for the ontology. When an ontology refers to an element from an extended ontology, this prefix and a period is appended before the element's name. In this way, references are guaranteed to be unambiguous, even when two ontologies use the same term to mean different things. By chaining the prefixes, one can specify a path through the extended ontologies to an element whose definition is given in a more general ontology.

Sometimes an ontology may need to use a term from another ontology, but a different label may be more useful within its context. The ⟨DEF-RENAME⟩ tag allows the ontology to specify a local name for a concept from any extended ontology. This local name must be unique within the scope of the ontology in which the rename appears. Renaming allows domain-specific ontologies to use the vocabulary that is appropriate for a particular domain while maintaining interoperability with other domains.

```
<INSTANCE KEY="http://univ.edu/jane/">

<!-- Use the semantics from the ontology "university-ont", prefixed with a "u." -->
   <USE-ONTOLOGY ID="university-ont" VERSION="1.0" PREFIX="u"
                    URL="http://www.ontology.org/univ1.0.html">

<!-- Claim some categories for this instance and others. -->
   <CATEGORY NAME="u.Chair">
   <CATEGORY NAME="u.Student" FOR="http://univ.edu/john/">

<!-- Claim some properties and relationships. -->
   <RELATION NAME="u.name">
      <ARG POS="TO" VALUE="Jane Smith">
   </RELATION>

   <RELATION NAME="u.advises">
      <ARG POS="TO" VALUE="http://univ.edu/john/">
   </RELATION>

</INSTANCE>
```

Figure 2.2
Example SHOE instance.

2.3.2　SHOE Instances

Unlike RDF, SHOE makes a distinction between what can be said in an ontology and what can be said on an arbitrary Web page. Ordinary Web pages declare one or more instances that represent SHOE entities, and each instance
describes itself or other instances using categories and relations. An example
of a SHOE instance is shown in figure 2.2.

The syntax for instances includes an ⟨INSTANCE⟩ element that has an attribute for a KEY that uniquely identifies the instance. We recommend that
the URL of the Web page be used as this key, since it is guaranteed to identify
only a single resource. An instance commits to a particular ontology by
means of the ⟨USE-ONTOLOGY⟩ tag, which has the same function as the
identically named element used within ontologies. To prevent ambiguity in
the declarations, ontology components are referred to using the prefixing

mechanism described earlier. The use of common ontologies makes it possible to issue a single logical query to a set of data sources and enables the integration of related domains. Additionally, by specifying ontologies the content author indicates exactly what meaning he associates with his claims and does not need to worry that an arbitrary definition made in some other ontology will alter this meaning.

An instance contains ground *category claims* and *relation claims*. A category claim is specified with the ⟨CATEGORY NAME=*y* FOR=*x*⟩ tag and says that the instance claims that an instance *x* is an element of a category *y*. If the FOR attribute is omitted, then the category claim is about the instance making the claim. In the example in figure 2.2, the instance http://univ.edu/jane/ claims that http://univ.edu/jane/ is a Chair and http://univ.edu/john/ is a Student.

A relational claim is enclosed by the ⟨RELATION NAME=*foo*⟩ and ⟨\RELATION⟩ tags and says that the instance claims that an *n*-ary relation *foo* exists between some *n* number of appropriately typed arguments consisting of data or instances. In figure 2.2, the instance http://univ.edu/jane/ claims that there exists the relation advises between http://univ.edu/jane/ and her student http://univ.edu/john/ and that that the name of http://univ.edu/jane/ is Jane Smith.

2.3.3 SHOE's Semantics

In order to describe the semantics of SHOE, we will extend a standard model-theoretic approach for definite logic with mechanisms to handle distributed ontologies. For simplicity, this model intentionally omits some minor features of the SHOE language.

We define an ontology O to be a tuple $\langle V, A \rangle$ where V is the vocabulary and A is the set of axioms that govern the theory represented by the ontology. Formally, V is a set of predicate symbols, each with some arity > 0 and distinct from symbols in other ontologies,[2] and A is a set of definite program clauses that have the standard logical semantics.[3] We now discuss the contents of V and A, based upon the components that are defined in the ontology.

A ⟨USE-ONTOLOGY⟩ statement adds the vocabulary and axioms of the specified ontology to the current ontology. Because of the assumption that names must be unique, name conflicts can be ignored.

A ⟨DEF-RELATION⟩ statement adds a symbol to the vocabulary and, for each argument type that is a category, adds an axiom that states that an instance in that argument must be a member of the category. If the tag specifies a name R and has n arguments, then there is an n-ary predicate symbol R in V. If the type of the ith argument is a category C, then $[R(x1, \ldots, xi, \ldots xn) \rightarrow C(xi)] \in A$. This rule is a consequence of SHOE's open-world policy: since there is no way to know that a given object in a relation claim is *not* a member of a category appropriate for that relation, it is better to assume that this information is yet undiscovered than it is to assume that the relation is in error. However, when arguments are basic data types, type checking is performed to validate the relation. Basic data types are treated differently because they *are* different: they have syntax that can be checked in ways that category types cannot, which allows us to impose stringent input-time type checking on basic data types.

A ⟨DEF-CATEGORY⟩ adds a unary predicate symbol to the vocabulary and possibly a set of rules indicating membership. If the name is C, then $C \in V$. For each supercategory Pi specified, $[C(x) \rightarrow Pi(x)] \in A$.

A ⟨DEF-INFERENCE⟩ adds one or more axioms to the theory. If there is a single clause in the ⟨INF-THEN⟩, then there is one axiom with a conjunction of the ⟨INF-IF⟩ clauses as the antecedent and the ⟨INF-THEN⟩ clause as the consequent. If there are n clauses in the ⟨INF-THEN⟩ then there are n axioms, each of which has one of the clauses as the consequent and has the same antecedent as above.

A ⟨DEF-RENAME⟩ provides an alias for a nonlogical symbol. It is meant as a convenience for users and can be implemented using a simple preprocessing step that translates the alias to the original, unique nonlogical symbol. Therefore, it can be ignored for the logical theory.

A formula *F* is well-formed with respect to *O* if (1) *F* is an atom of the form $p(t1, \ldots, tn)$, where *p* is an *n*-ary predicate symbol such that $p \in V$, or (2) *F* is a Horn clause in which each atom is of such a form. An ontology is well-formed if every axiom in the ontology is well-formed with respect to the ontology.

Now we turn our attention to data sources, such as one or more Web pages, that use an ontology to make relation and category claims. Let $S = \langle OS, DS \rangle$ be such a data source, where $OS = \langle VS, AS \rangle$ is the ontology and *DS* is the set of claims. *S* is well-formed if *OS* is well-formed and each element of *DS* is a ground atom that is well-formed with respect to *OS*. The terms of these ground atoms are constants and can be instance keys or values of a SHOE data type.

We wish to be able to describe the meaning of a given data source, but it is important to realize that on the Web, the same data may have different meanings for different people. An agent may be able to draw useful inferences from a data source without necessarily agreeing with the ontology intended by the data's author. A common case would be when an agent wishes to integrate information that depends on two overlapping but still distinct ontologies. Which set of rules should the agent use to reason about this data? There are many possible answers, and we propose that the agent should be free to choose. To describe this notion, we define a *perspective* $P = \langle S, O \rangle$ as a data source $S = \langle OS, DS \rangle$ viewed in the context of an ontology $O = \langle V, A \rangle$. If $O = OS$, then *P* is the *intended perspective*; otherwise it is an *alternate perspective*. If there are elements of *DS* that are not well-formed with respect to *O*, these elements are considered to be irrelevant to the perspective. If *WS* is the subset of *DS* that is well-formed with respect to *O*, then *P* is said to result in a definite logic theory $T = WS \cup A$.

Finally, we can describe the semantics of a perspective *P* using a model-theoretic approach. An interpretation of the perspective consists of a domain, the assignment of each constant in *S* to an element of the domain, and an assignment of each element in *V* to a relation from the domain. A model of *P* is an interpretation such that every formula in its theory *T* is true with respect to it. We define a query on *P* as a Horn clause with no consequent that has the semantics typically assigned to such queries for a definite logic program *T*.

We also introduce one additional piece of terminology that will be used later in the chapter. If every ground atomic logical consequence of perspective *P* is also a ground atomic logical consequence of perspective *P'*, then *P'* is said to *semantically subsume P*. In such cases, any query issued against perspective *P'* will have at least the same answers as if the query was issued against *P*. If two perspectives semantically subsume each other, then they are said to be equivalent.

2.3.4   *Interoperability in Distributed Environments*

SHOE was designed specifically with the needs of distributed Internet agents in mind. A key problem in distributed systems is interoperability; SHOE attempts to maximize interoperability through the use of shared ontologies, prefixed naming, prevention of contradictions, and locality of inference rules. This section discusses each of these in turn.

Figure 2.3 shows how the ontology extension and renaming features of the SHOE language promote interoperability. When two ontologies need to refer

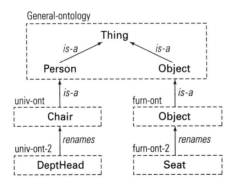

Figure 2.3
Interoperability in SHOE is based on shared ontologies.

to a common concept, they should both extend an ontology in which that concept is defined.

In this way, consistent definitions can be assigned to each concept while still allowing communities to customize ontologies to include definitions and rules of their own for specialized areas of knowledge. These methods allow the creation of high-level, abstract unifying ontologies extended by often-revised custom ontologies for specialized, new areas of knowledge. There is a trade-off between trust of sources far down in the tree (because of their fleeting nature) and the ease with which such sources can be modified on the fly to accommodate new important functions (because of their fleeting nature). In a dynamic environment, an ontology that is too stable will be too inflexible, but of course an ontology that is too flexible will be too unstable. SHOE attempts to strike a balance using simple economies of distribution.

The problems of synonymy and polysemy are handled by the extension mechanism and ⟨DEF-RENAME⟩ tag. Using this tag, ontologies can create aliases for terms, so that domain-specific vocabularies can be used. For example, in figure 2.3, the term DeptHead in univ-ont2 means the same thing as Chair in univ-ont, thanks to a ⟨DEF-RENAME⟩ tag in univ-ont2. Although the extension and aliasing mechanisms solve the problem of synonymy of terms, the same terms can still be used with different meanings in different ontologies. This is not undesirable; a term should not be restricted for use in one domain simply because it was first used in a particular ontology. As shown in figure 2.3, in SHOE different ontologies may also use the same term to define a different concept. Here, the term Chair means different things in univ-ont and furn-ont because the categories have different ancestors. To resolve any ambiguity that may arise, ontological elements are always referenced using special prefixes that define unique paths to their respective enclosing ontologies. Instances and ontologies that reference other ontologies must include statements identifying which ontologies are used, and each ontology is assigned a prefix that is unique within the scope of that ontology. All references to elements from that ontology must include this prefix, thereby uniquely identifying which definition of a particular term is desired.

Recall that each SHOE instance must be assigned a key and that this key is often the URL of the Web page describing the instance. In SHOE, it is assumed that each key identifies exactly one entity, but no assumptions are made about whether two distinct keys might identify the same entity. This is because many different URLs could be used to refer to the same page (because a single host can have multiple domain names and operating systems may allow many different paths to the same file). To solve problems that may arise in a practical setting from having multiple keys identifying the same entity, a canonical form can be chosen for the URL; an example rule might be that the full path to the file should be specified, without operating systems shortcuts such as "~" for a user's home directory. Even then, problems may still crop up with multiple keys possibly referring to the same conceptual object. At any rate, the solution implemented in SHOE ensures that the system will interpret two objects as being equivalent only when they truly are equivalent. Ensuring that two object references are matched when they conceptually refer to the same object is an open problem.

In distributed systems, a contradiction cannot be handled by simply retracting the most recent assertion; otherwise the system would give preference to those authors who provided their information first, regardless of whether it was true, false, or a matter of opinion. Rather than delve into complex procedures for maintaining consistency, we chose to keep SHOE easy to understand and implement. Therefore, we have carefully designed the language to eliminate the possibility of contradictions among agent assertions. SHOE does this in four ways:

- SHOE permits only assertions, not retractions.

- SHOE does not permit logical negation.

- SHOE does not have single-valued relations, that is, relational sets that may have only one value (or some fixed number of values).

- SHOE does not permit the specification of disjoint classes.

Although eliminating the possibility of contradictions in this way restricts the expressive power of the language, in our practical experience, we have not yet found it to be a significant problem. It should be noted that SHOE does not prevent "contradictions" that are not logically inconsistent. If claimant *A* says *father(Mark, Katherine)* and claimant *B* says *father(Katherine, Mark)*, the apparent contradiction is because one claimant is misusing the *father* relation. However, this does not change the fact that *A* and *B* made those claims.

A similar problem may occur in an ontology in which an inference rule derives a conclusion whose interpretation would be inconsistent with another ontology. Therefore, it is the ontology designer's responsibility to make sure that the ontology is correct and that it is consistent with all ontologies that it extends. It is expected that users will avoid ontologies that result in erroneous conclusions and that they will thus be weeded out by natural selection.

Yet another problem with distributed environments is the potential interference of rules created by other parties: a rule created by one individual could have unwanted side effects for other individuals. For these reasons, SHOE allows rules to be defined only in ontologies, and the only rules that can apply to a given claim are those that are defined in the ontologies used by the instance making the claim. Since rules can be expressed only in ontologies, the process of determining when a rule is applicable is simplified, and page authors can use this to control the side effects of their claims. If a user wishes to view an instance in a different context or use it in ways originally unintended by the author, then the user can employ an alternate perspective for the instance that is based on a different, but compatible, ontology.

2.3.5   Ontology Evolution

The Web's changing nature means that ontologies will have to be changed frequently to keep up with current knowledge and usage. Since physically revising an ontology can invalidate objects that reference it for vocabulary and definitions, it is useful to think of a revision as a new ontology that is a copy of the original ontology with subsequent modifications. In fact, this is exactly what SHOE does: each version of an ontology is a separate Web resource and is assigned a unique version number, and all references to an ontology must denote a specific version. How then, is a revision different from an ontology with a different identifier? The answer is that a revision can specify that it is backwardly compatible with an earlier version (using the backward-compatible-with attribute of the ontology), which allows interoperability among sources that use different versions of the same ontology.

Before we define backward compatibility, we will first characterize and compare different types of revisions using the formal model developed in section 2.3.3. To be succinct, we will discuss only revisions that add or remove components; the modification of a component can be thought of as a removal followed by an addition. In the rest of this section, O will refer to the original ontology, O' to its revision, P and P' to the perspectives formed by these respective ontologies and an arbitrary source $S = \langle O, DS \rangle$, and T and T' to the respective theories for these perspectives.

If a revision O' adds an arbitrary rule to ontology O, then for any source S, the perspective P' semantically subsumes P. Since the revision only adds a sentence to the corresponding theory $T' \supset T$, and since first-order logic is monotonic, any logical consequence of T is also a logical consequence of T'. Thus, when a revision that adds rules provides an alternate perspective of a legacy data source, there may be additional answers that were not originally intended by the author of the data. Similar reasoning is used to ascertain that if the revision removes rules, then P semantically subsumes P'.

If O' consists of the removal of categories or relations from O, then P semantically subsumes P'. This is because there may be some atoms in S that were well-formed with respect to O that are not well-formed with respect to O'. Informally, if categories or relations are removed, predicate symbols are removed from the vocabulary. If the ground atoms of S depend on these symbols for well-formedness, then when the symbols are removed, the sentences are no longer well-formed. Thus, $T' \subseteq T$, and because of the monotonicity of definite logic, every logical consequence of T' is a logical consequence of T.

Revisions of this type may mean that using the revised ontology to form a perspective may result in fewer answers to a given query.

Finally, if the revision only adds categories or relations, the corresponding perspective P' is equivalent to P. Since $T' \supset T$, it is easy to show that P' semantically subsumes P. The proof of the statement in the other direction depends on the nature of the axioms added: $R(x1, \ldots, xi, \ldots xn) \rightarrow C(xi)$ for relations and $C(x) \rightarrow Pi(x)$ for categories. It also relies on the fact that because of the definitions of categories and relations, the predicate of each antecedent is a symbol added by the new ontology and must be distinct from symbols in any other ontology. Therefore any atoms formed from these predicates are not well-formed with respect to any preexisting ontology. Thus, there can be no such atoms in S, since S must be well-formed with respect to some ontology $\neq O'$. Since the antecedents cannot be fulfilled, the rules will have no new logical consequences that are ground atoms. Since P semantically subsumes P' and vice versa, P and P' are equivalent. This result indicates that we can safely add relations or categories to the revision and maintain the same perspective on all legacy data sources.

We can now define backward compatibility: an ontology revision O' can be said to be backwardly compatible with an ontology O if for any data source $S = \langle O, DS \rangle$, the perspective $P' = \langle S, O' \rangle$ semantically subsumes the perspective $P = \langle S, O \rangle$. Put simply, if every logical consequence of the original is also a consequence of the revision, then the revision is backward compatible. By our analysis above, if a revision only adds categories, relations, or rules, then it is backwardly compatible with the original, whereas if it removes any of these components, then it is not backwardly compatible.

With this notion of backward compatibility, agents can assume with some degree of confidence that a perspective that uses the backwardly compatible revision will not alter the original meaning of the data source but instead supplement it with information that was originally implicit. Agents that don't wish to assume anything may still access the original version of the ontology, because it still exists at the original URL. However, it should be noted that this versioning mechanism is dependent on the compliance of the ontology designers. Since an ontology is merely a file on a Web server, there is nothing to prevent its author from making changes to an existing ontology version. This is the price we pay for having a system that is flexible enough to cope with the needs of diverse user communities while being able to change rapidly. However, we presume that users will gravitate toward ontologies from sources that they can trust and that ontologies that cannot be trusted will become obsolete.

Although ideally integration in SHOE is a by-product of ontology extension, a distributed environment in which ontologies are rapidly changing is not always conducive to this. Even when ontology designers have the best intentions, a very specialized concept may be simultaneously defined by two new ontologies. To handle such situations, periodic ontology integration must occur. Ontologies can be integrated using a new ontology that maps the related concepts using inference rules, by revising the relevant ontologies to map to each other, or by creating a new, more general ontology that defines the common concepts and revising the relevant ontologies to extend the new ontology. We discuss each of these solutions in more detail in Heflin and Hendler 2000a.

2.3.6 Scalability

The scalability of a knowledge representation depends on the computational complexity of the inferences that it sanctions. We intentionally omitted from SHOE features such as disjunction and negation that typically make knowledge representation systems intractable. Since SHOE is essentially a set of Horn clauses, a naive forward-chaining inference algorithm can be executed in polynomial time and space in the worst case. Of course, the expected size of an extensional database built from the Web makes this an undesirable option.

We carefully chose SHOE's set of semantic primitives so that it could be reduced to datalog, thus allowing the use of optimized algorithms such as magic sets (Ullman 1988). The semantics of SHOE categories can be described easily using a datalog rule. For example, category membership such as the fact that a Person is a Mammal may be expressed by using unary predicates and a rule of the form:

```
Mammal (X)  :- Person (x).
```

Since SHOE's inferential rules are basically Horn clauses, they also map directly to datalog. Furthermore, SHOE's more restrictive variable join rule ensures that all SHOE inference rules are safe. Thus, SHOE is equivalent to safe datalog without negation.

Obviously, SHOE systems can benefit from deductive database research, but the massive size of the resulting knowledge bases may at times yield unacceptable performance. Therefore SHOE has a modular design that allows systems to cleanly provide differing degrees of inferential capability. For example, a system may choose to implement only transitive category membership or may choose to implement no inference at all, thus providing access only to the extensional database. Although such systems might be incomplete reasoners with respect to the intended perspective (see section 2.3.3), they can be complete reasoners with respect to an alternate perspective (i.e., one that mirrors the intended perspective but omits all inference rules and/or category definitions).

2.4   Implementation

In the previous section we described the semantics of SHOE and discussed its treatment of some of the specific challenges for a Semantic Web language. In this section we describe a suite of tools and methods for using the language in practice and describe its application to the domains of computer science departments and food safety.

Although there are many possible ways to use the SHOE language, the simplest is one that parallels the way the Web works today. There are numerous tools that can be used to produce content, and this content is published on the Web by making it accessible via a Web server. A Web crawler can then gather relevant pages and store them in a repository, which can then be queried by some type of user interface. The key component of

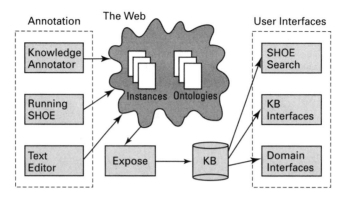

Figure 2.4
SHOE architecture.

a SHOE system is that both the content and the ontologies that provide semantics for the content are published on the Web. Since this information is structured and has semantics, the repository should be a knowledge base rather than an information retrieval system. This basic architecture is shown in figure 2.4.

The first step in using SHOE is to locate or design an appropriate ontology. To assist in this process, there should be a central repository of ontologies. A simple repository might be a set of Web pages that categorize ontologies, whereas a more complex repository might associate a number of characteristics with each ontology so that specific searches could be issued. A Web-based system that uses the latter approach is described in Vega 1999. If for a certain application no suitable ontology is available, any newly created ontology should always extend available ontologies that contain related concepts.

The process of adding semantic tags to a Web page is called annotation. There are a number of tools that can be used in this process, from simple text editors, to GUI-based editors, to semi- or fully automated techniques. Text editors have the advantage that they are commonplace but require that users become familiar with the syntax of SHOE. We have developed a GUI-based editor for SHOE called the Knowledge Annotator that allows the user to create markup by selecting from lists and filling in forms. However, there are cases in which the user may want to generate markup that corresponds to information from large lists or tables in preexisting Web pages. For such situations, our Running SHOE tool can be used to quickly create a wrapper for an existing document by specifying tokens that indicate records and fields and then mapping these records and fields to classes and relations from some ontology. This tool can be used to generate a large body of semantic markup from regular documents in minutes. Other approaches to generating markup can include machine learning, information extraction, and, in limited domains, natural-language processing techniques.

Once the necessary content and ontologies documents are published on the Web, they can be harvested by a Web crawler. Exposé, the SHOE Web crawler, searches for Web pages with SHOE markup and stores the information in a knowledge base. Whenever a page commits to an ontology unknown to the system, this ontology is also retrieved and stored in the knowledge base. The biggest drawback to a Web crawler approach is that the information stored in the knowledge base is only as recent as the last time the crawler visited the source Web page. In certain applications, such as comparison shopping, this level of timeliness may be unacceptable. An interesting direction for future research is the development of focused crawlers that seek answers to particular questions in real time.

As mentioned above, the Web crawler needs a knowledge base in which to store the results of its efforts. A knowledge base provides permanent storage for information and the ability to use knowledge to draw inferences from the information that has been explicitly stored in it. An important trade-off for candidate knowledge base systems is the degree to which they can make inferences sanctioned by the language (completeness) and the response time to queries (performance). We believe that users of SHOE systems should be able to specify their preferences with regard to this scale. Thus, many different knowledge base systems can be used for SHOE, with the appropriate trade-offs in mind.

At the completeness end of the scale sit systems such as XSB (Sagonas, Swift, and Warren 1994), a logic programming and deductive database system. XSB is more expressive than datalog and can thus be used as a complete reasoner for SHOE. At the performance end of the scale are relational database management systems (RDBMSs), which have traditionally been used for querying enormous quantities of data. However, a relational database provides no automated inferential capability and thus can only answer queries using the information that has been explicitly stored. In between these two extremes, one finds systems such as Parka (Evett, Andersen, and Hendler 1993; Stoffel, Taylor, and Hendler 1997), a high-performance knowledge representation system the roots of which lie in semantic networks and frame systems but which makes use of certain database technology such as secondary storage and indexing. Parka has better inferential capabilities than an RDBMS, but less than XSB while being faster than XSB but slower than an RDBMS.

Once information is stored in a knowledge base, it can be queried by a variety of front ends. SHOE Search (Heflin and Hendler 2000b) is a generic tool that gives users a new way to browse the Web by allowing them to submit structured queries and open documents by clicking on the URLs in the results in returns. The user first chooses an ontology against which the query should be issued and then chooses the class of the desired object from a hierarchical list. After the system presents a list of all properties that could apply to that object and the user has typed in desired values for one or more of these properties, the user issues a query and is presented with a set of results in a tabular form. If the user double-clicks on a binding that is a URL, then the corresponding Web page will be opened in a new window of the user's Web browser.

In order to evaluate the tools and techniques for SHOE, we have used them in two different domains. The first domain is that of computer science departments. We started by creating a simple computer science department ontology[4] by hand. The scope of this ontology includes departments, faculty, students, publications, courses, and research, for a total of 43 categories and 25 relations. The next step was to annotate a set of Web pages (i.e., add SHOE semantic markup to them). All members of the Parallel Understanding Systems (PLUS) Group marked up their own web pages. Although most members used the Knowledge Annotator, a few added the tags using their favorite text editors. To get even more SHOE information, we used the Running SHOE tool on the faculty, users, courses, and research groups Web pages from the Web sites of various computer science departments. Exposé was used to acquire the SHOE knowledge from the Web pages. This resulted in a total of 38,159 assertions, which were stored in both Parka and XSB. Although the knowledge base for this domain is very small when compared to the scale of the entire Web, the initial results are promising. For example, a query of the form member(http://www.cs.umd.edu, x) ∧ instance(Faculty, x) takes Parka less than 250 milliseconds to answer.

The possible benefits of a system such as this one are numerous. A prospective student could use it to inquire about universities that offered a particular class or performed research in certain areas. Or a researcher could design an agent to search for articles on a particular subject whose authors are members of a particular set of institutions and were published during some desired time interval. Additionally, SHOE can combine the information contained in multiple sources to answer a single query. For example, to answer the query "Find all papers about ontologies written by authors who are faculty members at public universities in the state of Maryland" one would need information from university home pages, faculty listing pages, and publication pages for individual faculty members. Such a query would be impossible for current search engines because they rank each page based upon how many of the query terms it contains.

The SHOE technology was also applied to the domain of food safety. The Joint Institute for Food Safety and Applied Nutrition (JIFSAN), a partnership between the Food and Drug Administration (FDA) and the University of Maryland, is working to expand the knowledge and resources available to support risk analysis in the food safety area. One of its goals is to develop a Web site that will serve as a clearinghouse for information about food safety risks. This Web site must serve a diverse group of users, including researchers, policymakers, risk assessors, and the general public, and thus must be able to respond to queries that vary widely in terminology, complexity, and specificity. This is not possible with keyword-based indices but can be accomplished using SHOE.

The initial TSE (transmissible spongiform encephalopathies) ontology was fleshed out in a series of meetings that included members of JIFSAN and a knowledge engineer. The ontology focused on the three main concerns for TSE risks: source material, processing, and end product use. Currently, the ontology has 73 categories and 88 relations.[5] Following the creation of the initial ontology, the TSE development team annotated Web pages. There are two types of pages that this system uses. Since the Web currently has little information on animal material processing, we created a set of pages describing many important source materials, processes, and products. The second set of pages are existing TSE pages that provide general descriptions of different diseases, make recommendations or regulations, and present experimental results. Early annotations were difficult because the original ontology did not have all of the concepts that were needed. When the initial set of pages was completed, we ran Exposé, using Parka as the knowledge base system. Since the TSE ontology currently does not define inference rules, Parka is able to provide a complete reasoning capability for it. The Parka knowledge base can be queried using SHOE Search as discussed earlier, but JIFSAN also wanted a special-purpose tool to help users visualize and understand the processing of animal materials.

To accommodate this, we built the TSE Path Analyzer, a graphical tool that can be used to analyze how source materials end up in products that are eventually consumed by humans or animals. This information is extremely valuable when one is trying to determine the risk of contamination given the chance that a source material is contaminated. It is expected that information on each step in the process will be provided on different Web sites (since many steps are performed by different companies); thus using a language like SHOE is essential to integrating this information. The TSE Path Analyzer allows the user to pick a source, process, and/or end product from lists that are derived from the taxonomies of the ontology. The system then displays all possible pathways that fulfill the query. Since these displays are created dynamically based on the semantic information in the SHOE Web pages, they are kept current automatically, even when the SHOE information on some remote site is changed.

2.5   Related Work

In recent years, work has been conducted in the area of using ontologies to help machines process and understand Web documents. Fensel et al. (1998) have developed Ontobroker, which proposes minor extensions to the common anchor tag in HTML. The theoretical basis for Ontobroker is frame logic, a superset of Horn logic that treats ontology objects as first-class citizens. However, this approach depends on a centralized broker, and as a result, the Web pages cannot specify that they reference a particular ontology, and agents from outside the community cannot discover the ontology information. Kent (1999) has designed the Ontology Markup Language (OML) and the Conceptual Knowledge Markup Language (CKML), which were influenced by SHOE but are based on the theories of formal concept analysis and information flow. However, the complexity of these theories makes it unlikely that this language will be accepted by the majority of existing Web developers and/or users. OIL (Decker et al. 2000) is a new Web ontology language that extends RDF and RDF Schema with description logic capabilities. Jannink et al. (1998) suggest a different approach from creating Web ontology languages and annotating pages: they propose that an ontology should be built for each data source and that generalization should then be accomplished by integrating these data sources. In this way, the data dictate the structure of the ontology rather than the other way around.

Querying the Web is such an important problem that a diverse body of research has been directed toward it. Some projects focus on creating query languages for the Web (Arocena, Mendelzon, and Mihaila 1997; Konopnicki and Shemueli 1995), but these approaches are limited to queries concerning the HTML structure of a document and the hypertext links. They also rely on index servers such as AltaVista or Lycos to search for words or phrases and thus suffer from the limitations of keyword search. Work on semistructured databases (McHugh et al. 1997) is of great significance to querying and processing XML, but the semistructured model suffers the same interoperability problems as XML. Even techniques such as data guides will be of little use when information developed by different communities in different contexts needs to be integrated. Another approach involves mediators (or wrappers), custom software that serves as an interface between middleware and a data source (Wiederhold 1992; Papakonstantinou et al. 1995; Roth and Schwarz 1997). When applied to the Web, wrappers allow users to query a page's contents as if it were a database. However, the heterogeneity of the Web requires that a multitude of custom wrappers be developed, and it is possible that important relationships cannot be extracted from the text based solely on the structure of the document. Semiautomatic generation of wrappers (Ashish and Knoblock 1997) is a promising approach to overcoming the first problem but is limited to data that has a recognizable structure.

In order to avoid the overhead of annotating pages or writing wrappers, some researchers have proposed machine learning techniques. Craven et al. (1998) have trained a system to classify Web pages and extract relations from them in accordance with a simple ontology. However, this approach is constrained by the time-consuming task of developing a training set and has difficulty in classifying certain kinds of pages because of the lack of similarities between pages in the same class.

2.6   Conclusion

In this chapter, we have described many of the challenges that must be addressed by research on the Semantic Web and have described SHOE, one of the first languages to address these problems explicitly. SHOE provides interoperability in distributed environments through the use of extensible, shared ontologies, the avoidance of contradictions, and the localization of inference rules. It handles the changing nature of the Web with an ontology versioning scheme that supports backward compatibility. It takes steps in the direction of scalability by limiting expressivity and allowing for different levels of inferential support. Finally, since the Web is an open world, SHOE does not allow conclusions to be drawn from lack of information.

To demonstrate SHOE's features, we have described applications that show the use of SHOE. We've developed a freely available ontology for computer science pages, and we've also worked with biological epidemiologists to design an ontology for a key food safety area. These applications show that SHOE can function on the Web and that tools using SHOE can be built and used.

Although we believe SHOE is a good language that has practical use, we do not mean to suggest that it solves all of the problems of the Semantic Web. We are at the beginning of a new and exciting research field, and there is still much work to do. Further research must be performed to determine how SHOE's method for interoperability scales to the thousands of ontologies that will be created on the Web, and the problem of ontology evolution must be studied more closely. Additionally, the appropriate level of expressivity for a Semantic Web language must be explored. For example, are negation and cardinality constraints necessary, and if so, how can they be used in a decentralized system such as the Web? Finally, more user-friendly tools need to be developed so that use of the Semantic Web can become routine for the layperson.

As pioneers in this field, we hope that our experience with SHOE can inspire and inform others. A key goal of this project is to raise the issues that are crucial to the development of the Semantic Web and encourage others to explore them. To this end, we have made SHOE freely available on the Web, including the Java libraries and our prototype tools. Interested readers are urged to explore our Web pages at http://www.cs.umd.edu/projects/plus/SHOE/ for the full details of the language and the applications.

Acknowledgments

This work was supported by the Army Research Laboratory under contract DAAL01-97-K0135 and the Air Force Research Laboratory under grants F306029910013 and F306020020578.

Notes

1. Prolog is not strictly declarative because the order of the rules determines how the system processes them.

2. In actuality, SHOE has a separate namespace for each ontology, but one can assume that the symbols are unique, because it is always possible to apply a renaming that appends a unique ontology identifier to each symbol.

3. A definite program clause is a Horn clause that has at least one antecedent and exactly one consequent.

4. This ontology is located at http://www.cs.umd.edu/projects/plus/SHOE/onts/cs1.0.html.

5. Those interested in the details of the ontology can view it at http://www.cs.umd.edu/projects/plus/SHOE/onts/tseont.html.

References

Arocena, G., A. Mendelzon, and G. Mihaila. 1997. Applications of a Web Query Language. *Computer Networks* 29:1305–1315.

Ashish, N., and C. Knoblock. 1997. Semi-Automatic Wrapper Generation for Internet Information Sources. In *Proceedings of the Second IFCIS Conference on Cooperative Information Systems (CoopIS), Charleston, South Carolina* (pp. 160–169). Los Alamitos, CA.: IEEE-CS.

Bobrow, D., and T. Winograd. 1977. An Overview of KRL, A Knowledge Representation Language. *Cognitive Science* 1(1):3–46.

Brachman, R., D. McGuinness, P. F. Patel-Schneider, L. Resnick, and A. Borgida. 1991. Living with Classic: When and How to Use a KL-ONE-like Language. In *Explorations in the Representation of Knowledge*, ed. J. Sowa. San Mateo, CA: Morgan-Kaufmann.

Brachman, R., and J. Schmolze. 1985. An Overview of the KL-ONE Knowledge Representation System. *Cognitive Science* 9(2):171–216.

Bray, T., J. Paoli, and C. Sperberg-McQueen. 1998. Extensible Markup Language (XML), W3C (World Wide Web Consortium). Available from http://www.w3.org/TR/1998/REC-xml-19980210.html.

Brickley, D., and R. V. Guha. 1999. Resource Description Framework (RDF) Schema Specification (candidate recommendation). W3C (World Wide Web Consortium. Available from http://www.w3.org/TR/2000/CR-rdf-schema-20000327.

Clark, J. 1999. XSL Transformations (XSLT). W3C (World Wide Web Consortium). Available from http://www.w3.org/TR/1999/REC-xslt-19991116.

Craven, M., D. DiPasquo, D. Freitag, A. McCallum, T. Mitchell, K. Nigram, and S. Slattery. 1998. Learning to Extract Symbolic Knowledge from the World Wide Web. In *Proceedings of the Fifteenth American Association for Artificial Intelligence Conference (AAAI-98)*. Menlo Park, CA/Cambridge, MA: AAAI/MIT Press.

Decker, S., D. Fensel, F. van Harmelen, I. Horrocks, S. Melnik, M. Klein, and J. Broekstra. 2000. Knowledge Representation on the Web. In *Proceedings of the 2000 International Workshop on Description Logics (DL2000), Aachen, Germany, August 2000*, ed. F. Baader and U. Sattler (pp. 89–97). Available from http://sunsite.informatik.rwth-aachen.de/Publications/CEUR-WS/Vol-33/.

Evett, M., W. Andersen, and J. Hendler. 1993. Providing Computational Effective Knowledge Presentation via Massive Parallelism. In *Proceedings of the 13th International Joint Conference on Artificial Intelligence, Chambéry, France, August 28–September 3, 1993*, ed. R. Bajcsy (pp. 1325–1331). San Mateo, CA: Morgan Kaufmann.

Farquhar, A., R. Fikes, and J. Rice. 1997. The Ontolingua Server: A Tool for Collaborative Ontology Construction. *International Journal of Human-Computer Studies* 46(6):707–727.

Fensel, D., S. Decker, M. Erdmann, and R. Studer. 1998. Ontobroker: The Very High Idea. In *Proceedings of the 11th International Flairs Conference (FLAIRS-98), Sanibel Island, Florida, USA, May*, ed. D. J. Cook (pp. 131–135). Menlo Park, CA: AAAI.

Gruber, T. 1993. A Translation Approach to Portable Ontology Specifications. *Knowledge Acquisition* 5:199–220.

Heflin, J., and J. Hendler. 2000a. Dynamic Ontologies on the Web. In *Proceedings of the Seventeenth National Conference on Artificial Intelligence (AAAI-2000)* (pp. 443–449). Menlo Park, CA/Cambridge, MA: AAAI/MIT Press.

Heflin, J., and J. Hendler. 2000b. Searching the Web with SHOE. In *Artificial Intelligence for Web Search. Papers from the AAAI Workshop* (pp. 35–40). WS-00-01. Menlo Park, CA: AAAI Press.

Heflin, J., and J. Hendler. 2000c. Semantic Interoperability on the Web. In Proceedings of Extreme Markup Languages 2000. Graphic Communications Association, Alexandria, VA. Available from http://www.gca.org/attend/2000_conferences/Extreme_2000/.

International Organization for Standardization (ISO). 1986. ISO 8879:1986(E). Information Processing—Text and Office Systems—Standard Generalized Markup Language (SGML). International Organization for Standardization, Geneva.

Jannink, J., S. Pichai, D. Verheijen, and G. Wiederhold. 1998. Encapsulation and Composition of Ontologies. *In AI and Information Integration: Papers from the 1998 Workshop* (pp. 43–50). Technical Report WS-98-14. Menlo Park, CA: AAAI Press.

Kent, R. E. 1999. Conceptual Knowledge Markup Language: The Central Core. In The Twelfth Workshop on Knowledge Acquisition, Modeling and Management. Available from http://sern.ucalgary.ca/KSI/KAW/KAW99/.

Konopnicki, D., and O. Shemueli. 1995. W3QS: A Query System for the World Wide Web. In *Proceedings of the 21st International Conference on Very Large Databases, Zurich, Switzerland, September 11–15, 1995*, ed. U. Dayal, P. M. D. Gray, and S. Nishio (pp. 54–65). San Francisco: Morgan Kaufmann.

Lassila, O. 1998. Web Metadata: A Matter of Semantics. *IEEE Internet Computing* 2(4):30–37.

Lenat, D., and R. Guha. 1990. *Building Large Knowledge Based Systems*. Boston: Addison-Wesley.

Luke, S., and J. Heflin. 2000. SHOE 1.01 (proposed specification). Available from http://www.cs.umd.edu/projects/plus/SHOE/spec.html, 2000.

Luke, S., L. Spector, D. Rager, and J. Hendler. 1997. Ontology-based Web Agents. In *Proceedings of the First International Conference on Autonomous Agents*, ed. W. L. Johnson (pp. 59–66). Marina del Rey, CA: ACM.

MacGregor, R. 1991. The Evolving Technology of Classification-Based Knowledge Representation Systems. In *Explorations in the Representation of Knowledge*, ed. J. Sowa (pp. 54–66). San Francisco: Morgan Kaufmann.

McHugh, J., S. Abiteboul, R. Goldman, D. Quass, and J. Widom. 1997. Lore: A Database Management System for Semistructured Data. *SIGMOD Record* 26(3):54–66.

Noy, N., and C. Hafner. 1997. The State of the Art in Ontology Design. *AI Magazine* 18(3):53–74.

Papakonstantinou, Y., A. Gupta, H. Garcia-Molina, J. D. Ullman. 1995. A Query Translation Scheme for Rapid Implementation of Wrappers. In *Proceedings of the Fourth Annual Conference on Deductive and Object-Oriented Databases (DOOD), Singapore, December 4–7, 1995*, ed. T. Wang Ling et al. (pp. 161–186). Berlin: Springer.

Roth, M., and P. Schwarz. 1997. Don't Scrap It, Wrap It! A Wrapper Architecture for Legacy Data Sources. *In Proceedings of 23rd International Conference on Very Large Databases, Athens, Greece, August 25–29, 1997*, ed. M. Jarke et al. (pp. 266–275). San Francisco: Morgan Kaufmann.

Sagonas, K., T. Swift, and D. S. Warren. 1994. XSB as an Efficient Deductive Database Engine. In *Proceedings of the 1994 ACM SIGMOD International Conference on Management of Data (SIGMOD'94)*, ed. R. T. Snodgrass and M. Winslett (pp. 442–453). Marina del Rey, CA: ACM.

Stoffel, K., M. Taylor and J. Hendler. 1997. Efficient Management of Very Large Ontologies. In *Proceedings of American Association for Artificial Intelligence Conference (AAAI-97), Providence, Rhode Island*. Menlo Park, CA/Cambridge, MA: AAAI/MIT Press.

Ullman, J. 1988. *Principles of Database and Knowledge-Based Systems*. Rockville, MD: Computer Science Press.

Vega, J., A. Gomez-Perez, A. Tello, and H. Pinto. 1999. How to Find Suitable Ontologies Using an Ontology-Based WWW Broker. In *International Work-Conference on Artificial and Natural Neural Networks (IWANN'99), Proceedings, Vol. II, Alicante, Spain*, ed. J. Mira and J. V. Sánchez-Andrés (pp. 725–739). Berlin: Springer.

Wiederhold, G. 1992. Mediators in the Architecture of Future Information Systems. *IEEE Computer* 25(3):38–49.

3   DAML-ONT: An Ontology Language for the Semantic Web

Deborah McGuinness, Richard Fikes, Lynn Andrea Stein, and James Hendler

3.1   Introduction

The DARPA Agent Markup Language (DAML) initiative is aimed at supporting the development of the Semantic Web. The program funds research in languages, tools, infrastructure, and applications for making Web content more accessible and understandable. It is funded by the U.S. Government yet represents collaborations among the Department of Defense, U.S. and European academia and business, and international consortia such as the W3C. Although the program covers the breadth of issues related to markup language development, deployment, and evolution, this chapter focuses on the markup language itself.

DAML is being developed in two pieces. The first portion—discussed in this chapter—is the ontology language, aimed at capturing definitions of terms: classes, subclasses, their properties, their restrictions, and individual object descriptions. The second portion of the language (called DAML-L) will address the issue of encoding inference and general logical implications.

In this chapter, we review the history and motivations for the development of the initial DAML ontology language, DAML-ONT. In the following section, we introduce the DAML-ONT language syntax and usage through a pedagogically ordered set of examples derived from the initial DAML walk-through document (Stein and Connolly 2000). In order to fully specify a knowledge representation language, one needs to describe both the syntax and the semantics of the language. The syntax description specifies what strings of characters are legal statements in the language. The semantic description specifies the intended meaning of each legal statement in the language. In the final section of this chapter, we explore an axiomatic semantics for DAML-ONT.

The DAML ontology language takes its motivation from many places, most notably the evolving Web languages, in particular RDF (Lassila 1998; Lassila and Swick 1999) (with the embedded XML) and RDFS (Brickley and Guha 2000), jointly referred to in this chapter as RDF/S. It is important for an ontology language to be backward compatible with existing Web standards for interoperability, given the growing user base of content, tools for these languages, and users who are comfortable with the languages. All of our examples below thus have the format of XML-based RDF. DAML-ONT extends RDF/S by capturing semantic relations in machine-readable form through more expressive term descriptions along with precise semantics. This is important for many reasons; arguably the most salient is to facilitate intercommunication among agents. Although compatibility with Web languages was the paramount consideration as we developed the language, we also recognized that markup representational needs went beyond what was conveniently expressible in RDF/S. Thus, an extended language was considered.

The language is also influenced by frame-based systems, including knowledge representation languages such as Ontolingua (Farquhar, Fikes, and Rice 1997) or KEE. Frame systems have enjoyed acceptance and perceived ease of use by broad populations and have been embraced relatively widespread use (Fikes and Kehler 1985; Karp 1992; Chaudhri et al. 1998). The goal of our language is to be accessible to the masses and thus it was important to use paradigms that are easy to explain and use.

Finally, DAML-ONT takes motivation from the field of description logics (www.dl.kr.org), which provide a formal foundation for frame-based systems.

Some early description logics–based systems include KL-ONE (Brachman and Schmolze 1985), CLASSIC (Borgida et al. 1989), and LOOM (MacGregor 1991), and a more recent example of a description logic-based system is OIL (Fensel et al. 2000; Bechhofer et al. 2000). Description logics emphasize clear, unambiguous languages supported by complete denotational semantics and tractable reasoning algorithms. Description logics have been heavily analyzed in order to understand how constructors interact and combine to affect tractable reasoning. (See, for example Donini et al. 1991a and 1991b, for early evaluations.) Also, the study of reasoning algorithms has produced knowledge about the efficiency of such algorithms. (See Horrocks and Patel-Schneider 1999 and Horrocks and Sattler 1999, for example). DAML-ONT draws on the general field of research in description logics and, in particular, on the latest description logic: OIL, designed to be an expressive description logic that is integrated with modern Web technology.

The resulting DAML ontology language is a combination of these three building blocks along with influence from KIF (the Knowledge Interchange Format), a first-order, logic-based proposed ANSI standard, SHOE (Simple HTML Ontology Language), and OKBC (Open Knowledge Base Connectivity), a standard applications programming interface for knowledge systems. The initial proposal for the language was written by MIT and W3C DAML contractors (Berners-Lee et al. 2000). It was subsequently taken over by a DAML language committee, which, in turn, expanded to become the Joint US/EU ad hoc Agent Markup Language Committee. The joint committee has had responsibility for all DAML ontology language releases to date. There is also expected to be a W3C ontology committee (under the Semantic Web Activity, http://www.w3.org/2001/sw/) that will have responsibility for future Semantic Web language releases.

It is worth noting that after DAML-ONT was released, the joint committee undertook a major effort to evolve the language. The initial language was heavily influenced by the existing Web languages. A primary initial goal of DAML-ONT was to provide a Web-compatible language expressive enough to handle markup requirements. Constructors were chosen initially by means of use-case analysis of experience with the current Web markup languages, mostly RDF and XML. A second primary goal was to produce a language quickly, so that experimentation could inform further development. An ontology library was also formed rapidly so that DAML ontologies could be submitted, stored, and reused by a larger community. Of these competing influences, Web language compatibility and timeliness were the first concerns. Usability issues, as informed by frame languages, were a secondary concern, and formal foundations—as found in description logics—came later. In a subsequent effort, Fikes and McGuinness (2001) produced an axiomatic semantics for DAML-ONT, providing a more precise foundation for semantic analysis of the language. Simultaneously, the joint committee undertook a concerted effort to improve the compatibility of DAML-ONT with more formal foundations. The resulting language, which was essentially a merging of DAML-ONT and OIL, is called DAML+OIL. It places much more emphasis on clear semantics for the language, provided by our updated axiomatic semantics (http://www.daml.org/2001/03/axiomatic-semantics.html) along with a model-theoretic semantics (http://www.daml.org/2001/03/model-theoretic-semantics.html). DAML+OIL also filters language constructors according to an understanding of the impact that they have on reasoning algorithms. It chooses its constructors carefully following the analysis done on the underlying formal description logic, typically referred to as SHIQ.[1]

An update to this chapter that begins with DAML+OIL is in preparation and will be available from www.ksl.stanford.edu/people/dlm/.

3.2   An Introduction through Examples

A language meant to capture terms and their meanings will need to be able to describe classes of objects, relations between objects, and ground objects in the domain of discourse. We will introduce the basic notions of the DAML ontology language through example. Readers interested in more information can also consider the following. The DAML Web site (www.daml.org) contains the full specification of the language along with an example file and an annotated walk-through. It also offers a DAML ontology library, along with numerous links to related work. Also, the documentation offered on the OIL site (www.ontoknowledge.org/oil) is useful in particular for language specification, documentation, semantics, and use cases. A white paper (Bechhofer et al. 2000) available on the site provides a nice introduction to OIL. Also available from the OIL site is the denotational semantics specification for OIL, which was the starting point for the denotational semantics for DAML+OIL. Later in this chapter, we provide our axiomatic semantics for DAML-ONT (which is, of course, the starting place for the axiomatic semantics for DAML+OIL).

The following sections, from the introduction through the extended example, are motivated by the walk-through available from the DAML home page.

3.2.1 Defining Classes and Properties

It is useful in describing objects to define types for the objects. For example, we may be interested in describing people and animals. First, some general classes should be defined. The first class defined is named animal:

```
<Class ID="Animal">
```

The class tag is used to state that there is a class known as Animal. It does not say anything else about what an animal is other than specifying the ID for that particular class. It is also not (necessarily) the sole source of information about Animals. By saying that the ID is Animal, it becomes possible, using the URI of the containing page followed by #Animal, for future sentences to refer to the definition of Animal given here. Thus, it is possible to add information to the definition of Animal at a later point.

Next, it may be desirable to annotate terms with labels and comments:

```
<label>Animal</label>
<comment>This class of animals is illustrative of a number
of ontological idioms.</comment>
```

These two lines introduce a label (a brief identifier of the enclosing element, suitable for graphical representations of RDF, etc.) and a comment (a atural-language—English, in this case—description of the element within which it is included). Neither a label nor a comment contributes to the logical interpretation of the DAML. The tag

```
</Class>
```

closes the current definition of the class Animal.

It may also be desirable to define types of animals, Male and Female:

```
<Class ID="Male">
    <subClassOf resource="#Animal"/>
</Class>
```

The subClassOf element asserts that its subject (Male) is a subclass of its object (the resource identified by #Animal).

When we define Female, we may want to state that no one can be simultaneously a Male and a Female. We do this using the disjointFrom tag in combination with the subClassOf tag below:

```
<Class ID="Female">
    <subClassOf resource="#Animal"/>
    <disjointFrom resource="#Male"/>
</Class>
```

3.2.2 Defining Individuals

The syntax that we've used to define classes can also be used to define individuals. For example, imagine that we want to say that Fred is a Male. Here we provide the syntax for defining the individual Fred. This piece of DAML begins with the type of the thing we're describing, in this case Male:

```
<Male ID="Fred">
    <label>Fred</label>
    <comment>Fred is a Male.</comment>
</Male>
```

The label and comment attributes are attached to this individual, Fred, but neither carries any semantics for the computer.

At this point, we can see the first benefit to be had from inference. Because we know that Fred is Male and because we are aware of the subclass relationship between Male and Animal, we know that Fred is also of type Animal.

3.2.3   *Relating Individuals through Properties*

Properties are used to relate items to each other. In this case we will be interested in connecting two animals via the parent property:

```
<Property ID="parent">
```

The property definition begins similarly to that of the class: there is a property called parent. Note, however, that this is not a closing tag; there's more to this definition. (There is a matching ⟨/Property⟩ tag below.)

We may want to say how many parents an animal can have. In this case we will state that things that have parents have exactly two parents:

```
<cardinality>2</cardinality>
```

Embedded elements, such as this one, are understood to describe their enclosing elements. So, this cardinality element describes the property whose ID is parent.

We may want to state that parent is a property that applies only to things that are animals:

```
<domain resource="#Animal"/>
```

This element also describes the property whose ID is parent. It says that the domain of the parent relation is Animal, by asserting that the domain (of the property with ID parent) is the resource known as #Animal. All properties may have domains and ranges specified. The resource attribute is used to refer to a "reference-able" item created with the ID tag.

Each of the names defined so far—Animal, Person, Male, and Female— refers to a name in this (i.e., the containing) document, since each reference begins with a #. The tag

```
</Property>
```

closes the property whose ID is parent.

3.2.4 Describing Attributes of Classes

Now we will define a class with an attribute:

```
<Class ID="Person">
<subClassOf resource="#Animal"/>
```

A Person is a kind of Animal. (See the definition of Animal, above.)

The next few lines describe a domain-specific range restriction. The parent of a Person is also a Person:

```
<restrictedBy>
    <Restriction>
      <onProperty resource="#parent"/>
      <toClass resource="#Person"/>
    </Restriction>
</restrictedBy>
```

The syntax used here is a cliché, that is, it is almost always used as shown, except for the name of the resource in the onProperty element, which will give the name of the property to be restricted, and the resource associated with the toClass element, which will give the name of the class to which the property is restricted. This is also sometimes referred to as a value restriction, since the type of the parent value is being restricted. The tag

```
</Class>
```

marks the end of the Person class definition at this point.

Suppose that we have a Person, Joe:

```
<Person ID="Joe">
    <label>Joe</label>
    <comment>Joe is a person.</comment>
</Person>
```

As we know, since Joe is stated to be of type Person, he will also be of type Animal (because of the subClassOf relationship). He will also have exactly two parents, because of the cardinality statement. Those objects that fill his parent property also are of type Person (thus, they also are of type Animal and also have exactly two parents who are of type Person).

We might also want to define Man as a kind of Male Person and Female as a kind of Female Person. This can be done as follows:

```
<Class ID="Man">
    <subClassOf resource="#Person"/>
    <subClassOf resource="#Male"/>
</Class>
<Class ID="Woman">
    <subClassOf resource="#Person"/>
    <subClassOf resource="#Female"/>
</Class>
```

The release of DAML+OIL will allow the definition of Man as exactly those things that are both person and male. Thus if something is known to be an instance of a male and a person, then it would be inferred to be of type Man. The definition above only uses the subClassOf relation, which states that a Man is simultaneously a subclass of Person and Male, but it does not state that everything that is simultaneously a Person and a Male is a Man.

3.2.5 Using Properties

The next several annotations illustrate features of properties.

Father is a property that is a kind of parent property, that is, *x*'s father is also *x*'s parent. In addition, range is used to ensure that *x*'s father must be Male and that *x* has only one father:

```
<Property ID="father">
    <subProperty resource="#parent"/>
    <range resource="#Man"/>
    <cardinality>1</cardinality>
</Property>
```

At this point if it is stated that Joe is John's father, then we can determine that Joe is of type Male because of the range restriction. Because Male is of type Animal, Joe is also of type Animal. Also, parents have a domain of Person, thus John is of type Person. He has exactly one father, now known to be Joe. Joe must further be of type Person, since Person has a domain-specific range restriction.

Mother is defined similarly to father but using a variant notation. A UniqueProperty is one with cardinality 1, so we can omit that subelement from mother's definition:

```
<UniqueProperty ID="mother">
    <subProperty resource="#parent"/>
    <range resource="#Woman"/>
</UniqueProperty>
```

Sometimes, synonyms are useful. For example, some applications may want to use the term "mom" rather than "mother." The tag equivalentTo allows us to establish this synonymy:

```
<Property ID="mom">
    <equivalentTo resource="#mother"/>
</Property>
```

Inverse relationships are supported as well using the inverseOf tag. If x's parent is y, then y is x's child:

```
<Property ID="child">
    <inverseOf resource="#parent"/>
</Property>
```

Transitive relationships are supported using the TransitiveProperty tag. The ancestor and descendent properties are transitive versions of the parent and child properties. We would need to introduce additional elements to explicitly specify the transitivity:

```
<TransitiveProperty ID="ancestor">
</TransitiveProperty>
<TransitiveProperty ID="descendant"/>
```

The cardinality property is exact. But sometimes we want to bound cardinality without precisely specifying it. A person may have zero or one job, but no more:

```
<Property ID="occupation">
    <maxCardinality>1</maxCardinality>
</Property>
```

In the release of DAML+OIL, cardinality may be stated in a class-dependent manner instead of requiring the cardinality statement to be universally applied to the property.

Classes, too, can be annotated in various ways:

```
<Class ID="Car">
    <comment>no car is a person</comment>
    <subClassOf>
```

The thing that Car is a subClassOf could in principle be specified using a resource=attribute. In this case, however, there is no preexisting succinct name for the thing we want. A car is a kind of nonperson. We build this by introducing a new—anonymous—class definition described using the complementOf tag:

```
<Class>
  <complementOf resource="#Person"/>
```

From the inside out: There's a thing that's the complement of Person, that is, all non-Persons.

```
</Class>
```

That thing is a class.

```
</subClassOf>
```

That thing—the class of all non-Persons—has a subclass.

```
</Class>
```

The class with ID Car is the thing that is a subclass of the class of all non-Persons. (There's a similar construction from the outside in: Car is a class that is a specialization of another class, the class that is left when you consider everything except Persons).

The next example shows an instance of further specifying a previously defined element by using the about attribute. These new assertions about the thing described above with ID Person have no more and no less authority than the assertions made within the ⟨Class ID="Person"⟩ element. (Of course, if the two assertions were in different documents, had different authors, etc., we might want to accord them different authority, but this would be as a result of information *about* those assertions rather than inherently from the assertions themselves.)

In this case, we identify the class Person with the disjoint union of the classes Man and Woman. Note that the disjointUnionOf element contains two subelements, the class Man and the class Woman. The parseType= "daml:collection" indicates that these subelements are to be treated as a unit, that is, that they have special RDF-extending meaning within the disjointUnionOf.

```
<Class about="#Person">
    <comment>every person is a man or a woman</comment>
    <disjointUnionOf parseType="daml:collection">
      <Class about="#Man"/>
      <Class about="#Woman"/>
    </disjointUnionOf>
</Class>
```

A Person has a height, which is a Height. (hasHeight is a property, or relation; Height is a class, or kind of thing.)

```
<Property ID="hasHeight">
    <domain resource="#Person"/>
    <range resource="#Height"/>
</Property>
```

Height is a class described by an explicitly enumerated set. We can describe this set using the oneOf element. Like disjointUnionOf, oneOf uses the RDF-extending parsetype="daml:collection".

```
<Class ID="Height">
    <oneOf parseType="daml:collection">
      <Height ID="short"/>
      <Height ID="medium"/>
      <Height ID="tall"/>
    </oneOf>
</Class>
```

3.3 Notes

Of course by giving an introduction using an example, we have not covered all portions of the language. Brief mention is made here of some other topics (see www.daml.org for more complete information).

DAML-ONT is consistent with the RDF namespace scheme, thus one can refer to RDF namespaces and create a base namespace for work. Ontologies will begin with an RDF start-tag and then include a specification of appropriate namespaces. The following is typical of a namespace declaration:

```
<rdf:RDF
  xmlns:rdf ="http://www.w3.org/1999/02/22-rdf-syntax-ns#"
  xmlns     ="http://www.daml.org/2000/10/daml-ont#"
  xmlns:daml="http://www.daml.org/2000/10/daml-ont#"
  >
```

In this document, the rdf: prefix should be understood as referring to things drawn from the namespace called http://www.w3.org/1999/02/22-rdf-syntax-ns#. This is a conventional RDF declaration appearing verbatim at the beginning of almost every RDF document.[2] The second declaration says that unprefixed element names in this document refer to terms in the namespace called http://www.daml.org/2000/10/daml-ont#. This is a conventional DAML-ONT declaration that should appear verbatim at the beginning of the current generation of DAML-ONT documents. The third declaration binds the daml: prefix to the same namespace name. So, for example, ⟨Thing/⟩ and ⟨daml:Thing/⟩ refer to the same thing in this document.[3]

This set of three namespaces would come at the beginning of the file, and then there would be a trailing closing tag at the end of the file: ⟨/rdf:RDF⟩.

One can also state information about version, import from other resources, etc. For example:

```
<versionInfo>$Id: daml-ex.daml,v 1.2 2000/10/07 03:21:17
connolly Exp $</versionInfo>
 <comment>An example ontology</comment>
<imports resource="http://www.daml.org/2000/10/daml-ont"/>
```

3.4 Language Extensions

When DAML-ONT was released, its authors were conscious that some expressive extensions would be made. Integrating a description logics–like methodology into DAML-ONT provided it with a more formal foundation.

Subsequently, two major features were added through expressive extensions. First, term definitions were introduced, allowing the definition of a term exactly equivalent to a combination of other terms. For example, one could define a term Man as exactly equivalent to the conjunction of a Person who was also a Male. Thus, if it were later stated that John was a Person and a Male, a system could *deduce* that John was a Man instead of waiting to be told that John is a Man.

A second addition was the introduction of concrete domains. It is important in any Web language to be able to make reference to ground objects such as the XML type system in order to appropriately encode things such as numbers and strings. The DAML+OIL extension adds XML types to the language.

3.5   An Axiomatic Semantics of DAML-ONT

3.5.1   Overview

As noted earlier in the chapter, full specification of a knowledge representation requires two things: a syntax description and a semantic description. The semantics of a representation language can be formally specified in multiple ways. We have chosen here to use the method of specifying a translation of the DAML-ONT language into another representation language that has a formally specified semantics. In particular, we have specified a translation of DAML-ONT into first-order predicate calculus, which has a well-accepted model-theoretic semantics. We specify how to translate a DAML-ONT ontology into a logical theory expressed in first-order predicate calculus that is claimed to be logically equivalent to the intended meaning of that DAML-ONT ontology.

There is an additional benefit to this approach. By translating a DAML-ONT ontology into a logically equivalent first-order predicate calculus theory, we produce a representation of the ontology from which inferences can automatically be made using traditional automatic theorem provers and problem solvers. For example, the DAML-ONT axioms enable a reasoner to infer from the two statements "Class Male and class Female are disjoint" and "John is type Male" that the statement "John is type Female" is false.

DAML-ONT is translated into first-order predicate calculus by applying a simple rule for translating an RDF statement into a first-order relational sentence and by including in the translation a prespecified set of first-order predicate calculus axioms that restrict the allowable interpretations of the properties and classes that are included in DAML-ONT. This creates a set of first-order sentences that include the specific terms in the ontology along with the prespecified set of axioms restricting the interpretations. The prespecified set of axioms and the rules for generating the translation of RDF statements into first-order sentences are the focus of this presentation, since this is the portion that is leveragable across all DAML-ONT (and RDF/S) ontologies. Since DAML-ONT is simply a vocabulary of properties and classes added to RDF and RDF Schema, and RDF Schema is simply a vocabulary of properties and classes added to RDF, all statements in DAML-ONT are RDF statements, and a rule for translating RDF statements is sufficient for translating DAML-ONT statements as well.

A logical theory that is logically equivalent to a set of DAML-ONT descriptions is produced as follows. Translate each RDF statement with property P, subject S, and object O into a first-order predicate calculus sentence of the form "(PropertyValue P S O)." Add to this translation the axioms that constrain the allowable interpretations of the properties and classes that are included in RDF, RDF Schema, and DAML-ONT.

Note that it is not necessary to specify a translation for every construct in RDF, since any set of RDF descriptions can be translated into an equivalent set of RDF statements (as described in the RDF and RDF Schema specification documents). Thus, the one translation rule above suffices to translate all of RDF and therefore all of DAML-ONT as well.

A notable characteristic of this axiomatization is that it is designed to minimize the constraints on the legal interpretations of the DAML-ONT properties and classes in the resulting logical theory. In particular, the axioms do not require classes to be sets or unary relations, nor do they require properties to be sets or binary relations. Such constraints could be added to the resulting logical theory if desired, but they are not needed to express the intended meaning of the DAML-ONT descriptions being translated.

We now present an informal description of the axioms that are added to the translation of each DAML-ONT ontology. Since DAML-ONT is specified as an extension to RDF and RDF Schema, the axiomatization includes axioms describing the properties and classes in both RDF and RDF Schema, as well as those in DAML-ONT itself.

3.5.2 The Axiom Language

The axioms are written in KIF (http://logic.stanford.edu/kif/kif.html), a proposed ANSI standard. The axioms use standard first-order logic constructs plus KIF-specific relations and functions dealing with lists and integers. Lists and integers as objects in the domain of discourse are needed in order to axiomatize RDF containers and the DAML-ONT properties dealing with cardinality.

As stated above, each RDF statement "Property P of resource R has value V" is translated into the KIF sentence "(PropertyValue P R V)." Because of the centrality of the "type" property in RDF, we define for convenience an additional binary relation called "Type" to provide a more succinct translation of RDF statements of the form "Property 'type' of resource R has value V." The meaning of the relation "Type" is specified by the following axiom:

Axiom 3.1   (<=> (Type ?r ?v) (PropertyValue type ?r ?v)).[4]

That is, saying that relation "Type" holds for objects R and V is logically equivalent to saying that relation "PropertyValue" holds for objects "type," R, and V.

The axiomatization also restricts the first argument of relation "Type" to be a resource and the second argument to be a class as follows:

Axiom 3.2 (=> (Type ?r ?c) (and (Type ?r Resource) (Type ?c Class)))[5]

3.5.3   Axioms for RDF

RDF is a language for

- declaring named resources to have type "Property" or "Class"

- declaring resources to have a given class as a type (e.g., "Clyde" is type "Elephant")

- stating that a given property of a given resource has a given value (e.g., that property "Color" of "Clyde" has value "Gray")

A property named "type" is used for declaring that the type of a resource R is T, so that such a declaration is actually a statement that a given property of a given resource has a given value, specifically that property "type" of resource R has value T. Thus, an RDF file can be considered to consist *entirely* of statements of the form "Property P of resource R has value V."

Our axiomatization provides axioms restricting the interpretation of the classes and properties that are included in RDF. The classes are "Resource," "Property," "Class," "Literal," "Statement," "Container," "Bag," "Seq," "Alt," and "ContainerMembershipProperty." The properties are "type," "subject," "predicate," "object," "value," "_1," "_2," "_3," and so on.

3.5.4   Axioms for RDF Schema

RDF Schema is simply a vocabulary of properties and classes added to RDF. Our axiomatization provides axioms restricting the interpretation of those classes and properties. The classes are "ConstraintResource" and "Constraint-Property." The properties are "subClassOf," "subPropertyOf," "seeAlso," "isDefinedBy," "comment," "label," "range," and "domain."

3.5.5   Axioms for DAML-ONT

DAML-ONT is simply a vocabulary of properties and classes added to RDF and RDF Schema. We present in sections 3.5.7 and 3.5.8 natural-language transcriptions of the axioms that restrict the interpretation of those classes and properties.

3.5.6   Example Translation and Inference

Consider the following DAML-ONT descriptions of class "Person" and of person "Joe":

```
<Class ID="Person">
    <subClassOf resource="#Animal" />
    <restrictedBy>
        <Restriction>
            <onProperty resource="#parent" />
            <toClass resource="#Person" />
        </Restriction>
    </restrictedBy>
</Class>
<Person ID="Joe">
    <parent resource="#John" />
</Person>
```

Those descriptions are equivalent to the following set of RDF statements:

```
(type Person Class)
(subClassOf Person Animal)
(type Restriction R)⁶
(restrictedBy Person R)
(onProperty R parent)
(toClass R Person)
(type Joe Person)
(parent Joe John)
```

Those RDF statements are translated by our axiomatic semantics into the following KIF sentences:

```
(Type Person Class)
(PropertyValue subClassOf Person Animal)
(Type R Restriction)
(PropertyValue restrictedBy Person R)
(PropertyValue onProperty R parent)
(PropertyValue toClass R Person)
(Type Joe Person)
(PropertyValue Parent Joe John)
```

Informally, the "toClass" restriction stated in these sentences is that parents of persons are also persons. Therefore, we should be able to infer from these sentences and the DAML-ONT axioms that "John" is type "Person." That inference can be made using the primary axiom (i.e., axiom 3.1) associated with property "toClass":

Axiom 3.1   (=> (and (PropertyValue restrictedBy ?c1 ?r)
                       (PropertyValue onProperty ?r ?p)
                       (PropertyValue toClass ?r ?c2))
                  (forall (?i ?v) (=> (and (Type ?i ?c1)
                                          (PropertyValue ?p ?i ?v))
                                     (Type ?v ?c2))))

The axiom says that if object R is a value of "restrictedBy" for object C1, object P is a value of "onProperty" for R, and object C2 is a value of "toClass" for R, then for all objects I and V, if I is of type C1 and V is a value of P for I, then V is type C2.

In this axiom, if variable ?c1 is bound to "Person," variable ?r is bound to "R," variable ?p is bound to "parent," and variable ?c2 is bound to "Person," then the sentences describing the "toClass" restriction on the parents of persons satisfy the conjunction that is the antecedent of the implication that is axiom 3.1. One can therefore infer the following corresponding instance of the consequence of that implication:

```
(forall (?i ?v) (=> (and (Type ?i Person)
                         (PropertyValue parent ?i ?v))
                    (Type ?v Person)))
```

If variable ?i is bound to "Joe" and variable ?v is bound to "John," then the sentences describing "Joe" satisfy the conjunction that is the antecedent of the above-inferred implication. One can therefore infer the following corresponding instance of the consequence of that implication:

```
(Type John Person)
```

That completes a proof that "John" is type "Person."

3.5.7   DAML-ONT Classes

This section describes the axioms for the classes that are included in DAML-ONT. For each of these classes C, there is an axiom stating that C is type "Class." The full logical specification of the axioms is available in Fikes and McGuinness 2000.

Thing

Axiom 3.2   Every object is type Thing.

Nothing

Axiom 3.3   Every object is not type "Nothing."

List

Axiom 3.4   An object of type "List" is also of type "Sequence."

Disjoint

Axiom 3.5 Saying that an object is type "Disjoint" is equivalent to saying that the object is type "List," that every item in the list is type "Class," and that the classes in the list are pairwise disjoint.[7]

Empty

Axiom 3.6 "Empty" and "Nothing" are the same class.[8]

Transitive Property

Axiom 3.7 Saying that an object P is type "TransitiveProperty" is equivalent to saying that P is type "Property" and that if object Y is a value of P for object X and object Z is a value of P for Y, then Z is also a value of P for X.

Unique Property

Axiom 3.8 Saying that object P is type "UniqueProperty" is equivalent to saying that P is type "Property" and that if objects Y and Z are both values of P for object X, then Y and Z are the same object.

Unambiguous Property

Axiom 3.9 Saying that an object P is type "UnambiguousProperty" is equivalent to saying that P is type "Property" and that if object V is a value of P for both objects X and Y, then X and Y are the same object.

Restriction, Qualification, and Ontology
No axioms other than those stating that each of these are type "Class."

3.5.8   *DAML-ONT Properties*

This section describes the axioms for the properties that are included in DAML-ONT. For each of these properties P, there is an axiom stating that P is type "Property." The full logical specification of the axioms is available in Fikes and McGuinness 2000.

disjointWith. Saying that object C2 is a value of property "disjointWith" for object C1 is equivalent to saying that C1 and C2 are each type "Class," that no object is both type C1 and type C2, and that there is at least one object that is type C1 or type C2.

unionOf. Saying that object L is a value of "unionOf" for object C1 is equivalent to saying that C1 is type "Class," L is type "List," every item in list L is type "Class," and an object is type C1 if and only if it is type of one of the items of list L.

disjointUnionOf. Saying that object L is a value of "disjointUnionOf" for object C is equivalent to saying that L is a value of property "unionOf" for C (i.e., that class C is the union of the classes in list L) and that L is type "Disjoint" (i.e., the classes in list L are pairwise disjoint).

intersectionOf. Saying that object L is a value of "intersectionOf" for object C1 is equivalent to saying that C1 is type "Class," L is type "List," all of the items in list L are type "Class," and an object is type C1 if and only if it is type of all of the items of list L.

complementOf. Saying that object C2 is a value of "complementOf" for object C1 is equivalent to saying that C2 is a value of "disjointWith" for C1 (i.e., C1 and C2 are disjoint classes) and all objects are either type C1 or type C2.

oneOf. Saying that object L is a value of "oneOf" for object C is equivalent to saying that C is type "Class," L is type "List," and the objects that are type C are exactly the items in list L.

asClass. Saying that object C is a value of "asClass" for object L is the equivalent of saying that something is of type C if and only if it is a member of the list L (i.e., it is the first of L or a member of the rest of L.)

first. Saying that object X is a value of "first" for object L is equivalent to saying that L is type "List," L has at least one item, and the first item of L is X.

rest. Saying that object R is a value of "rest" for object L is equivalent to saying that L is type "List," R is type "List," L has at least one item, and L has the same items in the same order as list R with one additional object as its first item.

item. Saying that object X is a value of "item" for object L is equivalent to saying that L is type "List" and either X is a value of "first" for L (i.e., X is the first item in list L) or there is an object R that is a value of "rest" for L (i.e., there is a list R that is the rest of list L) and X is a value of "item" for R (i.e., X is an item in the list R).

cardinality. Saying that object N is a value of "cardinality" for object P is equivalent to saying that P is type "Property" and for all objects X, any list containing no repeated items and containing exactly those objects V such that V is a value of P for X is of length N.

maxCardinality. Saying that object N is a value of "maxCardinality" for object P is equivalent to saying that P is type "Property" and for all objects X, the length of any list containing no repeated items and containing exactly those objects V such that V is a value of P for X is equal to or less than N.

minCardinality. Saying that object N is a value of "minCardinality" for object P is equivalent to saying that P is type "Property" and for all objects X, there exists a list of length at least N that contains no repeated items and contains only objects V such that V is a value of P for X.

inverseOf. Saying that object P2 is a value of "inverseOf" for object P1 is equivalent to saying that P1 is type "Property," P2 is type "Property," and object X2 is a value of P1 for object X1 if and only if X1 is a value of P2 for X2.

restrictedBy. If object R is a value of "restrictedBy" for object C, then R is type "Resource" and C is type "Class."

onProperty. If object P is a value of "onProperty" for object RQ, then P is type "Property" and RQ is either type "Restriction" or type "Qualification."

toValue. If object V is a value of "toValue" for object R, then R is type "Restriction." If object R is a value of "restrictedBy" for object C, object P is a value of "onProperty" for R, and object V is a value of "toValue" for R, then for all objects I of type C, V is a value of P for I (i.e., a "toValue" restriction of V on a property P on a class C constrains each object I of type C to have V as a value of property P).

toClass. If object C is a value of "toClass" for object R, then R is type "Restriction" and C is type "Class." If object R is a value of "restrictedBy" for object C1, object P is a value of "onProperty" for R, and object C2 is a value of "toClass" for R, then for all objects I and V, if I is of type C1 and V is a value of P for I, then V is type C2 (i.e., a "toValue" restriction of C2 on a property P on a class C1 constrains each P value of each object of type C1 to be type C2).

qualifiedBy. If object Q is a value of "qualifiedBy" for object C, then Q is type "Qualification" and C is type "Class."

hasValue. If object C is a value of "hasValue" for object Q, then C is type "Class" and Q is type "Qualification." If object Q is a value of "qualifiedBy" for object C1, object P is a value of "onProperty" for Q, and object C2 is a value of "hasValue" for Q, then for all objects I of type C1, there exists an object V such that V is a value of P for I and V is type C2 (i.e., a "hasValue" restriction of C2 on a property P on a class C1 constrains each object of type C1 to have a value of type C2).

versionInfo. If object V is a value of "versionInfo" for object O, then O is type "Ontology."

imports. If object O2 is a value of "imports" for object O1, then O1 is type "Ontology" and O2 is type "Ontology."

equivalentTo. Saying that object Y is a value of "equivalentTo" for object X is equivalent to saying that X and Y are the same object.

default. If object V is a value of "default" for object P, then P is type "Property."

3.6   Conclusion

The ontology language for a Semantic Web needs to be able to express common elements such as classes, properties, restrictions, and objects in the domain. We have provided a historical perspective on the evolution of the initial ontology language for the DAML program. We introduced the language through example. We also provided an axiomatization of the language (and in doing so, provided an axiomatization as well for the building blocks of the language: RDF). We presented a short proof using the axioms, showing how they can be used to make the inferences mentioned in the introduction by example.

We believe that this language is a useful starting point for describing Web content. It builds on decades of research in frame-based systems, description logics, and Web languages. It thus has the benefit of years of research on languages, complexity, and usability and may be positioned to be the foundation for the next evolution of Web access. It also provides the merging point for the eventual DAML ontology language formed by more tightly integrating the OIL language into DAML-ONT.

Acknowledgments

DAML-ONT is the result of work by many people. The U.S. Defense Advanced Research Projects Agency funds the DAML project. The ontology language originated within the program but has been heavily influenced by work beyond DARPA, in particular by work from the European Union–funded Semantic Web projects. This chapter is authored by two of the three original editors of the language release, the DAML program director, and the coauthor of the axiomatic semantics. We would explicitly like to acknowledge the impact of the other original co-editor—Dan Connolly—for his significant impact on the initial language release. The language has been influenced heavily by others, including Tim Berners-Lee, Frank van Harmelen, Ian Horrocks, Dan Brickley, Mike Dean, Stefan Decker, Pat Hayes, Jeff Heflin, Drew McDermott, Peter Patel-Schneider, and Ralph R. Swick. The evolving list of major contributors is maintained on www.daml.org. DAML-ONT has since merged into a new ontology language called DAML+OIL (see http://www. daml.org/2001/03/daml+oil-index for the release). We will be producing an updated chapter reflecting the larger language. Also, DAML is expected to include a logic language (DAML-L) and a service language (DAML-S).

Notes

1. SHIQ includes ALC plus transitive roles, inverse roles, and qualified number restrictions. For more on the theoretical analysis and reasoning issues, see Horrocks and Sattler 1999 and Horrocks, Sattler, and Tobies 1999.

2. The namespace prefix rdf is arbitrary. The name in this document would be the conventional choice.

3. Unprefixed attribute names are not associated with the default namespace name the way unprefixed element names are. This is expanded upon in myth 4, available in "Namespace Myths Exploded" at http://www.xml.com/pub/a/2000/03/08/namespaces/index. html?page=2.

4. KIF note: "<=>" means "if and only if." Relational sentences in KIF have the form "(⟨relation name⟩ ⟨argument⟩*)." Names whose first character is "?" are variables. If no explicit quantifier is specified, variables are assumed to be universally quantified.

5. KIF note: "=>" means "implies." RDF considers "Resource" to be a class and "Class" itself to be a class. The axiomatization specifies that semantics by including the axioms "(Type Resource Class)" and "(Type Class Class)."

6. The restriction is unnamed in the RDF markup. We use the arbitrary name "R" here to denote the restriction.

7. The DAML-ONT property "disjointWith" is used to express pairwise disjointness.

8. The DAML-ONT property "asClass" is used to express equivalence of classes.

References

Bechhofer, S., et al., An Informal Description of OIL-Core and Standard OIL: A Layered Proposal for DAML-O. Available from www.ontoknowledge.org/oil/downl/dialects.pdf.

Borners-Lee, T., D. R. Karger, L. A. Stein, R. R. Swick, and D. J. Weitzner. 2000. Semantic Web Development. Available from http://www.w3.org/2000/01/sw/DevelopmentProposal.

Borgida, A., R. J. Brachman, D. L. McGuinness, and L. Alperin Resnick. 1989.

CLASSIC: A Structural Data Model for Objects. *SIGMOD Record* 18(2):59–67.

Brachman, R. J., J. G. Schmolze. 1985. An Overview of the KL-ONE Knowledge Representation System. *Cognitive Science* 9(2):171–216.

Brickley, D., and R. V. Guha. 2000. Resource Description Framework (RDF) Schema Specification 1.0, W3C Candidate Recommendation. World Wide Web Consortium. Available from www.w3.org/TR/rdf-schema.

Chaudhri, V., A. Farquhar, R. Fikes, P. Karp, and J. Rice. 1998. OKBC: A Programmatic Foundation for Knowledge Base Interoperability. In *Proceedings of the Fifteenth National Conference on Artificial Intelligence and Tenth Innovative Applications of Artificial Intelligence Conference (AAAI-98), July 26–30, 1998, Madison, Wisconsin*. Menlo Park, CA/Cambridge, MA: AAAI/MIT Press.

Donini, F., M. Lenzerini, D. Nardi, and W. Nutt. 1991a. The Complexity of Concept Languages. In *Proceedings of the Second International Conference on Principles of Knowledge Representation and Reasoning (KR-91), Cambridge, Massachusetts, April 22–25, 1991*, ed. J. F. Allen et al. (pp. 151–162). San Francisco: Morgan Kaufmann.

Donini, F., M. Lenzerini, D. Nardi, and W. Nutt. 1991b. Tractable Concept Languages. In *Proceedings of the 12th International Joint Conference on Artificial Intelligence (IJCAI-91), Sydney, Australia, August 24–30*, ed. J. Mylopoulos and R. Reiter (pp. 458–465). San Francisco: Morgan Kaufmann.

Farquhar, A., R. Fikes, and J. Rice. 1997. The Ontolingua Server: A Tool for Collaborative Ontology Construction. *International Journal of Human-Computer Studies* 46:707–727.

Fensel, D., I. Horrocks, F. van Harmelen, S. Decker, M. Erdmann, and M. Klein. OIL in a Nutshell. In *Proceedings of the European Knowledge Acquisition Conference (EKAW-2000) Juan-les-Pins, France, October 2–6, 2000*, ed. R. Dieng and O. Corby. Berlin: Springer.

Fikes, R., and T. Kehler. 1985. The Role of Frame-Based Representation in Reasoning. *Communications of the ACM* 28(9):904–920.

Fikes, R., and D. L. McGuinness. 2000. An Axiomatic Semantics for DAML-ONT. Available from www.ksl.stanford.edu/people/dlm/daml-semantics.

Fikes, R., and D. L. McGuinness. 2001. An Axiomatic Semantics for RDF, RDF Schema, and DAML+OIL. KSL Technical Report KSL-01-01, Stanford University. Available from http://www.ksl.stanford.edu/people/dlm/daml-semantics/abstract-axiomatic-semantics.html.

Horrocks, I., and P. Patel-Schneider. 1999. Optimizing Description Logic Subsumption. *Journal of Logic and Computation* 9(3):267–293.

Horrocks, I., and U. Sattler. 1999. A Description Logic with Transitive and Inverse Roles and Role Hierarchies. *Journal of Logic and Computation* 9(3):385–410.

Horrocks, I., U. Sattler, and S. Tobies. 1999. Practical Reasoning for Very Expressive Description Logics. *Logic Journal of the IGPL* 8(3):239–263.

Karp, P. D. The Design Space of Frame Knowledge Representation Systems. Technical Report 520, SRI International AI Center. Available from ftp://www.ai.sri.com/pub/papers/karp-freview.ps.Z.

Lassila, O. 1998. Web Metadata: A Matter of Semantics. *IEEE Internet Computing* 2(4):30–37.

Lassila, O., and R. Swick, Resource Description Framework (RDF) Model and Syntax Specification (recommendation). World Wide Web Consortium. Available from www.w3.org/TR/REC-rdf-syntax.

MacGregor, R. M. 1991. Inside the LOOM Description Classifier. *SIGART Bulletin* 2(3):88–92.

Stein, L. A., and D. Connolly. 2000. Annotated DAML Ontology Markup. Available from www.daml.org/2000/10/daml-walkthru.

4 Ontologies and Schema Languages on the Web

*Michel Klein, Jeen Broekstra, Dieter Fensel, Frank van Harmelen,
and Ian Horrocks*

4.1 Introduction

For the past few years, information on the World Wide Web has mainly been intended for direct human consumption. However, to facilitate new intelligent applications such as meaning-based search, information brokering, and electronic transactions among several independent partners, the semantics of the data on the Internet should also be accessible for machines. Therefore, methods and tools to create such a Semantic Web have generated wide interest.

A major aspect of a Web of "machine-understandable" information is explicit models of the domains of interest that describe the vocabulary and structure of the information those domains contain. These models, often called ontologies, may play a key role in advanced information exchange, as they provide a shared and common understanding of a domain. However, how ontologies can be applied fruitfully to online resources is still an important question.

In this chapter, we will look at the relation between ontologies and two schema languages from the World Wide Web consortium that in some sense both aim at providing a mechanism for describing the common understanding of data in a specific domain. One is RDF Schema (Brickley and Guha 2000), a schema language for the RDF (Lassila and Swick 1999). RDF is a standard from the W3C for representing metadata on the Web. RDF Schema provides some modeling primitives that can be used to define a simple model of classes and their relations. This model can then act as a vocabulary for RDF statements that describe resources on the Web. The other schema language that we will consider is XML Schema (Thompson et al. 2000). This is a proposed standard for describing the structure and semantics of XML documents. It prescribes the way in which elements and attributes in an XML document are combined and can be used to validate the structure and content of a document.

The aim of this chapter is to investigate how these languages can be used to add ontology-based semantics to online resources. We will descibe their different roles in this process and illustrate the way in which they can play that role. In short, we will argue that XML Schema documents and ontologies refer to different abstraction levels on how to describe information and therefore also to different states in the process of developing online information sources. To illustrate this, we will provide a procedure for transforming ontologies into XML Schema documents. RDF Schema documents and ontologies, on the other hand, serve the same purpose, to a large extent, but generally differ in the level of expressiveness. We will show a method for capturing most of the expressive power of ontologies in RDF Schema documents by extending the RDF Schema language.

This chapter is organized as follows. In the next section, we offer an abstract introduction to ontologies, schemas, and their relationship. In section 4.3 we provide a short introduction to a specific ontology language, OIL (Fensel et al. 2000), that we will use as an example language throughout this chapter. Section 4.4 introduces XML Schema and compares it to ontology languages. Section 4.5 does the same for RDF Schema. In section 4.6, we give two examples of the application of ontologies to online resources, using, respectively, XML Schema and RDF Schema.

4.2 Ontologies and Schemas

Ontology, which has been a field of philosophy since Aristotle, has become a buzzword in information- and knowledge-based systems research (Guarino and Welty 2000). Various publications in knowledge engineering, natural-language processing, cooperative information systems, intelligent information integration, and knowledge management report on the applications of ontologies to developing and using systems. In general, ontologies provide a *shared and common* understanding of a domain that can be communicated between people and heterogeneous and distributed application systems. They have been developed in artificial intelligence to facilitate knowledge sharing and reuse.

Schemas, in particular, those for databases, have been developed in computer science to describe the structure and semantics of data. A well-known example is the relational database schema that has become the basis for most of the currently used databases (Elmasri and Navathe 2000). A database schema defines a set of relations and certain integrity constraints. A central assumption is the atomicity of the elements that are in certain relationships (i.e., first normal form). In a nutshell, an information source (or, more precisely, a data source) is viewed as a set of tables. However, many new information sources now exist that do not fit into such rigid schemas. In particular, the WWW has made available predominantly document-centered information based on natural-language text. Therefore, new schema languages have arisen that better fit the needs of richer data models. Some of them, like XML Schema (see Biron and Malhotra 2000; Thompson et al. 2000; and Walsh 1999), integrate schemas for describing documents (like HTML or SGML) with schemas designed for describing data. Other schema languages, such as RDF Schema, abstract from structure and representation issues and try to provide a general basis for data modeling on the Web.

And Their Relationship?   Ontologies applied to online information sources may be seen as explicit conceptualizations (i.e., *meta-information*) that describe the semantics of the data represented in such sources. Fensel (2001) points out the following common differences between ontologies and schema definitions:

- A language for defining ontologies is often syntactically and semantically richer than common approaches for databases.

- The information that is described by an ontology consists of semi-structured natural-language texts and not tabular information.

- An ontology must be a shared and consensual terminology because it is used for information sharing and exchange.

- An ontology provides a domain theory and not the structure of a data container, as most schema languages do.

However, these statements need to be formulated more precisely when one is comparing ontology languages with both the XML Schema language as the RDF Schema language and the purpose of ontologies with the purpose of those schema languages. These more precise formulations are presented in the next sections.

4.3   The Ontology Language OIL

To investigate the relations between ontology languages and schema languages, we will use one specific ontology language as reference and example. Horrocks et al. (2000) defines the *Ontology Inference Layer*. In this section we will give only a brief description of the OIL language. More detailed descriptions can be found elsewhere; a comparison of OIL with other ontology languages can be found in Horrocks et al. 2000 and Fensel et al. 2000.

A brief example ontology in OIL is provided in figure 4.1; the example is based on the country pages of the *CIA World Factbook* (http://www.odci.gov/cia/publications/factbook), which we will use as an example throughout this chapter. The OIL language has been designed so that (1) it provides most of the modeling primitives commonly used in frame-based and description logic (DL)–oriented ontologies, (2) it has a simple, clean, and well-defined semantics, and (3) automated reasoning support (e.g., class consistency and subsumption checking) can be provided. It is envisaged that this core language will be extended in the future by sets of additional primitives, with the proviso that full reasoning support may not be available for ontologies using such primitives.

```
 Ontology-container                           class-def
 title CIA Worldfact Book ontology          Geographical_Location
 creator Michel Klein                         slot-constraint name
 subject country information, CIA, world        value-type string
factbook                                      class-def City
 description A didactic example ontology       subclass-of
describing                                    Geographical_Location
      country information                       slot-constraint located_in
  description.release 1.02                       value-type Country
 publisher CIA                                class-def Country
 type ontology                                 subclass-of
 format pseudo-xml                           Geographical_Location
 identifier                                     slot-constraint capital
http://www.ontoknowledge.org/oil/wfb.xml        has-value City
 source                                       class-def LandBoundary
http://www.odci.gov/cia/publications/factbook/   slot-constraint
 language OIL                                neighbor_country
 language en-uk                                  cardinality 1 Country
                                                slot-constraint length
Ontology-definitions                            value-type
 slot-def capital                               (KilometerLength or
  domain Country                             MilesLength)
  range City                                  class-def KilometerLength
  inverse capital_of                           slot-constraint value
  properties functional                         has-value integer
 slot-def has_boundary                         slot-constraint unit
  domain Country                                has-value km
  range LandBoundary                         class-def MilesLength
 slot-def coastline                            slot-constraint value
  domain Geographical_Location                  has-value integer
  range (KilometerLength or MilesLength)       slot-constraint unit
 slot-def relative_area                         has-value mile
  domain Geographical_Location               class-def AreaComparison
  range AreaComparison                        slot-constraint
 slot-def value                              compared_to
  domain (KilometerLength or                    value-type
MilesLength)                                 Geographical_Location
  range integer                                slot-constraint proportion
  properties functional                        value-type string
```

Figure 4.1
Partial ontology in OIL.

An ontology in OIL is represented by an *ontology container* and an *ontology definition*. We will discuss both elements, starting with the ontology container and then discussing the backbone of OIL, the ontology definition.

For the *ontology container* part of the specification, OIL adopts the components defined by the Dublin Core Metadata Element Set, Version 1.1 (http://purl.org/DC/). Apart from the container, an OIL ontology consists of a set of *ontology definitions*:

- *import.* A list of references to other OIL modules that are to be included in the ontology. Specifications can be included, and the underlying assumptions is that names of different specifications are different (via different prefixes).

- *class and slot definitions.* Zero or more class definitions (*class-def*) and slot definitions (*slot-def*), the structure of which will be described below.

A class definition (class-def) associates a class name with a class description. It consists of the following components:

- *type.* The type of definition: either *primitive* or *defined*. If omitted, the type defaults to primitive. When a class is primitive, its definition (i.e., the combination of the following subclass-of and slot-constraint components) is taken to be a necessary but not a sufficient condition for membership in the class. When a class is defined, its definition is taken to be a necessary *and* a sufficient condition for membership in the class.

- *subclass-of.* A list of one or more class expressions, the structure of which will be described below. The class being defined in a particular class-def must be a subclass of each of the class expressions in the list.

- *slot-constraints.* Zero or more slot-constraints, the structure of which will be described below. The class being defined in a particular class-def must be a subclass of each of the slot-constraints in the list (note that a slot-constraint defines a class).

A *class expression* can be either a class name, a slot-constraint, or a boolean combination of class expressions using the operators *and*, *or*, and *not*. Note that class expressions are recursively defined, so that arbitrarily complex expressions can be formed.

In some situations it is possible to use a *concrete-type expression* instead of a class expression. A concrete-type expression defines a range over some data type. Two data types that are currently supported in OIL are *integer* and *string*. Ranges can be defined using the expressions (*min* X), (*max* X), (*greater-than* X), (*less-than* X), (*equal* X) and (*range* X Y). For example, (*min* 21) defines the data type consisting of all the integers greater than or equal to 21. As another example, (*equal* "xyz") defines the data type consisting of the string "xyz."

A *slot-constraint* is a list of one or more constraints (restrictions) applied to a *slot*. A slot is a binary relation (i.e., its instances are pairs of individuals), but a slot-constraint is actually a class definition—its instances are those individuals that satisfy the constraint(s). Typical slot-constraints are

- *has-value.* A list of one or more class expressions. Every instance of the class defined by the slot constraint must be related via the slot relation to an instance of each class expression in the list. For example, the has-value constraint:

```
slot-constraint eats
has-value zebra, wildebeest
```

defines the class each instance of which *eats* some instance of the class zebra and some instance of the class wildebeest. Note that this does not mean that instances of the slot-constraint eat *only* zebra and wildebeest: they may also be partial to a little gazelle when they can get it.

- *value-type.* A list of one or more class expressions. If an instance of the class defined by the slot-constraint is related via the slot relation to some individual x, then x must be an instance of each class expression in the list.

- *max-cardinality.* A nonnegative integer n followed by a class expression. An instance of the class defined by the slot-constraint can be related to at most n distinct instances of the class expression via the slot relation.

- *min-cardinality* (and, as a shortcut, *cardinality*).

A slot definition (*slot-def*) associates a slot name with a slot description. A slot description specifies global constraints that apply to the slot relation, for example, that it is a transitive relation. A slot-def consists of the following main components:

- *subslot-of.* A list of one or more slots. The slot being defined in a particular slot-def must be a subslot of each of the slots in the list. For example,

```
slot-def daughter
  subslot-of child
```

defines a slot *daughter* that is a subslot of *child*; that is, every pair of individuals that is an instance of *daughter* must also be an instance of *child*.

- *domain.* A list of one or more class expressions. If the pair $(x; y)$ is an instance of the slot relation, then x must be an instance of each class expression in the list.

- *range.* A list of one or more class expressions. If the pair $(x; y)$ is an instance of the slot relation, then y must be an instance of each class expression in the list.

- *inverse.* The name of a slot S that is the inverse of the slot being defined. If the pair $(x; y)$ is an instance of the slot S, then $(y; x)$ must be an instance of the slot being defined.

- *properties.* A list of one or more properties of the slot. Valid properties are *transitive, functional* and *symmetric*.

An *axiom* asserts some additional facts about the classes in the ontology, for example, that the classes carnivore and herbivore are disjoint (that is, have no instances in common). Valid axioms are

- *disjoint (class-expr)+.* All of the class expressions in the list are pairwise disjoint.

- *covered (class-expr) by (class-expr)+.* Every instance of the first class expression is also an instance of at least one of the class expressions in the list.

- *disjoint-covered (class-expr) by (class-expr)+.* Every instance of the first class expression is also an instance of exactly one of the class expressions in the list.

- *equivalent (class-expr)+.* All of the class expressions in the list are equivalent (i.e., they have the same instances).

Besides the "presentation syntax" described above, OIL also has an XML and an RDF representation. The technical report on OIL (Horrocks et al. 2000) defines a DTD and an XML Schema definition for the XML syntax. The representation of OIL in RDF is described in section 4.6.2 and also in Broekstra et al. 2000. We will now take a look at XML Schema and its relation to OIL.

4.4   XML Schema

4.4.1   Description of XML Schema

XML Schema is a means for defining constraints on the syntax and structure of valid XML documents (cf. Biron and Malhotra 2000; Thompson et al. 2000; Walsh 1999). A more easily readable explanation of XML Schema can be found in other sources such as Fallside 2000. XML Schemas have the same purpose as DTDs but provide several significant improvements:

- XML Schema definitions are themselves XML documents.

- XML Schemas provide a rich set of datatypes that can be used to define the values of elementary tags.

- XML Schemas provide a much richer means for defining nested tags (i.e., tags with subtags).

- XML Schemas provide the namespace mechanism to combine XML documents with heterogeneous vocabulary.

We will discuss these four aspects in more detail.

4.4.1.1   XML Schema Definitions as XML Documents

Figure 4.2 shows an XML Schema definition of an address. The schema definition for the address tag is itself an XML document, whereas DTDs would

```
<?xml version="1.0" encoding="UTF-8"?>
<xsd:schema xmlns:xsd="http://www.w3.org/2000/10/XMLSchema">
<xsd:complexType name="address">
<xsd:sequence>
<xsd:element name="name">
<xsd:complexType mixed="true">
<xsd:simpleContent>
<xsd:extension base="xsd:string"/>
</xsd:simpleContent>
</xsd:complexType>
</xsd:element>
<xsd:element name="street" type="xsd:string" maxOccurs="2"/>
<xsd:element ref="zip"/>
<xsd:element name="city" type="xsd:string"/>
<xsd:element name="country" type="xsd:string" minOccurs="0"/>
</xsd:sequence>
</xsd:complexType>
<xsd:element name="zip" type="zipCode"/>
<xsd:simpleType name="zipCode">
<xsd:restriction base="xsd:string">
<xsd:pattern value="[0-9]{5}(-[0-9]{4})?"/>
</xsd:restriction>
</xsd:simpleType>
</xsd:schema>
```

Figure 4.2
Example of a schema definition.

provide such a definition in an external second language. The clear advantage of having the definition be an XML document is that all tools developed for XML (e.g., validation or rendering tools) can be immediately applied to XML Schema definitions, too.

4.4.1.2 Datatypes

Datatypes are described in Biron and Malhotra 2000. We already saw the use of a datatype (i.e., string) in the example. In general, a datatype is defined as a 3-tuple consisting of a set of distinct values, called its *value space*, a set of lexical representations, called its *lexical space*, and a set of *facets* that characterize properties of the value space, individual values, or lexical items.

Value Space.   The value space of a given datatype can be defined in one of the following ways: enumerated outright (extensional definition), defined axiomatically from fundamental notions (intensional definition),[1] defined as the subset of values from a previously defined datatype with a given set of properties and defined as a combination of values from some already defined value space(s) by a specific construction procedure (e.g., a list).

Lexical Space.   A lexical space is a set of valid literals for a datatype. Each value in the datatype's value space is denoted by one or more literals in its lexical space. For example, "100" and "1.0E2" are two different literals from the lexical space of float that both denote the same value.

Facets.   A facet is a single defining aspect of a datatype. Facets are of two types: Fundamental facets that define the datatype and nonfundamental or constraining facets that constrain the permitted values of a datatype.

▪ *Fundamental facets.* Equality, order on values, lower and upper bounds for values, cardinality (can be categorized as "finite", "countably infinite," or "uncountably infinite"), numeric versus nonnumeric.

▪ *Constraining or nonfundamental facets.* Optional properties that can be applied to a datatype to constrain its value space: length constrains minimum and maximum, pattern can be used to constrain the allowable values using regular expressions, enumeration constrains the value space of the datatype to the specified list, lower and upper bounds for values, precision, encoding, etc. Some of these facets already constrain the possible lexical space for a datatype.

It is useful to categorize the datatypes defined in this specification along various dimensions, forming a set of characterization dichotomies:

▪ *Atomic versus list datatypes.* Atomic datatypes are those having values that are intrinsically indivisible. List datatypes are those having values that consist of a sequence of values of an atomic datatype. For example, a single token that matches NMTOKEN from XML 1.0 (Bray 1998) could be the value of an atomic datatype NMTOKEN, whereas a sequence of such tokens could be the value of a list datatype NMTOKENS.

▪ *Primitive versus generated datatypes.* Primitive datatypes are those that are not defined in terms of other datatypes; they exist ab initio. Generated datatypes are those that are defined in terms of other datatypes. Every generated datatype is defined in terms of an existing datatype, referred to as the basetype. Basetypes may be either primitive or generated. If type *a* is the basetype of type *b*, then *b* is said to be a subtype of *a*. The value space of a subtype is a subset of the value space of the basetype. For example, date is derived from the base type recurringInstant.

▪ *Built-in versus user-derived datatypes.* Built-in datatypes are those that are defined in the XML schema specification and may be either primitive or generated. User-derived datatypes are those derived datatypes that are defined by individual schema designers by giving values to constraining facets. XML Schema provides a large collection of such built-in datatypes, for example, string, boolean, float, decimal, timeInstant, and binary. In figure 4.2, "zipCode" is a user-derived datatype.

4.4.1.3 Structures

Structures use the datatypes to provide facilities for constraining the contents of elements and the values of attributes and for augmenting the information set of instances, for example, with defaulted values and type information (see Thompson et al. 2000). An example is the element "zip" that makes use of the datatype "zipCode." Another example is the definition of the element type "name." The value "true" for the "mixed" attribute of complexType allows strings to be mixed with (sub-)tags.

Attributes are defined by their *name*, a datatype that constraints their values, default or fixed values, and constraints on their presence (minOccurs and maxOccurs) (for example, ⟨attribute name="key" type="integer" minOccurs="1" maxOccurs="1"/⟩).

Elements can be constrained by reference to a simple datatype or by the specification of the allowed elements in their content (called the "rich content model").

• In the former case, i.e., constrained by datatype, *element declarations* associate an element name with a type, either by reference (e.g., "zip" in figure 4.2) or by incorporation (i.e., by defining the datatype within the element declaration).

• In the latter case, the content model consists of a simple grammar governing the allowed types of child elements and the order in which they must appear. If the "mixed" qualifier is present, text or elements may occur. Child elements are defined via an *element reference* (e.g., ⟨element ref="zip"/⟩ in figure 4.2) or directly via an *element declaration*. Elements can be combined in *groups* with a specific *order* (*all*, *sequence*, or *choice*). This combination can be recursive; for example, a sequence of some elements can be a selection from a different sequence or a sequence of different elements (i.e., the "( )", ",", and "|" of a DTD are present). Elements and their groups can be accompanied with *occurrence constraints*, for example, ⟨element name="street" minOccurs="1" maxOccurs="2" type="string"/⟩ in figure 4.2.

In the previous subsection we discussed the differences between primitive and generated datatypes, the latter being defined in terms of other datatypes (see Biron and Malhotra 2000). Defining a datatype in terms of other datatypes is possible not only for simple datatypes like integer, but also for complex types. Thompson et al. 2000 defines two mechanisms by which derived type definitions may be developed. Here the following two cases are distinguished:

• *Derivation by extension.* A new complex type can be defined by adding additional particles at the end of a type definition and/or by adding attribute declarations. An example of such an extension is provided in figure 4.3.

• *Derivation by restriction.* A new type can be defined by decreasing the possibilities made available by an existing type definition: narrowing ranges, removing alternatives, etc.

4.4.1.4 Namespaces
The facilities in XML Schema to construct schemas from other ones build on XML namespaces. An important concept in XML Schema is the *target*

```
<xsd:complexType name="personName">
<xsd:sequence>
 <xsd:element name="title" minOccurs="0"/>
 <xsd:element name="forename" minOccurs="0" maxOccurs="unbounded"/>
 <xsd:element name="surname"/>
</xsd:sequence>
</xsd:complexType>
<xsd:complexType name="extendedName">
<xsd:complexContent>
 <xsd:extension base="personName">
   <xsd:sequence>
    <xsd:element name="generation" minOccurs="0"/>
   </xsd:sequence>
 </xsd:extension>
</xsd:complexContent>
</xsd:complexType>
<xsd:element name="name" type="extendedName"/>

A snippet of a valid XML-file according to this schema is:
<name>
 <forename>Albert</forename>
 <forename>Arnold</forename>
 <surname>Gore</surname>
 <generation>Jr</generation>
</name>
```

Figure 4.3
Example of a derived type definition via extension.

namespace, which defines the URL that can be used to uniquely identify the definitions in the schema. XML Schema provides two mechanism for assembling a complete component set from separate original schemas (cf. Thompson et al. 2000):

▪ Via the *include* element (⟨include schemaLocation="http ..."/⟩). This include element brings in the definitions and declarations contained in the referred schema and make them available as part of the including schema target namespace. The effect is to compose a final effective schema by merging the declarations and definitions of the including and the included schemas. One important caveat in using this mechanism is that the target namespace of all included components must be the same as the target namespace of the including schema. The *redefine* mechanism is very much the same as the include mechanism but also allows the included types to be redefined.

- Via the *import* element (⟨import namespace="http …"/⟩). This element imports schemas with a different target namespace from that of the importing schema. It must coincide with a standard namespace declaration. XML Schema in fact permits multiple schema components to be imported, from multiple namespaces, into a single schema, and they can be referred to in both definitions and declarations.

In general, only inclusion is provided as means to combine various schemas, and the module name prefix is used to realize the nonequality of name assumptions (i.e., identifiers of two different schemas are by definition different).

4.4.2   The Relation between OIL and XML Schema

On the one hand, ontologies and XML schemas serve very different purposes. Ontology languages are a means to specify domain theories, and XML schemas are a means to provide integrity constraints for information sources (i.e., documents and/or semistructured data). It is therefore not surprising to encounter differences when comparing XML Schema with ontology languages like OIL. On the other hand, XML Schema and OIL have one main goal in common: both provide vocabulary and structure for describing information sources that are aimed at exchange. It is therefore legitimate to compare the two and investigate their commonalities and differences. In this section, we take a twofold approach to such an analysis: first, we analyze the main differences between the two, and second, we try to characterize their relation to one another.

4.4.2.1   Comparing OIL and XML Schema

Modeling Primitives.   XML Schema's main modeling primitives are elements. Elements may be simple, composed, or mixed. Simple elements have as their contents datatypes, like string or integer. Composed elements have as contents other (child) elements; they also specify a grammar that defines how they are composed from their child elements. Finally, mixed elements can mix strings with child elements. In addition, elements may have attributes.

OIL takes a different approach. Its basic modeling primitives are concepts and slots. Concepts in OIL can be roughly identified with elements in XML Schema, and XML Schema's child elements are roughly equivalent to OIL's slots defined for a concept. However, slots defined independently from concepts in OIL have no equivalents in XML Schema.

Datatypes.   XML Schema provides a large collection of built-in datatypes, such as string, boolean, float, decimal, timeInstant, and binary. OIL provides only string and integer as built-in datatypes, because of the difficulty of providing clear semantics and reasoning support for a large collection of complex datatypes.

In XML Schema all inheritance must be defined explicitly, so reasoning about hierarchical relationships is not an issue. In XML Schema, a datatype is defined by a value space, a lexical space, and a set of facets. Restriction of a value space (i.e., the membership of classes) is also present in OIL, however, OIL does not provide a lexical space and facets. These aspects are much more related to the representation of a datatype than to the aspect of modeling a domain. That is, date may be an important aspect of a domain, but various different representations of dates are not. This is a rather important point when we are talking about how information is represented. Finally, although XML Schema mentions the possibility of defining types intensionally via axioms, no language, no semantics, and no actual reasoning service is provided for this purpose. OIL, on the other hand, is a flexible language for the intensional, that is, axiomatic, definition of types. It provides facilities for the intensional definition of types (via defined concepts) that are completely lacking in XML Schema.[2]

Grammar.   OIL does not provide any grammar for the application of slots to concepts; that is, an instance of a concept comprises of a *set* of slots values.

XML Schema allows the definition of stronger requirements via a grammar: *sequence* and *choice* of attributes applied to an instance can be defined.

Inheritance.   XML Schema incorporates the notion of type derivation. However, this type derivation can be compared only partially with what is provided with inheritance in ontology languages. First, in XML Schema, all inheritance has to be modeled explicitly. In OIL, inheritance can be derived from the definitions of the concepts. Second, XML Schema does *not* provide a direct way to inherit from multiple parents. Types can be derived only from one basetype. OIL (like most ontology languages) provides for multiple inheritance.

Third, and most important, the is-a relationship has a twofold role in conceptual modeling that is not directly covered by XML Schema:

- Top-down inheritance of attributes from superclasses to subclasses. Assume *employee* as a subclass of a class *person*. Then *employee* inherits all attributes that are defined for *person*.
- Bottom-up inheritance of instances from subclasses to superclasses. Assume *employee* as a subclass of a class *person*. Then *person* inherits all instances (i.e., elements) that are an element of *employee*.

In XML Schema, both aspects can be modeled only in an artificial way. The top-down inheritance of attributes is difficult to model, because type derivations in XML Schema can either extend *or* restrict the base type. A "dummy" intermediate type has to be used to model full top-down inheritance of attributes with both extending and restricting derivations. For example, it is not possible to model a *student* as a *person* with a student number and age less than 28 in only one step. One first has to model a dummy type "young person," which *restricts* the age of persons to less than 28. After that it is possible to model a student as a "young person" *extended* with a student number.

The bottom-up inheritance of instances to superclasses is also not automatically available in XML Schema. For example, an instance of a *student* is not automatically a valid instance of a *person*, even if the student type inherits from the person type. However, using an additional attribute, it is possible to use an instance of a subclass wherever a superclass of it is expected. So to use a *student* as a filler of a "driver" element, which requires type *person*, we can write:

```
<driver xsi:type="student">
<name>John</name>
<studentnumber>0792098</studentnumber>
</driver>
```

The *type* attribute, which is part of the XML Schema instance namespace, explicitly declares that the current element is a derivation of the expected element.

4.4.2.2   The Relation between OIL and XML Schema

On the one hand, OIL provides much richer modeling primitives. It distinguishes classes and slots, and class (or slot) definitions can be used to derive the class's (or slot's) hierarchy (and its according inheritance). On the other hand, XML Schema provides richer modeling primitives concerning the variety of built-in datatypes and the grammar for structuring the content of elements. The latter is not of importance when one is building a domain model, but it is important when one is defining the structure of documents. Therefore, models in OIL can be viewed as high-level descriptions of a domain that is further refined when aiming at a document structure model.

The relation between ontology languages and XML Schema can be compared to the relation between the *entity relationship (ER) model* and the relational model.[3] We realize that this analogy is only partially valid, because ER is a model for analysis, whereas OIL is a language for design. Nevertheless, the metaphor illustrates the relation nicely. The ER model provides a framework for modeling information sources required for an application, and the relational model provides an implementation-oriented description of databases. The former provides entities (with attributes) and relationships, and the latter provides only relations. Elmasri and Navathe (2000) provide a procedure that translates models formulated as ER models into models based

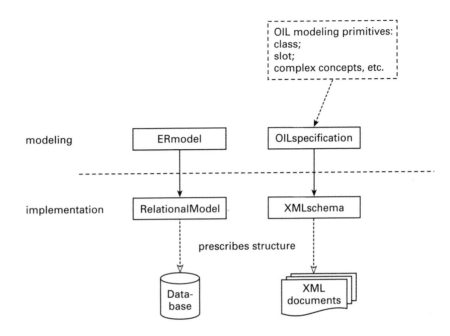

Figure 4.4
Relationship between schemas and ontologies, in a nutshell.

on the relational model. During system development, we start with a high-level ER model. Then we transform this model into a more implementation-oriented relational model. Both concepts and relationships are expressed as relations. A similar procedure can be used when transforming OIL specifications into XML Schema definitions. We illustrated this procedure in section 4.6.1.

Figure 4.4 depicts the overall relation between ER and the relational model, on the one hand, and OIL and XML Schema, on the other. The benefit of the procedure that we suggest in section 4.6.1 is that a document schema is created that is founded in a domain ontology. This schema in its turn can then be used to prescribe or validate document markup. Finally, this markup gives us a well-founded semantic annotation of actual data, which has two main advantages:

- It provides a way of representing instance data of an ontology in plain XML.

- An ontology can be used as a conceptual layer on top of a set of structured (XML) documents, because the markup of actual XML documents is founded in an ontology.

We want to stress that the relation that we describe here involves something completely different from expressing an ontology in some kind of XML format itself, although both approaches may use XML Schema documents. In our case, the XML Schema definition is a "simplified" version of the ontology, whereas in the other case, the XML Schema definition prescribes how an ontology should be encoded in XML. The latter approach can be found in Horrocks et al. 2000, in which an XML Schema definition is provided to write down an ontology in a plain XML document. In this chapter, we propose to produce a schema that captures the underlying semantics of an ontology, which can then be used for representing instances of an ontology in XML.

4.5   RDF Schema

We will now discuss the main features of RDF Schema (or RDFS, for short) and show how RDF Schema relates to ontology languages. We will first describe RDF itself, which is the basis of RDF Schema, and then RDF Schema.

4.5.1   RDF and RDF Schema

4.5.1.1   Introduction to RDF

A prerequisite for the Semantic Web is machine-processable semantics of information. RDF (Lassila and Swick 1999) is a foundation for processing metadata; it provides interoperability between applications that exchange machine-understandable information on the Web. Basically, RDF defines a data model for describing machine-processable semantics of data. The basic data model consists of three object types:

- *Resources.* A resource may be an entire Web page, a part of a Web page, a whole collection of pages, or an object that is not directly accessible via the Web (e.g., a printed book). Resources are always named by URLs.

- *Properties.* A property is a specific aspect, characteristic, attribute, or relation used to describe a resource.

- *Statements.* A specific resource, together with a named property plus the value of that property for that resource, constitutes an RDF statement. These three individual parts of a statement are called, respectively, the *subject*, the *predicate*, and the *object* of the statement.

In a nutshell, RDF defines object-property-value triples as basic modeling primitives and introduces a standard syntax for them. An RDF document will define properties in terms of the resources to which they apply. For example:

```
<rdf:RDF>
 <rdf:Description about="http://www.w3.org">
  <Publisher>World Wide Web Consortium </Publisher>
 </rdf:Description>
</rdf:RDF>
```

states that http://www.w3.org (the subject) has as publisher (the predicate) the W3C (the object). Since both the subject and the object of a statement can be resources, these statements can be linked in a chain:

```
<rdf:RDF>
 <rdf:Description about="http://www.w3.org/Home/Lassila">
  <Creator rdf:resource="http://www.w3.org/staffId/85740"/
  >
 </rdf:Description>
 <rdf:Description about="http://www.w3.org/staffId/85740">
  <Email>lassila@w3.org</v:Email>
 </rdf:Description>
</rdf:RDF>
```

states that http://www.w3.org/Home/Lassila (the subject) is created by staff member 85740 (the object). In the next statement, this same resource (staff member 85740) plays the role of subject to state that his email address (the object) is lassila@w3.org. Finally, RDF statements are also resources, so that statements can be applied recursively to statements, allowing their nesting. All this leads to the underlying data model being a labeled hypergraph (since each node can itself again contain an entire graph), with each statement being a predicate-labeled link between object and subject.

4.5.1.2 *Introduction to RDF Schema*

The modeling primitives offered by RDF are very basic. Therefore, the RDF Schema specification (Brickley and Guha 2000) defines further modeling primitives in RDF. That is, RDF Schema extends (or enriches) RDF by giving an externally specified semantics to specific resources (to rdfs:subclassOf, to rdfs:Class, etc.). It is only because of this external semantics that RDF Schema is useful. Moreover, this semantics cannot be captured in RDF: if it could then there would be no need for RDFS.

Figure 4.5 depicts the subclass-of hierarchy of RDFS according to Brickley and Guha (2000). The "rdf" prefix refers to the RDF namespace (i.e., primitives with this prefix are already defined in RDF) and "rdfs" refers to new primitives defined by RDFS. Note that RDFS uses a nonstandard object-meta model: the properties rdfs:subClassOf, rdf:type, rdfs:domain and rdfs:range are used both as primitive constructs in the definition of the RDF Schema

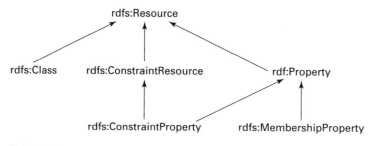

Figure 4.5
RDF Schema subclass-of hierarchy.

Specification and as specific instances of RDF properties. This dual role makes it possible to view, for example, rdfs:subClassOf as an RDF property just like other predefined or newly introduced RDF properties but introduces self-referentiality into the RDF schema definition, which makes it rather unique when compared to conventional model and metamodeling approaches and makes the RDF schema specification very difficult to read and to formalize (cf. Nejdl, Wolpers, and Capella 2000).

4.5.1.3 *The Modeling Primitives of RDF Schema*

In this section, we will discuss the main classes, properties, and constraints in RDFS.

• Core classes are rdfs:Resource, rdf:Property, and rdfs:Class. Everything that is described by RDF expressions is viewed to be an instance of the class rdfs:Resource. The class rdf:Property is the class of all properties used to characterize instances of rdfs:Resource; that is, each slot/relation is an instance of rdf:Property. Finally, rdfs:Class is used to define concepts in RDFS; that is, each concept must be an instance of rdfs:Class.

• Core properties are rdf:type, rdfs:subClassOf, and rdfs:subPropertyOf. The rdf:type relation models instance-of relationships between resources and classes. A resource may be an instance of more than one class. The rdfs:subClassOf relation models the subsumption hierarchy among classes and is supposed to be transitive. Again, a class may be subclass of several other classes, however, a class can be neither a subclass of its own nor a subclass of its own subclasses; that is, the inheritance graph is cycle-free. The rdfs:subPropertyOf relation models the subsumption hierarchy among properties. If some property $P2$ is a rdfs:subPropertyOf another property $P1$, and if a resource R has a $P2$ property with a value V, this implies that the resource R also has a $P1$ property with value V. Again, the inheritance graph is supposed to be cycle-free.

• Core constraints are rdfs:ConstraintResource, rdfs:ConstraintProperty, rdfs:range, and rdfs:domain. rdfs:ConstraintResource defines the class of all constraints. rdfs:ConstraintProperty is a subset of rdfs:ConstraintResource and rdf:Property covering all properties that are used to define constraints. It has two instances, rdfs:range and rdfs:domain, that are used to restrict the range and domain, respectively, of properties. Expressing more than one range constraint on a given property is not permitted. Multiple domain constraints are permitted, however, and are interpreted as the union of the domains.

4.5.2   The Relation between OIL and RDF Schema

RDF Schema and ontology languages aim, to a great extent, at the same goals. Both provide a kind of domain theory and a vocabulary that can be used in information exchange. However, there are some significant differences. We will now investigate those differences by comparing OIL with RDF Schema. After that, we will discuss the relation between OIL and RDF Schema in further detail.

4.5.2.1   Comparing OIL and RDF Schema

OIL and RDF Schema have a number of similarities and differences. The most important are the following:

- *Main modeling primitives.* The main modeling primitives of OIL and RDF Schema are the same. OIL uses concepts and slots; RDF Schema calls them classes and properties. In both languages, it is possible to form hierarchies of classes, using the subclass-of relation, and hierarchies of properties, using the subproperty-of relation. However, it is forbidden to form cyclic inheritance relations in RDF Schema, in contrast to OIL, which permits such relations.

- *Property restrictions.* OIL allows the specification of restrictions on properties on a per class basis. We will call this "local" property restrictions. For example, local property restrictions in OIL enable the fillers of a slot called "has_parent" in a class "dog" to be restricted to those of type "dog" as well, without requiring that the range of "has_parent" be "dog". In RDFS, in contrast, it is possible to specify domain and range restrictions on properties only on a global level.

- *Modeling primitives.* OIL has a number of modeling primitives that do not exist in RDFS: this allows a domain to be specified in more detail in OIL than in RDFS.

- *Cardinality.* To specify the number of fillers of a slot, OIL provides a "min-cardinality," "max-cardinality," and (exact) "cardinality" constructs.

- *Concrete types.* RDFS has only one datatype, which is called "literal." OIL distinguishes between "string" and "integer," and those datatypes can be used to specify constraints: for example, "young_persons" have an age less than "25."

- *Intensional class definitions.* Class membership in OIL can be derived from the characteristics of their properties. This enables the intensional definitions of classes. For example, if "young_persons" are defined as having an age less than "25," then it also holds that all persons with an age less than "25" are "young_persons." This can be specified in OIL with the "defined class" construct.

- *Characteristics of properties.* Specific characteristics can be given to properties in OIL. For example, properties can be defined in OIL as "transitive" or "functional."

- *Boolean class expressions.* In OIL, one can construct new anonymous classes as boolean combinations of other classes. To this end, OIL provides the operators "and," "or," and "not."

- *Axioms.* OIL provides axioms, like "disjointness" and "covering." RDFS does not.

- *Formal semantics.* A final—and important—difference between OIL and RDFS is in the formal semantics of each. The semantics of RDF Schema is defined only in textual descriptions. On the contrary, OIL has an exact mapping to an expressive description logic. This gives precise semantics to the constructs, which allows for reasoning on the ontologies. Reasoning on RDF schemas is very difficult, because of the unclear interpretation of some constructs.

4.5.2.2   Relating RDF Schema and Ontology Languages

We have seen that the main difference between OIL—and other ontology languages—and RDF Schema is not their purpose, but their expressiveness and formal semantics. Therefore, although the syntaxes of the two differ, their relation can be characterized as an extension relation. OIL adds formal semantics and some additional primitives to what is provided in RDF Schema.

Now, because the aim of this chapter is to investigate how schema languages can be used to apply ontology-based semantics to online resources, we have to make the additional expressiveness of ontology languages available to RDF Schema. This can be done in the same way as RDF Schema extends RDF. RDF Schema extends (or enriches) RDF by giving an externally specified semantics to specific resources (e.g., to rdfs:subclassOf, to *rdfs:Class*). OIL can be used to further extend (or enrich) RDF Schema by defining a semantics for specific resources. This provides added value by allowing the extension to capture meaning that cannot be captured in RDF Schema. Furthermore, if such an extension to RDF Schema is carefully designed, a partial interpretation without the additional semantics from the ontology language will still yield a valid RDF Schema interpretation.

In section 4.6.2, we will show how such an extension to RDF Schema can be created. We express OIL in terms of RDF Schema, thus enriching the latter with the required additional expressivity and the semantics of the former. The OIL extension of RDFS has been carefully engineered so that a partial interpretation of OIL metadata is still correct under the intended semantics of RDFS: simply ignoring the OIL-specific portions of an OIL document yields a correct RDF(S) document whose intended RDFS semantics is precisely a subset of the semantics of the full OIL statements. In this way, the approach ensures maximal sharing of metadata on the Web: even partial interpretation of metadata by less semantically aware processors will yield a correct partial interpretation of the metadata.

The result is an RDF Schema definition of OIL primitives, which allows one to express any OIL ontology in RDF Schema syntax. This enables the added benefits of OIL beyond RDF Schema, such as reasoning support and formal semantics, to be used on the Web while retaining maximal backward compatability with "pure" RDF.

4.6   *Applying Ontologies to Online Resources*

In the previous sections we have defined the relation between ontologies and XML Schema, on the one hand, and ontologies and RDF Schema, on the other. We will now show how these relations can be used in practice to apply the benefits of ontologies to online resources.

4.6.1   *Translating an Ontology into an XML Schema Prescription*

Just as (extended) ER models have to be translated into database schemas to enable them to be used in an actual DB system, an OIL ontology can be translated into an XML schema document to allow its use in an XML data exchange environment. We provide in this section a procedure for translating from an ontology to a specific XML Schema document that is very close in spirit to that provided in Elmasri and Navathe 2000 for ER models. ER models provide entities, attributes, and relationships as their primary modeling primitives. This closely corresponds to OIL, where we have concepts (i.e., entities), slot definitions for concepts (i.e., attributes), and global slot definitions (i.e., relationships). Extended ER models also incorporate the notion of inheritance, however, they require its explicit definition. On the other hand, the relation model provides only relations and the arguments (called attributes) of relations. Therefore, a translation step is required when we go from one type of model to the other. A similar procedure that translates a high-level conceptual description of a domain into a specific document definition via XML Schema is decribed below.

We assume a definition of an ontology in OIL. (An example is provided in figure 4.1.) We now describe its stepwise translation into an XML schema using the stepwise translation of this example as illustration.

```
Geographical_Location
Country                    <= Geographical_Location
City                       <= Geographical_Location
AreaComparison
KilometerLength-OR-MilesLength
  KilometerLength              <= KilometerLength-OR-MilesLength
  MilesLength                  <= KilometerLength-OR-MilesLength
  [,,,]
  coastline
  neighbor_country
```

Figure 4.6
Materializing the hierarchy.

1. *Materialize the hierarchy.* Give all complex class expressions that are used in subclass definitions and slot constraints names. Then materialize the hierarchy, that is, make all class and slot subsumptions explicit. This step is necessary because XML Schema lacks any notion of implicit hierarchy, and it is possible because subsumption can be defined in OIL. Actually, the FaCT system (via its CORBA interface if desired) can be used for this purpose (Bechhofer et al. 1999).[4] In this step, also make it explicit which slots can be applied to a particular class, exploiting the domain and range restrictions of the global slots definitions. Figure 4.6 provides the materialized hierarchy of our running example. Note that KilometerLength-OR-MilesLength is a new concept, constructed from a complex class expression. In our small example, there are no new class subsumptions derived, because all of them are already stated explicitly. (See Horrocks et al. 2000 or Fensel et al. 2000 for a more complex example that illustrates the derivation of implicit subsumptions.)

2. *Create a complexType definition for each slot definition in OIL.* Add a reference to the (still to be defined) element definition for the *range* component in the OIL slot-definition figure 4.7 begins with some example slot-definitions. If a slot has more than one range, an intermediate element must be used that is the conjunction of all the range components. The place of this intermediate element in the class hierarchy should be derived in the first step.

```
Part of the result of step 2: type definitions for slots:
<xsd:complexType name="capitalType">
<xsd:sequence>
 <xsd:element ref="City"/>
</xsd:sequence>
</xsd:complexType>
<xsd:complexType name="coastlineType">
<xsd:sequence>
 <xsd:element ref="KilometerLength-OR-MilesLength"/>
</xsd:sequence>
</xsd:complexType>
Part of the result of step 3: type definitions for classes:
<xsd:complexType name="CountryType">
<xsd:complexContent>
 <xsd:extension base="GeographicalLocationType">
  <xsd:sequence>
   <xsd:element name="capital" type="capitalType" minOccurs="1" maxOccurs="1"/>
   <xsd:element name="has-boundary" type="has_boundaryType" minOccurs="0"
maxOccurs="unbounded"/>
   <xsd:element name="relative_area" type="relative_areaType" minOccurs="0"
maxOccurs="unbounded"/>
  </xsd:sequence>
 </xsd:extension>
</xsd:complexContent>
</xsd:complexType>
<xsd:complexType name="AeraComparisonType">
<xsd:sequence>
  <xsd:element name="proportion" type="string" minOccurs="0"
maxOccurs="unbounded"/>
  <xsd:element name="compared_to" minOccurs="0" maxOccurs="unbounded">
   <xsd:complexType>
    <xsd:complexContent>
     <xsd:extension base="compared_toType">
      <xsd:sequence>
       <xsd:element ref="Country"/>
      </xsd:sequence>
     </xsd:extension>
    </xsd:complexContent>
   </xsd:complexType>
  </xsd:element>
 </xsd:sequence>
</xsd:complexType>
Part of the result of step 4: element definitions for slots and classes:
<xsd:element name="capital" type="capitalType"/>
<xsd:element name="GeographicalLocation" type="GeographicalLocationType"/>
<xsd:element name="Country" type="CountryType"/>
<xsd:element name="City" type="CityType"/>
<xsd:element name="AeraComparison" type="AeraComparisonType"/>
```

Figure 4.7
The result of steps 2 and 3.

3. *Also create a complexType definition for each class definition in OIL.* Add the names of the slots that can be applied to the classes as elements in the type definition. The facets on the slot-constraints are translated in the following way: has-value facets give a minOccurs="1" attribute in the element- element, value-type facets give minOccurs="0" and min-cardinality, max-cardinality, and cardinality give minOccurs="value," maxOccurs="value," or both, respectively, as attributes. If a slot has the property "functional," it will get the attribute maxOccurs="1". See, for example, the attributes of "capital" in "CountryType" in figure 4.7: the value of minOccurs is 1 because of the has-value constraint, and the value of maxOccurs is 1 because of the "functional" property.

For the slots that appear in explicit slot-constraints (i.e., those that are actually described in a class definition, not those that can be applied to a class according to their domain), an anonymous type is defined that is derived from the appropriate slot type defined in step 2. The extension of the base type consists of the reference to the class that must be the filler of the slot.

For slots that can be applied to the classes (according to their domain) but that are not present in explicit slot-constraints, the type of the element is directly the slot type from step 2, with the attributes minOccurs="0" and maxOccurs="unbounded". The second part of figure 4.7 gives an example.

4. *Create an element definition for each slot and class.* Each slot and each class definition is translated into an element definition in the XML schema. The type of the elements will obviously be the complexType definitions that are created in steps 2 and 3. See also figure 4.7.

5. *Define a grammar for each entity, associate basic datatypes with built-in datatypes if desired, and add lexical constraints on datatypes if desired.* This step adds an additional level of expressiveness that is not present in OIL. It is purely concerned with document structure and appearance.

6. *Replace the module concept of OIL with the namespace and inclusion concept of XML Schema.* This step is straightforward because the concepts only differ syntactically.

```
<?xml version="1.0" encoding="UTF-8"?>
<Country xmlns="worldfactbook.xsd"
   xmlns:xsi="http://www.w3.org/1999/XMLSchema/instance">
<name>The Netherlands</name>
<capital><City><name>Amsterdam</name></City></capital>
<relative_area>
 <AeraComparison>
  <proportion>slightly less than twice the size of</proportion>
  <compared_to><Country><name>New Jersey</name></Country></compared_to>
 </AeraComparison>
</relative_area>
<has_boundary>
 <LandBoundary>
<neighbor_country><Country><name>Belgium</name></Country></neighbor_country>
   <length xsi:type="KilometerLength"><value>450</value><unit>km</unit></length>
 </LandBoundary>
 <LandBoundary>
<neighbor_country><Country><name>Germany</name></Country></neighbor_country>
   <length xsi:type="KilometerLength"><value>577</value><unit>km</unit></length>
 </LandBoundary>
</has_boundary>
<coastline><KilometerLength><value>451</value><unit>km</unit></KilometerLength>
</coastline>
 </Country>
```

Figure 4.8
XML document conforming to the generated schema.

4.6.1.1 *Using the Schema for Document Markup*

The schema resulting from the transformation described in steps 1–6 above can be used to create XML instance documents. The structure of these documents must conform to the schema. As an example, we show in figure 4.8 an XML document that could constitute a Web page in the *World Factbook*. Together with a appropriate style sheet, this document can be used to produce a page like the one shown in figure 4.9. Note that we now have a Web page that looks similar to the original HTML version but has a markup that is well-founded on an ontology.

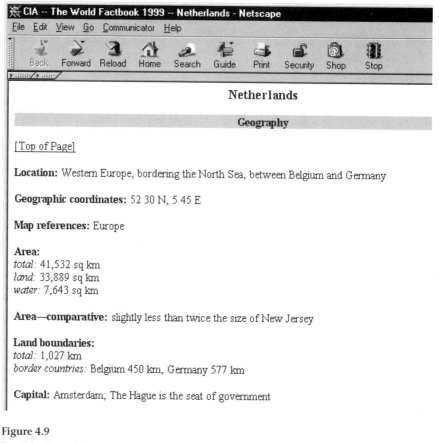

Figure 4.9
Possible view of data from Figure 4.8.

4.6.1.2 Problems in the Translation Procedure

In this section, we return to some of the points that arose when we investigated the relation between ontologies and XML schemas. First, multiple inheritance forms a problem in the translation procedure. As we discussed in section 4.4.2.1, in XML Schema there is no explicit way to define multiple inheritance. It is not possible to simulate multiple inheritance by inheriting from different superclasses in several type definitions, because the XML Schema specification does not allow more than one definition for a type.

Because of this lack of multiple inheritance, XML Schema is not well suited to be an ontology language. This is not meant as a criticism, because XML Schema is not designed for ontological modeling; it is designed for describing valid structures of documents.

Second, the question may arise as to whether the translation process can be automated and whether it is reversible. Concerning the first question, we can state that most of the steps can be completely automatic. The fifth step can be partially automated, for example, by using sequence as standard grammar for applying slots to classes. Final tuning via human interference may be necessary. Translation in the reverse direction is possible but more difficult; a high degree of automatization should be achievable, however.

4.6.2   Defining an Ontology Language as Extension to RDF Schema

We have shown a mechanism by which to use XML Schema for applying ontologies to online resources, and we now discuss a second method. In this section we show how OIL ontologies can be written down in RDF, using existing RDFS constructs as much as possible, but where necessary extending RDFS with additional constructs.

4.6.2.1   Class Definitions

In RDFS, classes are simply declared by giving them a name (with the ID attribute). In OIL, a class definition links a class with a name, a documentation, a type, its superclasses, and the attributes defined for it. We therefore need to extend the schema language to capture all the knowledge contained in an OIL ontology. To illustrate the use of these extensions, we will walk through them by means of some example OIL class definitions that need to be represented in RDFS syntax:

```
class-def defined herbivore
 subclass-of animal
  slot-constraint eats
   value-type (plant or (slot-constraint is-part-of plant))
```

```
class-def elephant
 subclass-of herbivore mammal
 slot-constraint eats
  value-type plant
 slot-constraint color
  has-filler "grey"
```

The first defines a class "herbivore," a subclass of animal, whose instances eat plants or parts of plants. The second defines a class "elephant", which is a subclass of both herbivore and mammal.

OIL distinguises between primitive classes and defined classes. To express a class's type in the RDFS syntax, we choose to introduce two extra classes, "oil:PrimitiveClass" and "oil:DefinedClass," as extension to RDFS. In a particular class definition, we can use one of these metaclasses to express the type. For example:

```
<oil:DefinedClass rdf:ID="herbivore">
</oil:DefinedClass>
```

This way of making an actual class an instance of either DefinedClass or PrimitiveClass introduces a nice object-meta distinction between the OIL RDFS schema and the actual ontology: using rdf:type, the class "herbivore" can be considered to be an instance of DefinedClass. (In OIL in general, if it is not explicitly stated that a class is defined, the class is assumed to be primitive.)

Next, we have to translate the subclass-of statement into RDFS. This also can be done in a straightforward manner, simply reusing existing RDFS expressiveness:

```
<oil:DefinedClass rdf:ID="herbivore">
 <rdfs:subClassOf rdf:resource="#animal"/>
</oil:DefinedClass>
```

To define a class as a subclass of a class expression (which is not possible in RDFS), we introduced the additional "oil:subClassOf property" in the RDFS extension.

We still need to serialize the slot-constraint on the class "herbivore." In RDFS, there is no mechanism for restricting the attributes of a class on a local level. This is due to the property-centric nature of the RDF data model: properties are defined globally, with their domain description coupling them to the relevant classes. To overcome this problem, we introduce the property "oil:hasPropertyRestriction" in the RDFS extension, which is an rdf:type of rdfs:ConstraintProperty (analogous to rdfs:domain and rdfs:range). Here we take full advantage of the intended extensibility of RDFS. We also introduce oil:PropertyRestriction as a placeholder class for specific classes of slot constraints, such as has-value, value-type, and cardinality. For the three cardinality constraints, an extra property, "number," is introduced and used to assign a concrete value to the cardinality constraints. In our example ontology, the first part of the slot constraint would be serialized using the primitives introduced above as follows:

```
<oil:DefinedClass rdf:ID="herbivore">
 <rdfs:subClassOf rdf:resource="#animal"/>
 <oil:hasPropertyRestriction>
  <oil:ValueType>
   <oil:onProperty rdf:resource="#eats"/>
   <oil:toClass> </oil:toClass>
  </oil:ValueType>
 </oil:hasPropertyRestriction>
</oil:DefinedClass>
```

The slot constraint has not yet been completely translated: the toClass element is not yet filled. Here we come across another feature of OIL that is not available in RDFS: the class expression. A class expression is an expression that evaluates to a class definition. Such an expression can be a simple class name, or it can be a boolean expression of classes and/or slot-constraints. In the example, we have a boolean "or" expression that evaluates to the class of all things that are plants or that are parts of a plant. We introduce oil:ClassExpression and oil:BooleanExpression to hold the operators "and," "or," and "not" as subclasses.

Also, since a single class is a essentially a simple kind of class expression, rdfs:Class itself should be a subclass of oil:ClassExpression. The "and," "or," and "not" operators are connected to operands using the newly introduced "oil:hasOperand" property. This property again has no direct equivalent in OIL primitive terms but is a helper to connect two class expressions, because in the RDF data model one can relate two classes only by means of a property.

We can now fill the toClass part of our example as follows:

```
<oil:toClass>
 <oil:Or>
  <oil:hasOperand rdf:resource="#plant"/>
  <oil:hasOperand>
   <HasValue>
    <oil:onProperty rdf:resource="#is-part-of"/>
    <oil:toClass rdf:resource="#plant"/>
   </HasValue>
  </oil:hasOperand>
 </oil:Or>
</oil:toClass>
```

4.6.2.2 Slot Definitions

Both OIL and RDFS allow slots as first-class citizens of an ontology. Therefore, slot definitions in OIL map nicely onto property definitions in RDFS. Also the "subslot-of," "domain," and "range" properties in OIL have almost direct equivalents in RDFS. However, there are a few subtle differences between domain and range restrictions in OIL and their equivalents in RDFS. First, the specification of OIL is very clear on multiple domain and range restriction: these are allowed, and the semantic is the intersection of the individual statements (conjunctive semantics). In RDFS, multiple domain statements are allowed, but their interpretation is the union of the classes in the statements (disjunctive semantics).

Secondly, in contrast to RDFS, OIL allows, as range and domain of properties, not only classes, but also class expressions, and (for range) concrete-type expressions. It is not possible to reuse rdfs:range and rdfs:domain for these sophisticated expressions, because of the conjunctive semantics of multiple range statements: we cannot extend the range of rdfs:range or rdfs:domain, we can only restrict it. Therefore, we introduce two new ConstraintProperties oil:domain and oil:range. They have the same domain as their RDFS equivalent (i.e., rdf:Property) but have a broader range. For domain, class expressions are valid fillers; for range, both class expressions and concrete-type expressions may be used.

When translating a slot definition, rdfs:domain and rdfs:range should be used for simple (one-class) domain and range restrictions, whereas for more complicated statements, the oil:range or oil:domain properties should be used. For example:

```
slot-def age
 domain animal
  range    (range 0 120)
```

is in the RDFS representation:

```
<rdf:Property rdf:ID="age">
<rdfs:domain rdf:resource="#elephant"/>
 <oil:range>
  <oil:Range>
   <oil:integerValue>0</oil:integerValue>
   <oil:integerValue>120</oil:integerValue>
  </oil:Range>
 </oil:range>
</rdf:Property>
```

However, global slot definitions in OIL allow specification of more aspects of a slot than property definitions in RDFS do. Besides the domain and range restrictions, OIL slots can also have an "inverse" attribute and qualities like "transitive" and "symmetric." We therefore add a property, "inverseRelationOf," with "rdf:Property" as domain and range. We also add the classes "TransitiveProperty," "FunctionalProperty," and "Symmetric-

Property" to reflect the different qualities of a slot. In the RDFS serialization of OIL, the rdf:type property can be used to add a quality to a property. For example, the OIL definition of

```
slot-def has-part
  domain is-part-of
  range   (range 0 120)
```

is in RDFS

```
<oil:TransitiveProperty rdf:ID="has-part">
<oil:inverseRelationOf rdf:resource="#is-part-of"/>
</oil:TransitiveProperty>
```

This way of translating the qualitities of properties features the same nice object-meta distinction between the OIL RDFS schema and the actual ontology as the translation of the "type" of a class (see section 4.4.2). In an actual ontology, the property "has-part" can be considered as an instance of a TransitiveProperty. Note that making a property an instance of more than one class, and thus giving it multiple qualities, is allowed.

4.6.2.3 Representing Axioms

Axioms in OIL are factual statements about the classes in the ontology. They correspond to n-ary relations between class expressions, where n is 2 or greater. RDF knows only binary relations (properties). Therefore, we cannot simply map OIL axioms to RDF properties. Instead, we choose to model axioms as classes, with helper properties connecting them to the class expressions involved in the relation. Since axioms can be considered objects, this is a very natural approach toward modeling them in RDF (see also Staab and Madche 2000; Staab et al. 2000). Observe also that binary relations (properties) are modeled as objects in RDFS as well (i.e., any property is an instance of the class rdf:Property). We simply introduce a new primitive alongside rdf:Property for relations with higher arity.

We introduce a placeholder class "oil:Axiom" and model specific types of axioms as subclasses and do likewise for Equivalent. We also introduce a property to connect the axiom object with the class expressions that it relates to each other: oil:hasObject is a property connecting an axiom with an object class expression. For example, to serialize the axiom that herbivores, omnivores, and carnivores are (pairwise) disjoint:

```
<oil:Disjoint>
<oil:hasObject rdf:resource="#herbivore"/>
<oil:hasObject rdf:resource="#carnivore"/>
<oil:hasObject rdf:resource="#omnivore"/>
</oil:Disjoint>
```

For modeling covering axioms, we introduce a separate placeholder class, "oil:Covering," which is a subclass of "oil:Axiom." The specific types of coverings available are modeled as subclasses of "oil:Covering" again. Furthermore, two additional properties are introduced: "oil:hasSubject," to connect a covering axiom with its subject, and "oil:isCoveredBy," which is a subproperty of "oil:hasObject," to connect a covering axiom with the classes that cover the subject. For example, we serialize the axiom that the class animal is covered by carnivore, herbivore, omnivore, and mammal (i.e., every instance of animal is also an instance of at least one of the other classes) as follows:

```
<oil:Cover>
<oil:hasSubject rdf:resource="#animal"/>
<oil:isCoveredBy rdf:resource="#carnivore"/>
<oil:isCoveredBy rdf:resource="#herbivore"/>
<oil:isCoveredBy rdf:resource="#omnivore"/>
<oil:isCoveredBy rdf:resource="#mammal"/>
</oil:Cover>
```

4.6.2.4   Compatability with RDF Schema

Figure 4.10 shows the resulting is-a hierarchy of the OIL constructs that we introduced to define OIL ontologies in RDFS representation. The hierarchy nicely illustrates that the new OIL language representation includes RDF

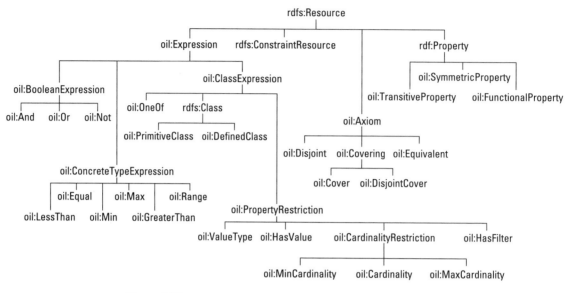

Figure 4.10

Is-a hierarchy of RDFS primitives with OIL extensions.

Schema as a sublanguage. As a result, all RDF Schema expressions are actually also valid and meaningful OIL expressions. This is called backward compatibility. Of course, since OIL is an extension of RDF Schema, not all OIL definitions are interpretable as RDF Schema definitions. However, the way in which this extension is defined ensures that all OIL definitions are still valid RDF Schema expressions, although only partly meaningful in RDF Schema. Such a partial interpretation results from simply ignoring any statement not from the rdf or rdfs namespaces (in our example, those from the oil namespace). For example, an RDF Schema processor will interpret the above definition of "herbivore" simply as stating that herbivores are a subclass of animals and that they have some other property that it cannot interpret. This is a correct, albeit partial, interpretation of the definition. Furthermore, because OIL is built on top of RDF Schema, it shares with it the mechanism for representing instance information.

Together, this gives another important compatibility result besides backward compatibility: even if an ontology is written in the richer modeling language (OIL), a processor for the simpler ontology language (RDF Schema) can still fully interpret all the instance information of the ontology and partially interpret the class structure of the ontology.

This can be called *partial forward compatibility*. Such partial interpretability of semantically rich metadata by semantically poor programs or agents is a crucial step toward the sharing of metadata on the Semantic Web. We cannot realistically hope that all of the Semantic Web will be built on a single standard for semantically rich metadata. The backward and partial forward capability shows that multiple semantic modeling languages do not have to lead to metadata that are totally uninterpretable by others. Instead, simpler processors can still pick up as much of the metadata from rich processors as they can "understand" and safely ignore the rest in the knowledge that their partial interpretation is still correct with respect to the original intention of the metadata.

4.7   Conclusion

In this chapter, we have discussed two important schema languages for the Web. We have compared these languages with full-fledged ontology languages and described the relation between them. Moreover, we have shown in two procedures how these schema languages can be used to apply ontologies to online resources.

When we compare OIL with the proposed XML Schema, our main conclusion is that an ontology language and XML Schema refer to a different level of abstraction. Therefore, OIL and XML Schema each play a role in a different phase of describing the semantics of online information sources. OIL is suitable for domain modeling; XML Schema can be used to prescribe how the information in a domain is structured. Our comparison has also revealed that the XML Schema type hierarchy can be used to express some conceptual knowledge. Although there are still some questions about the best way to create this type hierarchy, with the help of some artifices it is possible to capture the central is-a relationship of an ontology in an XML Schema definition.

We exploited this possibility in a procedure for translating from an OIL ontology to an XML structure prescription, which we provided as an illustration of the relation between the two. As a result of the translation procedure, a document schema is created that is founded in a domain ontology. The main advantage of this translation is that an ontology can be used as a conceptual layer on top of a set of structured (XML) documents, because the markup of actual XML documents is founded on an ontology. Another benefit of this procedure is that it yields an XML schema that can be used to encode instance data of an ontology in plain XML.

We have also, in this chapter, compared RDF Schema with OIL. We have observed that there is a big difference in the level of expressiveness between the two. However, we have shown how full-fledged ontology languages can be applied in the Resource Description Framework, by representing the modeling primitives as defined by OIL in RDF Schema. The OIL extension of RDFS has been carefully engineered so that a partial interpretation of OIL metadata is still correct under the intended semantics of RDFS: simply ignoring the OIL-specific portions of an OIL document yields a correct RDF(S) document whose intended RDFS semantics is precisely a subset of the semantics of the full OIL statements. In this way, the approach ensures maximal sharing of metadata on the Web: even partial interpretation of metadata by less semantically aware processors will yield a correct partial interpretation of the metadata.

We can conclude that, despite the similarity in their names, RDF Schema and XML Schema fulfill a different role. First, XML Schemas, and also DTDs, prescribe the order and combination of tags in an XML document. In contrast, RDF Schemas provide information about the interpretation of the statements given in RDF data (i.e., RDF Schema is a simple type system for RDF), but they do not constrain the syntactical appearance of an RDF description. From another point of view, RDF Schema and XML Schema can be considered orthogonal to one another: RDF is mainly intended for describing explicit metadata about Web resources as a whole; XML Schema gives semantics to the actual markup of a document (i.e., the tags and their stucture) and answers the question of how the structure of documents is related to conceptual terms.

This chapter has provided an illustration of how these two orthogonal mechanisms can be used to apply ontologies to online resources. XML Schema and RDF Schema each play a different role in this process. The semantically grounded document markup that is provided by XML Schema complements the kind of semantic description that is provided by RDF-based approaches. We think that both mechanisms are important building blocks for the Semantic Web. Finally, we believe that this way of translating and extending is generally applicable across other ontology languages than OIL.

Notes

1. However, XML Schema does not provide any formal language for these intensional definitions.

2. Actually primitive datatypes are defined in prose or by reference to another standard. Derived datatypes can be constrained along their facets (maxInclusive, maxExclusive, etc.).

3. A general comparison of type systems and description logics can be found in Borgida 1992.

4. OilEd is an integrated tool for building OIL ontologies and exploiting the FaCT reasoner; it can found at: http://img.cs.man.ac.uk/oil/.

References

Bechhofer, S., I. Horrocks, P. F. Patel-Schneider, and S. Tessaris. 1999. A Proposal for a Description Logic Interface. In *Proceedings of the International Workshop on Description Logics (DL'99), Linköping, Sweden, July 30–August 1, 1999*, ed. P. Lambrix et al. Available from http://CEUR-WS.org/Vol-22/.

Biron, P. V., and A. Malhotra. 2000. XML Schema Part 2: Datatypes (candidate recommendation). Available from http://www.w3.org/TR/2000/CR-xmlschema-2-20001024/.

Borgida, A. 1992. From Type Systems to Knowledge Representation: Natural Semantics Specifications for Description Logics. *International Journal of Intelligent and Cooperative Information Systems* 1(1):93–126.

Bray, T., J. Paoli, C. Sperberg-McQueen, and E. Maler. 1998. Extensible Markup Language (XML) 1.0 (recommendation). World Wide Web Consortium. Available from http://www.w3.org/TR/REC-xml.

Brickley, D., and R. V. Guha. 2000. Resource Description Framework (RDF) Schema Specification 1.0 (candidate recommendation). World Wide Web Consortium. Available from http://www.w3.org/TR/2000/CR-rdf-schema-20000327.

Broekstra, J., M. Klein, D. Fensel, S. Decker, F. van Harmelen, and I. Horrocks. 2001. Enabling Knowledge Representation on the Web by Extending RDF Schema. In *Proceedings of the 10th World Wide Web Conference, Hong Kong, May 1–5, 2001*. Available from http://www.cs.vu.nl/~mcaklein/papers/www10/.

Elmasri, R., and S. B. Navathe. 2000. *Fundamentals of Database Systems*, 3rd ed. Reading, MA: Addison Wesley.

Fallside, D. C. 2000. XML-Schema Part 0: Primer (candidate recommendation). World Wide Web Consortium. Available from http://www.w3.org/TR/2000/CR-xmlschema-0-20001024/.

Fensel, D. 2001. *Ontologies: Silver Bullet for Knowledge Management and Electronic Commerce*. Berlin: Springer.

Fensel, D., I. Horrocks, F. van Harmelen, S. Decker, M. Erdmann, and M. Klein. 2000. OIL in a Nutshell. In *Proceedings of EKAW-2000: The 12th International Conference on Knowledge Engineering and Knowledge Management*, ed. R. Dieng and O. Corby. Berlin: Springer.

Guarino, N., and C. Welty. 2000. A Formal Ontology of Properties. In *Proceedings of EKAW-2000: The 12th International Conference on Knowledge Engineering and Knowledge Management*, ed. R. Dieng and O. Corby (pp. 97–112). Berlin: Springer.

Horrocks, I., D. Fensel, J. Broekstra, S. Decker, M. Erdmann, C. Goble, F. Van Harmelen, M. Klein, S. Staab, and R. Studer. 2000. OIL: The Ontology Inference Layer. Technical Report IR-479, Vrije Universiteit Amsterdam, September. Available from http://www.ontoknowledge.com/oil.

Lassila, O., and R. R. Swick. 1999. Resource Description Framework (RDF): Model and Syntax Specification (recommendation). World Wide Web Consortium. Available from http://www.w3.org/TR/REC-rdf-syntax/.

Nejdl, W., M. Wolpers, and C. Capella. 2000. The RDF Schema Revisited. In *Modelle und Modellierungssprachen in Informatik und Wirtschaftsinformatik, Modellierung 2000 (Models and Modeling Languages in Computer Science, Modeling 2000), St. Goar*. Koblenz: Foelbach Verlag.

Staab, S., M. Erdmann, A. Madche, and S. Decker. 2000. An Extensible Approach for Modeling Ontologies in RDF(S). In *First Workshop on the Semantic Web at the Fourth European Conference on Digital Libraries, Lisbon, Portugal, 2000*. Available at http://www.ics.forth.gr/proj/isst/SemWeb/proceedings/session2-1/paper.pdf.

Staab, S., and A. Madche. 2000. Axioms Are Objects, Too: Ontology Engineering beyond the Modeling of Concepts and Relations. In *Proceedings of the Workshop on Applications of Onto-*

logies and Problem-solving Methods, 14th European Conference on Artificial Intelligence (ECAI-2000), Berlin, Germany, 2000, ed. V. Benjamins et al. Available from http://delicias.dia.fi. upm.es/WORKSHOP/ECAI00/8.pdf.

Thompson, H. S., D. Beech, M. Maloney, and N. Mendelsohn. 2000. XML Schema, Part 1: Structures (candidate recommendation). World Wide Web Consortium. Available from http://www.w3.org/TR/2000/CR-xmlschema-1-20001024/.

Walsh, N. 1999. Schemas for XML. Available from http://www.xml.com/pub/1999/07/schemas/ index.html.

5 UPML: The Language and Tool Support for Making the Semantic Web Alive

Borys Omelayenko, Monica Crubézy, Dieter Fensel, Richard Benjamins, Bob Wielinga, Enrico Motta, Mark Musen, and Ying Ding

5.1 Introduction

Originally, the World Wide Web grew mainly around representing static information using the HTML language, which provided a standard for document layout and was interpreted by browsers in a canonical way to render documents. On the one hand, it was the simplicity of HTML that enabled the fast growth of the Web. On the other hand, its simplicity seriously hampered more advanced Web application in many domains and for many tasks. The Semantic Web (Berners-Lee and Fischetti 1999) will transform the current World Wide Web into a network of resources structured with annotations defining their meaning and relationships. In this context, computers not only provide more efficient access to Web resources but are also able to perform intelligent tasks with those resources. The explicit representation of the semantics of data, accompanied with domain theories (i.e., ontologies), will enable the development of a Web that provides a qualitatively new level of service. It will weave an incredibly large network of human knowledge and will complement it with machine processibility. Various automated services will help users achieve their goals by accessing and providing necessary information in a machine-understandable form. This process might ultimately create an extremely knowledgeable system with various specialized reasoning services—the systems that can support us in many aspects of life.

Many steps need to be taken to make this vision become a reality. Languages and tools for enriching information sources with machine-processible semantics must be developed (cf. Fensel et al. 2001; Fensel, van Harmelen, et al. 2000). Web-based reasoning services need to be developed, services that employ these semantic-enriched information sources to provide intelligent support to human users in task achievement. Specifically, such services will need to support users not only in finding and accessing information but also in achieving their goals based on this information.

The objective of the IBROW project (http://www.swi.psy.uva.nl/projects/ibrow/home.html) is to develop an intelligent broker able to configure knowledge systems from reusable components on the World Wide Web (Fensel and Benjamins 1998; Benjamins et al. 1999). IBROW (INtelligent BRokering service for knowledge-component reuse on the Web) brokers will handle Web requests for some classes of knowledge systems (e.g., diagnostic systems) by accessing libraries of reusable reasoning components on the Web and selecting, adapting, and configuring them in accordance with the domain in question. The TBROW project integrates research on heterogeneous databases, interoperability, and Web technology with knowledge system technologies, namely, ontologies and problem-solving methods.

Nowadays, ontologies (Gruber 1993) represent mainly *static* and declarative knowledge about a domain of expertise. The way to apply domain knowledge to achieve user tasks, or *dynamic* knowledge, is usually encoded in inference algorithms, which reason on the contents of the domain ontologies. Making this dynamic knowledge explicit and generic and regarding it as an important part of the entire knowledge contained in a knowledge-based system (KBS) is the rationale that underlies *problem-solving methods* (PSMs) (cf. Stefik 1995; Benjamins and Fensel 1998; Benjamins and Shadbolt 1998; Motta 1999; Fensel 2000).

PSMs provide reusable components for implementing the reasoning part of KBSs.[1] PSMs refine inference engines to allow a more direct control of the reasoning process of a system to achieve a task. PSMs encode control knowledge independently of an application domain: they can therefore be reused for different domains and applications. PSMs decompose the reasoning task of a knowledge-based system into a number of subtasks and inference actions, which are connected by knowledge roles representing the "role" that knowledge plays in the reasoning process. Several libraries of problem-solving methods have been developed (cf. Marcus 1988; Chandrasekaran, Johnson, and Smith 1992; Puppe 1993; Breuker and van de Velde 1994; Benjamins 1995; Musen 1998; and Motta 1999), and a number of problem-solving method specification languages have been proposed, ranging from informal notations (e.g., Conceptual Modeling Language [CML] [Schreiber et al. 1994]) to formal modeling languages (see Fensel and van Harmelen 1994; Fensel 1995; and Gomez Perez and Benjamins 1999 for summaries).

Ontologies and PSMs provide the components that need to be combined by the IBROW broker to configure a particular knowledge system on the Web. As a central requirement, both types of components, ontologies and PSMs, need to be properly marked up to be localized on the Web and assembled into a working system by the broker. In the IBROW project, we have developed the Unified Problem-Solving Method Development Language (UPML)[2] (www.cs.vu.nl/~upml) to specify problem-solving components and their software architectures to facilitate their semiautomatic reuse and adaptation (see Fensel and Benjamins 1998; Fensel, Benjamins, Decker, et al. 1999; Fensel, Benjamins, Motta, and Wielinga 1999; Fensel et al. in press). Concisely, UPML is a framework for specifying knowledge-intensive reasoning systems based on libraries of generic problem-solving components. Since its first definition, UPML has been adopted by the members of the IBROW consortium and has been used to specify a design library (http://webonto.open.ac.uk) (Motta, Gaspari, and Fensel 1998) at the Open University, a library for classification problem solving (Motta and Lu 2000), and parts of the PSM library at Stanford University (cf. Musen 1998).

The goal of this chapter is to provide an overview of the UPML framework and tools and to demonstrate how this language provides the enabling technology for the next level of service of the World Wide Web: to provide users of the Web with online, ready-to-use problem-solving resources. In section 5.2, we discuss the mission of IBROW in the context of the future Web and the central role of a specification language such as UPML. In section 5.3, we

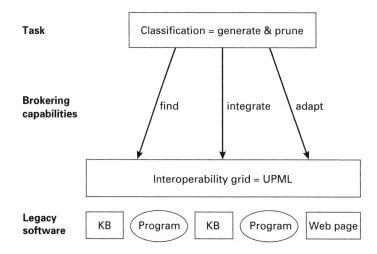

Figure 5.1
The IBROW approach. Based on user requirements about a task to be solved, the IBROW broker needs to find, integrate, and adapt a set of suitable knowledge components (i.e., knowledge bases and problem-solving methods) on the Web to solve a user-specified task. UPML is a central interoperability element of the IBROW approach.

introduce the UPML language for component markup. Tool support for UPML is provided by the Protégé environment, as presented in section 5.4. Concluding remarks are presented in section 5.5.

5.2 Brokering Reasoning Components on the Web

The mission of the IBROW project is to develop an intelligent brokering service capable of retrieving a set of knowledge components from the Web that, when combined, can solve the users' problem according to stated requirements (Benjamins et al. 1999). As illustrated in figure 5.1, the main goal of the IBROW broker is to identify the components needed to solve the problem and to adapt and configure them into a running reasoning service. In the context of the World Wide Web, the task of the broker includes reusing third-party components available on the Web and operating problem solvers and knowledge bases together in a distributed, plug-and-play fashion.

The IBROW approach offers a number of innovative aspects. Most of today's Web brokers (e.g., Metacrawler [www.metacrawler.com], Ariadne [www.isi.edu/ariadne], Ontobroker [www.aifb.uni-karlsruhe.de/Projekte/ontobroker/inhalt_en.html]) handle only static information, whereas the IBROW broker is capable of managing dynamic information.[3] As a result, our approach offers an opportunity for a new type of electronic marketplace where reasoning services can be configured dynamically out of independent components to solve a specific task. In particular, IBROW will enable the construction of "throw-away" applications for Web users.

A key issue in the IBROW approach is that reasoning components themselves need to be available on the Web. Moreover, components must be marked up with machine-processable data, so that an IBROW broker can identify their capabilities and reason about them. This requirement calls for the development of a language for component markup, which must support the specification of the capabilities and assumptions of available problem solvers, the goal and assumptions of tasks, and the properties of domains. In addition, this markup language must hold nonfunctional, pragmatics descriptions of available reasoning components. The language must be formal enough to express characteristics of reasoning components at the knowledge level, and it should also have a Web-compatible syntax, to allow the components to be distributed as Web resources. As explained in section 5.3, the first achievement of the IBROW project was to develop the UPML language, which meets these requirements for brokering reasoning components on the Web.

Based on UPML, the IBROW broker can reason about component annotations to determine the localization of the components and select appropriate components by matching them to the user's requirements. Reasoning capabilities are required from the broker to recognize and analyze the user's problem, to find relevant problem solvers for each (sub)task of the problem, and to check the applicability of problems solvers according to the knowledge bases available. Once the broker has selected a suitable set of knowledge components, it needs to adapt them and enable their integration into a single service. Finally, the broker needs to execute the configured running

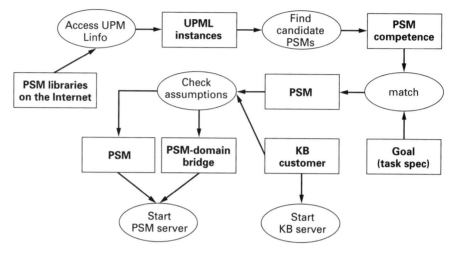

Figure 5.2
The brokering process in IBROW, in which the UPML markup language plays a central role.

system to solve the user's task. Figure 5.2 shows a view of the brokering process: libraries of problem-solving methods are marked up with UPML and correspond to UPML instances, which are selected by the broker on the basis of their competence and the user's task specification. Given the user's domain model (shown as a "KB customer" in the figure), the broker selects the PSMs, which make proper assumptions about the domain model via special adaptation elements in UPML: PSM-Domain bridges. Finally, the broker passes the PSMs on to a PSM server able to execute them. Again, the UPML language for component markup, discussed in the next section, plays a kernel role at each stage of the brokering process.

5.3 UPML: The Language for Knowledge Component Markup

UPML is a software architecture specially designed to describe knowledge systems. The UPML architecture presented in figure 5.3 consists of six different kinds of elements. A task defines the problem to be solved by the

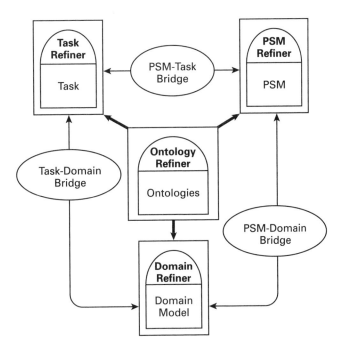

Figure 5.3
The UPML architecture.

knowledge system. A problem-solving method defines the reasoning process used to solve the problem. A domain model defines the domain knowledge available to solve the problem. Each of these elements is described independently to enable reuse of task descriptions in different domains, problem-solving methods for different tasks and domains, and domain knowledge for different tasks and problem-solving methods. Ontologies provide the terminology used in the tasks, problem-solving methods, and domain definitions. Again this separation enables knowledge sharing and reuse. For example, different tasks or problem-solving methods can share parts of the same vocabulary and definitions. Further elements of the specification are adapters, which are necessary to adjust other (reusable) elements to each other and to the specific application problem. UPML provides two types of adapters:

bridges and refiners. Bridges explicitly model the relationships between two specific parts of the architecture (e.g., between a domain and a task or a task and a problem-solving method). Refiners can be used to express the step-wise adaptation of other elements of the specification (e.g., generic problem-solving methods and tasks can be refined to more specific ones by applying to them a sequence of refiners) (Fensel 1997; Fensel and Motta 2001). Again, separating the generic and specific parts of a reasoning process enhances reusability. The main distinction between bridges and refiners is that bridges change the input and output of the components to make them fit together. Refiners, by contrast, may change only the internal details (e.g., the subtasks of a problem-solving method). This provides UPML with a structured and principled approach for developing and refining heuristic reasoning components. This approach provides a three-dimensional design space where different types of adapters correspond to different types of moves in that space (Fensel 2000; Fensel and Motta 2001).

5.3.1   Overview of the UPML Framework

UPML relies on a meta-ontology that defines the concepts and relations that are then instantiated for specific knowledge components. As shown in figure 5.4, this ontology is based on a root class, *Entity*, which specifies that each UPML concept and relation is represented with a list of attributes of a certain type. The root ontology of UPML defines two basic classes: *concept* and *binary relation*, both of which are subclasses of the Entity class. All UPML concepts and relations are subclasses of these two root classes. The hierarchy of classes used to define UPML is also presented in figure 5.4. The main classes of this hierarchy are discussed in the remainder of this section. The concepts of UPML define parts of a problem-solving system, as described in section 5.3.2. Binary Relations specify the interactions between the concepts, as described in section 5.3.3. *Architectural constraints and design guidelines* for UPML, which make it a full-fledged software architecture, are described in Fensel and Groenboom 1999 and Fensel et al. in press. The Web syntaxes for UPML are discussed in section 5.3.4.

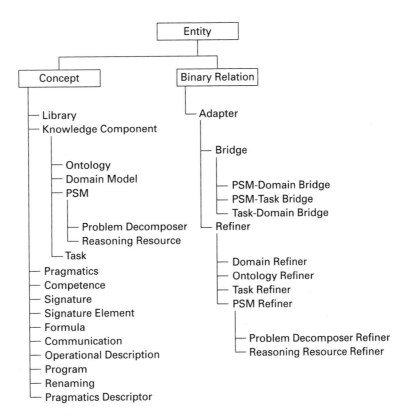

Figure 5.4
Class hierarchy of UPML. Each concept or relation in the UPML ontology is derived from the root ontology entities represented by the boxes.

5.3.2   Concepts

The Library concept is the overarching concept of UPML architecture: it contains a pointer to each component of a UPML specification (figure 5.5). The subclass-of relationship between two entities is denoted by the symbol <. Each concept or relation is represented as a list of attribute-type pairs (attribute : type) in which the type is either a primitive type (STRING) or a class of the hierarchy. The parentheses around the types denote that the corresponding attribute can have multiple values.

```
Library < Concept
pragmatics : (Pragmatics)
tasks : (Task)
domain models : (Domain Model)
problem decomposers : (Problem Decomposer)
reasoning resources : (Reasoning Resource)
ontologies : (Ontology)
ontology refiners : (Ontology Refiner)
problem decomposer refiners : (Problem Decomposer Refiner)
reasoning resource refiners : (Reasoning Resource Refiner)
task refiners : (Task Refiner)
domain refiners : (Domain Refiner)
psm-domain bridges : (PSM-Domain Bridge)
psm-task bridges : (PSM-Task Bridge)
task-domain bridges : (Task-Domain Bridge)
```

Figure 5.5
The Library concept.

There are four main types of knowledge components in UPML: Ontology, Domain Model, Task, and PSM (see figure 5.6). All types of components are defined as subclasses of the root concept Knowledge Component, also presented in figure 5.6. Each component has a pragmatics description and relies on one or more ontologies, which define its universe of discourse. All attributes represented in the figure model part-of relationships, in addition to uses.[4]

An Ontology (cf. Fensel 2001) is used in the definition of tasks, PSMs, and domain models. An ontology provides an explicit specification of a conceptualization, which can be reused and shared by multiple reasoning components. It enables, through a *signature*, *theorems*, and *axioms*, the definition of reusable terminology used by all other components. Ontologies are the key instrument of interchange among knowledge components. The core of an ontology specification in UPML is its signature definition, which captures the ontological elements used by a component, or signature elements. Signature elements are expressed in a modeling language. An ontology also provides *axioms* that characterize logical properties of the signature elements. Additional theorems may list useful statements that are implied by the axioms.

```
Knowledge Component < Concept          Task < Knowledge Component
Pragmatics : Pragmatics                Uses : (Task)
Ontologies : (Ontology)                Input roles : (Signature Element)
Ontology < Knowledge Component         Output roles : (Signature Element)
Signature : Signature                  Competence : Competence
Theorems : (Formula)                   Assumptions : (Formula)
Axioms : (Formula)                     PSM < Knowledge Component
Domain Model < Knowledge Component     Communication : Communication
uses : (Domain Model)                  Input roles : (Signature Element)
properties : (Formula)                 Output roles : (Signature Element)
metaknowledge : (Formula)              Competence : Competence
knowledge : (Formula)
```

Figure 5.6
UPML knowledge components: Ontology, Domain Model, Task, and PSM.

The Task concept specifies the task to be achieved by the PSMs of the library. The input roles and output roles together with the competence property define the input/output specification of the task. The input roles specify the input of case data, and the output roles specify the output of case data. The Competence concept represents the functional input/output specification of the Task component. Competence includes preconditions that restrict valid inputs and postconditions that describe the output of a method or task. The assumptions property of Task imposes requirements regarding the knowledge used to define the goal. A Task can import and refine other tasks via its uses attribute.

The Domain Model concept introduces domain knowledge (merely the formulas used by the problem-solving methods and tasks). The Domain Model consists of three elements: properties, metaknowledge, and the domain knowledge itself. Metaknowledge captures the implicit and explicit assumptions made in the domain model of the real world. Metaknowledge is assumed to be true. In other words, it has not been proven or cannot be proven and corresponds to our assumptions about the domain. Domain knowledge is the knowledge base of the domain necessary to define the task in a given application domain and to carry out the inference steps of the selected problem-solving method. Knowledge is specified under the

```
Problem Decomposer < PSM
Subtasks : (Task)
operational description : (Operational Description)
Reasoning Resource < PSM
knowledge roles : (Signature Element)
assumptions : (Formula)
```

Figure 5.7

Problem Decomposer and Reasoning Resource.

assumption that the metaknowledge is true. Properties (a synonym for theorems) can be derived from domain knowledge.

The *PSM* component represents a problem-solving method, defined by its competence and communication properties. The input roles and output roles of the PSM specify its inputs and outputs, functioning similarly to their role in the Task component. The PSM's communication property describes its interaction protocol with its environment, in particular with other (PSM) components.

The PSM concept has the following two subclasses: Problem Decomposer and Reasoning Resource, as presented in figure 5.7. A Problem Decomposer decomposes a task to be solved into a set of subtasks. Its Operational Description specifies the control structure over the subtasks and internal data flow among the subtasks. A Reasoning Resource solves a primitive step (or subtask) of a problem provided by the problem decomposer. It specifies assumptions regarding the domain knowledge, which must be fulfilled in order to perform a primitive reasoning step. Its internal structure is usually not specified, as it is considered an implementational aspect of no interest to the architectural specification of a problem-solving system. The knowledge roles attribute specifies the input of the (domain) knowledge to the reasoning resource.

Considering knowledge components to be Web resources themselves, UPML defines the concept of Pragmatics, which holds attributes that describe practical and reference information about a component. Pragmatics attributes are derived mainly from the Dublin Core (http://dublincore.org) metadata recommendation for annotating Web resources.

```
Adapter < Binary Relation
argument1 : Knowledge Component
argument2 : Knowledge Component
pragmatics : Pragmatics
ontologies : (Ontology)
renamings : (Renaming)
```

Figure 5.8
Adapter.

```
Bridge < Adapter
uses : (Bridge)
mapping axioms : (Formula)
assumptions : (Formula)
Refiner < Adapter
In : Knowledge Component
 Out : Knowledge Component
```

Figure 5.9
Bridge and Refiner.

UPML does not commit to any particular logical language to express formulas about the knowledge components or to any particular procedural language to describe the operational control of a problem decomposer. In several places, developers can extend UPML with additional concepts to hold the primitives of their languages of choice.

5.3.3 Binary Relations

Binary Relations specify the interactions among the UPML knowledge components. The root binary relation of UPML is the Adapter (figure 5.8). The Adapter connects two components, called arguments, through a set of renaming correspondences between the terms of both arguments. Like knowledge components, an Adapter holds pragmatics information and refers to specific ontologies. UPML introduces two subclasses of Adapter: a Bridge and a Refiner, shown in figure 5.9.

The *Bridge* relation connects two Knowledge Components of different kinds. It defines mapping axioms and additional assumptions about the components it relates. The Bridge relation has three subrelations: a PSM-Domain Bridge connects a PSM with a Domain Model, a *PSM-Task Bridge* connects a PSM and a Task, and a Task-Domain Bridge connects a Task and a Domain Model.

The Refiner relation connects two knowledge components of the same type and so expresses the stepwise adaptation of one component to the other. Very generic problem-solving methods and tasks can be refined to more specific ones by applying a sequence of refiners to them. A Refiner assumes that its two attributes, *in* and *out*, have the same type. This serves to ensure that the refiner modifies a given component, as opposed to mapping it to a different kind of component via the Bridge relation.

Each main UPML component has its own associated type of refiner. Consequently, the Refiner relation has four component-specific subrelations: a Domain Refiner, an Ontology Refiner, a Task Refiner, and a PSM Refiner. The definition of a refiner includes the attributes specific to each kind of component. Each refiner has its own restrictions on input and output: the Domain Refiner contains redefined properties, metaknowledge, and knowledge in the refined component. Similarly, the Ontology Refiner contains refined signature, theorems, and axioms. The Task Refiner refines competence and assumptions, and the PSM Refiner refines communication and competence.

The separation of generic and specific parts of a reasoning process maximizes reusability. UPML offers two ways of combining components of the same type. Both serve a similar purpose, however, they provide complementary means of accomplishing that purpose. First, a component can import another component via the uses attribute. Hence, the component can make use of definitions imported from the other component, monotonically refine them, and extend them. In this case, the uses relationship is modeled not by an explicit entity in the UPML specification, but rather via an attribute of an existing component (the one that imports another component). This first approach corresponds to a monotonic extension of a component. Second, a component can be defined as a refinement of another component via the Refiner relation. In this case, the former component can rewrite the aspects of the latter component via the renamings attribute. Also, in this case we model the uses relationship by means of an explicit entity of the UPML specification (i.e., a Refiner). This second approach enables nonmonotonic modification of a component via an explicit element of the architecture. As mentioned earlier, this provides UPML with a structured and principled approach for developing and configuring heuristic reasoning components by adapting and refining generic components (cf. Fensel 2000; Fensel and Motta 2001).

5.3.4   Web Syntaxes

In this section we describe the Web syntaxes for the UPML meta-ontology based on XML and RDF. A Web syntax is crucially important for UPML because UPML is posed as a standard for knowledge component markup on the Web. The syntaxes consist of three documents: an XML DTD definition for UPML, an XML Schema definition for UPML, and an RDF Schema definition for UPML, as described in the next section.

5.3.4.1   XML Syntax

XML (www.w3c.org/xml) is one of the Web standards that can be used to describe UPML. XML is a widely supported, domain-independent language for representing, storing, sharing, and exchanging data. It provides the means for marking up the semantics of data, as well as for validating and exchanging data structures. XML documents consist of XML tags, which have their names and associated values. The tags can be nested into one another to represent the hierarchical structure of a document. This structure provides a mechanism by which to impose constraints on the storage layout and logical structure of the document.

XML Schema (www.w3.org/XML/Schema) is a W3C standard aimed to specify the structure of XML documents. Parts of a document are specified with a set of data types, either primitive or complex, which can be inherited

```
<xsd:complexType name="upml:Knowledge_component" base="upml:Concept">
 <xsd:element name="upml:pragmatics" type="upml:Pragmatics" minOccurs="1"
maxOccurs="1"/>
 <xsd:element name="upml:ontology" type="upml:Ontology" minOccurs="1"
maxOccurs="unbounded"/>
 </xsd:complexType>
```

Figure 5.10
Part of the XML schema defining the XML representation of the Knowledge Component
concept.

```
<!ELEMENT upml:library (upml:pragmatics, upml:ontology+, upml:domain_models+,
upml:complex_psms+, upml:primitive_psms+, upml:tasks+, upml:ontology_refiners+,
upml:problem_decomposer_refiners+,
```

Figure 5.11
Part of the DTD for UPML defining the Library concept.

from one another. This inheritance of data structures allows explicit encoding of UPML structures as XML Schema structures.

Figure 5.10 shows a fragment of XML Schema syntax for the Knowledge
Component concept.

A relatively new standard, XML Schema is still not widely supported by
industry. Hence, we also provide a *DTD* specification for UPML, part of
which is presented in figure 5.11. However, DTDs are capable of representing
only the structure of document instances; they cannot capture the hierarchy
of the UPML structures. Both the full XML Schema and the full DTD for
UPML are available from the UPML website (www.cs.vu.nl/~upml).

5.3.4.2 RDF Syntax

RDF (www.w3c.org/rdf) is an upcoming standard for representing machine-
processable semantics of online information resources. Unlike XML, which
enables serialization of trees, RDF provides extensive representation of options to perform knowledge-level markup. The foundation of RDF is a model
for representing named properties and property values. RDF properties may

be thought of as attributes of resources. In this respect, they correspond to traditional attribute-value pairs used in UPML. RDF properties also represent relationships among resources. The RDF model can therefore resemble an entity relation diagram.

The structure of RDF documents is specified with RDF Schema (Brickley and Guha 2000). RDF resources represent some components and correspond to the Concept class in the UPML hierarchy. Hence, in the RDF Schema of UPML we define *Entity* as a subclass of rdfs:resource and *Concept* as a subclass of *Entity*. We define all other concepts of UPML as direct or indirect subclasses of the RDF class *Concept*.

RDF properties are conceptually equivalent to the UPML Binary Relations. Hence, the latter can be represented as RDF properties. However, RDF Schema does not allow properties of properties to be defined. Accordingly, if we were to define Binary Relation as a subclass of rdfs:property, then we would have no way of describing the attributes of binary relations. Consequently, in the RDF Schema of UPML we defined the Binary Relation as a subclass of Entity.

As a result, we used RDF classes to define both the Concepts and the Binary Relations. Each attribute of Concepts and Binary Relations is defined as a property of the corresponding class in RDFS. Each property has the corresponding class as its domain and the type of this attribute, as defined in the UPML specification, as its range.

The RDF syntax of UPML is generated from the Protégé-2000[5] knowledge acquisition tool, which supports import and export of ontologies from and to RDF. For example, a sample of the RDFS specification for the Knowledge Component concept is shown in figure 5.12; the whole specification is available from the UPML website. The tool for specifying UPML components is discussed in the next section.

5.4   An Editor for UPML Specifications Based on Protégé-2000

As described in the previous section, the UPML framework can be seen as an ontology composed of classes and relations describing reusable knowledge components. Instances of these classes and relations are particular

```
<s:Class rdf:about="&a;Knowledge_Component">
 <a:ROLE>Abstract</a:ROLE>
 <s:subClassOf rdf:resource="&a;Concept"/>
</s:Class>
<rdf:Property rdf:about="&a;pragmatics">
 <a:SLOT-MAXIMUM-CARDINALITY>1</a:SLOT-MAXIMUM-CARDINALITY>
 <s:domain rdf:resource="&a;Adapter"/>
 <s:domain rdf:resource="&a;Knowledge_Component"/>
 <s:range rdf:resource="&a;Pragmatics"/>
</rdf:Property>
<rdf:Property rdf:about="&a;ontologies">
 <s:domain rdf:resource="&a;Adapter"/>
 <s:domain rdf:resource="&a;Knowledge_Component"/>
 <s:domain rdf:resource="&a;Library"/>
 <s:range rdf:resource="&a;Ontology"/>
</rdf:Property>
```

Figure 5.12

Fragment of the RDF schema for UPML.

knowledge components and adapters (e.g., a classification task and a heuristic classifier problem decomposer). To enable developers to specify and annotate libraries of knowledge components, we created an editor for UPML using Protégé-2000 (http://protege.stanford.edu). Protégé is an extensible ontology-editing and knowledge acquisition environment assisting users in the construction of large electronic knowledge bases (Grosso et al. 1999). Protégé-2000 allows users to create, browse, and edit domain ontologies using a frame-based representation, compliant with the Open Knowledge Base Connectivity (OKBC) knowledge model (Chaudhri et al. 1998).

In Protégé-2000, an ontology is represented with a multiple-inheritance hierarchy of the classes of concepts that are important in a domain. Slots are attached to these classes and define their attributes. Facets restrict the type of value that a slot can take. Protégé automatically generates a graphical knowledge acquisition tool from the ontology, which enables application specialists to enter the detailed content knowledge required to define specific applications (Puerta et al. 1992). Protégé allows developers to tailor this knowledge acquisition tool directly by configuring graphical entities on forms that are attached to each class in the ontology for the acquisition of instances (particular exemplars of the classes). Consequently, application specialists can enter domain information by filling in the blanks of intuitive forms and by drawing diagrams composed of selectable icons and connectors. Protégé-2000 is able to store the knowledge bases in several formats, including RDF (Noy et al. in press).

We modeled the set of concepts and relationships of UPML as a hierarchy of classes in Protégé-2000, with slots and facets attached to them. Both concepts and binary relations in UPML are reified as classes in Protégé, so they can have attributes and be subclassed.

Figure 5.13 shows most of the hierarchy of the classes we used to model UPML and the definition of the class Library. The UPML ontology in Protégé reflects the fact that UPML does not commit to any logical or procedural language to express the formulas and programs that define knowledge components and adapters. By means of the ontology extension and ontology inclusion mechanisms of Protégé, developers can extend the UPML ontology with the primitives necessary to write expressions in their object language of choice. For example, we recently used the UPML editor to specify a library of classification problem-solving components (Motta and Lu 2000). The components of the library are coded using the logical and operational OCML (Operational Conceptual Modeling Language) language (Motta 1999). First, we modeled the OCML set of basic primitives (such as classes, relations, axioms, and functions) themselves as a meta-ontology in Protégé-2000. We then included this ontology in the UPML editor (as partially shown in the lower left part of figure 5.13). From there, we were able to extend (subclass) the UPML concepts Signature, Signature Element, Formula, and Program with the definitions that refer to the OCML primitives, as presented in figure 5.13.

Given this model of UPML, Protégé-2000 automatically generated an RDF Schema representation holding the UPML classes and properties for annotating reasoning resources. Based on the UPML ontology, Protégé-2000 also generated a graphical editor for instantiating specific UPML specifications, for example, the components of the library for classification problem solving. We then tailored this editor to center the knowledge acquisition process

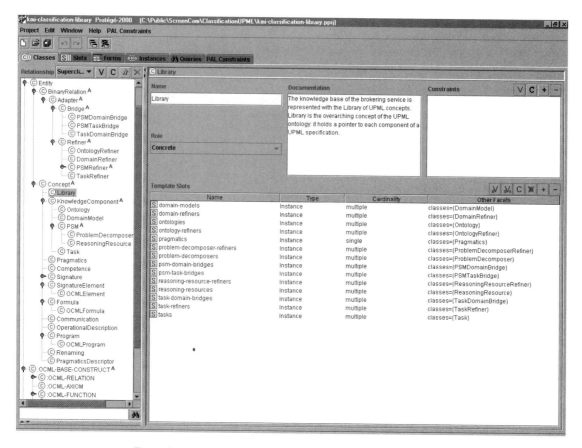

Figure 5.13

Snapshot of the Protégé-based UPML editor: the ontology of UPML modeled in Protégé as a hierarchy of classes, extended with OCML-specific classes (left panel) and the definition of the Library concept, which holds a pointer to every component in the architecture (right panel).

on the use of diagrammatic metaphors. In particular, we defined specific kinds of diagrams to enter the task decomposition (*inference structure*) of a problem decomposer and the control regime of its corresponding operational description (*control structure*).

As shown in figure 5.14, the UPML editor makes it possible to browse the list of instances of a selected class and to view and edit the knowledge acquisition form associated with the selected instance. In the figure, the editor displays the "heuristic optimal solution classifier" instance of the Problem Decomposer class. The knowledge acquisition form for a Problem Decomposer PSM contains a number of user interface components for entering the values of the slots defined for the Problem Decomposer class. For example, this form contains a subform (on the right) specifying the operational description slot of the PSM. This subform includes an inference structure diagram, which helps users specify the competence slots of the PSM (input roles, output roles and subtasks) by directly drawing nodes and links in the diagram, which, in turn, automatically creates and fills in the corresponding instances of the Signature Element and the Task classes.

Once created, the specification of a set of UPML knowledge components (instances) can be exported as a corresponding set of RDF statements, which refer to the RDF Schema of UPML. When Protégé-2000 generates an RDF specification from an ontology, it resolves the differences between the knowledge models of Protégé and RDF Schema by adding specific RDF statements to express facets such as cardinality constraints on slots or multiple domains or ranges for a given slot. Consequently, the resulting RDF code for UPML contains the complete translation of the UPML ontology; however, some parts of the ontology are understandable only by Protégé-2000 (see Noy et al. in press for a discussion).

As a result, the UPML editor in Protégé-2000 provides a guided framework that helps developers to define the UPML specifications and to annotate the knowledge components that they want to publish on the Web. Protégé-2000 is extensible through its application programming interface (API) (Musen et al. 2000). We envision enhancing the UPML editor with services that will

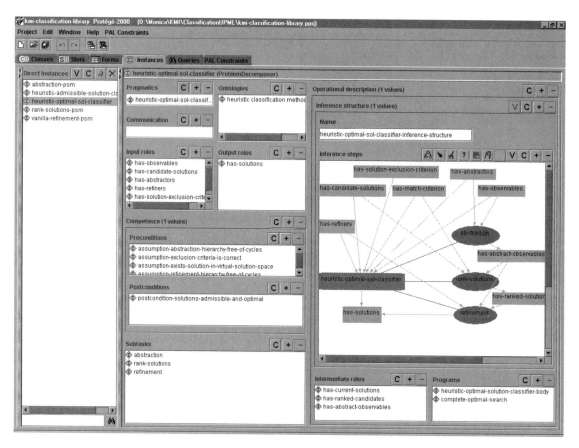

Figure 5.14

Snapshot of the Protégé-based UPML editor: the "heuristic optimal solution classifier" instance of the Problem Decomposer class, with its inference structure diagram on the right.

help users to configure the reasoning resources and problem decomposers for different domains and tasks in connection with the IBROW broker. The resulting configurations of problem solvers will help augment the UPML specification of the libraries available with the appropriate bridges and refiner components.

5.5   *Conclusion*

UPML defines an architecture for describing heuristic reasoning components (cf. Berners-Lee and Fischetti 1999 for the vision of the latter) for the Semantic Web. UPML is language-neutral in the sense that different formal languages can be plugged in to describe the elementary slots defined by UPML. We have already used order-sorted logic (Fensel, Groenboom, and de Lavalette 1998), frame logic (Kifer, Lausen, and Wu 1995), and OCML (Motta 1999) successfully for adding formal semantics to UPML specifications (cf. Fensel et al. in press). We have also tried to use the OIL language (Fensel et al. 2001) that has been developed within the Ontoknowledge (www.ontoknowledge.org) project (cf. Fensel, van Harmelen, et al. 2000) as a Web-based ontology language. OIL was a significant source of inspiration for the ontology language called DAML+OIL (http://www.cs.man.ac.uk/~horrocks/DAML-OIL/), developed in a joint European Union/United States working group on language standardization, which is currently a W3C working group on the Semantic Web. However in the case of OIL, the results achieved were somewhat disappointing (cf. Fensel, Crubézy, et al. 2000). OIL does not provide adequate expressive power for many of the axiomatic parts of UPML specifications. Extending the expressive power of OIL seems to be absolutely necessary for making it usable in this context.

In general, UPML is concerned with describing the dynamic reasoning aspect of the Semantic Web. Therefore, it defines a new layer on top of the currently developed language standards for the Semantic Web. This layer provides machine-processable semantics for the dynamic information sources of the Semantic Web (see chapter 1 for relevant discussion).

UPML is a description language and does not require operational semantics. However, the IBROW broker must be able to reason about expressions in the description language it encounters. In that sense, one can view the broker as a special-purpose "interpreter" of the language. The current priority in the IBROW project is to use UPML for annotating large libraries of problem-solving methods and implementing UPML-based reasoning services to enable their intelligent brokering on the Web. Here we can employ many concepts of the component retrieval area developed for software engineering. The use of formal techniques for software component retrieval is discussed in Jeng and Cheng 1992, 1995; Penix and Alexander 1995; Jiliani et al. 1997; Mili 1997; Mili, Mili, and Mittermeir 1997; and Zaremski and Wing 1997.

In many aspects the RETSINA project (http://www.cs.cmu.edu/~softagents/retsina.html) (cf. Sycara et al. 2001) is similar to IBROW. Although it is focused on multiagent systems, the RETSINA project deals with aspects similar to those we encounter in IBROW. Heterogeneous agents must be able to communicate with each other by means of a common language. The language needs to be coordinated effectively across distributed networks of information. An agent capability description language called LARKS (Language for Advertisement and Request for Knowledge Sharing) has been developed (cf. Sycara et al. 2001) that addresses the problem of agent interoperability. This common language is used by middle or matchmaking agents to pair service-requesting agents with service-providing agents that meet the requesting agents' requirements. The matching engine of the matchmaker agent contains five different filters, one each for context matching, word frequency profile comparison, similarity matching, signature matching, and constraint matching. The user configures these filters to achieve the desired trade-off between performance and matching quality. The main differences between UPML and LARKS are

- UPML defines a richer architecture for describing the reasoning components than LARKS.

- UPML is a full-fledged methodological framework for developing Web-enabled libraries of such components.

- LARKS fixes the language used to describe the competence of these components, whereas UPML "merely" provides an architecture into which several languages can be plugged.

Finally, it must be acknowledged that the actual retrieving component in RETSINA is far more developed than the current brokering support in IBROW. This also indicates the main direction for further development in IBROW. In particular, we foresee that the scope of the knowledge components to be brokered in IBROW will need to be broadened from traditional problem-solving methods to agent-based components capable of performing reasoning steps autonomously. Both UPML and the broker will need to take into account these new kinds of components (Abasolo et al. 2001).

During the early phase of the IBROW project, we demonstrated how our brokering approach based on UPML could be used for the toy problem of classifying apples for users (http://www.swi.psy.uva.nl/projects/ibrow). The broker used an approach based on Prolog and CORBA to localize, compose, and integrate the heterogeneous components of the configured system, such as knowledge bases of the apple domain and classification problem-solving methods (Benjamins et al. 1999). The results of this experiment appeared very promising and form the foundations for the work that we have planned for the next phases of the IBROW project. Consequently, we are expecting even more promising results from this stage, results that will help to make the vision of the Semantic Web a reality.

Notes

1. As such, PSMs are a special type of software architectures (Shaw and Garlan 1996).

2. The recent version is described in Omelayenko et al. 2000.

3. Note that we distinguish this from automatically generated Web pages, which are called dynamic, as opposed to static HTML pages.

4. Uses is a very important attribute that will be explained later in the chapter.

5. See the next section for a detailed description.

References

Abasolo, C., J.-L. Arcos, E. Armengol, M. Gómez, J.-M. López-Cobo, M. López-Sánchez, R. López de Màntaras, E. Plaza, C. van Aart, and B. Wielinga. 2001. Libraries for Information Agents. IBROW Project IST-1999-19005: An Intelligent Brokering Service for Knowledge-Component Reuse on the World-Wide Web. Available from http://www.swi.psy.uva.nl/projects/ibrow/home.html.

Benjamins, V. R. 1995. Problem Solving Methods for Diagnosis and Their Role in Knowledge Acquisition. *International Journal of Expert Systems: Research and Application* 8(2):93–120.

Benjamins, V. R., and D. Fensel. 1998. Special Issue on Problem-Solving Methods. *International Journal of Human-Computer Studies* 49(4).

Benjamins, V. R., and N. Shadbolt. 1998. Special Issue on Knowledge Acquisition and Planning. *International Journal of Human-Computer Studies* 48(4).

Benjamins, V. R., B. Wielinga, J. Wielemaker, and D. Fensel. 1999. Brokering Problem-Solving Knowledge at the Internet. In *Knowledge Acquisition, Modeling, and Management, Proceedings of the European Knowledge Acquisition Workshop (EKAW-99), May,* ed. D. Fensel. Berlin: Springer.

Berners-Lee, T., and M. Fischetti. 1999. Weaving the Web. San Francisco: Harper.

Breuker, J., and W. van de Velde, eds. 1994. *The CommonKADS Library for Expertise Modeling*. Amsterdam: IOS Press.

Brickley, D., and R. Guha. 2000. Resource Description Framework (RDF) Schema Specification 1.0 (candidate recommendation). World Wide Web Consortium. Available from http://www.w3.org/TR/rdf-schema.

Chandrasekaran, B., T. Johnson, and J. Smith. 1992. Task Structure Analysis for Knowledge Modeling. *Communications of the ACM* 35(9):124–137.

Chaudhri, V., A. Farquhar, R. Fikes, P. Karp, and J. Rice. 1998. OKBC: A Programmatic Foundation for Knowledge Base Interoperability. In *Proceedings of the 15th National Conference on Artificial Intelligence (AAAI-98) and of the 10th Conference on Innovative Applications of Artificial Intelligence (IAAI-98)* (pp. 600–607). Menlo Park, CA/Cambridge, MA: AAAI/MIT Press.

Fensel, D. 1995. Formal Specification Languages in Knowledge and Software Engineering. *The Knowledge Engineering Review* 10(4):361–404.

Fensel, D. 1997. The Tower-of-Adapter Method for Developing and Reusing Problem-Solving Methods. In *Knowledge Acquisition, Modeling and Management: Proceedings of the 10th*

European Workshop (EKAW-97), Sant Feliu de Guixols, Catalonia, Spain, October 15–18, ed. E. Plaza and R. Benjamins. Berlin: Springer.

Fensel, D. 2000. *Problem-Solving Methods: Understanding, Description, Development, and Reuse*, LNAI 1791, Berlin: Springer.

Fensel, D. 2001. *Ontologies: Silver Bullet for Knowledge Management and Electronic Commerce*. Berlin: Springer.

Fensel, D., and V. Benjamins. 19998. Key Issues for Problem-Solving Methods Reuse. In *Proceedings of the 13th European Conference on Artificial Intelligence (ECAI-98), Brighton, UK, August 23–28, 1998*, ed. H. Prade (pp. 63–67). Chichester: Wiley.

Fensel, D., V. R. Benjamins, S. Decker, M. Gaspari, R. Groenboom, W. Grosso, M. Musen, E. Plaza, G. Schreiber, R. Studer, and B. Wielinga. 1999. The Unified Problem-Solving Method Development Language UPML. IBROW3 ESPRIT Project 27169: An Intelligent Brokering Service for Knowledge-Component Reuse on the World Wide Web, Deliverable 1.1. Available from http://www.swi.psy.uva.nl/projects/ibrow/home.html.

Fensel, D., V. Benjamins, E. Motta, and B. Wielinga. 1999. UPML: A Framework for Knowledge System Reuse. In *Proceedings of the Sixteenth International Joint Conference on Artificial Intelligence (IJCAI-99), Stockholm, Sweden, July 31–August 6, 1999*, ed. T. Dean (pp. 16–23). San Francisco: Morgan Kaufmann.

Fensel, D., M. Crubézy, F. van Harmelen, and I. Horrocks: OIL and UPML: A Unifying Framework for the Knowledge Web. In *Proceedings of the Workshop on Applications of Ontologies and Problem-solving Methods. In 14th European Conference on Artificial Intelligence (ECAI-2000), Berlin, Germany August 20–25, 2000*. Available from http://delicias.dia.fi.upm.es/WORKSHOP/ECAI00/.

Fensel, D., and R. Groenboom. 1999. An Architecture for Knowledge-Based Systems. *The Knowledge Engineering Review* 14(3):153–173.

Fensel, D., R. Groenboom, and G. Renardel de Lavalette. 1998. Modal Change Logic (MCL): Specifying the Reasoning of Knowledge-based Systems. *Data and Knowledge Engineering* 26(3):243–269.

Fensel, D., I. Horrocks, F. van Harmelen, D. McGuiness, and P. Patel-Schneider. 2001. OIL: Ontology Infrastructure to Enable the Semantic Web. *IEEE Intelligent Systems* 16(2):38–45.

Fensel, D., and E. Motta. 2001. Structured Development of Problem Solving Methods. *IEEE Transactions on Knowledge and Data Engineering* 13(6):913–932.

Fensel, D., and F. van Harmelen. 1994. A Comparison of Languages which Operationalize and Formalize KADS Models of Expertise. *The Knowledge Engineering Review* 9(2):105–146.

Fensel, D., F. van Harmelen, H. Akkermans, M. Klein, J. Broekstra, C. Fluyt, J. van der Meer, H.-P. Schnurr, R. Studer, J. Davies, J. Hughes, U. Krohn, R. Engels, B. Bremdahl, F. Ygge, U. Reimer, and I. Horrocks. 2000. OnToKnowledge: Ontology-Based Tools for Knowledge Management. In *Proceedings of the eBusiness and eWork 2000 Conference (EMMSEC-2000), Madrid, Spain, October 18–20, 2000.* Available from http://www.ebew.net/.

Gomez Perez, A., and V. R. Benjamins. 1999. Applications of Ontologies and Problem-Solving Methods. *AI Magazine* 20(1):119–122.

Grosso, W., H. Eriksson, R. Fergerson, J. Gennari, S. Tu, and M. Musen. 1999. Knowledge Modeling at the Millennium (The Design and Evolution of Protégé-2000). In *Proceedings of the Twelfth Workshop on Knowledge Acquisition, Modeling, and Management (KAW-99), Banff, Alberta, Canada, October 16–21, 1999.* Available from http://smi-web.stanford.edu/pubs/SMI_Abstracts/SMI-1999-0801.html.

Gruber, T. 1993. Towards Principles for the Design of Ontologies Used for Knowledge Sharing, In *Formal Ontology in Conceptual Analysis and Knowledge Representation*, ed. N. Guarino and R. Poli (pp. 907–928). Deventer, the Netherlands: Kluwer Academic.

Jeng, J.-J., and B. H. Cheng. 1992. Using Automated Reasoning Techniques to Determine Software Reuse. *International Journal of Software Engineering and Knowledge Engineering* 2(4):523–546.

Jeng, J.-J., and B. H. Cheng. 1995. Specification Matching for Software Reuse: A Foundation. In *Proceedings of the ACM SIGSOFT Symposium on Software Reusability (SSR-95), Seattle, Washington, April, 1995*, ed. M. H. Samadzadeh and K. Zand (pp. 97–105). Marina del Rey, CA: ACM.

Jilani, L., J. Desharnais, M. Frappier, R. Mili, and A. Mili. 1997. Retrieving Software Components That Minimize Adaptation Effort. In *Proceedings of the 12th IEEE International Conference on Automated Software Engineering (ASEC-97), Incline Village, Nevada, November 3–5, 1997* (pp. 255–262). Los Alamitos, CA: IEEE.

Kifer, M., G. Lausen, and J. Wu. 1995. Logical Foundations of Object-Oriented and Frame-Based Languages. *Journal of the ACM* 42(4):741–843.

Marcus, S. (ed.): Automating Knowledge Acquisition for Experts Systems, Kluwer Academic Publisher, Boston, 1988.

Mili, F. 1997. Transformational Based Problem Solving Reuse. In *Proceedings of the 9th International Conference on Software Engineering and Knowledge Engineering (SEKE-97), Madrid, Spain, June 18–20, 1997.* Available from http://www.cs.pitt.edu/~jung/seke97/.

Mili, R., A. Mili, and R. Mittermeir. 1997. Storing and Retrieving Software Components: A Refinement Based System. *IEEE Transactions on Software Engineering* 23(7):445–460.

Motta, E. 1999. *Reusable Components for Knowledge Modeling.* Amsterdam: IOS Press.

Motta, E., M. Gaspari, and D. Fensel. 1998. UPML Specification of a Parametric Design Library. IBROW3 ESPRIT Project 27169: An Intelligent Brokering Service for Knowledge-Component Reuse on the World Wide Web. Deliverable D4.1. Available from http://www.swi.psy.uva.nl/projects/ibrow/home.html.

Motta, E., and W. Lu. 2000. A Library of Components for Classification Problem Solving. In *Proceedings of the 2000 Pacific Rim Knowledge Acquisition Workshop, Sydney, Australia, December 11–13, 2000.*

Musen, M. 1998. Modern Architectures for Intelligent Systems: Reusable Ontologies and Problem-Solving Methods. In 1998 AMIA Annual Symposium, Orlando, FL, ed. C. G. Chute. Available from http://www.amia.org/meetings/archive/f98/f98main.htm.

Musen, M., R. Fergerson, W. Grosso, N. Noy, M. Crubezy, and J. Gennari. 2000. Component-Based Support for Building Knowledge-Acquisition Systems. In *Proceedings of the Conference on Intelligent Information Processing (IIP-2000) of the International Federation for Information Processing World Computer Congress (WCC-2000), Beijing, 2000.* Available from http://smi-web.stanford.edu/pubs/SMI_Abstracts/SMI-2000-0838.html.

Noy, N., M. Sintek, S. Decker, M. Crubézy, R. Fergerson, M. Musen. In press. One Size Does Fit All: Acquiring Semantic Web Contents with Protégé-2000. *IEEE Intelligent Systems* 16(2):60–71.

Omelayenko, B., M. Crubézy, D. Fensel, Y. Ding, E. Motta, and M. Musen. 2000. Meta Data and UPML. IBROW Project IST-1999-19005: An Intelligent Brokering Service for Knowledge-Component Reuse on the World-Wide Web. Deliverable 5. Available from http://www.cs.vu.nl/~upml/.

Penix, J., and P. Alexander. 1995. Design Representation for Automating Software Component Reuse. In *Proceedings of the First International Workshop on Knowledge-Based Systems for the (Re)use of Program Libraries, Sophia Antipolis, France, November 23–24, 1995.* Available from http://www.ittc.ku.edu/Projects/SLDG/pub/kbup95.html.

Puerta, A., J. Egar, S. Tu, and M. Musen. 1992. A Multiple-Method Knowledge-Acquisition Shell for the Automatic Generation of Knowledge-acquisition Tools. *Knowledge Acquisition* 4(2):171–196.

Puppe, F. 1993. *Systematic Introduction to Expert Systems: Knowledge Representation and Problem-Solving Methods.* Berlin: Springer.

Schreiber, A., B. Wielinga, J. Akkermans, W. van de Velde, and R. de Hoog. 1994. CommonKADS: A Comprehensive Methodology for KBS Development. *IEEE Expert* 9(6):28–37.

Shaw, M., and D. Garlan. 1996. *Software Architectures: Perspectives on an Emerging Discipline.* Upper Saddle River, NJ: Prentice-Hall.

Stefik, M. 1995. *Introduction to Knowledge Systems.* San Francisco: Morgan Kaufmann.

Sycara, K., M. Paolucci, M. van Velsen, and J. Giampapa. 2001. The RETSINA MAS Infrastructure. Robotics Institute Technical Report #CMU-RI-TR-01-05, 2001. Available from http://www.cs.cmu.edu/~softagents/publications.html.

Zaremski, A., and J. Wing. 1997. Specification Matching of Software Components. *ACM Transactions on Software Engineering and Methodology* 6(4):335–369.

6   *Ontologies Come of Age*

Deborah L. McGuinness

6.1   *Introduction: The Web's Growing Needs*

We may be poised for the next major evolution of online environments. In the early days of the Web, HTML pages were generated by hand. The pages contained information about how to present information on a page. Early users took to the Web quickly, since it provided a convenient method for information sharing. Arguably, the generation of tools for machine generation and management of Web pages allowed the Web to really take off. Tool platforms allowed nontechnical people to generate and publish Web pages quickly and easily. The resulting pages typically included content and display information and targeted human readers (rather than programs or automatic readers).

The Web continues to grow at an astounding rate, with Web pages ubiquitously integrated into many aspects of business and personal life. However, Web pages still preserve much of their early character of being aimed at human consumption. Thus, applications such as search still require humans to review results pages in order to find the right answer to their queries. Although search engine advances such as Google have improved the situation (Guglielmo and Babcock 2000), most people agree that finding the exact information one is seeking on the Web today is not as easy as one would hope.

One reason for this difficulty in getting exact answers to Web queries is that answers to search queries typically are a rank-ordered list of Web pages that may contain the answer to the query. The answers rarely are just the portion of the page that the search engine "thought" contained the answer to the query. Additionally, Web pages typically do not contain markup information about the contents of the page. If pages were marked up with information concerning what information or services could be obtained via a particular page (and how that information or service could be obtained), then a page could be used more effectively by programs to return the portion of the page (or the answer from a service) that contained a specific answer to a question. Once Web pages are aimed for machine or program consumption, instead of human consumption, the next generation of the Web can be realized. The proliferation of markup languages aimed at marking up content and services instead of just presentation information can be viewed as support for this position. Markup languages such as XML (Bray et al. 2000), RDF (Lassila 1998; Lassila and Swick 1999), RDFS (Brickley and Guha 2000), and DAML (Hendler and McGuinness 2000) are becoming more accepted as users and application developers see the need for more understanding of what is available from Web pages.

The view presented in this chapter is consistent with the vision being put forward by Tim Berners-Lee of the W3C. In a widely cited presentation at the XML 2000 conference, Berners-Lee (2000) presented his vision of the Semantic Web as being machine processible. I support this view as well. I believe that the next Web evolution will require machines to understand the content of pages: both what information can be obtained from pages and what that information means. Markup languages allow specification of this information. Berners-Lee offered an architecture diagram (http://www.w3. org/2000/Talks/1206-xml2k-tbl/slide10-0.html) in his presentation that provides a nice outlook. I include it here as figure 6.1.

Berners-Lee's architecture shows the markup languages at the base (just above Unicode) for use in term specification (or in Webspeak, "resource definition"). The next layer up, one we will consider in this chapter, is the ontology layer. In this layer, we can define terms and their relationships to

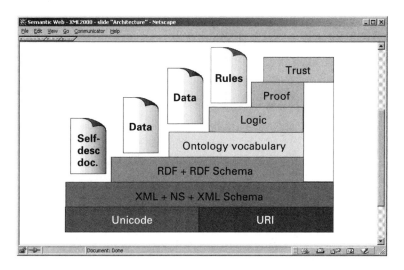

Figure 6.1
Berners-Lee's architecture.

other terms. The next layer is the logic layer. In this layer, the other we will discuss in the chapter, we can deduce information, thereby allowing us to deduce implications of the term definitions and relationships. In the rest of this chapter, we will discuss the ontology and logic layers, what they have come to mean on the Web, and how one might generate ontologies and use them in applications.

6.2   Ontologies

The term "ontology" has been in use for many years. Merriam Webster (http://www.m-w.com/home.htm), for example, dates ontology as originating circa 1721 and provides two definitions: (1) a branch of metaphysics concerned with the nature and relations of being and (2) a particular theory about the nature of being or the kinds of existents. These definitions provide an abstract philosophical notion of ontology. Mathematical or formal ontologies have also been written about for many years. Smith (1998) points out that at least as early as 1900, the philosopher Husserl distinguished the notion of a formal ontology from formal logic. Although ontologies (even formal ontologies) have had a lengthy history, for a long time they remained largely the topic of academic interest among philosophers, linguists, librarians, and knowledge representation researchers.

Ontologies have recently been gaining interest and acceptance in computational audiences (in addition to philosophical audiences). Guarino (1998) provides a list of fields that embrace ontologies, including knowledge engineering, knowledge representation, qualitative modeling, language engineering, database design, information retrieval and extraction, and knowledge management and organization. That list, put together in early 1998, did not include nearly the Web emphasis that such a list would show if combined today. Now we would also have to include the areas of library science (Dublin Core Metadata Initiative 1999), ontology-enhanced search (e.g., eCyc (http://www.e-Cyc.com/) and FindUR [McGuinness 1998]), possibly the largest one, e-commerce (e.g., Amazon.com, Yahoo Shopping), and configuration.

In this chapter, we will be restricting the sense of "ontology" to those ontologies we see emerging on the Web. Today's use of ontology on the Web has a different slant from the previous philosophical notions. One widely cited definition of an ontology is Gruber's (1993): "specification of a conceptualization" (p. 199). We will use this notion and expand upon it in our use of the term.

People (and computational agents) typically have some notion or conceptualization of the meaning of terms. Software programs sometimes provide a specification of the inputs and outputs of a program, which could be used as a specification of the program. Similarly ontologies can be used to provide a concrete specification of term names and term meanings. Within the line of thought in which an ontology is a specification of the conceptualization of a term, there are still a number of potential interpretations. Web ontologies may be viewed as a spectrum according to the detail in their specification. One might visualize a simple (linear) spectrum of definitions, as in figure 6.2.[1]

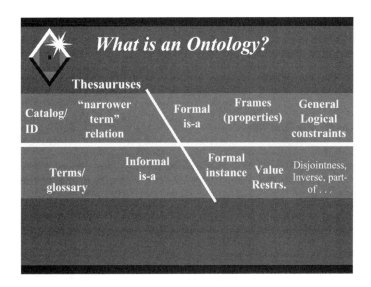

Figure 6.2
An ontology spectrum.

One of the simplest notions of a possible ontology may be a controlled vocabulary, that is, a finite list of terms. Catalogs are an example of this category. Catalogs can provide an unambiguous interpretation of terms: for example, every use of a term—say, "car"—will denote exactly the same identifier—say, "25."

Another potential ontology specification is a glossary (a list of terms and meanings). The meanings in the glossary are specified typically as natural-language statements. This provides a kind of semantics or meaning, since humans can read the natural-language statements and interpret them. Typically, interpretations are not unambiguous, and so these specifications are not adequate for computer agents; thus glossary definitions would not meet the requirement of being machine-processable.

Thesauruses provide some additional semantics in their treatments of relations between terms. They provide information such as synonym relationships. In many cases the relationships they discuss may be interpreted unambiguously by agents. Typically thesauruses do not provide an explicit hierarchy of terms (although with narrower and broader term specifications, one could deduce a simple hierarchy).

Early Web specifications of term hierarchies, such as Yahoo's, provide a basic notion of generalization and specialization. Yahoo, for example, provides a small number of top-level categories, such as apparel, and subordinate categories, such as dresses as a kind of (women's) apparel. Some people consider the previous categories (of catalogs, glossaries, and thesauruses) to be ontologies, but many prefer to require that an explicit hierarchy included before something is considered an ontology. Yahoo, for example, does provide an explicit hierarchy. Its hierarchy is not a strict subclass or "is-a" (Brachman 1983) hierarchy, however. This point was distinguished in figure 6.2, since it seems to capture many of the naturally occurring taxonomies on the Web. In Yahoo's organization schemes, typically an instance of a more specific class is also an instance of the more general class that includes that specific class, but this arrangement is not always enforced. For example, the general category apparel includes a subcategory women (which should more accurately be titled women's apparel), which then includes subcategories accessories and dresses. Although it is the case that every instance of a dress is an instance of apparel (and probably an instance of women's dress), it is not the case that a dress is a woman, and it is also not the case that a fragrance (an instance of a women's accessory) is an instance of apparel. This mixing of categories is not unique to Yahoo: it appears in many Web classification schemes.[2] Without true subclass (or true is-a) relationships, as we will see, certain kinds of deductive uses of ontologies become problematic.

The next point on the figure involves strict subclass hierarchies. In these systems if A is a superclass of B, then if an object is an instance of B, it necessarily follows that the object is an instance of A. For example, if "Dress" is a subclass of "Apparel," and "MyFavoriteDress" is an instance of "Dress", then it follows that "MyFavoriteDress" is an instance of "Apparel." Strict subclass hierarchies are necessary for exploitation of inheritance. The next point on the ontology spectrum involves formal instance relationships.

Some concept classification schemes include only class names, whereas others include ground individual content, including instances of classes.

The next point in the figure involves frames.[3] Here classes include property information. For example, the "Apparel" class may include the properties of "price" and "isMadeFrom." My specific dress may have a price of $100 and may be made from cotton. Properties become more useful for knowledge modeling when they are specified at a general class level and then inherited consistently by subclasses and instances. In a consumer hierarchy, a general category like "consumer product" might have a "price" property associated with it. Possibly apparel would be the general category with which the property "isMadeFrom" is associated. This would mean that the domain of "isMadeFrom" is apparel. All subclasses of such categories would inherit the properties associated with those categories.

A more expressive point on the ontology spectrum in figure 6.2 involves value restrictions. Here we may place restrictions on what can fill a property. For example, a "price" property might be restricted to have a filler that is a number (or a number in a certain range), and "isMadeFrom" may be restricted to have fillers that are a kind of material. One can now see a possible problem with a classification scheme that does not support a strict is-a or subclass relationship. For example, if "Fragrance" were a subclass of "Apparel," it would inherit the property "isMadeFrom" and the value restriction of material that was stated above.

As ontologies need to express more information, their expressive requirements grow. For example, we may want to fill in the value of one property based on a mathematical equation using values from other properties. Some languages allow ontologists to express arbitrary logical statements. Very expressive ontology languages such as Ontolingua (Farquhar, Fikes, and Rice 1997) or CycL allow ontologists to specify first-order logic constraints on terms as well as more detailed relationships, such as disjoint classes, disjoint coverings, inverse relationships, and part-whole relationships.

In this chapter, we will require the following properties to hold in order for something to be considered an ontology (specifications possessing these properties will be referred to as "simple ontologies"):

- finite controlled (extensible) vocabulary
- unambiguous interpretation of classes and term relationships
- strict hierarchical subclass relationships between classes

We will consider the following properties typical but not mandatory:

- property specification on a per-class basis
- individual inclusion in the ontology
- value restriction specification on a per-class basis

Finally, the following properties may be desirable but are not mandatory nor typical:

- specification of disjoint classes
- specification of arbitrary logical relationships between terms
- distinguished relationships, such as inverse and part-whole

The diagonal line in figure 6.2 is drawn such that everything to the right of it will be referred to in this chapter as an ontology and considered to meet at least the first three conditions stated above. Additionally, everything to the right of the line can be used as a basis for inference.

6.3   Simple Ontologies and Their Uses

We now consider ontologies and their impact on applications. We break this section into two parts, uses of simple ontologies and uses for more sophisticated ontologies, because we acknowledge that building the more complicated ontologies may be cost prohibitive for certain applications.

Simple ontologies are not as costly to build as more complex ones, and potentially more importantly, many are available. Simple ontologies are available in many forms: many exist as freeware on the Web today, and many also exist as internal information organization structures within companies, universities, and the like. Some collaborative efforts exist, such as DMOZ (Directory Mozilla) (www.dmoz.com), that are generating large simple ontologies.

DMOZ, for example, leverages over 45,000 volunteer editors and as this book went to press had over 460,000 classes in its taxonomy. Additionally, a number of more sophisticated ontologies are available today. For example, the unified medical language system (UMLS) (http://www.nlm.nih.gov/research/umls/ and Humphreys and Lindberg 1993), developed by the National Library of Medicine, is a large, sophisticated ontology about medical terminology. Some companies, such as Cycorp (www.cyc.com), are making available portions of large, detailed ontologies. I will address further the issue of ontology acquisition and maintenance later in the chapter, but for now, I just want to make the point that many simple and some sophisticated ontologies are readily available today.

Now let's consider some of the ways that simple ontologies may be used in practice. First, they provide a *controlled vocabulary* for their domain. This by itself can provide great impact, since users, authors, and databases can all use terms from the same vocabulary. In addition programs can generate interfaces that encourage usage of the controlled terms an ontology contains. The result is that people share the same set of terms. Of course, some of the terms may still be used with different senses, but common term usage is a start for interoperability.

Second, a simple taxonomy may be used for *site organization and navigation support*. Many Web sites today expose the top levels of a generalization hierarchy of terms as a kind of browsing structure. The categories are typically hot, and a user may click on them to expand the subcategories.

Third, taxonomies may be used to support *expectation setting*. It is important as a user interface feature that users be able to have realistic expectations of a site. If they may explore even the top-level categories of the site's hierarchy, they can quickly determine if the site might have content (and/or services) of interest to them.

Fourth, taxonomies may be used as *"umbrella" structures from which to extend content*. Some freely available ontologies are attempting to provide the high-level taxonomic organization from which many efforts may inherit terms. The Universal Standard Products and Services Classification (UNSPSC) (www.unspsc.org) is one such categorization scheme. It was jointly developed by the United Nations Development Program and Dunn & Bradstreet and was aimed at providing the infrastructure for interoperability of terms in the domains of products and services. It provides a classification scheme (with associated numbers) for products and services. For example, Category 50 (Food, beverage, and tobacco products) has a subclass family 5010 (Fruits and vegetables and nuts and seeds),[4] which in turn contains a subclass 501015 (Vegetables), which in turn has a subclass commodity 50101538 (Fresh vegetables). The numbers provide a unique identification for each term and also encode the hierarchy. A number of e-commerce applications today are looking for such umbrella organization structures, and in fact many have chosen to be compliant with the UNSPSC. Most applications will need to extend these ontologies with their specific hierarchies of categories, but if applications need to communicate among a number of content providers, it is convenient to use a shared umbrella or upper-level ontology.

Fifth, taxonomies may provide *browsing support*. Content on a site may be tagged with terms from the taxonomy. This may be done manually in the style of Yahoo or automatically (possibly using a clustering approach). Once a page (or service) is metatagged with a term chosen from a controlled vocabulary, then search engines may exploit the tagging and provide enhanced search capabilities.

Sixth, taxonomies may be used to provide *search support*. A query expansion method may be used to expand a user query with terms from more specific categories in the hierarchy. We exploited this approach in our work on FindUR, a knowledge-intensive search engine for complex Web sites (McGuinness 1998), and found that under certain conditions (such as short document length and limited content areas), query expansion can radically improve search results.

Seventh, taxonomies may be used to *sense disambiguation support*. If the same term appears in multiple places in a taxonomy, an application may move to a more general level in the taxonomy in order to find the sense of the word. For example, if an ontology contains the information that Jordan is an instance of a BasketballPlayer and also an instance of a country, an application may choose to query a user searching for Jordan if she is interested in basketball players or countries. Sense disambiguation using ontologies may be seen in the work of eCyc, along with Hotbot and Lycos.

6.4   Structured Ontologies and Their Uses

Up to this point, we have focused on simple taxonomies for usage in applications. As ontologies begin to have more structure, however, they can provide more power in applications. Once ontologies have more structure than simple generalization links, their property information enables them to be used in many forms.

First, these more structured ontologies can be used for simple kinds of *consistency checking*. If ontologies contain information about properties and value restrictions on the properties, then type checking can be done within applications. For example, if a class called "Goods" has a property called "price" that has a value restriction of number, then something that is known to be of type "Goods" that has its "price" property filled in with a value that is not a number can be flagged as an error. This just exploits simple value restrictions that designate the type of a value. A value restriction might include a range, for example, a number between 10 and 100. Then if the "price" is 10,000, it is out of the range and can be signaled as an error.

Second, more structured ontologies may be used to provide *completion*. An application may obtain a small amount of information from a user, such as the fact that she is looking for a high-resolution screen on a PC, and then have the ontology expand the range of the number of pixels that the user expects. This can be accomplished simply by defining what the term "High-ResolutionPc" is with respect to a particular pixel range on two dimensions: "verticalResolution" and "horizontalResolution". Similarly, information may be reused. For example, a medical system may obtain information from an ontology that if a patient is stated to be a man, then the gender of the patient is "male," and that information may be used to determine that a question concerning whether or not the patient is pregnant should not be asked, since there could be information in the system that things whose gender is male are disjoint from things that are pregnant.

Third, more structured ontologies may be able to provide *interoperability support*. Controlled vocabularies enhance interoperability support, since different users and applications are using the same set of terms. In simple taxonomies, we can recognize when one application is using a term that is more general or more specific than another term and facilitate interoperability. In more expressive ontologies, we may have a complete operational definition for how one term relates to another term, and thus we can use equality axioms or mappings to express one term precisely in terms of another and thereby support more "intelligent" interoperability. For example, an ontology may include a definition that a "StanfordEmployee" is equal to a "Person" whose "employer" property is filled with the individual "StanfordUniversity." This definition may be used to expand the term "StanfordEmployee" in an application that does not understand either "StanfordEmployee" or "Employee" but does understand the terms "Person," "employer," and "StanfordUniversity."

Fourth, more structured ontologies may be used to *support validation and verification testing* of data (and schemas). If an ontology contains class descriptions, such as "StanfordEmployee," these definitions may be used as queries to databases to discover what kind of coverage currently exists in data sets. For example, if one was going to expose the class "Stanford-Employee" on an interface to some application, it would be useful to know first if the data set contained any instances of "Person" whose "employer" property was filled with the value "Stanford University." Additionally, if in a simple data model, we stated that a "Person" had at most one "employer," then we could use that information to check to see if any current information on "Person"s in the data set contained more than one "employer" value. Similarly, checks could be conducted to determine if there were currently "Person"s in the data set that were known to be "Employee"s yet did not have a value for the "employer" property (thereby showing that the data set was not complete). Chimaera (McGuinness, Resnick, and Isbell 2000) is an example ontology evolution environment that provides a set of diagnostic tests for checking ontologies for problems in the ontology definitions as well as problems with the instance data. It looks for provable inconsistencies as well as conditions that reflect situations in which an ontology or the data may need to be fixed.

Fifth, more structured ontologies containing markup information may *encode entire test suites*. An ontology may contain a number of definitions of terms and some instance definitions, then include a term definition that is considered to be a query: find all terms that meet the following conditions. Markup information could be encoded with this query to include what the answer should be, thus providing enough information to encode regression testing data. We provide one such example ontology at http://ksl. stanford.edu/projects/DAML/chimaera-jtp-cardinality-test1.daml. The ontology contains a regression test suite for checking cardinality inferences (such as persons having two employers yet being restricted to having at most one employer) in a Stanford Theorem prover (http://www.ksl.Stanford.EDU/ software/jtp/).

Sixth, more structured ontologies can provide the foundation for *configuration support*. Class terms may be defined so that they contain descriptions of what kinds of parts may be in a system. Additionally interactions among properties can be defined so that filling in a value for one property can cause another value to be filled in for another slot. For example, one may generate an ontology of information about home theater products, as is done in a small configurator example using a simple description logic–based system (McGuinness, Resnick, and Isbell 1995). Terms such as "Television", "Amplifier", and "Tuner" are defined. Additionally, information connecting the terms is included. A class of "HighQualityTelevision"'s is defined so that users may choose from this class, and the configurator will automatically fill in limited sets of manufacturers to choose from, minimum diagonal values, minimum price ranges, and so on. Also, information is encoded that propagates restrictions from one component to another. For example, some of the components in this system are meant to be sold in pairs. If one buys one particular kind of speaker (which is sold only in pairs, thus two speakers are added to the parts list), then restrictions on particular speaker stands appear in the configuration specification.

Seventh, more structured ontologies can *support structured, comparative, and customized search*. For example, if one is looking for televisions, a class description for television may be obtained from an ontology, its properties may be obtained (diagonal, price, manufacturer, etc.), and then a comparative presentation may be made of televisions by presenting the values of each of the properties for each television. Those properties can also be used to provide a form for users to fill in so that they may provide a detailed set of specifications about the items they are looking to find. This also provides the foundation for providing a number of different search interfaces: a simple text box in which the user is expected to type a textual query, as well as search interfaces exposing important properties of products that can provide a structured search query. More sophisticated ontologies may be generated that mark which properties are most useful to present in comparative analyses so that users may have concise descriptions of products instead of comparisons offering complete details. Thus, ontologies with markup information may also be used to prune comparative searches.

Eighth, more structured ontologies may be used to *exploit generalization/ specialization information*. If a search application finds that a user's query generates too many answers, it might dissect the query to see if any terms in it appear in an ontology, and if so, then the search application may suggest specializing that term. For example, if one did a search for concerts in the San Francisco Bay area and obtained too many answers, a search engine might look up "concert" in an ontology and discover that there are subclasses of concert (and it may also discover that there are specific concert locations in the Bay area). The search engine could then choose to present the user with the option of looking for a particular kind of concert (say, rock concert), which would restrict the search, thereby returning fewer answers. Further, the search engine could proactively run queries in the background while waiting for user input or cache information from popular queries. Then the search engine could also present a list of subclasses of concerts and provide the user with the approximate number of retrievals the user would get if she specialized her query in various manners.

These are just some of the ways in which more structured ontologies may be used to refine search queries. We could also look at the ontology to provide alternative values (by looking at siblings in the ontology) for terms specified in the search query.

We have not claimed to present an exhaustive list of the ways in which ontologies may be used in applications. The above lists are illustrative of some ways that ontologies have been used to support intelligent applications.

6.5   Ontology Acquisition

Having presented some of the ways ontologies are useful components in applications, we now examine some sources of ontologies. As mentioned previously, many ontologies exist in the public domain. It may be possible to start with an existing industry standard and use that as the ontology starting point. Most likely application developers will need to modify and/or extend ontologies that are available and were developed for other uses, to meet application-specific requirements.

Another methodology for obtaining ontologies is to semiautomatically generate a starting point. Many taxonomic structures exist on the Web or in the table of contents of Web documents. One might crawl certain sites to obtain a starting taxonomic structure and then analyze, modify, and extend it.

One question is where to look for existing ontologies or sources of information to be crawled. Many controlled vocabularies are being made available today. Sometimes standards organizations, such as the National Institute of Standards and Technology (NIST) (http://www.nist.gov/), support efforts to produce controlled vocabularies and ontologies. Some consortiums are forming to generate ontologies, for example, RosettaNet (http://www.rosettanet.org) in the area of information technology, electronic technology, electronic components, and semiconductor manufacturing. They are creating industry-wide open e-business standards and providing a language for business processes. Sometimes trade organizations provide class hierarchies on their sites that can also be used as a standard structured controlled vocabulary. There are also broad sources of class structures. Essentially every e-commerce site today encodes at least a taxonomic organization of terms. Sites like Amazon, in organizing its book and music information, provide a very broad organization of information. Also, some government programs are generating large ontologies that are being put into the public domain for reuse, such as many ontologies generated in the DARPA High Performance Knowledge Base Program and the Rapid Knowledge Formation Program (http://reliant.teknowledge.com/RKF/).

Another emerging trend is the use of markup languages such as XML, RDF, and DAML for annotating Web pages. The pages including the annotations may be using markup terms from controlled vocabularies. Some libraries of ontologies that are potentially of use for markup are emerging. For example, the DAML program maintains a library of DAML ontologies at http://www.daml.org/ontologies/.

Much of this section has introduced the idea of obtaining either a simple or complex ontology as a starting point and then analyzing, modifying, and maintaining it over time. In the next section, I address the issue of implications of and needs arising from ontology-based applications.

6.6 Ontology-Related Implications and Needs

When one is starting an ontology-based application, the two major concerns are language and environment.

6.6.1 Language

When considering ontology-related applications, inevitably the issue of *ontology language* will arise. An ontology must be encoded in some language. If one is using a simple ontology, few issues arise concerning the language used for encoding. However, if one is considering a more complex ontology, the expressive power of a representation and reasoning needs to be considered. As with any problem involving the choice of a language, the language chosen must be epistemologically adequate: it must be able to express the concepts in the domain. For example, if one wants to do range checking in an e-commerce application, then it would be unwise to choose a simple language that contains only subclass and instance relationships and does not include property specification with value restrictions. There are a number of candidate ontology languages; in fact there are so many that some research efforts arose in the last decade to produce standard specification languages (such as the Knowledge Representation System Specification [KRSS] effort [Patel-Schneider and Swartout 1993]), interchange formats (such as the Knowledge Interchange Format [KIF], which is now a proposed ANSI standard [KIF 1991]), and common application programming interface standards (such as Open Knowledge Base Connectivity [OKBC] [Chaudhri et al. 1998]).

One does not want only to consider representational constructs in a language; one also wants to consider the reasoning that may be supported in the language. Some fields, such as description logics (www.dl.kr.org), make this a central focus in language design. They look for trade-offs that maintain the expressive power needed by applications and also consider what it takes to provide inference engines that can make deductions based on the constructs represented in the language. For example, if a language supports the notion of stating that two classes are disjoint, then a reasoning engine should be able to be built that enforces the constraint that the classes are disjoint. Thus, an inference engine should be able to warn a user if she is creating an instance or subclass of two disjoint classes.

Also, a language should be usable with existing platforms and should be something that nonexperts can use to do their conceptual modeling. Frame-based systems have had a long history of being thought of as conceptually easy to use; thus a frame paradigm may be worth considering while choosing a language for the Semantic Web.

Language efforts underway today attempt to take the best of the research on expressive power along with reasoning power and provide representationally powerful languages that have known reasoning properties and, of course, are efficient in their implementations. The DARPA Agent Markup

Language program, for example, attempted to take the emerging Web languages of today such as XML and RDF and create a language that is Web compatible, incorporates the ease of use of frame-based systems, and draws on the 20-year history of description logics in choosing language constructs along with reasoning paradigms. The resulting language, DAML+OIL, attempts to merge the best of existing Web languages, description logics, and frame-based systems. OIL, a modern description logic aimed also at Web compatibility (Bechhofer et al. 2000), attempts to provide a layered approach to language design.

6.6.2   Environment

Another consideration in developing ontology-based applications is how to generate, analyze, modify, and maintain an ontology over time. If the ontology is to be generated and maintained by subject matter experts (and not to require knowledge experts), some ontology support tools will be needed. There are a number of simple ontology tools available commercially. Some information retrieval companies, such as Verity (www.verity.com), have provided simple editors for generating and browsing simple generalization hierarchies. Verity has for years provided a "topic editor" that will support users in generating taxonomies and utilizing them in search queries. Research efforts have existed for many years in producing ontology toolkits. Stanford University's previously mentioned tools Ontolingua (Farquhar, Fikes, and Rice 1997) and Chimaera (McGuinness et al. 2000) are just two examples, however, examples abound, including OilEd (http://img.cs. man.ac.uk/oil/) from Manchester University and Protégé (Protégé Project 2000) from Stanford Medical Informatics, just to name a few. Application developers may choose commercial vendors as their toolkit provider, sophisticated research applications as the base, or something in between. Some companies with extensive ontology needs such as VerticalNet (http:// www.verticalnet.com/) have developed or are developing their own ontology tools to build ontologies that meet the needs of a sophisticated commercial ontologist. Their tools are built after analysis of existing research prototypes and are then designed to meet the commercial standards required in diverse, collaborative e-commerce applications of today.

When choosing to use or build an ontology environment, a number of issues should be considered including the following:

- *Collaboration and distributed workforce support.* Some ontology environments allow users to share a common workspace, that is, to see each other's work environments. This can be particularly useful for debugging ontologies. Ontolingua, for example, supports this notion through its use of sessions. Additionally, when workers are distributed in location, it becomes important to have an environment that allows access from multiple places. This is becoming much more typical today with server/client architectures. Finally, collaboration may require concurrency control, locking, and a kind of versioning and permission system.

- *Platform interconnectivity.* As applications become embedded in more complex platforms, it becomes important for environments to be able to read and write compatible formats, to be able to be integrated with multiple hardware/software environments, and so on. Java-based applications provide a convenient approach to this problem, but other systems that support multiple input and output formats, understand common standards, and provide translation and mapping services may also help.

- *Scale.* Ontology applications today may need to scale a few orders of magnitude larger than past applications. It is important to look at scaling in terms of size of ontologies as well as numbers of simultaneous users.

- *Versioning.* As applications become long-lived and also are deployed in different environments, possibly internationally, it becomes important to be able to support many versions of ontologies. In typical software engineering environments, source code control systems and versioning address these issues, and special ontology-oriented change management systems are evolving.

- *Security.* Some applications will have needs for differing levels of access to portions of the ontology. Thus, it is important to have an environment that can expose only portions of the ontology, based on a security model. The security model may need to support both read and write access.

- *Analysis.* Environments are expected to support acquisition, evolution, and maintenance of ontologies. Thus, it would be common to expect ontologies to have periods when they are incomplete and incorrect. Analysis support that can focus the user's attention on areas that are likely to need modification can be quite useful. The Chimaera ontology environment, for example, supports a number of diagnostic tests aimed at helping users identify provably incorrect ontologies as well as possible problems.

- *Life cycle issues.* As ontologies become larger and longer lived, application developers may be maintaining ontologies over many years. Additionally, they may be constantly merging new ontologies into their system as their applications interconnect with more diverse systems. Thus, it becomes important to consider support for ontology evolution issues such as merging terms, breaking apart terms, multiple namespaces, source code control systems, truth maintenance systems, and regression testing systems.

- *Ease of use.* Even if an environment has everything an application developer may need, if it is difficult for the user to decide how to use parts of the environment, they may not get used. Thus training materials, tutorials, conceptual modeling support, graphical browsing tools, and the like all may be necessary. We have written separately on some of the issues required to make description logic–based systems usable in the mainstream (Brachman et al. 1999).

- *Diverse user support.* Some environments are made for power users and some for naïve users, and some have settings that allow users to customize environments as appropriate to the type of user. It is important to determine if a particular environment can support all of the types of users anticipated. The support should be in all areas along the spectrum from initially generating the ontology in the planning and conceptual modeling state, to evolving it, diagnosing it, maintaining it, and so on.

- *Presentation style.* Possibly closely related to user type is presentation style. Some users need to see extensive detail, some need pruned information, and some need abstractions. Presentation of information may be textual, graphical, or other. Although no one environment needs to support all presentation styles, it is important that an environment be extensible enough to have new presentation methods added when needed.

- *Extensibility.* It will be impossible to anticipate all of the needs an application will have. Thus, it is important to use an environment that can adapt along with the needs of the users and the projects.

6.7　Conclusion

In this chapter, I have noted the emergence of ontologies from academic obscurity into mainstream business and practice on the Web. I have introduced the term "ontology," along with a spectrum of properties that ontologies may exhibit. I have provided criteria necessary, prototypical, and desirable for simple and complex ontologies. I have also identified ways that ontologies (both simple and complex) are being and may be used to provide value in many types of applications. I have dealt with the issue of acquiring ontologies and then addressed the issues of maintenance and evolution. Finally, I have identified a number of ontology-related issues that arise from the emergence of ontologies, focusing on ontology language and environment. Finally, I concluded with issues that are gaining importance as ontologies grow in their importance and centrality in diverse applications.

Acknowledgments

This chapter evolved as a result of a talk initially presented at the Semantics for the Web Seminar of the Dagstuhl Seminar series in March 2000 (http://www.dagstuhl.de/DATA/Reports/00121/ and http://www.semanticweb.org/events/dagstuhl2000/). The ideas have been enhanced by many people, including many of my collaborators on past ontology environments, in particular collaborators on the CLASSIC (particularly Patel-Schneider), FindUR, and Chimaera environments. It also benefited from joint work with Ora Lassila using it as a foundation for a portion of work on the role of frame-based representation on the Semantic Web. Additionally, support from the DARPA HPKB, RKF, and DAML programs has helped finance it, motivate it, and guide it. Finally, it is the result of a long-standing interest in ontologies and the meanings of terms, first inspired by Richard McGuinness, my father. He generated the first spark many years ago and then helped inspire me to take the work to the masses. His influence was still felt in the initial Dagstuhl talk, but he has since passed away, and thus my continuing work is dedicated to him.

Notes

1. The spectrum depicted in figure 6.2 arose out of a conversation in preparation for an ontology panel at AAAI '99. The panelists (Lehman, McGuinness, Ushold, and Welty), chosen because of their years of experience in ontologies, found that they encountered many forms of specifications that different people termed ontologies. McGuinness refined the picture to the one included here.

2. Some prominent hierarchies such as Yahoo have renamed their classes as broad, disjunctive categories, such as "Apparel, Accessories, and Shoes," presumably to provide for stricter subclass relationships. Disjunctive categories make inheritance more problematic, however, with class-specific properties.

3. Frames were introduced by Minsky (1975) and have been widely adopted; see for example Fikes and Kehler 1985, Karp 1992, and Chaudhri et al. 1998.

4. Note that if one is using the common logical meanings of connectives, this class should really be named "Fruits or vegetables or nuts or seeds."

References

Bechhofer, S., J. Broekstra, S. Decker, M. Erdmann, D. Fensel, C. Goble, F. van Harmelen, I. Horrocks, M. Klein, D. McGuinness, E. Motta, P. Patel-Schneider, S. Staab, and R. Studer. 2000. An Informal Description of Standard Oil and Instance OIL. Available from http://www.ontoknowledge.org/oil/downl/oil-whitepaper.pdf.

Berners-Lee, T. 2000. Semantic Web on XML. Keynote presentation for XML 2000. Slides available from http://www.w3.org/2000/Talks/1206-xml2k-tbl/slide1-0.html. Reporting available from http://www.xml.com/pub/a/2000/12/xml2000/timbl.html.

Brachman, R. J. 1983. What ISA Is and Isn't: An Analysis of Taxonomic Links in Semantic Networks. *IEEE Computer* 16(10):30–36.

Brachman, R. J., A. Borgida, D. L. McGuinness, and P. F. Patel-Schneider. 1999. Reducing CLASSIC to Practice: Knowledge Representation Theory Meets Reality. *Artificial Intelligence* 114(1–2):203–237.

Bray, T., J. Paoli, C. M. Sperberg-McQueen, and Eve Maler, ed. 2000. Extensible Markup Language (XML) 1.0 (second edition) (recommendation). World Wide Web Consortium. Available from http://www.w3.org/TR/2000/REC-xml-20001006.

Brickley, D., and R. V. Guha. 2000. Resource Description Framework (RDF) Schema Specification 1.0 (candidate recommendation). World Wide Web Consortium. Available from http://www.w3.org/TR/rdf-schema/.

Chaudhri, V., A. Farquhar, R. Fikes, P. Karp, and J. Rice. 1998. OKBC: A Programmatic Foundation for Knowledge Base Interoperability. In *Proceedings of the Fifteenth National Conference on Artificial Intelligence and Tenth Innovative Applications of Artificial Intelligence Conference (AAAI-98), Madison, Wisconsin, July 26–30, 1998*. Menlo Park, CA/Cambridge, MA: AAAI/MIT Press.

Dublin Core Metadata Initiative. 1999. Dublin Core Metadata Element Set, Version 1.1: Reference Description. Available from http://purl.org/dc/documents/rec-dces-19990702.htm.

Farquhar, A., R. Fikes, and J. Rice. 1997. *The Ontolingua Server: A Tool for Collaborative Ontology Construction. International Journal of Human-Computer Studies* 46(6):707–727.

Fikes, R., and T. Kehler. 1985. The Role of Frame-Based Representation in Reasoning. *Communications of the ACM* 28(9):904–920.

Gruber, T. R. 1993. A Translation Approach to Portable Ontologies. *Knowledge Acquisition* 5(2):199–220.

Guarino, N. 1998. Formal Ontology and Information Systems. In *Proceedings of Formal Ontology in Information Systems (FOIS-98), Trento, Italy, June 1998*, ed. N. Guarino (pp. 3–15). Amsterdam: IOS Press.

Guglielmo, C., and C. Babcock. 2000. Gaga over Google. *Interactive Week*. Available from http://www.zdnet.com/intweek/stories/news/0,4164,2651081,00.html and http://www.google.com/about.html.

Hendler, J., and D. McGuinness. 2000. The DARPA Agent Markup Language. *IEEE Intelligent Systems Trends and Controversies* (November/December). Available from http://www.ksl.stanford.edu/people/dlm/papers/ieee-daml01-abstract.html.

Humphreys, B. L., and D. A. B. Lindberg. 1993. The UMLS Project: Making the Conceptual Connection between Users and the Information They Need. *Bulletin of the Medical Library Association* 81(2):170.

Husserl, E. 1900–1901. *Logische Untersuchungen (Logical Investigations)*. 1st ed. Halle: Niemeyer.

Knowledge Interchange Format. 1991. Language Description (draft proposed national standard)/ NCITS.T2/98-004. Available from http://logic.stanford.edu/kif/kif.html.

Karp, P. D. 1992. The Design Space of Frame Knowledge Representation Systems. Technical Report 520, SRI International AI Center. Available from ftp://www.ai.sri.com/pub/papers/karp-freview.ps.Z.

Lassila, O. 1992. Web Metadata: A Matter of Semantics. *IEEE Internet Computing* 2(4):30–37.

Lassila, O., and R. Swick. 1999. Resource Description Framework (RDF) Model and Syntax Specification (recommendation). World Wide Web Consortium. Available from http://www.w3.org/TR/REC-rdf-syntax/.

McGuinness, D. L., L. A. Resnick, and C. Isbell. 1995. Description Logic in Practice: A CLASSIC: Application. In *Proceedings of the 14th International Joint Conference on Artificial Intelligence (IJCAI-95), Montreal, Canada, August, 1995* (pp. 2045–2046). San Francisco: Morgan Kaufmann.

McGuinness, D. L. 1998. Ontological Issues for Knowledge-Enhanced Search. In *Proceedings of Formal Ontology in Information Systems (FOIS-98), Trento, Italy, June 1998*, ed. N. Guarino (pp. 302–316). Amsterdam: IOS Press.

McGuinness, D. L., R. Fikes, J. Rice, and Steve Wilder. 2000. An Environment for Merging and Testing Large Ontologies. In *Proceedings of the Seventh International Conference on Principles of Knowledge Representation and Reasoning (KR-2000), Breckenridge, Colorado, USA. April 12–15, 2000* (pp. 483–493). San Francisco: Morgan Kaufmann.

Minsky, M. 1975. A Framework for Representing Knowledge. In *The Psychology of Computer Vision*, ed. P. H. Winston. New York: McGraw-Hill.

Patel-Schneider, P. F., and B. Swartout. 1993. Description-Logic Knowledge Representation System Specification. KRSS Group of the ARPA Knowledge Sharing Effort. Available from http://www-db.research.bell-labs.com/user/pfps/papers/krss-spec.ps.

The Protege Project. 2000. Available from http://protege.stanford.edu.

Smith, B. 1998. Basic Concepts of Formal Ontologies. In *Proceedings of Formal Ontology in Information Systems (FOIS-98), Trento, Italy, June 1998*, ed. N. Guarino. Amsterdam: IOS Press.

Woods, W. A. 1975. What's in a Link: Foundations for Semantic Networks. In *Representation and Understanding: Studies in Cognitive Science*, ed. D. G. Bobrow and A. M. Collins (pp. 35–82). New York: Academic.

II   *Knowledge Support*

7

Sesame: An Architecture for Storing and Querying RDF Data and Schema Information

Jeen Broekstra, Arjohn Kampman, and Frank van Harmelen

7.1   Introduction

The Resource Description Framework (Lassila and Swick 1999) is a W3C recommendation for the notation of metadata on the World Wide Web. RDF Schema (Brickley and Guha 2000) extends this standard by providing developers with the means to specify domain vocabulary and to model object structures.

These techniques will enable the enrichment of the Web with machine-processable semantics, thus giving rise to what has been dubbed the Semantic Web. However, simply having these data available is not enough. Tooling is needed to process the information, to transform it, and to reason with it. As a basis for this, we have developed Sesame, an architecture for efficient storage and expressive querying of large quantities of RDF metadata. Sesame is being developed by Aidministrator Nederland b.v. (http://www.aidministrator.nl) as part of the European IST project On-To-Knowledge (www.ontoknowledge.org) (Fensel et al. 2000).

This chapter is organized as follows: in section 7.2 we give a short introduction to RDF and RDF Schema. This section can be skipped by readers already familiar with these languages. In section 7.3 we discuss why a query language specifically tailored to RDF and RDF Schema is needed, over and above existing query languages such as XQuery. In sections 7.4 and 7.5 we look in detail at Sesame's architecture. Section 7.6 discusses our experiences with Sesame until now, and section 7.7 looks into possible future developments. Finally we provide our conclusions in section 7.8.

7.2   RDF and RDF Schema

RDF (Lassila and Swick 1999) is a W3C recommendation originally designed to standardize the definition and use of metadata descriptions of Web-based resources. However, RDF is equally well suited to representing arbitrary data, whether they are metadata or not.

7.2.1   RDF

The basic building block in RDF is an object-attribute-value triple, commonly written as $A(O;V)$. That is, an object O has an attribute A with value V. Another way to think of this relationship is as a labeled edge between two nodes: $[O]\_A![V]$. This notation is useful, because RDF allows objects and values to be interchanged. Thus, any object from one triple can play the role of a value in another triple, which amounts to chaining two labeled edges in a graphic representation. The graph in figure 7.1, for example, expresses the following relationships:

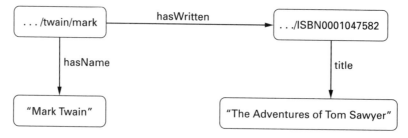

Figure 7.1
Example RDF data graph, capturing three statements.

```
HasName ('http://www.famouswriters.org/twain/mark', "Mark
Twain")
hasWritten ('http://www.famouswriters.org/twain/mark',
'http://www.books.org/ISBN0001047582')
title ('http://www.books.org/ISBN0001047582', "The
Adventures of Tom Sawyer")
```

RDF also allows a form of reification[1] in which any RDF statement itself can be the object or value of a triple. This means graphs can be nested as well as chained. On the Web this allows us, for example, to express doubt or support for statements created by other people. Finally, it is possible to indicate that a given object is of a certain type, such as stating that "ISBN0001047582" is of the type Book, by creating a type edge referring to the Book definition in an RDF schema:

```
type ('http://www.books.org/ISBN0001047582', 'http://
www.description.org/schema#Book')
```

The RDF Model and Syntax Specification also proposes an XML syntax for RDF data models. One possible serialization of the above relations in this syntax would look like this:

```
    <rdf:Description
rdf:about="http://www.famouswriters.org/twain/mark">
    <s:hasName>Mark Twain</s:hasName>
    <s:hasWritten
rdf:resource="http://www.books.org/ISBN0001047582"/>
    </rdf:Description>
    <rdf:Description
rdf:about="http://www.books.org/ISBN0001047582">
    <s:title>The Adventures of Tom Sawyer</s:title>
    <rdf:type
rdf:resource="http://www.description.org/schema#Book"/>
    </rdf:Description>
```

Since the proposed XML syntax allows many alternative ways of recording information (and indeed still other syntaxes may be introduced), the above XML syntax is just one of many possibilities for writing an RDF model in XML. It is important to note that RDF is designed to provide a basic object-attribute-value model for Web data.

Other than this intentional semantics—described only informally in the standard—RDF makes no commitments with respect to data modeling. In particular, no reserved terms are defined for further data modeling. As with XML, the RDF data model provides no mechanisms for declaring property names that are to be used.

7.2.2 RDF Schema

RDF Schema (Brickley and Guha 2000) is a mechanism that lets developers define a particular vocabulary for RDF data (such as hasWritten) and specify the kinds of objects to which these attributes can be applied (such as Writer). RDF Schema does this by prespecifying some terminology, such as Class, subClassOf, and Property, which can then be used in application-specific schemata. RDF Schema expressions are also valid RDF expressions—in fact, the only difference between RDF Schema expressions and "normal" RDF expressions is that in RDF Schema an agreement is made on the *semantics* of certain terms and thus on the *interpretation* of certain statements.

For example, the subClassOf property allows the developer to specify the hierarchical organization of classes. Objects can be declared to be instances of these classes using the type property. Constraints on the use of properties can be specified using domain and range constructs.

Above the dotted line in figure 7.2, we see an example RDF schema that defines vocabulary for the RDF example we saw earlier: Book, Writer, and FamousWriter are introduced as classes, and hasWritten is introduced as a property. A specific instance is described in terms of this vocabulary below the dotted line.

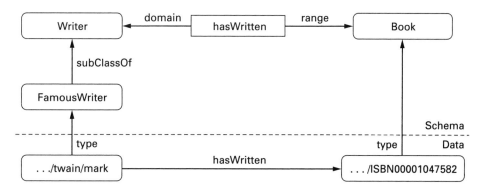

Figure 7.2
Example RDF Schema, defining vocabulary and a class hierarchy.

7.3 The Need for an RDF/S Query Language

RDF documents and RDF schemata can be considered at three different levels of abstraction:

1. At the *syntactic level* they are XML documents.

2. At the *structure level* they consist of a set of triples.

3. At the *semantic level* they constitute one or more graphs with partially predefined semantics.

We can query these documents at each of these three levels. We will briefly consider in the next sections the pros and cons of doing so for each level. This will lead us to conclude that RDF(S) documents should really be queried at the semantic level. We will briefly discuss RQL, a language for querying RDF(S) documents at the semantic level.

7.3.1 Querying at the Syntactic Level

As we have seen in section 7.2, any RDF model (and therefore any RDF schema) can be written in XML notation. It would therefore seem reasonable to assume that we can query RDF using an XML query language (for example, XQuery [Chamberlin et al. 2001]). However, this approach disregards the fact that RDF is not just an XML dialect but has its own data model that is very different from the XML tree structure. Relationships in the RDF data model that are not apparent from the XML tree structure become very hard to query.

In an XML query language such as XQuery (Chamberlin et al. 2001), expressions to traverse data structures are tailored toward traversing a node-labeled tree. However, the RDF data model in this instance is a graph, not a tree, and moreover, both its edges (properties) and its nodes (subjects/objects) are labeled.

In querying at the syntax level, this is literally left as an exercise for the query builder: one cannot query the relation between the resource signifying "Mark Twain" and the resource signifying "The Adventures of Tom Sawyer" without knowledge of the syntax that was used to encode the RDF data in XML. Ideally, we would want to formulate a query like "Give me all the relationships that exist between Mark Twain and The Adventures of Tom Sawyer." However, using only the XML syntax, we are stuck with formulating an awkward query like "Give me all the elements nested in a Description element with an about attribute with value 'http://www.famouswriters.org/twain/mark' of which the value of its resource attribute occurs elsewhere as the about attribute value of a Description element that has a nested element title with the value 'The Adventures of Tom Sawyer.'"

Not only is this approach inconvenient, it also disregards the fact that the XML syntax for RDF is not unique: different ways of encoding the same information in XML are possible and in use currently. This means that one query will never be guaranteed to retrieve all the potential "correct" answers from an RDF model.

7.3.2 Querying at the Structure Level

When we abstract from the XML linearization syntax, any RDF document represents a set of triples, each triple representing a statement of the form object-attribute-value. A number of query languages have been proposed and implemented that regard RDF documents as such a set of triples and that allow such a triple set to be queried in various ways (see http://perso.enst.fr/~ta/web/rdf/rdf-query.html for a recent overview).

The RDF/RDF Schema example from figure 7.2 corresponds to the following set of triples:

```
(type Book Class)
(type Writer Class)
(type FamousWriter Class)
(subClassOf FamousWriter Writer)
(type hasWritten Property)
(domain hasWritten Writer)
(range hasWritten Writer)
(type twain/mark FamousWriter)
(type ISBN0001047582 Book)
(hasWritten twain/mark ISBN0001047582)
```

An RDF query language would allow us to query which resources are known to be of type FamousWriter:

```
select ?x from ... where (type ?x FamousWriter)
```

The clear advantage of such a query is that it directly addresses the RDF data model and that it is therefore independent of the specific XML syntax that has been chosen to represent the data. However, a major shortcoming of any query language at this level is that it interprets *any* RDF only as a set of triples, including those elements that have been given a special semantics in RDF Schema. For example, since http://www.famouswriters.org/twain/mark is of type FamousWriter, and since FamousWriter is a subclass of Writer, http://www.famouswriters.org/twain/mark is also of type Writer, by virtue of the intended RDF Schema semantics of type and subClassOf. However, there is no triple that explicitly asserts this fact. As a result, the query

```
SELECT ?x FROM (type ?x Writer)
```

will fail, because the query looks only for explicit triples in the store, whereas the triple (type /twain/mark Writer) is not explicitly present in the store but is implied by the semantics of RDF Schema. Notice that simply expanding the query into something like

```
SELECT ?x ?c1 ?c2 ?c3
FROM (type ?x ?c1),
(subClassOf ?c2 ?c3)
WHERE ?c1 = ?c2
```

will solve the problem in this specific example but does not accommodate a chain of subClassOf triples, etc.

7.3.3   Querying at the Semantic Level: RQL

What is clearly required is a query language that is sensitive to the semantics of the RDF Schema primitives. RQL (Karvounarakis et al. 2000; Alexaki et al. 2000) is the first (and to the best of our knowledge currently the only) proposal for a declarative query language for RDF and RDF Schema. It is being developed within the European IST project C-Web and its follow-up project MESMUSES by the Institute of Computer Science at FORTH, in Greece (http: www.ics.forth.gr/).

RQL adopts the syntax of OQL (Cattel et al. 2000). Like OQL, RQL is a functional language: the output of RDF Schema queries in RQL is again legal RDF Schema code, which allows the output of queries to function as input for subsequent queries.

RQL is defined by means of a set of core queries, a set of basic filters, and a way to build new queries through functional composition and iterators. The core queries are the basic building blocks of RQL, which give access to the RDF Schema–specific contents of an RDF triple store with queries such as Class (retrieving all classes), Property (retrieving all properties) or Writer (returning all instances of the class with name Writer). This last query also returns of course all instances of subclasses of Writer, since these are also instances of the class Writer, by virtue of the semantics of RDF Schema. We can ask for all *direct* instances of Writer (i.e., ignoring all instances of subclasses) through the query Writer.

RQL can also query the structure of the subclass hierarchy. In our example, the query subClassOf(Writer) would return the class FamousWriter as its only result. In general, this would return all direct and indirect subclasses of Writer, since RQL is aware of the transitivity of the subclass relation. The query subClassOf^(Writer) would return only the immediate subclasses.

Of course, being based on OQL, RQL also allows a select-from-where construct. A final crucial feature of RQL is the path expressions. These allow us to match patterns along entire paths in RDF/RDF Schema graphs, such as the one depicted in figure 7.2. For example, the query

```
SELECT Y FROM FamousWriter {X}. hasWritten {Y}
```

returns all books written by famous writers, effectively doing pattern matching along a path in the graph of figure 7.2.

7.3.4   Conclusion

The previous subsections have argued that RDF data should not be queried at the level of their (rather incidental) XML encoding and that RDF Schema data should not be regarded as simply a set of RDF triples, since all intended semantics of the RDF Schema primitives are then lost. Consequently, we should be using a query language that is sensitive to this RDF Schema semantics. RQL is a powerful (and currently the only) candidate for such a language.

In the next few sections, we discuss the architecture we have designed for a query engine for RQL.

7.4   Sesame's Architecture

The Sesame system is a Web-based architecture that allows persistent storage of RDF data and schema information and subsequent online querying of that information. In section 7.4.1, we present an overview of Sesame's

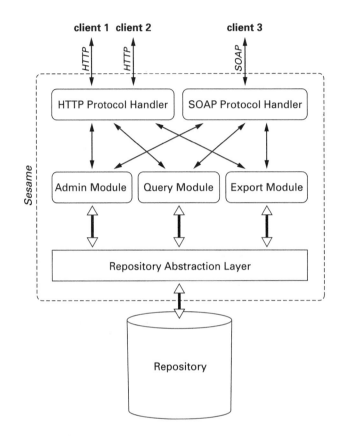

Figure 7.3
Sesame's architecture.

architecture. In the sections following that, we look in more detail at several components of Sesame.

7.4.1   Overview

An overview of Sesame's architecture is shown in figure 7.3. In this section we will give a brief overview of the system's main components. For persistent storage of RDF data, Sesame needs a scalable repository. Naturally, a database management system (DBMS) comes to mind, as these have been used for decades for storing large quantities of data. Over those decades, a large number of DBMSs have been developed, each having its own strengths and weaknesses, targeted platforms, and application programming interfaces (APIs). Also, for each of these DBMSs, the RDF data can be stored in numerous ways.

As we would like to keep Sesame independent of any particular DBMS and it is impossible to know which way of storing data is best fitted for which DBMS, all DBMS-specific code is concentrated in a single architectural layer of Sesame: the *repository abstraction layer (RAL)*. This RAL offers RDF-specific methods to its clients and translates these methods into calls to its specific DBMS. An important advantage of the introduction of such a separate layer is that it makes it possible to implement Sesame on top of a wide variety of repositories without changing any of Sesame's other components. Section 7.4.3 describes a number of possible repository implementations.

Sesame's functional modules are clients of the RAL. Currently, there are three such modules:

- *The RQL query module.* This module evaluates RQL queries posed by the user (see section 7.5.1).

- *The RDF administration module.* This module allows incremental uploading of RDF data and schema information, as well as the deleting of information (see section 7.5.2).

- *The RDF export module.* This module allows the extraction of the complete schema and/or data from a model in RDF format (see section 7.5.3).

Depending on the environment in which Sesame is deployed, different ways of communicating with the Sesame modules may be desirable. For example, communication over HTTP may be preferable in a Web context, but in other contexts protocols such as RMI (Remote Method Invocation) (http://java.sun.com/j2se/1.3/docs/guide/rmi/spec/rmiTOC.html) or SOAP (Simple Object Access Protocol) (Box et al. 2000) may be more suited.

To incorporate maximum flexibility, the actual handling of these protocols has been placed outside the scope of the functional modules. Instead, protocol handlers are provided as intermediaries between the modules and their clients, each handling a specific protocol.

The introduction of the RAL and the protocol handlers makes Sesame a generic architecture for RDF(S) storage and querying, rather than just a particular implementation of such a system. Adding additional protocol handlers makes it easy to connect Sesame to different operating environments. The construction of concrete RALs will be discussed in the next section.

Sesame's architecture has been designed with extensibility and adaptability in mind. The possibility of using other kinds of repositories has been mentioned before. Adding other modules or protocol handlers is also possible. The only part that is fixed in the architecture is the RAL.

7.4.2   The Repository Abstraction Layer

As we have seen in the previous section, the RAL offers a stable, high-level interface for talking to repositories. This RAL is defined by an API that offers functionality to add data to, or to retrieve or delete data from, the repository. RAL implementations translate calls to the API methods into operations on the underlying repository.

Rather than adopting or extending an existing RDF API, such as the "Stanford API" proposed by Sergey Melnik (2000), we have created a completely new API. The main differences between our proposal and the Stanford API are that

1. the Stanford API is very much targeted at data that are kept in memory, whereas our API is considerably more "lightweight," as all data are returned one at a time in data streams.

2. our API supports RDF Schema semantics, such as subsumption reasoning, whereas the Stanford API offers only RDF-related functionality.

The advantage of returning data in streams (point 1) is that at any one time only a small portion of the data is kept in memory. This streaming approach is also used in the functional modules and even in the protocol handlers, which give results as soon as they are available. This approach is needed to enable Sesame to scale to large volumes of data without requiring exceptionally expensive hardware. In fact, Sesame requires close to zero memory for data and only a small amount of memory for the program to run. This, together with the option of using a remote data store for the repository (see section 7.4.3), makes Sesame potentially suitable for use as infrastructure in highly constrained environments such as portable devices.

Of course, reading everything from a repository and keeping nothing in memory seriously hurts performance. This performance problem can be solved by selectively caching data in memory.[2] For small data volumes it is even possible to cache all data in memory, in which case the repository serves only as a persistent storage. Sesame's architecture allows all of this to be done in a completely transparent way, as will be shown in the next section.

7.4.2.1   *Stacking Abstraction Layers*

An important feature of the RALs in Sesame is that it is possible to put one on top of another. To Sesame's functional modules (the admin, query, and export modules) this is completely transparent, as they will only see the RAL at the top of the stack (see figure 7.4). The RAL at the top can perform some action when the modules make calls to it and then forward these calls to the RAL beneath it. This process continues down the stack of RALs until one of them finally handles the request.

One good example in which such stacking of RALs makes sense is when implementing a cache. We implemented a RAL that caches all schema data in a dedicated data structure in main memory. These schema data are often very limited in size and are requested very frequently. At the same time, the schema data are the most difficult to query from a DBMS because of the transitivity of the subClassOf and subPropertyOf properties. This schema-caching RAL can be placed on top of arbitrary other RALs, handling all calls concerning schema data. The rest of the calls are forwarded to the RAL underlying the schema-caching RAL.

7.4.3   *The Repository*

Thanks to the repository abstraction layer, Sesame can be based on any kind of repository that is able to store RDF. The following is a list of possible concrete implementations of the repository, each with its own advantages.

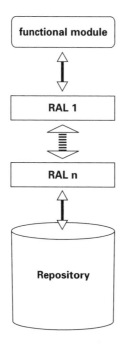

Figure 7.4
RALs can be stacked to add functionality.

- *DMBSs.* Any kind of database can be used: relational databases (RDBMSs), object-relational databases (ORDBMSs), etc.

- *Existing RDF stores.* A number of RDF stores are currently in development (Guha 2001; Reggiori 2001; Beckett 2001; Wagner 2001). Sesame can use a particular RDF store if a RAL is written that knows how to talk to that specific RDF store.

- *RDF files.* Files containing RDF can be used as repositories too. A flat file is not very practical on its own, as it will be painfully slow in storing and retrieving data. However, when combined with a RAL that caches all of the data in memory, it becomes a good alternative for small volumes of data.

- *RDF network services.* Apart from performance, there is no need for the repository to be located close to Sesame, which can use any network service that offers basic functionality for storing, retrieving, and deleting RDF data. An example of a system offering such functionality is, of course, Sesame itself. Many of the RDF stores mentioned above can also be approached as Web services.

The last option in particular is very interesting. An initial query is sent to a Sesame server somewhere on the Web. This server can use not only its local repository to answer the query, but also any number of remote repositories that it knows about. In turn, some of these remote repositories might themselves either answer the query using local data stores or in turn again approach yet other remote repositories. This opens up the possibility of a highly distributed architecture for RDF(S) storing and querying that has been unexplored until now, but that is truly in the spirit of the Semantic Web.

7.4.3.1 *PostgreSQL*

The first and, so far, only repository that has been used with Sesame is PostgreSQL (http://www.postgresql.org/). PostgreSQL is a freely available (opensource) object-relational DBMS that supports many features that normally can be found only in commercial DBMS implementations.

One of the main reasons for choosing PostgreSQL as a repository for Sesame is that it is an object-relational DBMS, meaning that it supports subtable relations between its tables. As these subtable relations are also transitive, we use these to model the subsumption reasoning of RDF Schema.

The RAL implemented on top of PostgreSQL uses a dynamic database schema that was inspired by the schema shown in Karvounarakis et al. 2000. New tables are added to the database whenever a new class or property is added to the repository. If a class is a subclass of other classes, the table created for it will also be a subtable of the tables for the superclasses. Likewise for properties being subproperties of other properties. Instances of classes and properties are inserted as values into the appropriate tables. Figure 7.5 gives an impression of the contents of a database containing the data from figure 7.2.

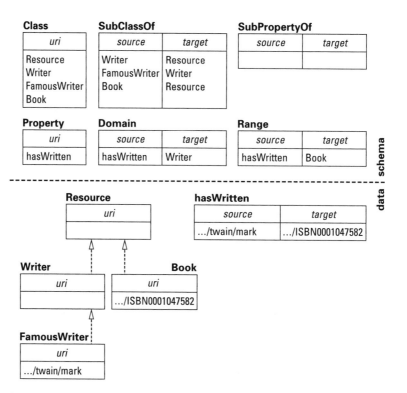

Figure 7.5
Impression of the object-relational schema currently used with PostgreSQL.

The actual schema involves one more table, called *resources*. This table contains all resources and literal values, each mapped to a unique ID. These IDs are used in the tables shown in the figure to refer to the resources and literal values. The resources table is used to minimize the size of the database. It ensures that resources and literal values, which can be quite long, occur only once in the database, saving potentially large amounts of memory.

7.5 Sesame's Functional Modules

In this section, we briefly describe the three modules that are currently implemented in Sesame.

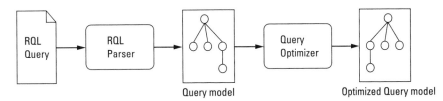

Figure 7.6
A query is parsed and then optimized into a query object model.

7.5.1   The RQL Query Module

As we have seen in section 7.4.1, one of the three modules currently implemented in Sesame is an RQL query engine. The version of RQL implemented in Sesame is slightly different from the language proposed by Karvounarakis et al. (2000). It features better compliance with W3C specifications, including support for optional domain and range restrictions as well as multiple domain and range restrictions (see Broekstra and Kampman 2001 for details). The query module follows the path depicted in figure 7.6 when handling a query. After parsing the query and building a query tree model for it, this model is fed to the query optimizer, which transforms the query model into an equivalent model that will evaluate more efficiently.

The optimized model of the query is subsequently evaluated in a streaming fashion, following the tree structure into which the query has been broken down. Each object represents a basic unit in the original query and evaluates itself, fetching data from the RAL where needed. The main advantage of this approach is that results can be returned in a streaming fashion, without the entire result set having to be built up in memory first.

In Sesame, RQL queries are translated (via the object model) into a set of calls to the RAL. This approach means that the main bulk of the actual evaluation of the RQL query is done in the RQL query engine itself. For example, when a query contains a join operation over two subqueries, each of the subqueries is evaluated, and the join operation is then executed by the query engine on the results.

Another possible approach would be to directly translate as much of the RQL query as possible into a query specific for the underlying repository. An advantage of this approach would be that, when using a DBMS, we would get all its sophisticated query evaluation and optimization mechanisms for free. However, a large disadvantage would be that the implementation of the query engine would be directly dependent on the repository being used and the architecture would lose the ability to switch easily between repositories.

This design decision on how queries are to be translated is one of the major differences between Sesame and the RDF Suite implementation of RQL by ICS-FORTH (see Alexaki et al. 2000), which relies on the underlying DBMS for query optimization. However, this dependency means that RDF Suite cannot as easily be transported to run on top of another storage engine.

A natural consequence of our choice to evaluate queries in the RAL is that we need to devise several optimization techniques in the engine, since we cannot rely on any given DBMS to do this for us.

7.5.2   The Admin Module

In order to be able to insert RDF data and schema information into a repository, Sesame provides an admin module. The current implementation is rather simple and offers two main functions: incrementally adding RDF data/ schema information and clearing a repository.

The admin module retrieves its information from an RDF(S) source (usually an online RDF(S) document in XML-serialized form) and parses it using a streaming RDF parser currently, we use ARP (Another RD Parser), developed by Hewlett-Packard. The parser delivers the information to the admin module on a per-statement basis: *(S;P;O)*. The admin module subsequently checks each statement for consistency with the information already present in the repository and infers implied information if necessary, as follows:

- If *P* equals *type*, then the admin module infers that *O* must be a class.

- If *P* equals *subClassOf*, then the admin module infers that both *S* and *O* are classes.

▪ If *E* equals *subPropertyOf*, then the admin module infers that both *S* and *O* are properties.

▪ If *P* equals *domain* or *range*, the admin module infers that *S* must be a property and *O* must be a class.

In all these cases, the admin module checks whether the inferred information is consistent with the current contents of the repository and if so, the inferred information is added to the repository. If the admin module encounters a duplicate statement (i.e., a fact that is already known in the repository), this is reported; otherwise it is ignored.

7.5.3   The RDF Export Module

The RDF export module is a very simple module. It module is able to export the contents of a repository formatted in XML-serialized RDF. The idea behind this module is that it supplies a basis for using Sesame in combination with other RDF tools, as all RDF tools will at least be able to read this format. Some tools, like ontology editors, need only the schema part of the data. On the other hand, tools that don't support RDF Schema semantics will probably need only the nonschema part of the data. For these reasons, the RDF export module is able to selectively export the schema, the data, or both.

7.6   Experiences

Our implementation of Sesame can be found at http://sesame. aidministrator.nl and is freely available for noncommercial use. This implementation follows the general architecture described in this chapter, using the following concrete implementation choices for the modules:

▪ As discussed above, the repository is realized by PostgreSQL.

▪ A protocol handler is realized using HTTP.

▪ The admin module uses the SiRPAC RDF parser.

In this section, we briefly report on our experiences with various aspects of this implementation.

7.6.1   Using RQL

As we have seen in section 7.5.1, Sesame supports querying using RQL. RQL is a very powerful declarative language that offers very expressive querying capabilities. One of the most distinguishing features of RQL is its built-in support for RDF Schema semantics and the possibility it affords us to combine data and schema information in a single query. However, RQL currently lacks support for semantically querying reified statements, mainly because reification is poorly defined in the RDF specification. The direct result of this lack of support is that it is not possible to query such constructs semantically. When Sesame is confronted with a reified statement, RQL queries will have to be formulated in terms of the structure of such a statement.

7.6.2   Application: On-To-Knowledge

Sesame is currently being deployed as the central infrastructure of the European IST project On-To-Knowledge (http://www.ontoknowledge.org). On-To-Knowledge aims at developing ontology-driven knowledge management tools. Figure 7.7 shows how Sesame serves as the central data repository for a number of such tools:

▪ OntoExtract, developed by CognIT a.s., extracts ontological conceptual structures from natural-language documents. These ontologies are uploaded for storage in Sesame.

▪ The resulting ontologies can be downloaded into OntoEdit, an editor for ontologies developed by the the Institute AIFB of the University of Karlsruhe. When the user has edited an ontology, the result is again stored in Sesame.

▪ The resulting ontologies are downloaded into RDF Ferret, a user front-end, developed by BT Adastral Park Research Labs, that provides search and query facilities for Web data based on the ontologies.

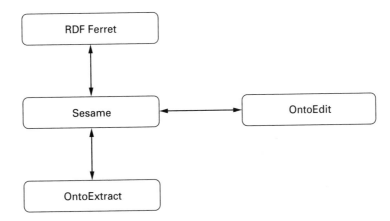

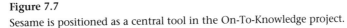

Figure 7.7
Sesame is positioned as a central tool in the On-To-Knowledge project.

Because Sesame is a server-based application, all this functionality is integrated simply by establishing HTTP connections to Sesame. We are currently in the process of applying this architecture in a number of knowledge management applications.

7.6.3 Ontologies and RDF Schema

While developing Sesame, many ambiguities in the RDF Schema specification were uncovered. One of the reasons for these ambiguities is that RDF Schema is defined in natural language: no formal description of its semantics is given. As a result of this, even the RDF Schema specification contains some inconsistencies.

Another reason why RDF Schema is so hard to understand is that RDF Schema is self-describing in the sense that the definition of its terms is itself done in RDF Schema. This leads to strange circular dependencies in the term definitions (e.g., the term *Class* is both a subclass of and an instance of *Resource*, which is itself an instance of *Class* again). In fact, primitives from different metalevels of description have been mapped to identical terms, resulting in a rather unclear specification (see also Nejdl, Wolpers, and Capella 2000).

One of the consequences of these circular dependencies is that RDF Schema is not only a language for, but also a part of, ontologies. This means that all primitives defined in RDF Schema (i.e., subClassOf, subPropertyOf, domain, range, etc.) are also in the ontology. We would argue that this is counterintuitive. At the very least, this approach deviates from approaches taken by most other ontology languages.

7.6.4   Using PostgreSQL

Our experiences with the database schema in PostgreSQL, as shown in section 7.4.3.1, have not been completely satisfactory. Both data retrieval and data insertion are not as fast as we would like. In particular, incremental uploads of schema data can be very slow, since table creation is very expensive in PostgreSQL. Even worse, when a new subClassOf relation between two existing classes is added, the complete class hierarchy starting from the subclass needs to broken down and must then be rebuilt again, because subtable relations cannot be added to an existing table; all subtable relations have to be specified when a table is created. Once created, the subtable relations are fixed.

7.6.5   Scalability Issues

We have conducted experiments using Sesame with several data sets and/or ontologies that are currently available on the Web. The largest set of data that we have uploaded and subsequently queried was the collection of nouns from Wordnet,[3] consisting of about 400,000 RDF statements. This data set almost completely consists of RDF data (i.e. hardly any schema information). Although we have not performed any structured benchmark testing, the following points are noteworthy.

First of all, all experimenting has been done using a desktop computer (Sun UltraSPARC 5 workstation, 256MB) to run Sesame. Java servlets running on a Web server were used as protocol handlers to communicate over HTTP. The database schema described in section 7.4.3.1 in combination with Post-greSQL version 7.1.1 was used as repository.

The uploading of the information in this setup has not been not as fast as we would like, mainly because of the database schema being used. Just adding a data statement to the database involves the following steps:

- Check whether the property is already known. If not, add it and create a table for it.
- Check whether the subject is already known, adding it if not.
- Check whether the object is already known, adding it if not.
- Add a row representing the statement to the appropriate table.

Most of these steps have to be performed in sequential order, which is very time intensive. Uploading the Wordnet nouns took approximately 94 minutes, which comes down to 71 statements per second. As was to be expected, the upload did not show any significant signs of slowing down as the amount of data in the repository increased (the amount of data is really not very large by DBMS standards).

Querying the information proved to be quite slow, too, for exactly the same reasons. Because of the database's distributed storage over multiple tables, retrieving data from the repository means doing many joins on tables, hindering performance.

7.7   Future Directions

7.7.1   DAML+OIL

Currently, Sesame understands the semantics of RDF and RDF Schema. We would like to extend this to more powerful languages like DAML+OIL (Horrocks et al. 2001). DAML+OIL is an extension of RDF Schema and offers additional primitives for creating schemata. Examples of the additional expressive power of DAML+OIL are

- the use of arbitrary class expressions, including disjunction, conjunction, and negation (complement) of classes.

- cardinality constraints on properties, expressing the minimum and maximum number of values a property can have for each object.

- symmetric, transitive, and inverse properties.

Since DAML+OIL allows more expressiveness and has more inferencing capabilities than RDF schema, a reasoner/query language that understands its semantics is significantly more complicated than the current reasoning service in Sesame.

7.7.2 Other Repositories

We are planning to implement support for other DMBS/schema combinations so that we can compare the pros and cons of each approach. A first option will be to implement a RAL based on a traditional relational DBMS, that is, one that only uses standard SQL queries. Such a RAL can be used on numerous DBMSs, as almost all DBMSs support such queries.

7.7.3 Admin Module

The admin module currently offers very limited functionality for administering the contents of repositories. More fine-grained functionality is needed for the module to be really useful. We are currently investigating the options for accomplishing this. One of these options is to extend RQL with primitives for updating and deleting data, just as SQL does.

7.8 Conclusion

In this chapter we have presented Sesame, a flexible architecture for storing and querying both RDF data and RDF Schema information. Sesame is an important step beyond the currently available storage and query devices for RDF, since it is the first publicly available implementation of a query language that is aware of the RDF Schema semantics.

An important feature of the Sesame architecture is its abstraction from the details of any particular repository used for the actual storage. This makes it possible to port Sesame to a large variety of different repositories, including relational databases, RDF triple stores, and even remote-storage services on the Web.

Sesame itself is a server-based application and can therefore be used as a remote service for storing and querying data on the Semantic Web. As with storage layers, Sesame abstracts from any particular communication protocol, so that Sesame can easily be connected to different clients by writing different protocol handlers.

We have constructed a concrete implementation of the generic architecture, using PostgreSQL as a repository and using HTTP as communication protocol handlers. Important next steps to expand Sesame toward a full-fledged storage and querying service for the Semantic Web include its extension from RDF Schema to DAML+OIL and implementations for different repositories, notably those that can live elsewhere on the Web.

Notes

1. From Latin *rem facere*, "to make into a thing."

2. A good DBMS implementation will also cache query results to improve performance.

3. This collection can be found in RDF form at http://www.semanticweb.org/library/.

References

Alexaki, S., V. Christophides, G. Karvounarakis, D. Plexousakis, and K. Tolle. 2000. The RDFSuite: Managing Voluminous RDF Description Bases. Technical report, Institute of Computer Science, FORTH, Heraklion, Greece. Available from http://www.ics.forth.gr/proj/isst/RDF/RSSDB/rdfsuite.pdf.

Beckett, D. 2001. Redland RDF Application Framework. Available from http://www.redland.opensource.ac.uk/.

Box, D., D. Ehnebuske, G. Kakivaya, A. Layman, N. Mendelsohn, H. F. Nielsen, S. Thatte, and D. Winer. 2000. Simple Object Access Protocol (SOAP) 1.1 (note). World Wide Web Consortium. Available from http://www.w3.org/TR/SOAP/.

Brickley, D., and R. Guha. 2000. Resource Description Framework (RDF) Schema Specification 1.0 (candidate recommendation). World Wide Web Consortium. Available from http://www.w3.org/TR/2000/CR-rdf-schema-20000327.

Broekstra, J., and A. Kampman. 2001. Query Language Definition: On-To-Knowledge (IST-1999-10132). Deliverable 9, Aidministrator Nederland b.v. Available from http://www.ontoknowledge.org/.

Cattel, R., D. Barry, M. Berler, J. Eastman, D. Jordan, C. Russell, O. Schadow, T. Stanienda, and F. Velez. 2000. The Object Database Standard: ODMG 3.0. San Francisco: Morgan Kaufmann.

Chamberlin, D., D. Florescu, J. Robie, J. Simeon, and M. Stefanescu. 2001. XQuery: A Query Language for XML (working draft). World Wide Web Consortium. Available from http://www.w3.org/TR/xquery/.

Fensel, D., F. van Harmelen, M. Klein, H. Akkermans, J. Broekstra, C. Fluit, J. van der Meer, H.-P. Schnurr, R. Studer, J. Hughes, U. Krohn, J. Davies, R. Engels, B. Bremdal, F. Ygge, T. Lau, B. Novotny, U. Reimer, and I. Horrocks. 2000. On-To-Knowledge: Ontology-Based Tools for Knowledge Management. *Proceedings of the eBusiness and eWork (EMMSEC-2000) Conference, Madrid, Spain, October.* Available from http://www.ebew.net/.

Guha, R. 2001. rdfDB. Available from http://web1.guha.com/rdfdb/.

Horrocks, I., F. van Harmelen, P. Patel-Schneider, T. Berners-Lee, D. Brickley, D. Connoly, M. Dean, S. Decker, D. Fensel, P. Hayes, J. Heflin, J. Hendler, O. Lassila, D. McGuinness, and L. A. Stein. 2001. DAML+OIL. Available from http://www.daml.org/2001/03/daml+oil-index.html.

Karvounarakis, G., V. Christophides, D. Plexousakis, and S. Alexaki. 2000. Querying Community Web Portals. Technical report, Institute of Computer Science, FORTH, Heraklion, Greece. Available from http://www.ics.forth.gr/proj/isst/RDF/RQL/rql.pdf.

Lassila, O. and R. R. Swick. 1999. Resource Description Framework (RDF): Model and Syntax Specification (recommendation). World Wide Web Consortium. Available from http://www.w3.org/TR/REC-rdf-syntax/.

Melnik, S. 2000. RDF API Draft. Public draft, Database Group, Stanford University. Available from http://www-db.stanford.edu/~melnik/rdf/api.html.

Nejdl, W., M. Wolpers, and C. Capella. 2000. The RDF Schema Revisited. In *Modelle und Modellierungssprachen in Informatik und Wirtschaftsinformatik, Modellierung 2000 (Models and Modeling Languages in Computer Science, Modeling 2000), St. Goar.* Koblenz: Foelbach Verlag.

Reggiori, A. 2001. RDFStore. Available from http://rdfstore.jrc.it/.

Wagner, H. 2001. Extensible open rdf. Available from http://eor.dublincore.org/.

8   Enabling Task-Centered Knowledge Support through Semantic Markup

Rob Jasper and Mike Uschold

8.1   The Evolving Web

The current evolution of the Web can be characterized from various perspectives:

- *Locating resources.* The way people find things on the Web is evolving from simple keyword search into more sophisticated semantic techniques for both search and navigation.
- *Users.* Web resources are evolving from being primarily intended for human consumption into being intended for use both by humans and machines—most notably, software agents.
- *Semantics.* The information resources the Web contains are evolving from those that have little or no explicit semantics into those having a rich semantic infrastructure.

There is considerable activity going on, and significant progress being made in each of these areas, by various communities, including research, standards organizations, and commercial interests.

8.1.1 Locating Resources

Commercial companies have made great progress in developing search engines for the Web, primarily focusing on keyword-based search and text categorization techniques.

8.1.2 Users

More and more, software programs are accessing and processing Web pages automatically. Metasearch engines are one good example. There is a growing number of B2C Web sites that operate in a similar manner, by checking and comparing many different Web sites—for example, those for selling books or those for online travel. This works fine but often requires customization of Web sites by humans to figure out what the information on a particular site "means." By looking at the text and analyzing the underlying structure of the Web site, it is possible to write CGI scripts, perform some computation, collate the results, and return them to the user. For various reasons, these sites are not a panacea for information integration on the Web. But more important, perhaps, is the fact that there is no systematic and agreed-upon way to represent and interpret the semantics of the information about product or service offers. This brings us to the semantic web.

8.1.3 The Semantic Web

There has been and continues to be a tremendous amount of activity on the part of the W3C and research groups to address the issue of semantics with respect to the Web. From the perspective of the W3C, the idea of a Semantic Web is to make the information available on the Web machine-sensible. The research community is working with the W3C to realize the dream of a Semantic Web (DAML 2001). A major part of this quest will entail representing and reasoning with semantic metadata and/or providing semantic markup of information resources available on the Web. A key benefit should be that this will make it much easier and much faster for humans to find what they require on the Web, compared, say, to today's "nonsemantic" search engines. However, this remains an unproven and largely untested hypothesis. The main intent of the Semantic Web is to give machines much better access to information resources so they can be information intermediaries in support of humans.

Currently, much of the research on semantic markup has focused on providing common languages and infrastructure to enhance information retrieval and support e-business applications. Although we believe this work is important, these applications often fail to recognize or support the underlying tasks users are performing when they search the Web. Users are seldom simply searching for documents but are doing so in the context of performing some larger task (e.g., selling a car, moving to a new city).

Consider the user interfaces presented by most information retrieval or knowledge management systems. These interfaces typically capture a set of keywords, or at best, a complex boolean query but fail to identify the broader task the user is performing in submitting those keywords or queries. Understanding the user and his underlying task is critical in determining which resources are most appropriate in response to his search. For example, a system that understood whether a user's task was purchasing, selling, or repairing a car would be much better at supporting the user's ultimate goal in conducting a search on the keyword "car." Other researchers (e.g., Dumais 1999) have identified the need for understanding the underlying task a user is performing, but little work has been done on capturing and exploiting this information.

8.1.4   A Place to Do Things

In his presentation at the Knowledge Technologies 2001 conference, Reid Smith, vice president of knowledge management at Slumberger, introduced another perspective from which to view the evolution of the web. The web, according to Smith, will evolve from being primarily a place to *find* things into being a place to *do* things as well.

Smith's perspective is the focus of this chapter. We describe some important first steps in this evolution of the Web into a place to perform tasks. Provision of semantics for the Web is a necessary foundation on which to build our task-centered approach. It enables new kinds of applications that better support a user's broader goals. We describe a semantics-based prototype focused on supporting users' tasks in the domain of aerospace customer support.

8.2   Web Problem Solving

People use the Web in a variety of contexts to solve many different kinds of problems. The effectiveness of task-centered knowledge support relies on identifying a convenient mechanism for expressing the user's intentions, matching those intentions with the relevant resources, and integrating them into a consistent view. In the short run, this requires that the application anticipate the kinds of problems that users want to solve and that those problems occur with some degree of regularity.

In this section we note some key distinctions or dimensions that define a notional space of web problem solving (see figure 8.1). Different points and regions in this space require different problem-solving techniques. We identify two dimensions of variation: frequency of occurrence and how easy it is to anticipate a specific task that some user might have. Our task-centered approach supports a space of problems that occur with some regularity and that are possible, but perhaps not easy to anticipate.

8.2.1   Dimensions of Variation

Anticipatability   The anticipatability dimension represents a continuum ranging from questions that are very easy to anticipate to those that are very difficult to anticipate. In the domain of U.S. history, a user might present a simple task such as determining who was the 19th U.S. president. This task is fairly easy to anticipate, and the answer can easily be found using a standard search engine. Tasks that are easy to anticipate will often have existing Web resources that address them. In this case there is a whole Web page (IPL 2001) devoted to the 19th president, Rutherford Birhard Hayes. At the other end of this continuum are tasks that are virtually impossible to anticipate. An example would be the task of determining whether Rutherford Birhard Hayes is related to artificial intelligence researcher Pat Hayes. We were unable to locate a Web page that had the answer to this question. A task somewhere in the middle of this continuum would be that of finding out how many vice presidents were older than the president they served. It is rather harder to anticipate this specific question than the first one. However, it is possible to set up a database that contains information about past presidencies that can answer this and a wide variety of other similar questions. Each such question is not by itself easy to anticipate.

Frequency   The other dimension, frequency, represents a continuum of problems ranging from those that occur frequently to those that occur infrequently. A simple task that might arise frequently would be finding out who the current U.S. president is or what the capital city is for a particular country or state.

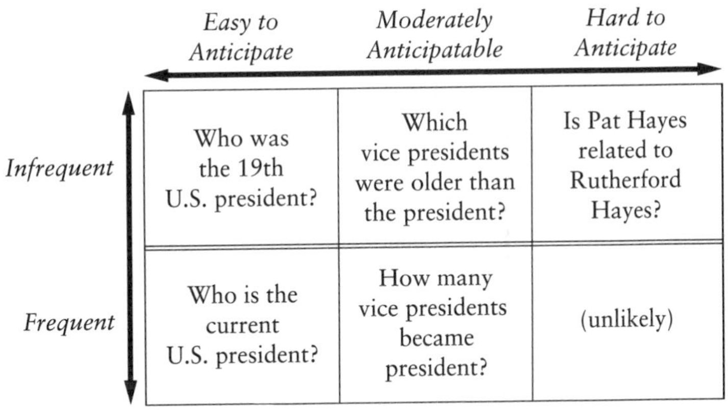

	Easy to Anticipate	*Moderately Anticipatable*	*Hard to Anticipate*
Infrequent	Who was the 19th U.S. president?	Which vice presidents were older than the president?	Is Pat Hayes related to Rutherford Hayes?
Frequent	Who is the current U.S. president?	How many vice presidents became president?	(unlikely)

Figure 8.1
Notional space of problems.

These dimensions are distinct and largely orthogonal (see figure 8.1). Easy-to-anticipate tasks may arise frequently ("Who is the current U.S. president?") or infrequently ("Who was the 19th U.S. president?"). Tasks in the middle of the anticipatability continuum may also arise frequently ("How many vice presidents became president?") or less frequently ("Which vice presidents were older than the president they served?"). The dimensions are partially correlated, in that frequently arising tasks will often be easier to anticipate. Also, very few tasks that are very difficult to anticipate will arise frequently. By limiting the domain (e.g., U.S. presidents), one can better anticipate the kinds of tasks or problems in that domain that people might be working on.

8.2.2 Supporting Technologies

Figure 8.2 depicts how different technologies may be used to support problem solving in different areas of this notional space. Some commercial applications attempt to support portions of this space, but in a very limited way. Ask Jeeves (www.ask.com) focuses on classifying the responses from previous searches. This requires the ability to match natural-language queries against categories of questions asked previously by users. Jeeves attempts to answer

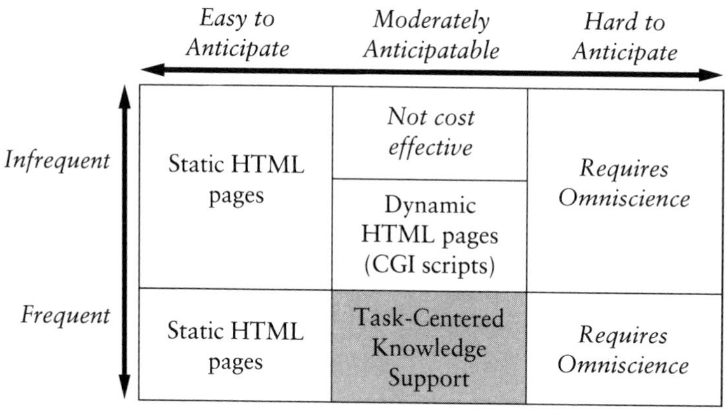

	Easy to Anticipate	Moderately Anticipatable	Hard to Anticipate
Infrequent	Static HTML pages	Not cost effective	Requires Omniscience
		Dynamic HTML pages (CGI scripts)	
Frequent	Static HTML pages	Task-Centered Knowledge Support	Requires Omniscience

Figure 8.2
Problem approaches.

very general questions in a virtually unrestricted domain. It is successful only to the extent that similar questions have been asked before. It has limited ability to leverage domain knowledge, as it doesn't restrict the domain of potential user queries at all.

The Ask Jeeves interface encourages the expressions of queries as questions, which may in some instances correspond to the goal of the user. For example, the question "How do you build a home?" may indicate some interest in the user's desire to build a home. In fact, the results from Jeeves on this question led to better results than the simple query "build home" on a standard search engine site. The Jeeves interface provides some additional insight into the task the user is performing over standard search engines. The query "build home" could also imply that the user is trying to build a home page. The Jeeves interface provides at least some hope of disambiguation between home building and home page building. Nevertheless, the interface doesn't elicit the task the user is performing, only the question she is asking. In some cases these coincide; in other cases they don't. In general, task information cannot be leveraged from a purely question-based interface.

Specific kinds of questions and tasks can easily be supported by standard HTML or dynamic HTML, especially if the tasks are sufficiently easy to anticipate that someone has already put together a Web page that can help solve it. Suppose a user is trying to determine who the 19th president of the United States was. This question is easy to anticipate, which in part explains why someone has built a Web page featuring the 19th president, Rutherford Birhard Hayes. On the other hand, if the user's task was to determine whether President Hayes was related to Pat Hayes (very difficult to anticipate), she would have a much more difficult time.

Our goal in describing this framework is primarily to emphasize that task-centered knowledge support focuses on the space of frequently asked questions not supported easily by standard static or dynamic HTML interfaces. In the middle area along the anticipatability dimension, we can define spaces that are domain specific and context rich. Limiting the domain of a search provides for simpler mechanism for expression of the underlying task and allows for leveraging of domain knowledge. Boeing's Service Engineering organization provides an example of a context-rich specific domain to illustrate the concept of task-centered knowledge support.

8.3   The Domain

In this section, we give an overview of the domain of aerospace customer support and describe a problem-solving scenario that we are supporting.[1]

8.3.1   Aerospace Customer Service

Airline operators require assistance from manufacturers in solving service-related problems with their airplanes. There is a constant stream of incoming requests that need to be handled. Solving these kinds of problems requires significant human and computational infrastructure. People handling these requests rely on dozens of different resources scattered throughout the company. In addition, they must also coordinate their work with a number of other people:

- Customers: people responsible for maintenance and safety of the aircraft they operate.

- Federal Aviation Administration (FAA) officials and representatives responsible for safety and certification of aircraft in the United States.

- Service representatives (SRs) typically located on site with the airline, functioning as first line of support to customers.

- Help desk workers responsible for coordinating activities and making sure that requests are given to the appropriate people for efficient and effective resolution.

- Engineers: specialists in aircraft engineering and maintenance, including the original designers.

A typical flow of events is as follows:

1. Airline customers experiencing some problem with their airplane contact an on-site SR, who can fix many general and routine problems directly.

Nevertheless, SRs are generalists and often don't have the knowledge or expertise to solve specialized engineering problems.

2. SRs enter problems requiring specialized knowledge into a help desk system that describes the specific problem. The requests for service are called help desk requests (HD requests, for short).

3. Each HD request is routed to the engineer whose expertise is most appropriate to the given request. The engineer coordinates her activities with other engineers as appropriate. The engineers also rely on a number of paper and online resources in responding to the HD request. Different resources are required for different kinds of problems.

4. Critical or safety-related changes that require FAA approval are passed on to the appropriate FAA representative.

8.3.2 Scenario

In this section, we outline a scenario for how a task-centered approach can support aerospace customer service. A key requirement is quick and reliable location of the appropriate engineering resources required to solve customers' problems. Different kinds of tasks require different resources, and even the same kind of task will require different resources depending on the nature of the underlying request.

Required resources for dealing with customers' problems include engineering databases, design documents, and drawings, as well as the appropriate individuals for bringing closure to a particular problem. A large amount of the expertise an engineer brings to the table is knowing the location of these resources. The kinds of resources needed are dictated by the specific task the engineer is working on. Tasks can be grouped by several factors, including aircraft model, engineering area (e.g., systems, structures, payloads), location (e.g., fuselage, empennage), or problem category (e.g., part substitution, FAA approval, animal infestation and drawing request). Example problem categories are shown in figure 8.3 as request types.

In our prototype, we support location of relevant resources through understanding of the underlying task and key concepts from the original request.

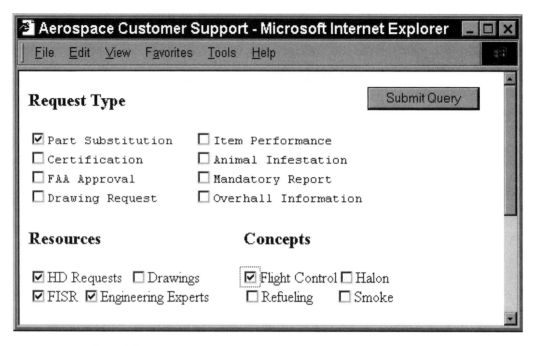

Figure 8.3
Query Web form.

For example, an engineer might be working on the task of part substitution in the area of flight control. This requires him to locate related HD requests, engineering experts, and fleet in service summary reports (FISRs).

To submit such a query, the user fills out a Web form (see figure 8.3). For the prototype, we have enumerated typical problem categories (request types) and four kinds of resources: HD requests, drawings, FISRs, and engineering experts. We have a small handful of concepts to select from for demonstration purposes. In the future, we expect that these would come from a controlled vocabulary of concepts.

The user begins by checking boxes that identify the category of the task (i.e., request type) he is working on. In some cases, multiple categories are appropriate. Each task category or combination has a set of associated resource types that are deemed relevant to that category. The system automatically identifies these through a set of predefined mappings. In the future, we could apply some form of online learning (e.g., relevance feedback) to improve resource selection.

In addition, the user identifies concepts central to the current task (or request) by checking boxes. A future enhancement would be to extract these concepts from the underlying HD request. For demonstration purposes, we used a fixed set of concepts that had to be identified by the user. The selected concepts act as a search filter, so that only relevant resources are returned. At this point, the user can press the SUBMIT QUERY button to locate the relevant resources.

In addition to these factors, the content of the incoming HD message often contains keywords that help identify the appropriate resources. We believe the combination of these factors and the underlying text of the message can be used to identify the resources relevant to the problem the engineer is solving.

8.4   Enabling Infrastructure

This is the main section of this chapter. Here we describe the details of our infrastructure and architecture for using semantic metadata to enable task-centered knowledge support. We start by presenting the main components of the architecture and we discuss some of the reasons for our choices. Section 8.4.2 gives full details of the information/knowledge repository, and section 8.4.3 describes how queries are handled. In the next section, we provide a complete, worked example.

8.4.1   Main Components

Figure 8.4 summarizes our prototype architecture for enabling task-centered knowledge support. The two central classes of functions provided by this architecture are

- *semantic metadata services*—representing, querying, and inferencing over metadata about diverse engineering resources (e.g., databases, documents, engineers).

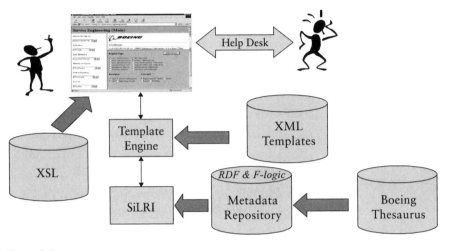

Figure 8.4
Prototype architecture.

- *user interaction*—task identification and presentation of links to appropriate resources.

8.4.1.1 Semantic Metadata Services

We chose Frame Logic (F-logic) (Kifer 1990) and the Resource Description Framework for representing facts, rules, and queries about the metadata describing key resources required to solve customer problems. We chose the Simple Logic-Based RDF Interpreter (SiLRI) developed at University of Karls-ruhe (Decker et al. 1998) for processing the queries. The RDF Model and Syntax Specification (Lassila and Swick 1999) defines a formal set-theoretic data model that can have several isomorphic representations. The SiLRI engine uses the RDF triples representation. The underlying technology behind SiLRI has been commercialized by Ontoprise (2001).

Because Boeing is such a large and diverse enterprise, language use among its employees tends to be specialized. This not only causes problems during oral communication but can lead to difficulties in querying for resources (e.g., databases) controlled by another group. To help reduce such problems, we chose to integrate a large aerospace thesaurus into our architecture (Clark et al. 2000). The Boeing Thesaurus was developed by the Boeing Technical Libraries for the purpose of classifying and retrieving documents. It has been under development for many years and consists of a vast network of approximately 37,000 concepts with approximately 100,000 links among them. This thesaurus has been enhanced and exploited in a knowledge-based search application for locating experts in a given subject area.

This demonstrated that an existing corpus of knowledge could be suitably enhanced and exploited in a context not originally anticipated, that is, searching for experts, rather than for documents. The thesaurus can be thought of as a conceptual vocabulary or "lightweight ontology." Current research at Boeing is focused on continuing to enhance the thesaurus's representational aspects. We continued to improve the thesaurus as required for a variety of other applications. In doing so, we were faced with the realization that people will resist imposition of a global vocabulary, and therefore ways must be developed to reap the advantages of a standard vocabulary while allowing individuals to continue to use their own terms locally. Terms and their associated relations in the thesaurus were automatically converted into RDF syntax for use by SiLRI.

8.4.1.2 User Interaction

To support interaction with the user, we chose to build a template engine that supports (1) collection of user inputs, (2) processing of those inputs, and (3) generating the content of the output to the user. User input parameters and RDF queries represented in F-logic specify how templates are to be instantiated and expanded by a template engine. The queries are embedded in the uninstantiated template and are sent to the SiLRI engine for evaluation, which may result in additional bound or partially bound, but still unevaluated, expressions. The query evaluation drives the template instantiation process, which continues until there are no unevaluated query expressions left in the template. The expanded template contains the content of the output to the user in XML format. Before it is presented to the user, it is first converted to HTML by the browser (Internet Explorer 5.0) using a predefined style sheet written in XSL (see figure 8.4).

8.4.1.3   Rationale

We chose RDF because it is a standard way to represent metadata on the Web. This was an important consideration in the Boeing environment, where central management and control over these resources doesn't exist. Many of the resources used by the customer support organization are not owned or controlled by them. Other mechanisms for representing metadata, including topic maps (TopicMaps 2001), didn't have the kinds of support tools required when we started the project. Since then, more tools have been developed to support topic maps. SiLRI provided a convenient mechanism for querying the underlying RDF and, as a bonus, supported representation of and inferencing over rules. This turned out to be an important part of our architecture.

We chose a template-driven approach to the user interface because of its generality and the ability it provided us to update the look and feel without programming. Originally, the templates contained HTML with embedded queries to the SiLRI engine. After experimenting with this approach for several weeks, we kept wanting to extend the template language to support sorting, filtering, and other common operations. We realized that XSL could support many of the operations we desired without our having to build them ourselves. At this point, we chose to use XML as our template language rather than HTML and to use the facility in Internet Explorer 5.0 to translate the XML into HTML using XSL.

8.4.2   Information/Knowledge Repository

Here we give the formal details of how the information described in the previous section is represented and used. Various kinds of information needs to be stored and/or referred to in the resource metadata, encoded in F-logic:

- Concepts—the Boeing thesaurus, converted to F-logic syntax.

- Resources—FISRs, HD requests, engineering experts.

- Rules—characterize important relationships and are used to specify queries.

8.4.2.1   Concepts

We have translated the Boeing Thesaurus into F-logic syntax. F-logic is a declarative language that mixes features of object-oriented and frame-based languages. It has a model-theoretic semantics and a sound and complete resolution-based proof theory. The main components of F-logic syntax are summarized below:

- F [S1 => A; S2 =>> B]

declares that

- F is a frame with two slots, S1 and S2.
- slot S1 has values of frame type A.
- slot S2 is multivalued and has values of frame type B.

- F1::F2

declares that F1 is a subtype of F2.

- I:F[S1 –> V; S2 –>> {V1, V2, ..., Vn}]

declares that

- I is an instance of frame type F.
- slot S1 of I has value V.
- multivalued slot S2 of I has values V1–Vn.

Note that double arrows (e.g., "=>" or "=>>") are used for defining the frames. Single arrows (e.g., "–>" or "–>>") are used for defining instances. Also, two right angle brackets in a row (e.g., "–>>" or "=>>") denotes a multivalued slot; otherwise a slot is single-valued.

Example 8.1   A concept from the thesaurus has four slots: name, related_to, broader_than, and narrower_than. These are standard for a thesaurus. The definition for a concept and a few examples are given below.

```
Concept::Object
[Name => String;
 related_to =>> Concept;
 broader_than =>> Concept;
 narrower_than =>> Concept].
```

```
halon:Concept
[name -> "halon";
 related_to ->> flight_control]

flight_control:Concept
[name -> "flight control";
 related_to ->> halon]
```

We also define a simple rule for indicating that concepts are near each other. F-logic rules are written as backward implications, just like Prolog rules:

- near(1, C1, C2) is true when C1 is "related_to" C2 or C1 is a broader or narrower term than C2:

```
FORALL C1,Y near(1, C1, C2) <-
    C1[related_to ->> C2]      or
    C1[broader_term ->> C2]    or
    C1[narrower_term ->> C2]
```

By creating rules of this sort, one can specify different degrees of relatedness, which can be exploited to provide greater flexibility to the user in locating resources.

8.4.2.2 Resources

Although it makes sense to refer to the F-logic code as metadata from the perspective of its role in characterizing resources, from the perspective of an F-logic user, such code is more likely to be thought of as a knowledge base. Hence, we shall refer to the F-logic KB, which is the metadata for the resource base.

Engineering Experts   We define a frame or class called Person that has three slots: a name, an employee ID, and a list of subjects the employee has expertise in. The "subjects" that fill the last slot must be of type Concept, another F-logic frame. The F-logic syntax defining the frame Person and two instances are given below.

```
Person::Object
[Name   => String;
 ID => Integer;
 SubjectsExpertIn =>> Concept].

person1:Person
[Name -> "Robert Jasper";
 ID -> "139988";
 SubjectsExpertIn ->> {refueling, flight_control, smoke}].

person2:Person
[Name -> "John Thompson";
 ID -> "42549";
 SubjectsExpertIn ->> {smoke, halon}].
```

For convenience in specifying queries, we define the following predicates (again, the style is very Prolog-like):

▪ has_expertise(P, C) is true when P is an instance of Person and the slot SubjectsExpertIn contains Concept C.

▪ has_expertise_related_to(P, C) is true when P is an instance of Person, and either P has_expertise in C, or there is another concept, C0, which is "near" to C (in the concept thesaurus), and P has_expertise in C0.

```
FORALL P,C has_expertise(P,C) <-
    P:Person[SubjectsExpertIn ->> C].
FORALL P,C has_expertise_related_to(P,C) <-
    has_expertise(P,C).
FORALL P,C has_expertise_related_to(P,C) <-
    (EXISTS C0 has_expertise(P,C0) and near(1,C0,C)).
```

Fleet Issues Summary Reports   We define a frame called FISR that has five attributes: a URL, a model number, a title, a list of references that pertain to this FISR, and a set of concepts that this FISR relates to. The last slot has the metadata tag that refers to the resource, which is used when searching for FISRs relevant to the task at hand. In our prototype, this tagging is done manually, but much of the information already exists in another form. Techniques such as wrapper induction (Ashish and Knoblock 1997), could also be used for this tagging.

We also define a separate frame for the references. This frame has four slots: a label, a date, a URL and a location, which indicates where the hard copy of the FISR is physically located. These two frames, with examples, are given below, in F-logic:

```
FISR::Object
[URL => String;
 Model => String;
 Title => String;
 References =>> Reference;
 Related_Concepts =>> Concept].
Reference :: Object
[RefLabel => String;
 RefDate => Date;
 RefURL => URL;
 RefLocation =>> String].

id_787_0066:FISR
[URL-> "yadayada.boeing.com/cgi?model=787& ...";
 Model -> "787";
 Title -> "Lateral Flight Control";
 References       ->> {id_787_8801, id_787_039A};
Related_Concepts->> flight_control].

id_787_8801:Reference
[RefLabel -> "787 8801";
 RefDate -> "14-JAN-88":String;
 RefLocation ->> {"Joe's Office", "Renton Library"};
 RefURL-> "yadayada.boeing.com/787_8801-fisr-ref.html"].
```

For convenience in specifying queries, we define the following predicates to determine which FISRs are related to a given concept:

- fisr_related_to(C, U, L, M) is true when there is a FISR related to Concept C, and U is the FISR's URL, L [abel] is the FISR's title, and M is the FISR's model. The relationship may be direct, or it may be via an intermediate concept, C0, as in the example with engineering experts.

- fisr_directly_related_to(C, U, L, M) is true when there is a FISR directly related to concept C and U is the FISR's URL, L [abel] is the FISR's title, and M is the FISR's model.

These predicates are given below as straightforward recursive definitions in F-logic:

```
FORALL C, U, L, M //for Concept, URL, Label, Model
fisr_related_to(C, U, L, M) <-
    fisr_directly_related_to(C, U, L, M).

FORALL C, U, L, M
fisr_related_to(C, U, L, M) <-
    (EXISTS C0 fisr_directly_related_to(C0, U, L, M) and
      near(1, C0, C) and
      (EXISTS F   F:FISR[URL -> U; Title -> L; Model ->
      M].

FORALL F, C, U, L, M
fisr_directly_related_to(C, U, L, M) <-
    F:FISR[Related_Concepts ->> C] and
    F:FISR[URL -> U; Title -> L; Model -> M].
```

HD Requests We define a frame, HD_Request, which has slots for URL, subject, task type, and related concepts. There is a predicate called hd_related_to that is exactly analogous to fisr_related_to. This predicate is summarized below (we include fewer details to avoid repetitiveness).

- hd_related_to(C, U, S, T) is true when there is a HD request related to Concept C and U is the HD's URL, S is the HD's subject, and T is the HD's task type. The relationship may be direct, or it may be via an intermediate concept, C0, as in the above examples.

```
HD_Request::Object
[URL => String;
 Subject => String;
 TaskType => String;
 Related_Concepts =>> Concept].
```

8.4.3 Handling Queries

An illustrated above, we have added metadata that explicitly relate resources to concepts. The concepts that the user specifies act like search keywords, except that we are employing concept-based search (Clark et al. 2000), which enables resources to be located that are tagged with concepts that do not exactly match any string that is input by the user. The metadata for the resources are stored as F-logic facts and rules and act as a database to be queried. In response to the user's request for information (enacted by pressing the SUBMIT QUERY button in figure 8.3), the system will generate an XML file containing all the relevant resources it identifies. This is then rendered via an XSL style sheet. Determining exactly which resources are related to the specified concepts requires querying the metadata. Furthermore, we require that the degree of relatedness be able to be variable and tailored to different users' needs. The question is: how can many different queries be issued from a single Web page, specifying different tasks and/or different concepts, such that a different set of resources, just the ones the user needs, will be produced?

To support this kind of response, tailored to the user's specific tasks, we require a more flexible and general mechanism for generating Web pages than is provided using standard CGI scripts alone. The key idea is to, in effect, add a template feature to the XML language. Viewed another way, we have designed an XML-based template language. By convention, these templates have an .xmlt file extension. These files are preprocessed by a Perl script that expands the templates and outputs an .xml file, which is rendered on the Web page using an XSL style sheet. This style sheet is the response to the user's query.

Templates contain standard XML mixed with variable references and queries written in F-logic. Note that we have *two entirely different kinds of queries*. The first is issued by the user by filling out the Web form and clicking the SUBMIT QUERY button. The other kind is a query to the metadata that is encoded using the template language and processed by the F-logic inference engine, SiLRI. The first kind is a query from the user's perspective, so we refer to queries of this type as *user queries*. The second kind is invisible to the user; we refer to queries of this type as *metadata queries*. Our architecture is general, so any language and query engine could be used to express and process the metadata queries. In our prototype, all metadata queries are expressed in F-logic and handled by SiLRI.

The .xmlt file is transformed into an .xml file through a process of instantiation and expansion that occurs on the server through CGI scripts written in Perl. There are two kinds of variables in the template, which differ according to when they get instantiated. The first kind gets instantiated when the user submits her query. We refer to these as *global variables,* because wherever they occur in the templates in the .xmlt file, they refer to the same thing and are instantiated to have the same value. They are bound in the usual fashion via CGI. The other variables are called *metadata variables*, because they refer to elements in the metadata and are instantiated during the process of answering metadata queries. They are local to an individual template; that is, different metadata variables can have the same name if they are in different templates in the same .xmlt file.

The raw .xmlt template file contains a number of global variables whose values are specified by the user when she fills out the Web form. In our prototype, these variables identify the category of task the user is working on, the kinds of resources she is interested in, and the concepts that the resources are related to (figure 8.4). When the user submits her query, an interim, partially instantiated template is created with all the global variables instantiated. If there are *no* metadata queries in the template, then this is the final result; no significant template language functionality would have been exercised. If there *are* metadata queries in the template, the partially instantiated template is the starting point for the expansion process. At this point, the template will still contain unbound metadata variables, local to individual templates. In order for these variables to be bound, they must also be embedded in a metadata query. The expansion engine delegates processing of the queries to SiLRI. With the queries answered, some of the metadata variables will now be bound. However, nesting is possible, so the resulting template may still contain unbound metadata variables and unevaluated metadata queries. Templates are expanded recursively until all metadata queries are executed and all free metadata variables are bound. (This process is illustrated with a worked example in the next section.) The final XML document is translated by the Internet Explorer browser into HTML via an XSL style sheet. (This step could have just as easily been accomplished via a server-based XSL engine such as Xalan [Apache Project 2001].)

We employ the F-logic language to enable tailoring of rules, which can be used to fine tune what is meant by "related-to." For example, one can easily specify degrees of relatedness based on how far away concepts are from one another in the thesaurus. A user can submit his queries for relevant resources using different degrees of "related to." This would have the effect of increasing the recall but decreasing the precision, or vice versa.

The power and flexibility of this approach derives from the fact that the Perl script queries the metadata to retrieve zero or more resources of each type. Each resource results in an instantiation of the template in XML.

8.5   Worked Example

The template language extends standard XML by adding three special tags (⟨GLOBAL-SUBST⟩, ⟨META-SUBST⟩, and ⟨HTML-TEMPLATE⟩) and a syntax for referring to template variables that will be bound to values as the template is expanded. Template variables are strings prefixed with the symbol "@" (e.g., "@Cnpt"). They always occur inside an ⟨HTML-TEMPLATE⟩; an "@" symbol occurring outside an ⟨HTML-TEMPLATE⟩ has no special significance and is treated as raw XML. Below is an example showing how these template variables are used.

```
<GLOBAL-SUBST>
<HTML-TEMPLATE>
<FISRS>
<META-SUBST QUERY="FORALL URL,Label,Model <-
selected("@show_fisrs") and
fisr_related_to(@Cnpt, URL, Label, Model).">
<HTML-TEMPLATE>
<FISR>
<URL><![CDATA[\/@URL]]></URL>
<Model>@Model</Model>
<Title>@Label</Title>
</FISR>
</HTML-TEMPLATE>
</META-SUBST>
</FISRS>

<HDS>
<META-SUBST QUERY="forall URL,Label <-
selected("@show_hds") and
EXISTS X hd_related_to(@Cnpt, URL, Label, X).">
<HTML-TEMPLATE>
<HD>
<URL><![CDATA[\/@URL]]></URL>
<Title>@Label</Title>
</HD>
</HTML-TEMPLATE>
</META-SUBST>
</HDS>
```

```
<EXPERTS>
<META-SUBST QUERY="FORALL N,Id <-
selected("@show_experts") and
EXISTS P has_expertise_related_to(P,@Cnpt) and
P[Name -> N; ID->Id].">
<HTML-TEMPLATE>
<EXPERT>
<Name>@N</Name>
<ID>@Id</ID>
</EXPERT>
</HTML-TEMPLATE>
</META-SUBST>
</EXPERTS>
</HTML-TEMPLATE>
</GLOBAL_SUBST>
```

The ⟨GLOBAL-SUBST⟩ and ⟨META-SUBST⟩ tags are for specifying the scope of substitutions for global variables and metadata variables, respectively. The ⟨HTML-TEMPLATE⟩ tag is used in conjunction with a specification of variable substitutions of the following form:

```
{[VarA=valA1,VarB=valB1,..., VarN=valN1],
[VarA=valA2,VarB=valB2,..., VarN=valN2],...}
```

In this case, there are two complete sets of variable substitutions. This would result in the ⟨HTML-TEMPLATE⟩ getting instantiated and included in the final .xml file twice, once for each set of substitutions. Multiple inclusions of instantiated templates is what we mean by "expansion." The use of an ⟨HTML-TEMPLATE⟩ immediately following the ⟨GLOBAL-SUBST⟩ tag is a special case, in that the query string passes only a single set of variable substitutions, so that template is instantiated only once. The server generates this substitution specification when the user presses the SUBMIT QUERY button. It is contained in the query string that's passed to the CGI script. The relevant part of the query string for our example is:

```
show_fisrs=T&show_hds=T&show_experts=T&Cnpt=flight_control
```

This is the substitution specification for the global variables. Performing this substitution results in the instantiation of the outermost ⟨HTML-TEMPLATE⟩, that is, the one that occurs between the ⟨GLOBAL_SUBST⟩ tags. The first three are boolean variables that are "T" if and only if the corresponding resource type box is checked (see figure 8.3).

The substitution specifications resulting from the ⟨META-SUBST⟩ tag are more interesting in that multiple instantiations of the ⟨HTML-TEMPLATE⟩ may result. In the example, we saw that there were four FISRs. This is because the F-logic query for related FISRs returned four sets of variable bindings as follows:

```
{[Url="http://...foo...", Model=797, Label="Refueling
Valves"]
  [Url="http://...bar...", Model=787, Label="Halon
  Concentration ... Barrier"],
  [Url="http://...baz...", Model=787, Label="Lateral
  Flight Control"],
  [Url="http://...gaz...", Model=787, Label="Warm Flight
  Deck Temperatures"]}.
```

This is the substitution specification that is used for the instantiation and expansion of the second ⟨HTML-TEMPLATE⟩. The ⟨FISRS⟩ and ⟨/FISRS⟩ tags are outside the ⟨HTML-TEMPLATE⟩ tags and contain no global variables, so they pass through to the output .xml file unchanged. The resulting .xml code for the FISRS is

```
<FISRS>
<FISR>
<URL><![CDATA[\/yadayada.boeing.com/cgi?model=
797&foo...]]></URL>
<Model>797</Model>
<Title>Refueling Valves</Title>
```

```
</FISR>
<FISR>

<URL><![CDATA[\/yadayada.boeing.com/cgi?model=
787&bar...]]></URL>
      <Model>787</Model>
      <Title>Halon Concentration for Smoke Barrier</Title>
      </FISR>
      <FISR>
      <URL><![CDATA[\/yadayada.boeing.com/cgi?model=
      787&baz...]]></URL>
      <Model>787</Model>
      <Title>Lateral Flight Control</Title>
      </FISR>
      <FISR>

<URL><![CDATA[\/yadayada.boeing.com/cgi?model=
787&gaz...]]]></URL>
      <Model>787</Model>
      <Title>Warm Flight Deck Temperatures</Title>
      </FISR>
      </FISRS>
```

The query to find related HD request fails, because there are none found in the F-logic database. It returns the null set—thus the next ⟨HTML-TEMPLATE⟩ results in no .xml code at all. Again, the ⟨HDS⟩ ⟨/HDS⟩ pass through to the output .xml file unchanged. The resulting .xml code for the HDs is just

```
<HDS>
</HDS>
```

Finally, the query to find related experts results in the single set of substitution bindings:

```
{ [Name="John Thompson", Id="42549] }.
```

Thus the ⟨HTML-TEMPLATE⟩ is instantiated exactly once. The resulting .xml code for the experts is

```
<EXPERTS>
<EXPERT>
<Name>John Thompson</Name>
<ID>42549</ID>
</EXPERT>
</EXPERTS>
```

The final step is to present the information to the user in a convenient format (see Figure 8.5). We used the XSL processor embedded in the Internet Explorer 5.0 browser.

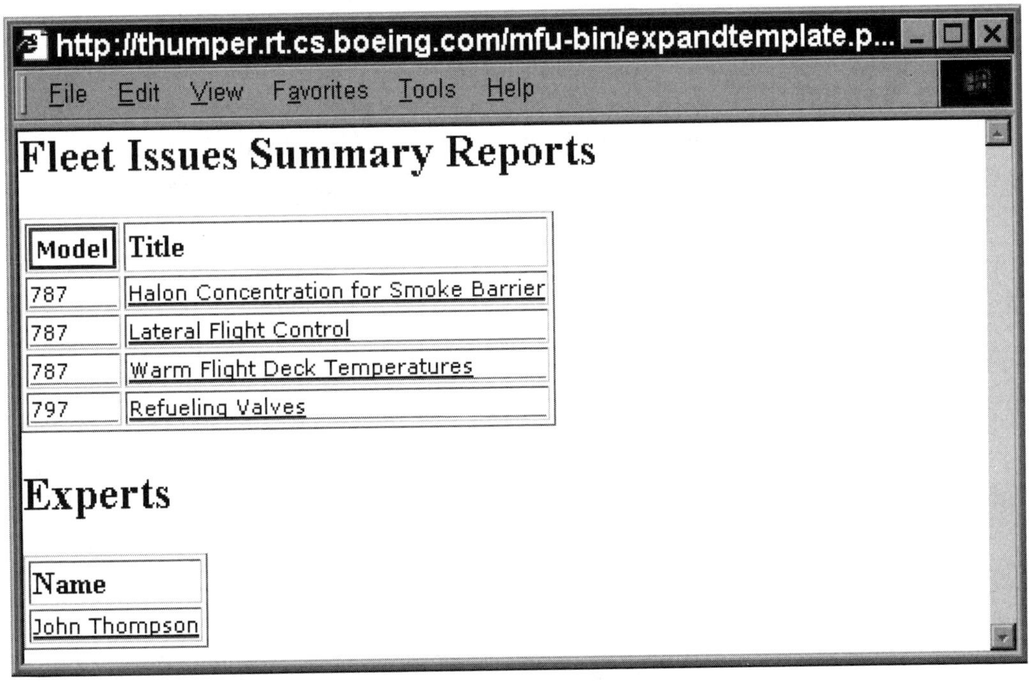

Figure 8.5
Sample output.

8.6   Conclusion

The Semantic Web opens up opportunities for fundamentally redefining our relationship with the Web by defining resources in such a way that they are not only human-sensible but also machine-sensible. Users are seldom just searching for documents on the Web but are often in the process of performing some larger task when they conduct Web searches. Current interfaces for Web search tools often don't provide any means for the user to communicate her intentions; therefore systems can't leverage task information in support of the user. Making Web resources machine-sensible will gradually shift the primary consumers of raw Web content from humans to agents that will play the role of information intermediaries. These agents will collect and integrate information based on the task users are currently performing.

Unless the Semantic Web community provides a means of capturing and exploiting task information, newly built semantics-based systems will likely be only moderately better at supporting users than current systems. Our modest prototype simply highlights the need for and promise of taking a task-centered approach to the Semantic Web.

Future research should focus on better mechanisms for identifying and characterizing user tasks in a way that can be exploited by semantics-based tools. We also believe there is potentially fruitful research to be conducted in mixing semantics-based technologies with existing information retrieval technologies, as it is doubtful that all Web resources will ever be fully characterized in a way that will eliminate the need for standard information retrieval techniques. In addition, there is significant opportunity for exploiting online machine learning techniques to improve performance of task-centered systems over time.

Note

1. The details presented in this description are of course fictional to protect Boeing's propriety information. Even with the fictionalized details, however, the description serves the purpose of illustrating our technology.

References

Apache Project. 2001. Xalan. Available from http://xml.apache.org/xalan/.

Ashish, N., and C. Knoblock. 1997. Semi-Automatic Wrapper Generation for Internet Information Sources. In *Proceedings of the Second IFCIS Conference on Cooperative Information Systems (CoopIS), Charleston, South Carolina* (pp. 160–169). Los Alamitos, CA.: IEEE-CS.

Clark, P., J. Thompson, H. Holmback, and L. Duncan. 2000. Exploiting a Thesaurus-Based Semantic Net for Knowledge-Based Search. In *Proceedings of the Seventeenth National Conference on Artificial Intelligence and Twelfth Conference on Innovative Applications of AI (AAAI, IAAI-2000), Austin, Texas, July 30–August 3, 2000* (pp. 988–995). Menlo Park, CA/Cambridge, MA: AAAI/MIT Press.

DARPA Agent Markup Language (DAML). 2001. Available from http://www.daml.org/.

Decker, S., D. Brickley, J. Saarela, and J. Angele. 1998. A Query Service for RDF. The Query Languages Workshop, 1998. Available from http://www.w3.org/TandS/QL/QL98/pp/queryservice.html.

Dumais, S. 1999. Inductive Learning and Representation for Text Categorization. Lecture presented at University of Washington. Available from http://murl.microsoft.com/LectureDetails.asp?177.

Internet Public Library (IPL). 2001. Available from http://www.ipl.org/ref/POTUS/rbhayes.html.

Kifer, M., G. Lausen, and J. Wu. 1990. Logical Foundations of Object-Oriented and Frame-Based Languages. *Journal of the ACM* 42(4):741–843.

Lassila, O., and R. Swick. 1999. The Resource Description Framework (RDF) Model and Syntax (recommendation). World Wide Web Consortium. Available from http://www.w3.org/TR/PR-rdf-syntax/.

Ontroprise. 2001. Available from http://www.ontoprise.de/.

Smith, R. 2001. What's Required in Knowledge Technologies: A Practical View. In *Proceedings of Knowledge Technologies 2001*. Available from http://www.gca.org/attend/2001_conferences/kt_2001/default.htm.

TopicMaps. 2000. Available from http://www.topicmaps.org/.

9 Knowledge Mobility: Semantics for the Web as a White Knight for Knowledge-Based Systems

Yolanda Gil

No man is an island
Entire of itself.
Every man is a piece of the continent....
—John Donne (1572–1631)

9.1 Introduction

One of the challenges for knowledge-based systems is interoperation with other software, intelligent or not. In recent years, our research group has participated in various integration efforts in which interoperation was supported through translation techniques, mostly at the syntactic level and more recently through ontology-based approaches. In this chapter, I argue that the interoperation challenge will not be met with current approaches, since they entail trapping knowledge into formal representations that are seldom shareable and often hard to translate, seriously impairing their mobility. I propose an approach to develop knowledge bases that captures at different levels of formality and specificity how each piece of knowledge in a system was derived from original sources, which are often Web sources. If a knowledge base contains a trace of information about how each piece of knowledge was defined, it will be possible to develop interoperation tools that take advantage of this information. The contents of knowledge bases will then be more mobile and no longer be confined within a formalism. The

Semantic Web will provide an ideal framework for developing knowledge bases in this fashion. We are investigating these issues in the context of TRELLIS,[1] an interactive tool for eliciting from users the rationale for the choices and decisions they make as they analyze information that may be complementary or contradictory. Starting from raw information sources, most of them originating on the Web, users are able to specify connections between selected portions of those sources. These connections are initially very high level and informal, and our ultimate goal is to develop a system that will help users to formalize them further.

9.2   The Need for Knowledge Mobility

This section argues the need for knowledge mobility from two viewpoints. First, knowledge-based systems need to be built to facilitate interoperability, and thus the knowledge they contain needs to be more accessible to external systems. Second, our knowledge bases capture knowledge in such a way that it is very hard to extract or translate what they contain.

9.2.1   No Knowledge Base Is an Island

Knowledge-based systems are no longer built to function in isolation. Every application that we have built with the EXPECT architecture (Blythe et al. 2001; Kim and Gil 2000; Gil and Tallis 1997; Gil and Melz 1996) in recent years has been integrated within a larger end-to-end system in order to provide the overall functionality required. This section describes several integration efforts that illustrate important challenges in terms of knowledge mobility:

- *Significant differences in representation languages.* We have found on several occasions that different systems use representations and languages that adequately support certain functionality or problem-solving capabilities. Requiring that all the systems in the integration adopt the same representation may be an option in some cases, but many times doing this may be technically challenging or simply unfeasible in practice. An alternative approach that ends up being more acceptable is to allow each problem solver to use different languages and representations and then have ways of mapping back and forth between the languages and representations.

- *Discrepancies in modeling styles.* Even when different knowledge bases are developed in similarly expressive languages, different knowledge engineers practice different modeling styles and approaches. Translators between different languages help import knowledge bases written by different developers, but they only translate one syntactic expression into another and do not address deeper differences in representational styles. The rationale for modeling the original knowledge as a certain suite of expressions is never captured in the knowledge base.

- *Maintaining consistency among related pieces of knowledge.* A single domain description may be modeled piecemeal in separate parts of a knowledge base to reflect different views or functions of the description. The individual pieces may not be explicitly related in the knowledge base, especially when different pieces are used only by different components of the overall integration. In general, very few of the many and varied relations between individual pieces of knowledge are captured in the resulting knowledge bases.

9.2.1.1 Plan Generation and Evaluation

Figure 9.1 shows the architecture of a knowledge-based system for work-arounds analysis that we developed for the DARPA High Performance Knowledge Bases (HPKB) Battlespace Challenge Problem (Cohen et al. 1999). This system estimates the delay caused to enemy forces when an obstacle is targeted (e.g., a bridge is destroyed or a road is mined) by reasoning about how they could bypass, breach, or reduce the obstacle in order to continue movement (e.g., by repairing a damaged bridge or installing a temporary one, fording a river, removing mines, choosing an alternative route). Several general ontologies relevant to battlespace (e.g., military units, vehicles), anchored on the HPKB upper ontology, were used and augmented with

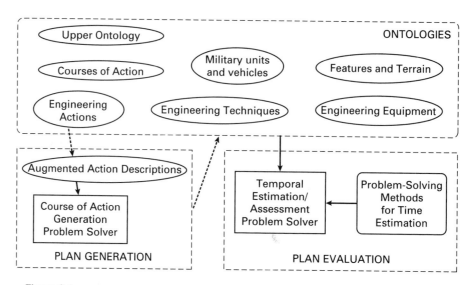

Figure 9.1
Knowledge-based system for plan generation and evaluation.

ontologies needed to reason about work-arounds (e.g., engineering equipment). These ontologies were represented in LOOM, a knowledge representation and reasoning system based on description logic (MacGregor 1991).
The system also includes two main problem solvers. A Course of Action
Generation problem solver creates several alternative solutions to the problem. Each solution lists several engineering actions for that particular workaround (e.g., deslope the banks of the river, then install a temporary bridge),
includes information about the resources used (e.g., what kind of earth-
moving equipment or bridge is used), and states temporal constraints among
the individual actions to indicate which can be executed in parallel. This
problem solver was developed using a state-of-the-art planner (Veloso et al.
1995). A Temporal Estimation/Assessment problem solver, developed in
EXPECT, evaluates each of the alternatives and selects one as the most likely
choice for an enemy workaround. It used the information about engineering
equipment and techniques included in the ontologies as well as several
dozen problem-solving methods to estimate how long it would take to carry

out a given workaround plan generated by the Course of Action Generation problem solver. This system was the only one among those submitted in response to this DARPA challenge problem to attempt full coverage and demonstrated the best performance at this task of all the entries.

One of the challenges for integration illustrated by this system is differences in representation. We found a huge gap between the representations used in the state-of-the-art knowledge representation and reasoning systems and those of a special-purpose reasoner, in our case a state-of-the-art plan generation system. The ontology of engineering actions shown in figure 9.1 was sufficient to support the temporal estimation problem solver, but it needed to be significantly augmented by knowledge engineers to develop the action descriptions required by the planner. These descriptions could not be represented declaratively in the ontology and thus had to be separately developed and maintained. Conversely, the planner generated very detailed plans that included many causal and temporal links among the actions, as well as steps and bindings that were helpful for plan generation but had no counterpart in an engineering plan. Thus, only portions of the final plan were incorporated into the knowledge base. It is important to notice that the issue was not a difference in content, but in the expressivity of the language regarding planning-specific knowledge. Although it may be possible (though certainly nontrivial) to coerce the planner's representations into the ontology, it is not clear that the ontology is a superior representation for that kind of knowledge.

Another problem was maintaining consistency in the knowledge base. We needed to keep three different parts of the knowledge base closely aligned: the ontology of engineering actions, the ontology of engineering techniques, the methods for time estimation, and the planner's augmented engineering actions. Since each of these ontologies required different expertise, different knowledge engineers were resposible for each of them. The EXPECT knowledge acquisition tools (Kim and Gil 1999) were very useful in pointing out inconsistencies between the methods and some of the ontologies, but the planner's actions were not accessible to EXPECT. Consistency across the different parts of the knowledge base therefore had to be maintained largely by hand. Some of the performance problems encountered during the evaluation of this system were traced to these kinds of inconsistencies.

9.2.1.2 Mixed-Initiative Plan Generation

Another active area of research within our project is mixed-initiative tools to help users create strategic plans, in particular in air campaign planning. In order to plan what air operations will be conducted in a campaign, military planners use a strategies-to-task methodology in which low-level tasks are derived from higher-level national and campaign goals. For example, a campaign objective like attaining air superiority results in an operational subobjective of suppressing enemy air sorties, which in turn creates an operational task of damaging key air base support facilities. Ultimately, these objectives are turned into missions stating which specific aircraft, crews, and airfields will be used to accomplish the lower-level tasks. At the higher, strategic levels of planning, users prefer to maintain control of the planning process and specify the objectives themselves, leaving automatic plan generation to the lower levels of the planning process. A series of plan editors were built to allow a user to define objectives and decompose them into subobjectives, possibly invoking automated plan generation tools to flesh out the plan at the lower levels. Because the plan creation process is mostly manual (at least at the higher levels), it is prone to error. This is aggravated by the size of the plans (several hundreds of interdependent objectives and tasks) and by the number of different people involved in a plan's creation. In order to help users detect potential problems as early as possible in the planning process, we developed INSPECT, a knowledge-based system built with EXPECT that analyzes a manually created air campaign plan and checks for commonly occurring plan flaws, including incompleteness, problems with plan structure, and unfeasibility due to lack of resources. For example, INSPECT would point out that if one of the objectives in the plan was to gain air superiority over a certain area, then there was a requirement for special facilities for storing JPTS fuel that had not been taken into account. Without INSPECT, this problem might have been found only when a logis-

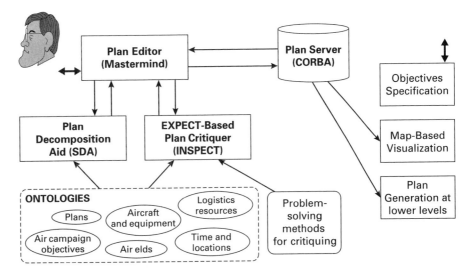

Figure 9.2
Integration framework for a plan critiquer.

tics expert checked the plan, a day or more after the execution of the overall plan was started. INSPECT reasoned about the kinds of objectives in the plan and noticed that gaining air superiority requires providing reconnaissance missions, which are typically flown in stealth aircraft that need specific kinds of fuel that must stored in special facilities. INSPECT was very well received by users, since it always found unintentional errors in the plans created by INSPECT's very own designers.

INSPECT was integrated in several architectures of very different natures. Figure 9.2 shows an integration of INSPECT with a few knowledge-based tools within a preexisting software architecture that was CORBA-based. The existing architecture included a plan server that contained not only air campaign plans but also those for land and maritime activities in joint operations. The plan server was not amenable to any major changes, so many of the plan details and constraints that were used by the knowledge-based tools never made it there. Figure 9.2 also shows the different ontologies in

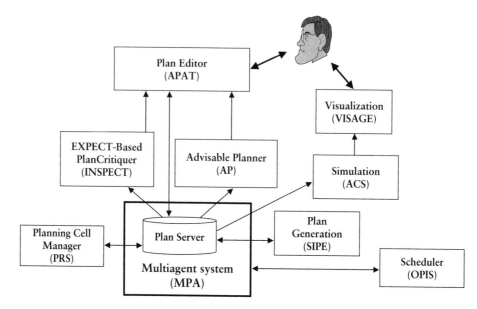

Figure 9.3

Integrating a plan critiquer into a multiagent system.

INSPECT's knowledge base, whose integration and development is described elsewhere (Valente et al. 1999).

Figure 9.3 shows another integration, this time with several other planning aids within a multiagent planning architecture. This integration is another illustration of a representational mismatch among different systems. The plan server in this architecture contained rich representations of plans regarding their hierarchical decomposition, causal and temporal dependencies, and overall planning process management. It lacked, however, rich representations of objectives that were needed by the plan editor and by INSPECT in order to analyze the requirements of each objective, and as a result these representations were not incorporated in the plan server and were not available to any other tool. We suspect that other modules found similar discrepancies between their particular representation formalisms and the plan server.

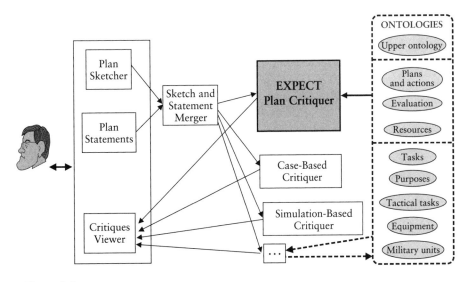

Figure 9.4
Critiquing courses of action.

9.2.1.3 Critiquing Courses of Action

Another important integration effort was to develop an end-to-end system, depicted in figure 9.4, to help users develop military courses of action. Users input a sketch on a map to specify the activities of each force and a statement of the objectives of the course of action. Several critiquers were developed by different groups to analyze different aspects of each course of action in order to give users feedback about possible problems in their design. We developed a critiquer with EXPECT to check for problems related to plan structure and use of resources. The other critiquers had complementary capabilities, since each of them addressed different kinds of critiques.

The application-specific ontologies used by our system were developed by other groups involved in this effort. Importing these ontologies into our knowledge base was a significant effort, as it involved transforming the input course of action into a format consistent with our representation.

Simpler translation issues arose in translating original ontologies in KIF into LOOM, although sometimes mapping different names was necessary (e.g., to map "TranslationLocationChange" into "Move"). More complex translations were required when there were deeper representational mismatches. At times, some of the decomposition structure of the course of action was implicit in the order of the statements, and we had to reconstruct that structure so that it would be available in our knowledge base. We used the OntoMorph rewrite engine to support these more complex mappings, which are described in more detail in Chalupsky 2000. In essence, supporting this integration was challenging even though the languages used by the different systems were comparable in terms of their expressivity. The differences in modeling approaches and representations were quite significant and required a complex translation system like OntoMorph.

9.2.1.4   *Translation among Intelligent Agents*

As part of the initial stages of a new project to develop ontology-based translation services for multiagent systems, we conducted a study of an existing multiagent system (not developed by us) to determine the requirements of such a translation service (Gil 2000). This multiagent system was developed to support noncombatant evacuation operations and was used to organize groups of helicopters to take people out of a dangerous area and to a safe place. The agents participating in the system included a suite of interface agents that interact with users to get the initial helicopter team composition and critical locations as well as unexpected threats to the mission (e.g., explosions), a route planner, a threat (SAM site) finder, and helicopter agents that can work in teams in a simulated environment. All of these agents were initially developed in radically different contexts and originally did not even share the application domain.

In a typical run, a few thousand messages are exchanged among the agents. We analyzed the content of messages that are representative of the communications regarding significant events and activities during the mission. Our findings included the following:

- Syntactic translators are relatively easy to build and are often readily available for many formats and languages. Yet in the years ahead we will see large communities of heterogeneous agents in which pairwise translations will become impractical. Each agent will have to advertise its capabilities and requirements in one (or just a few) formats and rely on translators and mediators to map those requirements into those of other agents. In the particular system under study, syntactic translations were often required, even though the developers often agreed to message formats that would minimize these needs. Even when the same kind of information was transmitted, different formats were used. For example, the latitude-longitude coordinates sometimes used the convention of an "X" and "Y" label; in other cases the coordinates were preceded by "-lat" and "-long" (when the critical locations are given to helicopters by the interface agents) or just ordered within parentheses (the format used by the threat finder to send threat sites to the helicopter agents). A complex case of syntactic mapping was required because the threat finder takes queries in SQL format.

■ Mismatches across representations were numerous and often due to modeling with different granularities and levels of abstraction. For example, the route generated by the route planner needed to be transformed to a coarser-grained route in order to be useful to the helicopter agents. The route planner sends a route composed of points that are 9 meters apart. The helicopters are tasked one route segment at a time, and when a helicopter is given a route that is of a small size (like 9 meters) it will say that the route is achieved without even taking off. Details must often be dropped from a plan when planning agents exchange plans. This may involve dropping steps or dropping parts of steps or may require a completely different plan altogether. Another example of the need for such transformations is that the helicopters consider routes to be composed of point-to-point segments, and the threat finder needed to be given a rectangular area to initiate its search. The route segment was made into the diagonal of the rectangular area, and as a result, threats were returned that were in the area but not very close to the route itself. Similarly, the interface agents specified helicopter landing zones as areas, whereas the helicopter agents take only a point as landing zone.

▪ Mapping among different representations may be complex, and invocations of third-party agents may be necessary. The route planner and the threat finder use a latitude-longitude coordinate system, the helicopters use an "x,y,cell" format, and the interface agents use UTM coordinates. Although it is possible to build ontology-based translators to mediate these communications, it may be more practical to use the ontologies simply to detect mismatches and then invoke a third party to do the conversion required to remedy them, since many such conversion systems are already available. Other cases in which invocation of other agents would be useful arise when an agent can fulfill a request but needs information that the requesting agent may not have. For example, the route planner require a map URL, the interface agents require a range around a location, and so on.

This particular multiagent system illustrates the challenges in supporting interoperation among intelligent systems, even on a relative small scale and in relatively small numbers of agents. It would not be simple to replace a subset of the agents involved with other agents of equivalent functionality, which could probably not be done without some additional changes and adaptations in the original remaining agents.

9.2.1.5 Summary

Current efforts in the knowledge-based systems community aim to support interoperability through shared ontologies and diverse translation tools. Drawing from past experiences within our own research project, this section illustrates several points:

▪ Shared ontologies do not address all integration issues. Content can be agreed upon, but representational needs are determined by the functionality required of the individual problem solvers and components within the system.

▪ Maintaining consistency in the knowledge used by several components is a great challenge. Some components may have some consistency-checking facilities, but that is often not the case with all the components in the overall system.

▪ Differences in modeling methodologies make translation an arbitrarily complex task. Syntactic translation and mappings are adequate only when such differences are minor.

To paraphrase John Donne, no knowledge-based system is an island. There is an increasing demand to have individually developed intelligent systems become part of larger end-to-end applications, and current paths to integration are not able to support interoperability appropriately to respond to this demand.

9.2.2   Educating Knowledge Bases

Large knowledge bases contain a wealth of information, and yet browsing through them often leaves one with an uneasy feeling that one has to take the developer's word for why certain things are represented in certain ways, why other things are not represented at all, and where one might find a piece of related information that one knows is related under some context. Although the languages that we use are quite expressive, they still *force knowledge into a straightjacket*: whatever fits the language will be represented, and anything else will be left out. Many other things are also left out, but for other reasons, such as available time and resources or perhaps lack of detailed understanding of some aspects of the knowledge being specified.

Furthermore, *knowledge ends up represented piecemeal*, compartmentalized in whatever expressions the modeling language supports. Many of the connections between different pieces of knowledge are never stated, nor can they be derived by the system given what it knows. We see no value in representing redundant information or alternative ways to deduce the same facts: if the system can derive something in one way, that may be more than sufficient.

Knowledge base developers may consult many sources presenting contradictory or complementary information, analyze the different implications of each alternative belief, and decide what and how to model the knowledge. In essence, developers often capture in the knowledge base only their final beliefs about some body of knowledge. *The rationale for modeling the*

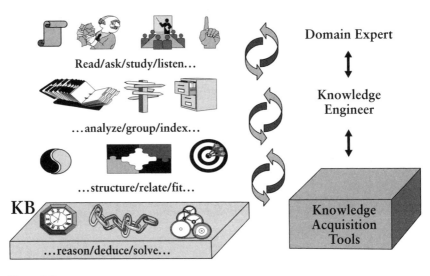

Figure 9.5
How knowledge bases are built today.

knowledge the way it appears in the knowledge base is not captured declaratively. Only consistent and complete information is captured. No indication of inconsistent but possible statements is added to the knowledge base.

As Minsky (1970) argues it: "There is a real conflict between the logician's goal and the educator's. The logician wants to minimize the variety of ideas, and does not mind a long thin path. The educator (rightly) wants to make the paths short and does not mind—in fact, prefers—connections to many other ideas." Knowledge base developers seem to prefer the role of logicians to seeing themselves as educators of intelligent systems.

Figure 9.5 illustrates the limited kinds of knowledge that are captured in final knowledge bases produced as described above. Developers (at least nonexperts) start by consulting manuals and tutorial material, asking questions, and requesting clarifications. Their main task is to analyze different information sources, grouping information, indexing related definitions and terms, and gathering as much raw material as possible in order to understand what needs to be represented and how. Next, they organize the information in semiformal ways by structuring it in tables and itemized lists and detecting opposite and complementary descriptions. Finally, they build the knowledge base itself by turning the refined results of this analysis into formal expressions that fit into the particular knowledge representation language used. Whatever documentation ends up in the knowledge base will be the only trace left of all the design and analysis process that was done to create it. None of the documentation is captured in declarative languages. The rationale of the knowledge base design is lost: the original sources, the analysis and structuring of the knowledge therein, and the trade-offs that were considering before deciding on the final formalization. As a result:

- It is hard to extend existing knowledge bases. When the knowledge base needs to be extended or updated, the rationale for their design is absent and needs to be at least partially reconstructed. The sources from which the knowledge base was constructed are no longer readily available and may need to be accessed.

- It is hard to reuse knowledge contained in knowledge bases. Although entire knowledge bases can be reused and incorporated into new systems, it is harder to extract only the portions of them that are relevant and appropriate in the new application. Parts of the knowledge base may be too inaccurate for the new task or may need to be modeled in a different way to take into account relevant aspects of the new application.

In summary, knowledge has a very modest degree of mobility once it is incorporated into existing systems. Some researchers are creating shared upper ontologies that can serve as a common substrate for the more detailed knowledge in specific knowledge bases, thus facilitating interoperation and reuse. Some have argued that the brittleness in our knowledge bases can be addressed by providing commonsense and other background knowledge to these systems. These approaches may be part of the solution, but they will not address some of the issues brought up here. Current intelligent systems are hard to integrate, maintain, and understand because their *knowledge bases have not been truly educated on the topics they are supposed to know about.*

9.3   A New Generation of Knowledge Bases: Resilient Hyper–Knowledge Bases

In order to empower intelligent systems, we believe we need to allow them to have access to the roots and rationale of the knowledge they contain. Furthermore, knowledge bases should not contain just a body of formalized expressions; rather, we should extend our view of knowledge bases to include a variety of formats and representations as well as alternative renderings of the same (or related) knowledge. They should include as many connections as possible, as stated in the original sources and as they result from the analysis of the knowledge base developer. This approach would create a new generation of knowledge bases, Resilient Hyper–Knowledge Bases (RHKBs), that will be more adaptable to change and reuse and will be more laden with connections and hyperlinks.

Figure 9.6 depicts a RHKB in contrast with the current approaches illustrated in figure 9.5. Originally, the development of an RHKB starts with

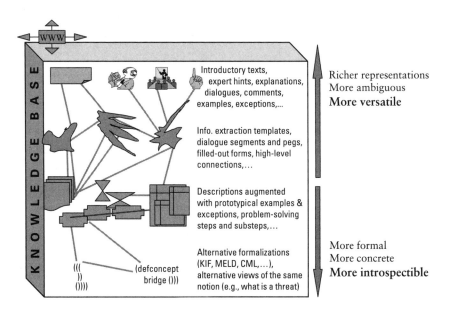

Figure 9.6
Resilient Hyper–Knowledge Base (RHKB).

documentation, examples, dialogues (perhaps with experts), detailed explanations of special cases, notes on exceptions, hints and comments on specific topics, and the like. From these sources, the developer extracts templates, relevant dialogue segments, itemized lists and tables to organize information, and so on, maintaining in all cases a trail of connections to the original sources. The developer can also indicate some connections between different portions of the original sources. It is our experience that many of the original sources either exist or are converted into resources on the Web, and as a result the developer can exploit the hyperlinks and connections that already exist in these original sources. As the developer continues this analysis, additional sources may be sought and incorporated at the higher levels, further enriching the grounding of the final RHKB that is being developed.

Next, the developer can identify descriptions and associate with them prototypical examples as well as exceptions, pieces of problem-solving knowledge in terms of steps and substeps, tables of parameters and values, and the like. These new distillations will continue to be connected to any other pieces in the knowledge base that they were derived from. The developer can also mark alternative views on the same knowledge, indicate contradictory statements by different sources, and dismiss some pieces of knowledge that may not seem useful for current purposes.

Finally, the developer can turn the more structured components into formalized expressions in one or more languages and formalisms. Contradictory statements can be formalized and connected and marked as contradictory for someone to pick and choose as she incorporates the knowledge into a reasoning engine. During this process, the developer can annotate the reasons for making certain decisions regarding which knowledge to model and how to model it.

I have described here the process of RHKB development to show the incremental nature of the analysis needed for such development, but there may be as many levels of refinement as the nature of the knowledge and the final system may require.

Note that in the higher levels of refinement, the representations may be richer and more versatile, but at the same time more ambiguous. In some sense, plain human language (i.e., text) may be the most mobile vehicle for stating knowledge. The many users of the World Wide Web use the same pages for a variety of purposes and tasks, the ultimate signature of true knowledge reuse. At the lowest levels of refinement, the representations are more formal, more concrete, and also more introspectible, lending themselves more to automated analysis and reasoning.

There are a number of benefits to the approach outlined above:

- *Knowledge can be extended more easily.* The formalized, final expressions in the RHKB may not necessarily contain every detail in every knowledge source, but if the need arises, the system is better positioned than a typical knowledge base to digest additional knowledge. Such additional knowledge could be handled in two ways: the developer could incorporate the additional knowledge, or perhaps the system could itself use some automated tools to extract the knowledge (since it has access to the sources and how they were originally processed).

- *Knowledge can be reused and translated at any level.* Another system can be built from the RHKB by reusing only the higher levels of the design process and incorporating other sources to create different final formalized expressions. Other developers can tap into any intermediate results of the analysis and do not have to start from scratch. Knowledge does not have to be reused only at the lowest level, as it is today.

- *Knowledge can be integrated and translated at any level to facilitate interoperability.* Translators can be built to transform and map knowledge at higher levels. The rationale and meaning of different pieces of knowledge can be available to support translation and interoperation.

- *Intelligent systems will be able to provide better explanations.* We find that many users are reluctant to accept solutions presented by systems and ask for explanations not of how the system derived an answer automatically, but instead of why the system starts out with a certain fact or belief. When users are shown the reasons for certain assumptions and the fact that certain sources were consulted to make those assumptions, they are reassured of the competence of the system to provide legitimate answers. Capturing this trail of sources within the knowledge base will enable the system to generate these kinds of justifications and explanations for the user.

▪ *Content providers will not need to be knowledge engineers.* Although only those trained in the art of designing, modeling, and writing formal expressions can build the more refined portions of RHKBs, anyone can contribute to the higher levels. Many people in diverse disciplines acquire analytical skills sufficient to organize and digest knowledge sources.

Many existing tools for text extraction (e.g., for extracting significant event descriptions from news articles) and discourse analysis (e.g., to segment text into meaningful portions) could be used to support these earlier steps of the analysis. Existing approaches to derive interdependencies among pieces of knowledge may be used to help users create connections among diverse pieces of knowledge. Other tools can be developed to support transformations at the lower levels (e.g., to turn tables into instances and role values). The overhead that may be incurred in creating knowledge bases using this approach is, in our view, not as significant as the analysis efforts that developers undertake. It may even save developers time if others can look up the rationale trail for the portion of the knowledge base they are developing instead of asking the developers detailed questions directly.

The approach presented here has many relations to software engineering methodologies for capturing the rationale for software development and to higher-level languages and frameworks for developing knowledge-based systems. Unfortunately, these methodologies are not common practice among developers of knowledge bases for lack of adequate tools to support developers in this process. Moreover, these methodologies are aimed at software and knowledge engineers and are not very accessible to other potential knowledge base developers, such as end users and/or domain experts.

The Semantic Web will provide an ideal substrate for grounding knowledge bases in their original knowledge sources and for containing progressively defined pieces of knowledge and the connections among them. More and more every day, knowledge originates and ends in the Web, and we find ourselves extracting knowledge from the Web, processing it inside of a knowledge base, then putting the results back on the Web. It only makes sense to integrate knowledge bases (their content and their reasoning) more closely with the Web.

9.4   TRELLIS: Building Resilient Hyper–Knowledge Bases

The TRELLIS project is our first step toward enabling the creation of RHKBs. In previous work within the EXPECT project, we have investigated several approaches to developing knowledge acquisition tools to enable end users to extend a knowledge base, including analysis of interdependency models and scripts for planing acquisition dialogue, exploiting problem-solving methods and other background knowledge, and creating English-based structured editors (Blythe et al. 2001; Kim and Gil 2000; Gil and Tallis 1997; Swartout and Gil 1995). EXPECT helps users enter knowledge at the lower levels of an RHKB and has been shown to be quite effective in several user evaluations with subjects not familiar with programming and formal languages. TRELLIS acquires more informal knowledge and is aimed to support the higher levels of development of RHKBs.

The key innovative ideas behind our approach are as follows:

▪ *Supporting users in creating knowledge fragments from original sources as well as from other fragments.* The key in such creation is to capture how a developer progressively generates new knowledge that results in value added to the original raw information sources. Our goal is to support users in highlighting key salient information from large reports and documents, in adding new knowledge fragments based on their analysis and integration of existing information, and finally in creating semiformal fragments.

▪ *Capturing and exploiting semantic interrelationships among information items.* TRELLIS will (1) facilitate semantic markup of relationships between different pieces of knowledge, (2) exploit semantic markups in given problem-solving contexts, and (3) suggest additional relationships based on those already specified by the user. Users will be encouraged to add and rewarded for adding valuable annotations over raw information sources, since the more annotations they add the more help the system can provide in their work. When the user chooses to do little or no annotation, the system will provide weaker support (based on default heuristics and strategies) but will still help the user as much as possible.

▪ *Extensible semantic markup of information items and their relationships.* Users will be able to draw from a core semantic markup language that will contain a basic domain-independent vocabulary to formulate annotations. They will also be able to extend this core language with additional terminology useful in their particular domain. Using this language, users will be able to annotate not only the information items themselves, but also the relationships among them, which will enable them to qualify and describe interdependencies among different information sources and how they relate to a new conclusion or assessment added by the developer. In essence, links between the information items will be first-class citizens in the knowledge base.

Figure 9.7 shows an overview of the architecture of TRELLIS. A user typically starts searching the Web for a certain document or indicating a pointer

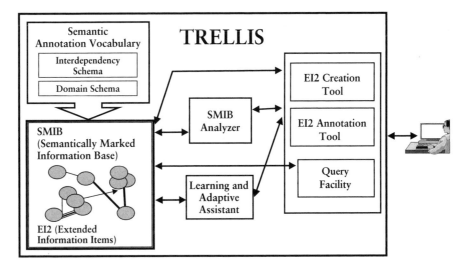

Figure 9.7
Overview of TRELLIS architecture.

to a specific Web resource that contains useful information. Each source is considered an information item. Information items may include raw information sources (an image, a text document, a video, etc.) as well as products of previous analysis (by the user or by other users). All the information items are in some sense the knowledge base that TRELLIS operates on, and we refer to this knowledge base as the Semantically Marked Information Base (SMIB). We refer to an information item as an EI2 (Extended Information Items).

Users extend the SMIB using two tools: the Annotation tool and the Creation tool. They can use the EI2 Annotation tool to add semantic annotations to an EI2 to describe its contents and to relate them to other EI2s. For example, an EI2 may be annotated as containing a map or an interesting event. The Annotation tool can also be used to relate EI2s to one another. The tool will provide an editor with a set of connectors. An example would be a connector for denoting that two EI2s are contradictory. Using such a connector, a user could link an EI2 that contains a description of a product as having a tag price of $20 to another EI2 that has the same product with a price of $25.

The Annotation tool draws on a library of semantic annotations and connectors that will be based on a core domain-independent language defined by the Semantic Annotation Vocabulary. An Interdependency schema defines a vocabulary for connectors based on a variety of dimensions: pertinence, reliability, credibility, structural (x is an example of y, x is part of y, x describes y, etc.), causality ($x1\ x2 \ldots xn$ contribute to y, $x1\ x2 \ldots xn$ indicate y, etc.), temporal ordering (x before y, x after y, x simultaneous with y, etc.), argumentation (x may be a reason for y, x supports y, etc.). The Domain schema contains a core vocabulary for annotating the content of documents that extends the Interdependency schema with domain terms. Our plan is that TRELLIS will provide a core vocabulary, and users will be able to extend it with additional terms.

The Creation tool enables users to create new EI2s. For example, a user may create an EI2 as an assessment that she formulates based on existing EI2s. If a combination of some subparts of EI2s lets a user conclude or decide on some definition, then the subparts can be captured in a new information

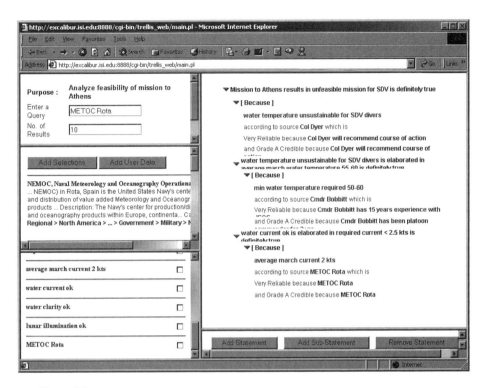

Figure 9.8
Snapshot of the current TRELLIS interface.

item that drops all other irrelevant parts of the original EI2s. A new EI2 can be added by extracting or summarizing some of the previous results.

Figure 9.8 shows a snapshot of the current user interface of TRELLIS. In this case, a user is using TRELLIS to decide whether a mission to take Navy SEALs to Athens is feasible. Given the Web sources consulted and the indicated capabilities of the SEAL team (shown on the left), the user has entered the rationale for deciding that the operation is not feasible.

We plan to extend TRELLIS with learning and adaptive techniques in order to offer the user improved and extended capabilities over time. As users annotate more EI2s and create new EI2s that capture their analysis, TRELLIS will be able to exploit this information and become increasingly more proactive. We also plan to add a query facility that will allow users to search the SMIB based on the semantic annotations of the EI2s. This facility will include a structured editor to guide users to formulate queries using the semantic annotation vocabulary defined in the schemas.

In summary, TRELLIS provides users with tools that enable them to specify information in increasingly more structured form and to specify semantic annotations that can be exploited for processing and integration of separate information items.

9.5   Conclusion

Integrating knowledge-based systems within end-to-end systems remains a challenge. In this chapter, we have shown some practical examples of the difficulties of enabling interoperability among knowledge bases. We have argued that current approaches will solve the interoperability problems only partially, since knowledge will continue to be trapped in low-level representations with no roots or connections to the rationale that was used in creating them. We have presented a different approach that would create Resilient Hyper–Knowledge Bases, which contain knowledge from its initial rendering in unstructured raw information sources and capture how it was refined and interrelated to produce the final formal representations the developer created. This new method of generating knowledge bases will be more resilient to changes and integrations and will contain highly interconnected knowledge fragments at all levels of abstraction. It will also enable people who have no training in knowledge engineering to contribute content, at least in the initial stages of development. The Semantic Web is an ideal substrate for these knowledge bases and will be a great contributor to resolving interoperability issues.

The spirit of the Web was clearly to empower all people to access and publish information. The Semantic Web will enable them to turn this information into knowledge that can be understood by machines. We must embrace this spirit and not continue to keep knowledge bases out of the reach of the public at large—or each other.

Acknowledgments

I would like to thank Jim Blythe, Jihie Kim, Larry Kite, Surya Ramachandran, and Pablo Yanez for their helpful discussions on TRELLIS and Varun Ratnakar for implementing its interface. I would also like to thank Jim Blythe, Jihie Kim, Surya Ramachandran, Bill Swartout, and Andre Valente for their participation in our group's integration efforts described in this chapter, which motivated much of this discussion, as well as other researchers, too numerous to list here, who contributed to the integration. The TRELLIS project is supported by a grant from the Air Force Office of Scientific Research with award number F49690-00-1-0337. The integrations of EXPECT's knowledge-based systems described here were funded under the DARPA High Performance Knowledge Bases program with award number F30602-97-1-0195, the DARPA/Rome Planning Initiative with award number DABT 63-95-C-0059, the DARPA Joint Forces Air Component Commander program with award number F30602-97-C-0118, and the DARPA Control of Agent-Based Systems program with award number F30602-97-1-0195.

Note

1. trellis.semanticweb.org.

References

Blythe, J., J. Kim, S. Ramachandran, and Y. Gil. 2001. An Integrated Environment for Knowledge Acquisition. In *Proceedings of the 2001 International Conference on Intelligent User Interfaces (IUI-2001), Santa Fe, New Mexico, January 14–17, 2001* (pp. 13–20). Marina del Rey, CA: ACM.

Chalupsky, H. 2000. OntoMorph: A Translation System for Symbolic Knowledge. In *Proceedings of the Seventh International Conference on Principles of Knowledge Representation and Reasoning (KR-2000), Breckenridge, Colorado, April 12–15* (pp. 471–482). San Francisco: Morgan Kaufmann.

Cohen, P., R. Schrag, E. Jones, A. Pease, A. Lin, B. Starr, D. Easter, D. Gunning, and M. Burke. 1998. The DARPA High Performance Knowledge Bases Project. In *Artificial Intelligence* 19(4):25–49.

Gil, Y. 2000. An Analysis of the CoABS TIE-1 Messages: Opportunities and Challenges for Agent Translation Services. USC/ISI Internal Project Report. Marina del Rey, CA.

Gil, Y., and E. Melz. 1996. Explicit Representations of Problem-Solving Strategies to Support Knowledge Acquisition. In *Proceedings of the Thirteen National Conference on Artificial Intelligence (AAAI-96), Portland, Oregon, August 4–8, 1996* (pp. 469–476). Menlo Park, CA/Cambridge, MA: AAAI/MIT Press.

Gil, Y., and M. Tallis. 1997. A Script-Based Approach to Modifying Knowledge Bases. In *Proceedings of the 14th National Conference on Artificial Intelligence (AAAI-97), July 27–31, 1997* (pp. 377–383). Menlo Park, CA/Cambridge, MA: AAAI/MIT Press.

Kim, J., and Y. Gil. 1999. Deriving Expectations to Guide Knowledge Base Creation. In *Proceedings of the Sixth National Conference on Artificial Intelligence (AAAI-99), July 18–22, 1999* (pp. 235–241). Menlo Park, CA/Cambridge, MA: AAAI/MIT Press.

Kim, J., and Y. Gil. 2000. Acquiring Problem-Solving Knowledge from End Users: Putting Interdependency Models to the Test. In *Proceedings of the Fifteenth National Conference on Artificial Intelligence (AAAI-2000), Austin, Texas, July 30–August 3, 2000 (pp. 223–229)*. Menlo Park, CA/Cambridge, MA: AAAI/MIT Press.

MacGregor, R. 1991. The Evolving Technology of Classification-Based Knowledge Representation Systems. In *Principles of Semantic Networks*, ed. J. Sowa (pp. 385–400). San Mateo, CA: Morgan Kaufmann.

Minsky, M. 1970. Form and Content in Computer Science. *Journal of the ACM* 17(2):197–215.

Swartout, B. and Y. Gil. 1995. EXPECT: Explicit Representations for Flexible Acquisition. In *Proceedings of the Ninth Knowledge Acquisition for Knowledge-Based Systems Workshop, Banff, Alberta, Canada, February 26–March 3, 1995*.

Valente, A., T. Russ, R. MacGregor, and W. Swartout. 1999. Building and (Re)Using an Ontology of Air Campaign Planning. *IEEE Intelligent Systems* 14(1):27–36.

Veloso, M., J. Carbonell, A. Perez, D. Borrajo, E. Fink, and J. Blythe. 1995. Integrating Planning and Learning: The PRODIGY Architecture. *Journal of Theoretical and Experimental AI* 7(1):81–120.

10 Complex Relationships for the Semantic Web

Sanjeev Thacker, Amit Sheth, and Shuchi Patel

10.1 Introduction

Relationships are fundamental to supporting semantics (Wiederhold 1997; Sheth 1996) and hence to the Semantic Web (Berners-Lee, Hendler, and Lassila 2001; Fensel and Musen 2001). To date, the focus in research on relationships has been on simple relationships, such as is-a and is-part-of, as in DAML+OIL (Ontology-Based Information Exchange 2001). In this work, we adapt our earlier work (Shah and Sheth 1998) to develop a framework for supporting complex relationships. A framework for managing complex relationships as discussed here becomes the basis for the discovery of knowledge from the information interlinked by the Semantic Web.

Our work primarily builds upon earlier research in integrating information systems that has also been applied to exploiting Web-accessible knowledge distributed across heterogeneous information sources. The primary focus of information integration systems has been to model these diverse data sources and integrate the data by resolving the heterogeneity involved to provide global views of domains (one-point access) for querying. We shift the focus from modeling of the information sources for purposes of querying to extracting useful knowledge from these information sources. This, we believe, can be achieved by modeling the complex relationships among the domains to study and explore the interaction that exists among them. In addition to information source and relationship modeling, operations are also modeled as part of the knowledge to exploit the semantics involved in executing complex information requests across multiple domains. The system's framework provides a support for knowledge discovery. Knowledge representation and support for relationships, which are fundamental to the concept of Semantic Web, are also described in this chapter.

Consider the capability provided by current research prototypes to support integration of information from diverse sources of data over a domain to provide the user with a unified structured (homogeneous) view of that domain for querying. On an integrated view of "earthquakes," one can make queries on the nature of "find information on all the earthquakes that have occurred in California since 1990." However, there is still a limitation on the type of queries that can be answered using such integrated domain views. Assuming views on earthquakes and nuclear tests exist, can one obtain answers to the question "Do nuclear tests cause earthquakes?" How can one study such relationships between two domains based on the data available on diverse Web-accessible sources? Let us consider a known relationship, such as that between air pollution and vegetation. Assuming the necessary views exist, can a question like "How does air pollution affect vegetation?" be answered using only the integrated views? These queries are beyond the realm of the existing systems. There is a compelling need to be able to model the semantic correlation of data across the domains and then be able to pose complex information requests involving these correlated data.

Support for semantic correlation involving complex relationships is demonstrated in the InfoQuilt,[1] which provides a framework and a platform for answering complex information requests of the above nature. The novel features of InfoQuilt are

- a mechanism for expressing and understanding complex semantic interdomain relationships.

- a powerful interface that can use the semantic knowledge about domains and their relationships to construct complex information requests known as Information Scapes (IScapes). Most information integration systems (e.g.,

SIMS [Arens, Knoblock, and Shen 1996]) focus on efficiently retrieving data on a single domain only. IScapes, on the other hand, are information requests that may span one or more domains and involve interdomain relationships, too. These information requests have a much higher degree of expressiveness compared to keyword-based search techniques provided by Web-based search tools and database queries that focus only on the syntax and structure of data.

- the ability, using IScapes, to analyze the data available from a multitude of heterogeneous, autonomous sources to explore and study potential relationships. Although InfoQuilt provides the tools necessary for data analysis, human involvement is a part of the process. This forms the basis of the knowledge discovery supported by InfoQuilt.

- a framework for supporting complex operations that can be used for postprocessing of data retrieved from sources (e.g., statistical analysis) and as complex operators needed to define interdomain relationships.

The major issues addressed in building the InfoQuilt system are as follows:

- A large portion of the data on the Web is either unstructured or semistructured. There are syntactic, structural, and semantic heterogeneities across different sources providing information about the same domain (Kashyap and Sheth 1997; Sheth 1999). In addition to these inconsistencies, there is overlapping of information across sources.

- The knowledge of domains and their sources needs to be modeled in such a way that the system is able to identify automatically the sources of data that could possibly provide useful information with respect to an information request while carefully pruning the others, maximizing the ability to obtain faster and more comprehensive results from the same available sources.

- Representation of complex relationships spanning multiple domains involves modeling the semantics involved in their interaction.

- Posing complex information requests containing embedded semantic information requires the system to able to understand the semantics of a request to retrieve relevant results corresponding to the request.

▪ Exploring new relationships, which is of special interest to us, might require an ability to postprocess the data obtained from sources in several ways.

This chapter focuses on our work on semantic correlation and complex relationships in the hope of supporting "deeper semantics" in the Semantic web. The chapter is organized as follows. Section 10.2 focuses on our approach to modeling the domains, interdomain relationships, information sources available to the system, and functions that form the system's knowledge base. Section 10.3 addresses the use of IScapes in our system to develop and deploy complex information requests that are answered using the system knowledge and the set of resources available to the system. Knowledge discovery, which is the ability of InfoQuilt to study domains, mine and analyze the data available from the sources, and explore relationships, is described in section 10.4. Section 10.5 discusses the use of visual toolkits that are provided to construct the knowledge base and construct and execute IScapes. We compare our approach to other state-of-the-art information integration systems in section 10.6 and present our conclusions and planned future improvements in section 10.7.

10.2   Knowledge Modeling

The representation of information sources in the system and the creation of an "integrated structured view" of the domain that the users can use are two of the critical issues that need to be addressed in any information integration system. Two main approaches are used for information integration (Duschka 1997):

▪ *Source-Centric.* In source-centric approaches, the integrated view of the domain is modeled first. Both user queries and source views are specified in terms of that view. For each information request, the integration system needs to plan how to answer it using the source views.

▪ *Query-Centric.* In query-centric approaches, user queries are formulated in terms of views synthesized at a mediator that are defined on source views.

After a view expansion at the mediator, queries are translated into a logical plan that is composed of source views.

The term "view" here implies some form of representation of the domain and not a view in a database. InfoQuilt adopts the source-centric approach, which has several advantages over the query-centric approach. First, in the source-centric approach, the integrated views of domains are created independent of their source views. Second, in the source-centric approach, the source views are independent of each other and are described in terms of their domain model. Hence, a source can be added, removed, or modified dynamically without affecting any other source views. In the query-centric approach, adding and removing sources additionally requires redefining the domain view, and the sources need to be mapped with each other, making schema integration difficult. Lastly, the source-centric approach is more suitable for sources other than databases.

The work on InfoQuilt has been built upon work reported in Bertram 1998 and Laksminarayanan 2000. InfoQuilt system knowledge comprises knowledge about domains, resources accessible to them, interdomain relationships, and complex operations like functions and simulations. We use ontologies to describe the domains to the system. An ontology is meant to capture useful semantics of the domain, such as the domain characteristics, the set of terms and concepts of interest involved, and their meanings. Section 10.2.1 describes how a domain is represented using an ontology. (We will use the terms *ontology* and *domain* interchangeably in the rest of the chapter unless we explicitly specify a distinction between them.) There can be multiple resources accessible to a system, and an ontology can have several resources that provide relevant data on it. Section 10.2.2 describes how we define resources in terms of ontologies. Section 10.2.3 describes how complex relationships between two or more domains are modeled. Finally, section 10.2.4 describes how we support operations such as simulations and functions in the system. InfoQuilt uses XML as the knowledge representation language. We provide a visual tool called Knowledge Builder that lets a user easily create and update the knowledge base of the system. Section 10.5.1 describes the Knowledge Builder and its functionalities in detail.

10.2.1   Ontology (Domain Modeling)

An ontology should be able to provide a good understanding of the domain it represents. This includes related terms/concepts, their definitions and/or meanings, their relationships with each other, and characteristics of the domain. It also helps in resolving differences between the models of the domain used by the available sources, by mapping the data available from all resources for the domain from the local model used by each resource to the model specified by the ontology, which the user can then use. The user can create a classification of real-world entities and represent them as ontologies in the system. This classification is based on the human perception of the world broken down into several domains and their subdomains and so on (real-world objects as perceived from a modeling standpoint). The representation of an ontology comprises related terms (attributes), their place in the domain hierarchy, domain rules, and functional dependencies. The ontology of a subdomain is said to inherit from the ontology of its parent domain. A child ontology inherits all attributes, domain rules, and functional dependencies of its parent ontology.

Example 10.1   Consider the domain of disasters. They could be subcategorized as natural disasters and man-made disasters. Natural disasters could be further subcategorized into earthquakes, volcanic eruptions, tsunamis, and so on. Similarly, man-made disasters could have subcategories like nuclear tests. An example hierarchy is shown in figure 10.1. An ontology's place in the domain hierarchy is represented by specifying its parent ontology, if any. However, it is not necessary for an ontology to be a part of a hierarchy.

10.2.1.1   Attributes

The terms and concepts of the domain are represented as attributes of the ontology. As mentioned earlier, an ontology inherits all attributes of its parent ontology. The meaning of each attribute and its syntax (type and format) are standardized so that the attribute has a precise interpretation and use.

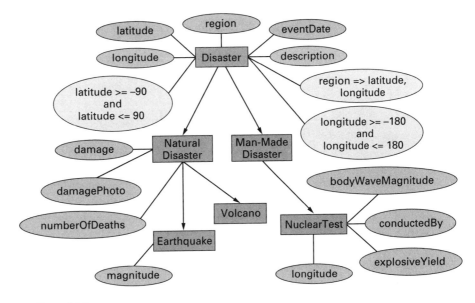

Figure 10.1
Example domain hierarchy.

Example 10.2   An earthquake can have attributes like the date it occurred, the region where it occurred, the latitude and longitude for its epicenter, a description of the earthquake, the number of people that died, the magnitude, and an image showing some damage or fault line, as seen in figure 10.1. We will use the following notation to represent an ontology:

```
Earthquake (eventDate, description, region, magnitude,
            latitude, longitude, numberOfDeaths,
            damagePhoto);
```

10.2.1.2   Domain Rules
The characteristics and semantics of a domain are described by domain rules and functional dependencies. Domain rules describe a condition that always holds true for all entities in the domain. They can be used for query validation and optimization of query plans.

Example 10.3 A simple fact, such as that the latitude of an earthquake should lie between −90° and 90°, can be described by the following rule on the ontology Earthquake:

```
latitude >= -90 and latitude <= 90
```

The ontology can then be represented as follows:

```
Earthquake (eventDate, description, region, magnitude,
            latitude, longitude, numberOfDeaths,
            damagePhoto,
            latitude >= -90 and latitude <= 90);
```

10.2.1.3 Functional Dependencies

A functional dependency (FD) specifies that two entities having the same values for all attributes appearing on the left-hand side of the FD will have the same values for the corresponding variables appearing on the right-hand side. Domain rules and FDs help in understanding the characteristics of domains. Web sources constitute a large portion of the set of resources available to the InfoQuilt system. The integrated domain model is a comprehensive model, and it is very likely to come across resources that do not contain certain attributes of the domain model and are incomplete. The system uses information about the FDs of a domain to retrieve information (attributes) that is missing from a resource by using another resource (an *associate resource*), thereby deducing additional information and retrieving more comprehensive results with the same available resources.

Example 10.4 A functional dependency on the ontology Earthquake could be that the region of a place implies the latitude and longitude of the place. This can be represented as:

```
region -> latitude longitude
```

The ontology can therefore be represented as follows:

```
Earthquake (eventDate, description, region, magnitude,
            latitude, longitude, numberOfDeaths,
            damagePhoto,
            latitude >= -90 and latitude <= 90,
            region -> latitude longitude);
```

Assume that the system has access to two sources that provide information about earthquakes: SignificantEarthquakesDB, which provides eventDate, description, region, magnitude, latitude, longitude, numberOfDeaths, and damagePhoto for significant earthquakes (say, with a magnitude greater than 5) all over the world, and EarthquakesAfter1990, which provides eventDate, region, magnitude, numberOfDeaths, and damagePhoto for earthquakes that occurred after January 1, 1990. Suppose the user has the following information request: "Find all earthquakes with epicenter in a 5,000-mile radius around the location at latitude 60.790 North and longitude 97.570 East."

Assume that the calculation of the distance between two locations, given their latitudes and longitudes, is possible. Also, assume that the ontology Earthquake does have attributes latitude and longitude that specify these characteristics. So the system should be able to answer the query. However, the resource EarthquakesAfter1990 does not supply values for the latitude and longitude attributes. Hence, we would need to return only the information that was available from the resource SignificantEarthquakesDB. The results that the user sees will include all significant earthquakes (with magnitude greater than 5) that occurred in the region defined by the query. But to be able to return *all* earthquakes, the system can use the domain's functional dependency *region −> latitude longitude*. The system can check to see if it can deduce the latitudes and longitudes of epicenters of any earthquakes in EarthquakesAfter1990 by checking the regions of earthquakes available from SignificantEarthquakesDB. For all the earthquakes for which the latitude and longitude of the epicenter can be deduced, the system can now check if they fall within the 5,000-mile radius area specified in the query. Using the resource EarthquakesAfter1990 to answer this query would not been impossible without the use of the FD.

10.2.2   Resources

Information sources in InfoQuilt are described in terms of their corresponding ontologies. Such a description is meant to supply details about the resource that can be used for efficient planning. It consists of a set of attributes, binding patterns, data characteristic rules, and local completeness rules. Sections 10.2.2.1 to 10.2.2.4 describe each of these and the rationale for including them in the knowledge base. The goal of the system concerning the support of resources is (Levy, Rajaraman, and Ordille 1996)

- to be able to add, modify, and delete resources for an ontology dynamically without affecting the system's knowledge.

- to be able to specify the sources of information in a manner that enables one to query them declaratively.

- to be able to identify the exact usefulness of some resources in the context of a particular IScape and prune those that are not useful.

10.2.2.1   Resource Attributes

Since the way a resource perceives its data can be different from our perception, represented by the ontology of the domain, data need to be mapped after they are retrieved. This allows for interoperability among sources with heterogeneous data (Guntamadugu 2000). Additionally, since the ontology is ideally a comprehensive perception of the domain, it is common to come across resources that supply only a part of the information modeled in the ontologies. In other words, a resource may not provide values for all the attributes of the ontology. The resource's description therefore lists the attributes that it can provide.

Example 10.5   Consider the resources SignificantEarthquakesDB and EarthquakesAfter1990. Example 10.2 offers a list of attributes that the resources provide values for. The resources would therefore be represented as follows:

```
SignificantEarthquakesDB (eventDate, description, region,
                          magnitude, latitude, longitude,
                          numberOfDeaths, damagePhoto);
EarthquakesAfter1990 (eventDate, region, magnitude,
                      numberOfDeaths, damagePhoto);
```

We will use the notation in example 10.5 to represent resources.

10.2.2.2 Binding Patterns

The sources accessible to the system that are not databases do not have the ability to execute queries. Most Web sources fall into this category. However, some Web sources do have a limited query capability that is supported by allowing users to search, based on some attributes. These Web sources require that values for some attributes be provided to retrieve results. The source can be queried only by specifying values for those attributes. Additionally, some sources may provide a finite number of optional ways to query (different sets of attributes). For example, a user may be able to query a site providing information about movies by actors, director, title, and so on. Such query limitations and characteristics of resources are important to consider while planning a query. There are a number of common motivations for having such limitations (Duschka 1997):

- *Privacy/Security.* For example, a company might not want users to be able to get a listing of all its employees but might allow a search on an employee by name.

- *Performance.* The data on a site could be indexed, and it would then be more efficient to query the source on the indexed attributes for efficient retrieval.

- *Efficiency.* The amount of data might be enormous, and hence it might not be efficient to query all of it. The values supplied for bound attributes might be used to narrow the search and limit the data retrieved.

The attributes are represented in the knowledge base as a set of binding patterns (BPs). A BP is a set of attributes that the system must be able to supply values for in order to query a particular resource. If the resource has several BPs, the system can select the most appropriate one. The values for the BP can be obtained from the query constraint or provided by some other resource.

Example 10.6 Consider the ontology Flight, which represents a flight from one city to another within United States. Most Web sites for air travel reservation have forms that require the user to specify source, destination, dates of travel, and similar information. The Web site could require one or more combinations of values as input as a condition for the Web site to obtain any useful information. One of the possible combinations of BPs could be

```
[fromCity, fromState, toCity, toState, departureDate]
```

Suppose we use the AirTran Airways Web site (www.airtran.com) as a source. The resource would then be represented as follows:

```
AirTranAirways (airlineCompany, flightNumber, fromCity,
                fromState, toCity, toState, departureDate,
                fare, departureTime, arrivalTime,
                [fromCity, fromState, toCity, toState,
                departureDate]);
```

10.2.2.3   Data Characteristic Rules

Data characteristic (DC) rules are similar to domain rules (discussed in section 10.2.1.2), but they apply only to a specific resource. Knowledge about the data characteristics of a particular resource can be useful to the system in predicting whether that resource will provide any useful results for a particular information request. This prediction can be used to prune a resource if it is possible to infer from the DC rules for that resource that the resource will not provide any useful results for the Iscape. It can also be used to optimize the query plan by eliminating a constraint on a particular resource if it can be deduced that the constraint will always be true for all the data retrieved from that resource. The DC rules are also used to select an appropriate associate resource for a resource with BPs or missing attributes.

Example 10.7   Consider the AirTranAirways resource introduced in example 10.6 that provides data for the ontology Flight. We know that it provides only information about flights operated by AirTran Airways. This characteristic of the resource can be represented as follows:

```
AirTranAirways (airlineCompany, flightNumber, fromCity,
                fromState, toCity, toState, departureDate,
                fare, departureTime, arrivalTime,
                [dc] airlineCompany = "AirTran Airways",
                [fromCity, fromState, toCity, toState,
                departureDate]);
```

We use [dc] and [lc] to distinguish data characteristic rules from local completeness rules, respectively. (Local completeness rules are described in section 10.2.2.4.)

Consider the following query using the ontology Flight: "Find all the flights operated by Delta Airlines from Boston, MA, to Los Angeles, CA, on February 19, 2001." Clearly, AirTranAirways will not provide any information about Delta flights. The system can use this knowledge to deduce that the resource AirTranAirways should not be used to answer this query.

Now suppose the user modifies the query to look for flights operated by AirTran Airways. This time the system knows that it can use the AirTranAirways resource. Additionally, it can also eliminate the check for "AirTran Airways," since all flights available from the AirTranAirways resource are known to be operated by AirTran Airways.

10.2.2.4 *Local Completeness Rules*

A local completeness (LC) rule for a resource has the same format as a DC rule or a domain rule, but it has a different interpretation. Overlapping and incomplete information is characteristic of Web sources. Hence, using just one source to answer an information request in many cases does not guarantee retrieval of all the possible information that is responsive to the request. The general approach to a solution for this problem has been to use all the sources (for the appropriate ontology) and compute a union of the results retrieved from all of them to provide the maximum possible information in response to every request. However, it is also possible to find sources that do provide complete information about some subset of a particular domain. LC rules are used to model this. They specify that a given resource is complete for a subset (or subsets) of information on a particular ontology. In other words, the information contained in the resource is specified to be *all* the information for that subset (specified by the LC rule) of the domain. Hence, the system cannot retrieve any additional information (for that subset) by querying other sources.

Example 10.8 Consider again the AirTranAirways resource used in earlier examples. We know that information about *all* flights operated by AirTran Airways will be available from it. It is thus locally complete for all flights with airlineCompany = "AirTran Airways".

```
AirTranAirways (airlineCompany, flightNumber, fromCity,
                fromState, toCity, toState, departureDate,
                fare, departureTime, arrivalTime,
                [dc] airlineCompany = "AirTran Airways",
                [lc] airlineCompany = "AirTran Airways",
                [fromCity, fromState, toCity, toState,
                departureDate]);
```

Now, any information request that needs only the subset of flights that are operated by AirTran Airways can use only AirTranAirways to retrieve data about all such flights. This would be faster than querying all sources available for Flight.

10.2.3 *Interontological Relationships*

Real-world entities that are classified into domains and subdomains can be related to each other in various ways. These relationships can be very simple, like the "is-a" relationship implied by inheritance. For example, a nuclear test is-a man-made disaster, and so on. They can also be very complex; for example, an earthquake can "cause" a tsunami. A relationship may involve more than two domains (ontologies). Such complex interontological relationships represent real-world concepts and characteristics. A novel feature of InfoQuilt is that it provides an infrastructure for modeling and learning about such complex relationships between different ontologies and to use them to specify information requests. Modeling such interontological relationships requires an understanding of the semantics involved in their interaction, and such relationships cannot be expressed using only simple relational and logical operators. Relationships already known can be directly modeled (defined) using InfoQuilt's Knowledge Builder toolkit (discussed in section 10.5.1). Additionally, we may want to explore hypothetical relationships and formalize them, if they can be established using the available information sources. Established relationships can then be used to study the interaction between the ontologies involved. Further, two relationships, "*A affects B*" and "*B affects C*," could lead to the transitive finding "*A affects C*."

Example 10.9 Consider the relationship between a nuclear test and an earthquake. We use the Earthquake ontology from example 10.4 here. Suppose we model the nuclear test as follows:

```
NuclearTest (testSite, explosiveYield, bodyWaveMagnitude,
testType,
           eventDate, conductedBy, latitude, longitude,
           bodyWaveMagnitude > 0,
           bodyWaveMagnitude < 10,
           testSite -> latitude longitude);
```

We can say that some nuclear test could have "caused" an earthquake if we see that the earthquake occurred "some time after" the nuclear test was conducted and "in nearby region." Notice the use of operators "some time after" and "in nearby region." These are specialized, user-defined operators that are not a part of the set of relational operators ($<$, $>$, $<=$, etc.). They are made possible by InfoQuilt's ability to support user-defined functions, as described in section 10.2.4. For now, assume that there are two functions called dateDifference and distance available to the system. The function dateDifference takes two dates as arguments and returns number of days from date1 to date2. The function distance takes the latitudes and longitudes of two places and calculates the distance between them. Given that we can use these functions, we can represent the relationship as follows:

```
NuclearTest Causes Earthquake:

dateDifference(NuclearTest.eventDate,
Earthquake.eventDate) < 30
                          AND
distance(NuclearTest.latitude, NuclearTest.longitude,
      Earthquake.latitude, Earthquake.longitude)
      <10000
```

The values 30 and 10,000 here are arbitrary. In fact, a user can try different values in analyzing the data. This is a part of the knowledge discovery support that the system's framework provides, as described further in section 10.4.

10.2.4   Operations

A distinguishing feature of InfoQuilt is its framework to support the use of operations. In example 10.9, we used the functions dateDifference and distance as operators to describe a complex interontological relationship between NuclearTest and Earthquake. Users can also use operators to specify constraints in their information requests.

Example 10.10   Consider the following information request: "Find all earthquakes with epicenter in a 5,000-mile radius around the location at latitude 60.790 North and longitude 97.570 East." The system needs to know how it can calculate the distance between two points, given their latitudes and longitudes, in order to check which earthquakes' epicenters fall in the range specified.

Operations are also used to resolve syntactic heterogeneities among sources by providing a fuzzy matching mechanism to map the two sources. Consider the use of the functional dependency region $->$ latitude longitude from example 10.4 to solve the missing attribute (latitude and longitude) problem of the source EarthquakesAfter1990. It is highly unlikely that the sources SignificantEarthquakesDB and EarthquakesAfter1990 will have exact same values for the attribute region. The value available from one source could be "Nevada, USA" and that from another source could be "NV, USA". The two are semantically equal but syntactically unequal (Kashyap and Sheth 1996).

Another important advantage of using operations is that the system can support complex postprocessing of data. An interesting form of postprocessing is the use of simulation programs. These independent programs can be integrated with the InfoQuilt system. For instance, researchers in the field of geographic information systems use simulation programs to forecast characteristics like urban growth in a region based on a model. InfoQuilt supports the use of such simulations as it does any other operation. They provide valuable additional information that is not often available from the resources directly.

Example 10.11   Clarke's Urban Growth Model (2001) is a model for forecasting the urban growth in a region based on information about the areas in the region where it is known that growth cannot occur for some reason, along with information about roads, slopes, and vegetation in the region. It requires that this information be specified as a set of maps and generates a series of maps showing the progressive urban growth using a specified time step. This simulation can be run on data that can be retrieved from some resource (or multiple resources) that has the maps needed, assuming that they are in the format that the program expects.

To be able to dynamically and easily add new operations and update and delete existing ones, InfoQuilt maintains what is known as a *Function Store*. The Function Store contains information about all the functions known to the system. (We will use the terms *function* and *operation* interchangeably in the rest of the chapter.) The description of a function contains its name, a description of its functionality, a list of arguments that it takes as inputs along with their types and descriptions of what they are, the type of value it returns, and information about how the system can use it. The user provides an implementation for the function. Once the implementation is provided and has been added to the Function Store, the system can make use of it as other operations.

10.3 Information Scapes

The goal of the InfoQuilt system is to develop a framework for knowledge discovery support through use of available resources of data. Users can form complex information requests to be executed on data available from multiple heterogeneous distributed resources. Note that we use the term *information request* rather than *query*. A query generally explicitly specifies the exact sources (tables in an RDBMS) that need to be used and how the data from these sources should be integrated (join conditions in an RDBMS). Additionally, it does not "understand" what the user is asking. An information request, on the other hand, can understand what the user is enquiring about by embedding semantic information within the request.[2] As noted earlier, in InfoQuilt, we refer to information requests as IScapes. The work on IScapes has built upon work presented in Palsena 2000 and Shah and Sheth 1998.

Example 10.12 Consider the following information request: "Find all earthquakes with epicenter in a 5000 mile radius around the location at latitude

60.790 North and longitude 97.570 East, and find all tsunamis that they might have caused." In addition to the obvious constraints, the system needs to understand what the user means by saying "find all tsunamis that they might have caused." The relationship "an earthquake caused a tsunami" is a complex interontological relationship.

Any system that needs to answer information requests like the one in example 10.12 would need a comprehensive knowledge of the terms involved and how they are related. An IScape is specified in terms of the components of the knowledge base of the system, such as ontologies, interontological relationships, and operations, that the system understands. This helps the system in understanding the semantics of the request. Additionally, it abstracts the user from having to know the actual sources that will be used by the system to answer the request and how the data retrieved from these sources will be integrated.

An IScape is defined as a set of information semantically related in a complex manner. We use XML to represent an IScape. It specifies the ontologies involved, interontological relationships, preset constraint, run time–configurable constraint, how the results should be grouped, any aggregations that need to be computed or constraints that need to be applied to the grouped data, and finally the information that needs to be returned to the user in the results. The ontologies in the IScape identify the domains that are involved in the IScape, and the interontological relationships specify how they are related to each other. The preset constraint and the run time–configurable constraint are filters used to describe the subset of data that the user is interested in. For example, a user may be interested only in earthquakes that occurred in a certain region and had a magnitude greater than 5. In the IScape template certain constraints are preset, whereas others can be configured at execution. The difference between the preset constraint and the run time–configurable constraint is that the run time–configurable constraint can be set at the time of the IScape is executed. The run time–configurable constraint forms an important mechanism for supporting knowledge discovery, as described in section 10.4. Constraints are essentially conjunctive boolean expressions.

The results of the IScape can be grouped based on attributes and/or specified functions. If the results are to be grouped, the user can also specify any aggregations that the user wants to be returned as a part of the results or specify additional constraints on the groups formed (similar to the HAVING clause in the SELECT statement in SQL). The aggregates supported by the system are sum (SUM), average (AVG), count (COUNT), minimum (MIN), and maximum (MAX). Finally, the user specifies a list of all the information that is to be returned as a part of the result. We refer to this as the *projection list*. It can include certain information modeled by the ontologies directly (attributes), aggregates, values of functions evaluated on the data, and results of some simulation programs.

A graphical toolkit known as the IScape Builder is available to the user for constructing and executing these IScapes and analyzing the results. It provides a platform for ease of development and deployment of IScapes using the knowledge base without having to understand the underlying formats used by the system.

10.4   Knowledge Discovery

InfoQuilt provides a conceptual framework that allows users to access data available from a multitude of diverse autonomous distributed resources and provide tools that help them to analyze the data to gain a better understanding of the domains and the interdomain relationships as well as to explore the possibilities of new relationships. This section discusses this conceptual framework using a series of examples; the next section discusses some of the software components of the InfoQuilt framework.

The interontological relationships defined in the knowledge base of the InfoQuilt system describe the interaction between domains that contain embedded semantic information. Existing relationships provide a scope for discovering new aspects of relationships through transitive learning, as discussed in example 10.13.

Example 10.13 Consider the ontologies Earthquake, Tsunami, and Environment. Assume that the relationships Earthquake Affects Environment, Earthquake Causes Tsunami, and Tsunami Affects Environment are defined and known to the system. We can see that since an earthquake causes a tsunami and a tsunami affects the environment, effectively this is another way in which an earthquake affects the environment (by causing a tsunami). If this aspect of the relationship between an earthquake and environment was not considered earlier, it can now be studied further.

Another valuable source of knowledge discovery is studying existing IScapes that make use of ontologies, their resources, and relationships to retrieve information that is of interest to users. The results obtained from IScapes can be analyzed further by postprocessing of the results data. For example, Clarke's Urban Growth Model forecasts future patterns of urban growth using various data, as noted in example 10.11.

For the users that are well-versed with a particular domain, the InfoQuilt framework supports exploring new relationships within that domain. Data available from various sources can be analyzed using charts, statistical analysis techniques, and the like to study and explore trends or aspects of the domain. Such analysis can also be used to hypothesize new relationships between domains and to determine whether the data invalidate the hypothesized relationships or support them sufficiently, as demonstrated by example 10.14.

Example 10.14 Several researchers in the past have expressed their concern over nuclear tests as one of the causes of earthquakes and have suggested that there could be a direct connection between the two. Underground nuclear tests cause shock waves, which travel as ripples along the crust of the earth and weaken it, thereby making it more susceptible to earthquakes. Although this issue has been addressed before, it still remains a hypothesis that is not conclusively and scientifically proven. Suppose we want to explore this hypothetical relationship.

Consider again the NuclearTest and Earthquake ontologies. We assume that the system has access to sufficient resources for both the ontologies such that they together provide sufficient information for the analysis to be undertaken. These resources include nontraditional, nondatabase sources based on the Web.

If the researchers' hypothesis is true, then we should be able to see an increase in the number of earthquakes that have occurred since nuclear testing started. We proceed as follows. First, we check to see when nuclear testing began:

IScape 1: "Find when the earliest recorded nuclear test was conducted."

We find that nuclear testing began in 1950. Next we check the trend in the number of earthquakes that have occurred since the nuclear testing started. It is believed that some earthquakes below the intensity of 5.8 on the Richter scale would have passed unrecorded in the earlier part of the century when measuring devices were less sensitive and less ubiquitous. But for stronger earthquakes, the records are detailed and believed to be complete (Whiteford 1989). We therefore check the number of earthquakes with a magnitude of 5.8 or higher occurring every year in this century:[3]

IScape 2: "Find the total number of earthquakes with a magnitude of 5.8 or higher on the Richter scale per year starting from year 1900."

With the results of IScape 2, we can plot a chart to analyze the trend in the number of earthquakes occurring every year. Such a chart reveals that there seems to be a sudden increase in the number of earthquakes after 1950. We modify the query to try to quantify this rise approximately.

IScape 3: "Find the average number of earthquakes with a magnitude of 5.8 or higher on the Richter scale per year for the period 1900–1949 and for the period 1950–present."

We see that in the period 1900–1949, the average rate of earthquakes of magnitude 5.8 or greater was 68 per year and that for 1950–present[4] has been 127 per year; that is, it almost doubled (Whiteford 1989).

Next, we try to analyze the same data grouping the earthquakes by their magnitudes.

```
IScape 4: "Find the average number of earthquakes with
magnitudes in the ranges 5.8—6, 6—7, 7—8, 8—9, and
magnitudes higher than 9 on the Richter scale per year
starting from year 1900."
```

The results of IScape 4 show that the average number of earthquakes with magnitude greater than 7 on the Richter scale has remained practically constant over the century (about 19 per year) (Whiteford 1989). We can therefore deduce that the earthquakes caused by nuclear tests usually are of magnitudes less than 7 on the Richter scale. We can then try to explore the data at a finer level of granularity by trying to look for specific instances of earthquakes that occurred within a certain period of time after a nuclear test was conducted in a nearby region.

```
IScape 5: "Find nuclear tests conducted after January 1,
1950, and find any earthquakes that occurred not later
than a certain number of days after the test and such that
the earthquake's epicenter was located no farther than a
certain distance from the test site."
```

Note the use of "not later than a certain number of days" and "no farther than a certain distance." The IScape does not specify the value for the time period and the distance. These are defined as run time–configurable parameters that the user can use to form a constraint while executing the IScape. The user can hence supply different values for each and execute the IScape repeatedly to analyze the data for different values without constructing it repeatedly from scratch. This is where the run time–configurable constraint feature of InfoQuilt is useful. Also, note the use of functions as user-defined operators to calculate the difference in date (dateDifference) and the distance between the epicenter of the earthquake and the nuclear test site (distance). Some of the interesting results that can be obtained by exploring earthquakes that occurred no later than 30 days after a nuclear test with their epicenters no farther than 5,000 miles from the test site are listed below.

China conducted a nuclear test on October 6, 1983, at the Lop Nor test site. The USSR conducted two tests, one on the same day and another on October 26, 1983, both at the Eastern Kazakh or Semipalatinsk test site. An earthquake of magnitude 6 on the Richter scale occurred in Erzurum, Turkey, on October 30, 1983, that killed about 1,300 people. The epicenter of the earthquake was about 2,000 miles away from the test site in China and about 3,500 miles away from the test site in USSR. The second USSR test took place just four days before the quake.

The USSR conducted a nuclear test on September 15, 1978, at the Eastern Kazakh or Semipalatinsk test site. There was an earthquake in Tabas, Iran, on September 16, 1978. The epicenter was about 2,300 miles away from the test site.

More recently, India conducted a nuclear test at its Pokaran test site in Rajasthan on May 11, 1998. Pakistan conducted two nuclear tests, one on May 28, 1998, at the Chagai test site and another on May 30, 1998, at the same site. Two earthquakes occurred soon after these tests. One was in Egypt and Israel on May 28, 1998, with its epicenter about 4,500 miles away from both test sites, and the other was in the Tajikistan region of Afghanistan on May 30, 1998, with a magnitude of 6.9 and its epicenter about 750 miles away from the Pokaran test site and 710 miles from the Chagai test site.

10.5   Visual Interfaces

This section describes the graphical tools we provide in InfoQuilt to aid in the creation of the system's knowledge base and the creation and execution of Iscapes and for monitoring the execution of Iscapes. These components of the InfoQuilt system described here are those most relevant to knowledge discovery, which is the focus of this chapter; the remaining components—primarily the distributed agent–based run time system—are described in Patel and Sheth 2001.

10.5.1   Knowledge Builder

The Knowledge Builder (KB) is InfoQuilt's graphical toolkit, which helps the user in creating the knowledge base of the system. It allows the user to declaratively specify ontologies, relationships, resources, and functions (including simulations). Use of KB provides the following advantages:

- The user does not need to know the format of the XML specification used by the system to represent ontologies, relationships, and functions. The KB provides an easy-to-follow graphical interface that users can use and thereby provides an abstraction from the details of the formats used internally by the system (See figure 10.2).

- The KB provides tools that help the user relate the information in the knowledge base in a convenient way. For example, the user can look at the entire knowledge base as a graphical tree that lists all the ontologies defined in the system; their details, including rules and FDs imposed on them; relationships involving the ontologies, with their details; and resources available for the ontologies, with their details, such as the attributes they supply, the data characteristic rules, the local completeness rules, and the binding patterns that they need.

- The KB structures knowledge in a manner that allows for easy access to that knowledge in a form that can help the user understand and learn about a domain.

- The KB also assists the user in trying to modify the knowledge base. For example, a user may want to remove an attribute from an ontology. The KB will not allow this if the attribute is being used in a rule on the ontology, a FD on the ontology, a set of attributes provided by some resource, a data characteristic rule on a resource, a local completeness rule on a resource, or a binding pattern on a resource. The KB requires the user to manually resolve such conflicts before removing the attribute. If the knowledge base is huge, it would be a tedious and error-prone task to go through all the various specifications to find where the attribute is being used. Even worse, the user

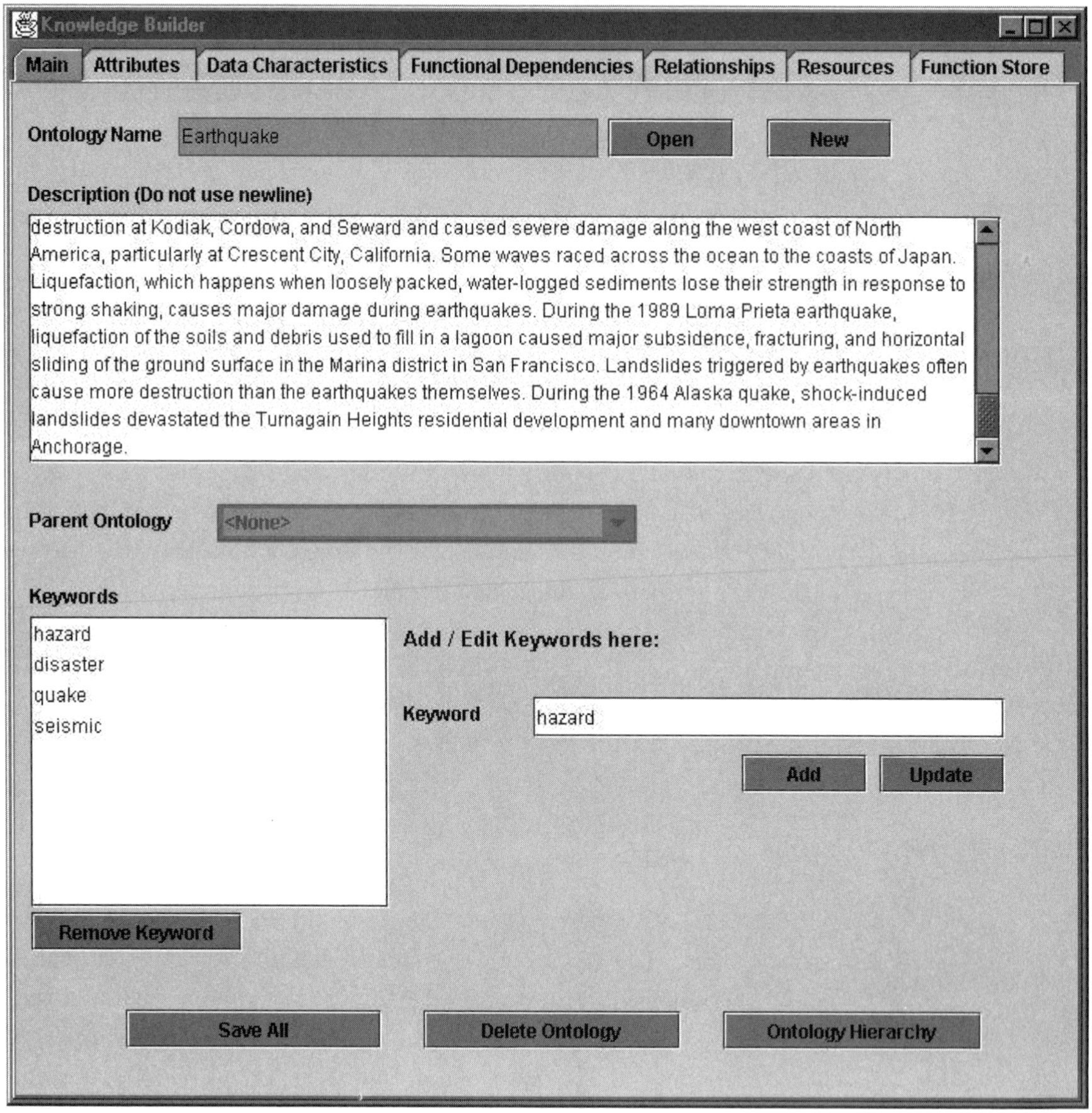

Figure 10.2
Knowledge Builder.

would have to go through the XML specifications in the absence of a tool like KB to correctly make the required modifications. Using the graphical tree display provided by the KB, however, the user finds it easier locate uses of the attribute (See figure 10.3).

10.5.2 IScape Builder

The IScape Builder (IB) is a stand-alone Java application that provides a graphical interface for creating and executing IScapes. Use of this tool has the following advantages:

- It provides a simple and intuitive interface that allows the user to create and execute IScapes step by step (see figure 10.4).

- The user does not need to be aware of the format of the XML specification used internally by the system to represent IScapes.

- The IB is aware of the knowledge base of the system. The user therefore does not need to look it up to create new IScapes. For example, names of ontologies, relationships, and functions appear, wherever required, in combo boxes, from which the user can easily make his selection.

- It implements basic validity checks to make sure that the IScape being created is valid. For example, if the proposed IScape involves use of a function call, the IB makes sure that the user has specified the places from which the values for all the arguments to the function should be supplied. It also performs a type match.

- It can provide various tools to help users better analyze the results of IScapes. For example, the current version of the IB provides a charting tool that allows the user to create charts to analyze IScape results. This helps in providing a learning environment for users.

10.5.3 Web-Accessible Interface to Execute IScapes

We also provide in InfoQuilt a Web-accessible interface that offers a learning environment and allows execution of existing IScapes by setting the run

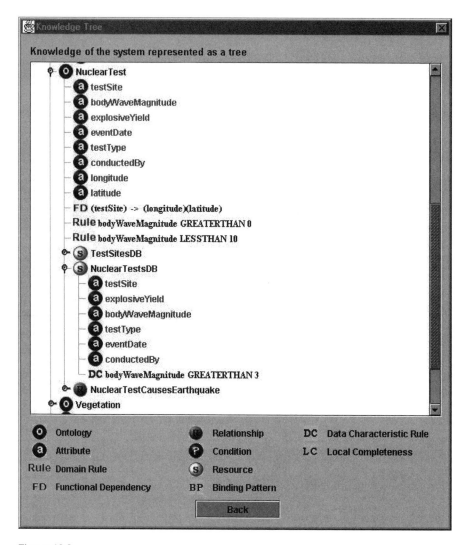

Figure 10.3
Ontology hierarchy.

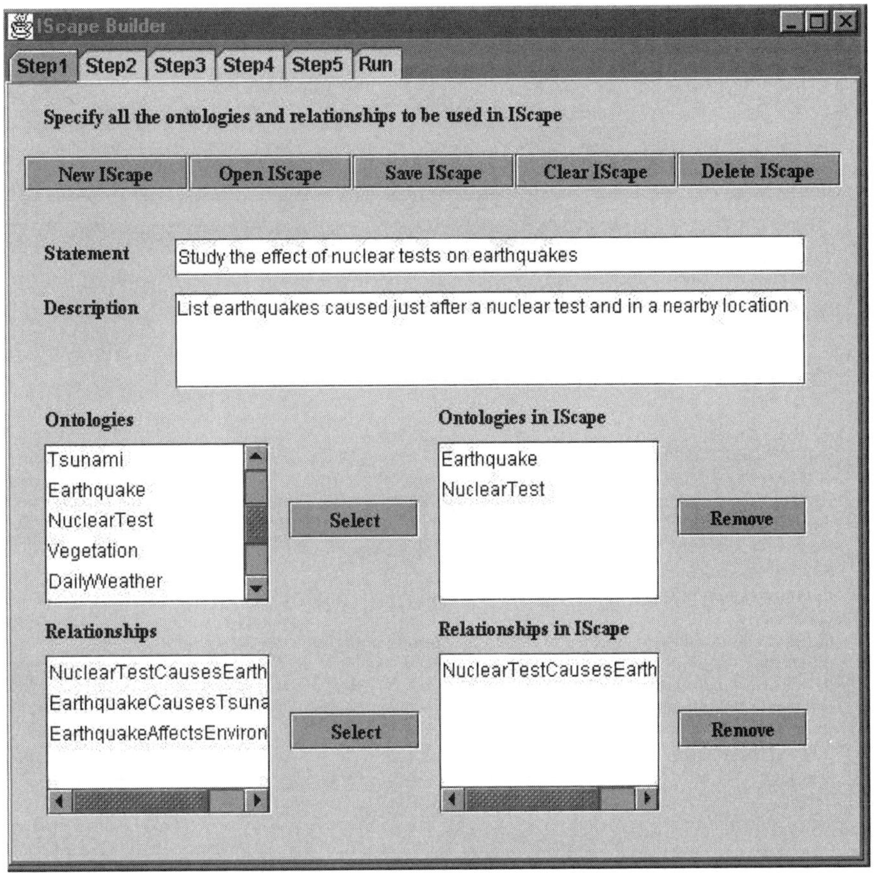

Figure 10.4
IScape Builder.

time–configurable constraint. However, it does not allow users to create new IScapes. The result of executing the NuclearTest Causes Earthquake IScape in example 10.14 is demonstrated in figure 10.5.

The interface describes the entire knowledge base of the system, which helps users understand the domains that are modeled by the ontologies, how the ontologies are related to each other in complex ways (interontological relationships like affects and causes), and the functions and simulations available in the system.

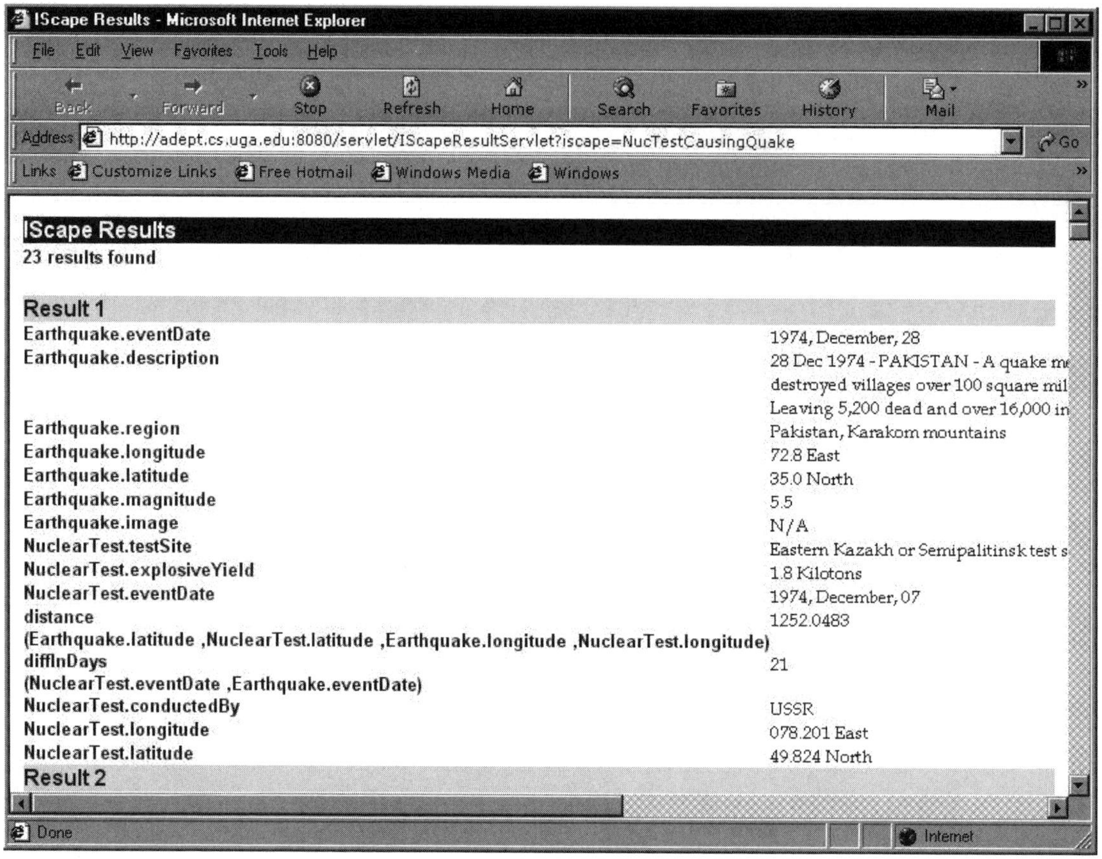

Figure 10.5
IScape results using the Web interface.

10.5.4 IScape Processing Monitor

The IScape Processing Monitor (IPM) (figure 10.6) is a graphical interface used to monitor the execution of IScapes. The user can choose to run an IScape with or without the IPM. The Web-accessible interface, however, does not support the use of the IPM.

The various agents in the run time system generate log entries that are sent to the monitor and displayed as a color-coded table. These log entries can

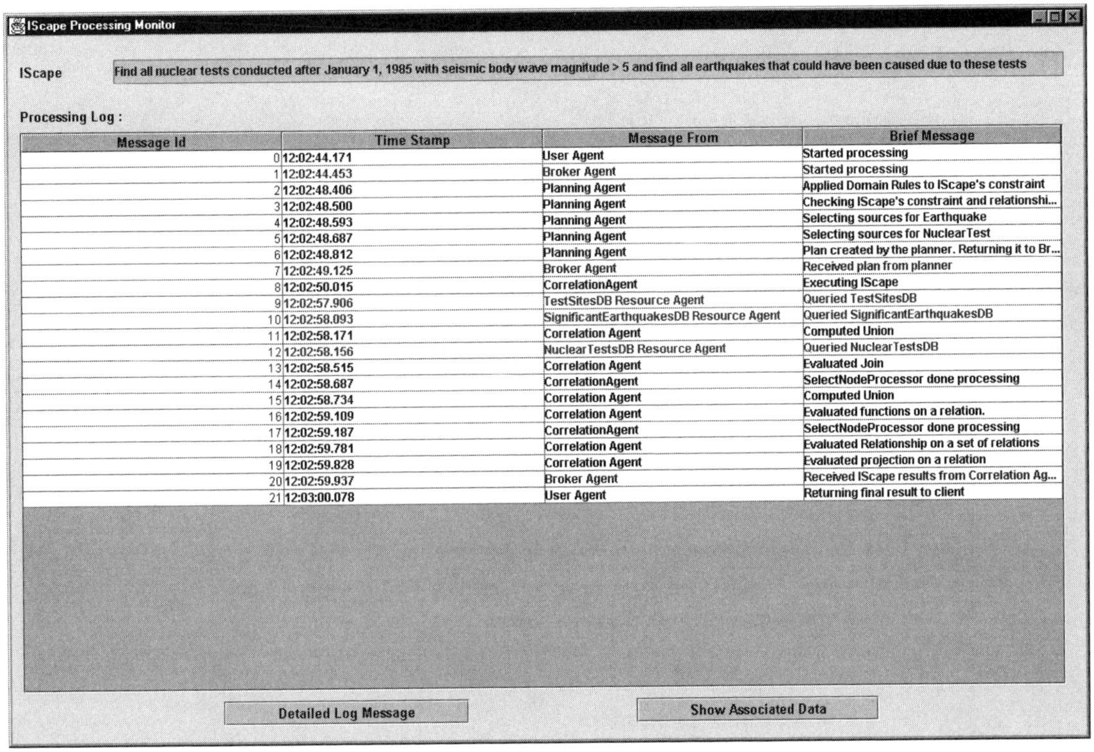

IScape Processing Monitor

IScape: Find all nuclear tests conducted after January 1, 1985 with seismic body wave magnitude > 5 and find all earthquakes that could have been caused due to these tests

Processing Log :

Message Id	Time Stamp	Message From	Brief Message
0	12:02:44.171	User Agent	Started processing
1	12:02:44.453	Broker Agent	Started processing
2	12:02:48.406	Planning Agent	Applied Domain Rules to IScape's constraint
3	12:02:48.500	Planning Agent	Checking IScape's constraint and relationshi...
4	12:02:48.593	Planning Agent	Selecting sources for Earthquake
5	12:02:48.687	Planning Agent	Selecting sources for NuclearTest
6	12:02:48.812	Planning Agent	Plan created by the planner. Returning it to Br...
7	12:02:49.125	Broker Agent	Received plan from planner
8	12:02:50.015	CorrelationAgent	Executing IScape
9	12:02:57.906	TestSitesDB Resource Agent	Queried TestSitesDB
10	12:02:58.093	SignificantEarthquakesDB Resource Agent	Queried SignificantEarthquakesDB
11	12:02:58.171	Correlation Agent	Computed Union
12	12:02:58.156	NuclearTestsDB Resource Agent	Queried NuclearTestsDB
13	12:02:58.515	Correlation Agent	Evaluated Join
14	12:02:58.687	CorrelationAgent	SelectNodeProcessor done processing
15	12:02:58.734	Correlation Agent	Computed Union
16	12:02:59.109	Correlation Agent	Evaluated functions on a relation.
17	12:02:59.187	CorrelationAgent	SelectNodeProcessor done processing
18	12:02:59.781	Correlation Agent	Evaluated Relationship on a set of relations
19	12:02:59.828	Correlation Agent	Evaluated projection on a relation
20	12:02:59.937	Broker Agent	Received IScape results from Correlation Ag...
21	12:03:00.078	User Agent	Returning final result to client

Detailed Log Message | Show Associated Data

Figure 10.6
IScape Processing Monitor.

be very detailed. They include a time stamp, the name of the agent sending the entry, a brief message, a more descriptive message, and associated data, if any. Associated data could be, for example, the execution plan generated by the planner or the results at various stages in the IScape execution.

The IPM is very useful in the following ways:

- It helps in monitoring the execution of the IScape as it proceeds and enables the user to locate any failures easily.
- The inclusion of time stamps with all log entries allows the development team to evaluate which phases of the IScape processing are taking the most

time. This helps us evaluate our system better and identify areas that need improvement.

- The detailed log messages generated by various agents describe in considerable detail exactly what is going on during processing. The IPM is therefore extremely useful to us as a high-level debugging tool.

10.6   *Related Work*

SIMS (Arens, Knoblock, and Shen 1996), TSIMMIS (Chawathe et al. 1994), Information Manifold (Levy, Rajaraman, and Ordille 1996), OBSERVER (Mena et al. 2000) and InfoSleuth (Bayardo et al. 1997) are some of the other efforts that have been made to integrate information from multiple heterogeneous sources for querying. Most other systems focus on retrieving and integrating "data" from multiple sources and not on the "learning, exploring, and understanding" aspects. The following features of InfoQuilt are not supported by any other systems:

- A framework for studying, analyzing, and learning about domains and interdomain relationships.

- Functions and simulations to postprocess the data retrieved from the resources, thereby adding value to the data.

- Modeling of complex relationships and constraints representing the semantic correlation of information across multiple domains that cannot be expressed using relational and logical operators.

- Powerful semantic query interface (IScapes).

Additionally, in comparing the general approach of information integration in the other systems, we identify the following noteworthy differences between those systems and InfoQuilt. The mediator in SIMS (Arens, Knoblock, and Shen 1996) is specialized to a single application domain that is source dependent and query dependent. An application domain in SIMS models a single hierarchy of classes. It does not support interontological relationships. SIMS uses LOOM, a member of the KL-ONE family of knowledge representation systems, to model domains as well as describe information sources. These systems do not consider use of local completeness information about sources and support only one binding pattern per Web resource.

OBSERVER (Mena et al. 2000) uses ontologies to describe information sources and interontology relationships like synonyms, hyponyms, and hypernyms across terms in different ontologies to be able to translate a query specified using some ontology that the user has selected into another query that uses related ontologies describing relevant information. This approach of using relationships to achieve interoperability between sources is limited to basic relationships.

TSIMMIS (Chawathe et al. 1994; Garcia-Molina et al. 1995) uses a mediator-based architecture (Wiederhold 1993) with a query-centric approach. It uses Mediator Specification Language (MSL) to define mediators. MSL specifications encode how the system should use available resources. The mediators are then generated automatically from these specifications. Since the MSL definitions need to be created manually, adding or removing information sources is not easy, as it requires updating them after determining how the sources should be used to answer the queries and then recompiling them. TSIMMIS has a set of predefined query templates that it knows how to answer. User queries are then answered by relating them to these existing query templates. The types of queries that can be answered using this approach are limited, compared to InfoQuilt.

Information Manifold (IM) (Levy, Rajaraman, and Ordille 1996) uses an approach similar to InfoQuilt's in that the user creates a *world view* (a collection of virtual relations and classes). The world view does not, however, capture semantics of the domains as InfoQuilt can using domain rules and FDs. Information sources are described to the system as a query over the relations in the world view. Locally complete resources cannot be modeled precisely. IM uses capability records to capture query capability limitations of sources. These records specify, among other things, a set of input parameters and a minimum and maximum number of inputs allowed. The system then arbitrarily selects a subset of the set of input parameters with at least the minimum number of allowed parameters in the set. Because the subset selected is arbitrary, the capability records cannot precisely specify the binding patterns.

Semantic network is a related concept in terms of modeling knowledge and relationships (Mylopoulu et al. 1990). Unlike information integration systems, the main purpose of semantic network is to create a logical, orderly, and aesthetically consistent relationship of pages (page is an elemental unit of semantic network). The relationships modeled are hierarchical or similarity based and can be used to understand semantics involved within and across domains but are limited in terms of their ability to model complex semantic relationships like "causes" or "affects."

10.7   Conclusion

This chapter discussed our approach for knowledge discovery on the evolving Semantic Web. This approach involves modeling knowledge in terms of complex relationships among Web-accessible semantically related but otherwise heterogeneous information. IScape, a representation used for this, comprises ontologies, interontological relationships, information sources, and complex operations, including functions and simulations. The chapter described the use of IScapes to construct and deploy complex information requests. Of particular interest was the use of interontological relationships and functions to answer those requests. Simulations can also be integrated with the system to perform postquery analysis on the results. IScapes also form the basis for knowledge discovery in the system, through the ability to study and explore new (complex) relationships.

IScapes, interontological relationships, support for functions, and knowledge discovery are the distinguishing features of InfoQuilt. The system can easily adapt to new sources of information and is very scalable. Further, the system has been implemented with and makes use of query planning and optimization with a multithreaded execution to exploit the parallelism in the query plans (Patel and Sheth 2001).

Some improvements to the system are planned. The system will be enhanced to allow the use of recursive query plans, which would further expand its query capability. It needs to make use of inductive learning to infer rules and use them appropriately, which can speed up query processing (Hsu and Crai 1994). In using the current framework to support simulations, further investigation might be necessary to support simulations with more complex interactions.

Notes

1. One of the incarnations of the InfoQuilt system, as applied to geographic information as part of the National Science Foundation Digital Library initiative, is the ADEPT-UGA system (http://alexandria.uscb.edu/).

2. Use of ontologies, context, and relationships are critical in defining information requests and in supporting semantics; see for example the DS-6 proceedings, especially Wiederhold 1997 and Sheth 1996.

3. The information presented in this example is based on the findings of Gary T. Whiteford published in the 1989 paper "Earthquakes and Nuclear Testing: Dangerous Patterns and Trends." Whiteford's paper has been recognized as the most exhaustive study yet of the correlation between nuclear testing and earthquakes.

4. The period "1950–present" in this example implies the period 1950–1989, since the data presented here were published by Whiteford in 1989.

References

Arens, Y., C. A. Knoblock, and W. Shen. 1996. Query Reformulation for Dynamic Information Integration. *Journal of Intelligent Information Systems* 6:99–130.

Bayardo, R. J. Jr., W. Bohrer, R. Brice, A. Cichocki, J. Fowler, A. Helal, V. Kashyap, T. Ksiezyk, G. Martin, M. H. Nodine, M. Rashid, M. Rusinkiewicz, R. Shea, C. Unnikrishnan, A. Unruh, D. Woelk. 1997. InfoSleuth: Agent-Based Semantic Integration of Information in Open and Dynamic Environments. In *Proceedings of the ACM SIGMOD International Conference on Management of Data (SIGMOD-97), Tucson, Arizona, May 13–15, 1997*, ed. J. Peckham (pp. 195–206). Marina del Rey, CA: ACM.

Berners-Lee, T., J. Hendler, and O. Lassila. 2001. The Semantic Web. *Scientific American*. Available from http://www.sciam.com/2001/0501issue/0501berners-lee.html.

Bertram, C. 1998. InfoQuilt: Semantic Correlation of Heterogeneous Distributed Assets. Master's thesis, Computer Science Department, University of Georgia, Athens.

Clarke's Urban Growth Model. 2001. Project Gigalopolis, Department of Geography, University of California, Santa Barbara. Available from http://www.ncgia.ucsb.edu/projects/gig/ncgia.html.

Chawathe, S., H. Garcia-Molina, J. Hammer, K. Ireland, Y. Papakonstantinou, J. Ullman, and J. Widom. 1994. The TSIMMIS Project: Integration of Heterogeneous Information Sources. In *Proceedings of 10th Anniversary Meeting of the Information Processing Society of Japan, Tokyo, Japan.* Available from http://www.ipsj.or.jp/.

Duschka, O. M. 1997. Query Planning and Optimization in Information Integration. Ph.D. thesis, Computer Science Department, Stanford University, Stanford, California.

Fensel, D., and M. A. Musen, eds. 2001. The Semantic Web: A Brain for Humankind. *Special Issue of IEEE Intelligent Systems on Semantic Web Technology* 16(2).

Garcia-Molina, H., Y. Papakonstantinou, D. Quass, A. Rajaraman, Y. Sagiv, J. Ullman, and J. Widom. 1995. The TSIMMIS Approach to Mediation: Data Models and Languages. In *Proceedings of the Second International Workshop on Next Generation Information Technologies and Systems (NGTIS-95) Naharia, Israel, June, 1995.* Available from http://www.site.uottawa.ca/kaml/CFP/775413258.html.

Guntamadugu, M. 2000. MÉTIS: Automating Metabase Creation from Multiple Heterogeneous Sources. Master's thesis, Computer Science Department, University of Georgia, Athens.

Hsu, C.-N., and C. A. Knoblock. 1994. Rule Induction for Semantic Query Optimization. In *Proceedings of the Eleventh International Conference on Machine Learning, Rutgers University, New Brunswick, New Jersey, July 10–13, 1994,* ed. W. W. Cohen and H. Hirsh (pp. 112–120). San Francisco: Morgan Kaufmann.

Kashyap, V., and A. Sheth. 1996. Schematic and Semantic Similarities between Database Objects: A Context-Based Approach. In *Very Large Databases (VLDB) Journal* 5(4):276–304.

Kashyap, V., and A. Sheth. 1997. Semantic Heterogeneity in Global Information Systems: The Role of Metadata, Context and Ontologies. In Cooperative Information Systems, ed. M. Papazoglou, and G. Schlageter (pp. 139–178). San Diego: Academic Press.

Kashyap, V., and A. Sheth. 2000. *Information Brokering across Heterogeneous Digital Data: A Metadata-Based Approach.* Boston: Kluwer Academic.

Laksminarayanan, S. 2000. Achieving Semantic Inter-Operability in Digital Libraries by Use of Inter-Ontological Relations. Master's thesis, Computer Science Department, University of Georgia, Athens.

Levy, A. Y., A. Rajaraman, and J. J. Ordille. 1996. Querying Heterogeneous Information Sources Using Source Descriptions. In *Proceedings of the 22nd International Conference on Very*

Large Databases (VLDB-96), Bombay, India, September 1996, ed. T. M. Vijayaraman, A. P. Buchmann, C. Mohan, and N. L. Sarda (pp. 251–262). San Francisco: Morgan Kaufmann.

Mena, E., A. Illarramendi, V. Kashyap, and A. P. Sheth. 2000. OBSERVER: An Approach for Query Processing in Global Information Systems Based on Interoperation across Pre-existing Ontologies. *International Journal on Distributed and Parallel Databases* 8(2):223–271.

Mylopoulus, J., A. Borgida, M. Jarke, and M. Koubarakis. 1990. Telos: Representing Knowledge about Information Systems. *ACM Transaction on Information Systems* 8(4):325–362.

Ontology-based information exchange for Knowledge Management and electronic Commerce. Available from http://www.ontoweb.org.

Palsena, N. 2000. A Collaborative Approach to Learning Using Information Landscapes. Master's thesis, Computer Science Department, University of Georgia, Athens.

Patel, S., and A. Sheth. 2001. Planning And Optimizing Semantic Information Requests on Heterogeneous Information Sources Using Semantically Modeled Domain and Resource Characteristics. LSDIS Technical Report, University of Georgia, Athens.

Shah, K., and A. Sheth. 1998. Logical Information Modeling of Web-Accessible Heterogeneous Digital Assets. In *Proceedings of the IEEE Forum on Research and Technology Advances in Digital Libraries (IEEE ADL-98), Santa Barbara, CA, April, 22–24, 1998*. Los Alamitos, CA: IEEE.

Sheth, A. 1996. Data Semantics: What, Where, and How? In *Data Semantics (IFIP Transactions)*, ed. R. Meersman and L. Mark (pp. 601–610). London: Chapman and Hall.

Sheth, A. 1999. Changing Focus on Interoperability: From System, Syntax, Structure to Semantics. In *Interoperating Geographic Information Systems*, ed. M. Goodchild, M. Egenhofer, R. Fegeas, and C. Kottman. Boston: Kluwer Academic.

Whiteford, G. T. 1989. Earthquakes and Nuclear Testing: Dangerous Patterns and Trends. *Pulse of the Planet* 1(2).

Wiederhold, G. 1993. Mediators in the Architecture of Future Information Systems. IEEE Computer 25(3):38–49.

Wiederhold, G. 1997. Value-Added Mediation in Large-Scale Information Systems. In *Database Application Semantics*, ed. R. Meersman. London: Chapman and Hall.

11   SEmantic portAL: The SEAL Approach

*Alexander Maedche, Steffen Staab, Nenad Stojanovic,
Rudi Studer, and York Sure*

11.1   Introduction

The widely agreed-upon core idea of the Semantic Web is the delivery of data
on a semantic basis. Intuitively the delivery of semantically apprehended
data should help with establishing a higher quality of communication between the information provider and the consumer. How this intuition may
be put into practice is the topic of this chapter. We discuss means for fur-
thering communication on a semantic basis. For this one needs a theory of
communication that links results from semiotics, linguistics, and philosophy
into actual information technology. We here consider *ontologies* as a sound
semantic basis that is used to define the meaning of terms and hence to
support intelligent access, for example, by semantic querying (Decker et al.
1999) or dynamic hypertext views (Staab et al. 2000). Thus, ontologies constitute the foundation of our SEAL (SEmantic portAL) approach. The origin
of SEAL lies in Ontobroker (Decker et al. 1999), which was conceived for semantic search of knowledge on the Web and has also been used for sharing
knowledge on the Web (Benjamins and Fensel 1998). It then developed into
an overarching framework for search and presentation offering access at a
portal site (Staab et al. 2000). This concept was then transferred to further
applications (Angele et al. 2000; Staab and Maedche 2001; Sure, Maedche,

and Staab 2000) and is currently being extended to a commercial solution (see http://www.time2research.de).

Here, we describe how we have applied SEAL to a real-world case study, namely, the AIFB Web site. From the history of SEAL and related projects, we have distilled a methodology for construction of ontology-based knowledge systems that has been applied for the construction of the AIFB web site (section 11.3). Following the description of this methodology and the experiences we have had with its application to the AIFB site, we describe the core modules of SEAL and its overall architecture (section 11.4). Thereafter, we discuss several technical details that are important for human and machine access to a semantic portal.

In particular, we describe a general approach for semantic ranking (section 11.5). The motivation for semantic ranking is that even with accurate semantic access, one will often find too much information in a Web search. Underlying semantic structures, such as topic hierarchies, give an indication of what should be ranked higher on a list of results. Then, we tackle the issue of semantic personalization (section 11.6). The principal idea of semantic personalization is that underlying semantics may be very useful for presenting personalized views on ontologies, because they allow content-based views to be placed onto the web site. Finally, we present mechanisms for delivering and collecting machine-understandable data (section 11.7). They extend previous means for better digestion of Web site data by software agents. Before we conclude (in section 11.9), we give a short survey of related work in section 11.8.

11.2 Ontologies and Knowledge Bases

For our AIFB intranet, we explicitly model relevant aspects of the domain in order to allow for a more concise communication between agents, namely, within the group of software agents, between software and human agents, and—last but not least—between different human agents. In particular, we describe a way of modeling an ontology that we consider appropriate for supporting communication between human and software agents.

11.2.1   Ontologies for Communication

Research in ontology has its roots in philosophy dealing with the nature and organization of being. In computer science, the term *ontology* refers to an engineering artifact, constituted by a specific vocabulary used to describe a particular model of the world, plus a set of explicit assumptions regarding the intended meaning of the words in the vocabulary. Both vocabulary and assumptions aid human and software agents in reaching common conclusions when communicating.

11.2.1.1   Reference and Meaning

The general context of communication (with or without ontology) is described by the meaning triangle (Odgen and Richards 1993). The meaning triangle defines the interaction among symbols or words, concepts, and things of the world (see figure 11.1). It illustrates the idea that although words cannot completely capture the essence of a reference (= concept) or of a referent (= thing), there is a correspondence between them.

As the meaning triangle illustrates, the relationship between a word and a thing is indirect. The correct linkage can be accomplished only when an interpreter processes the word invoking a corresponding concept and establishes the proper linkage between his concept and the appropriate thing in the world.

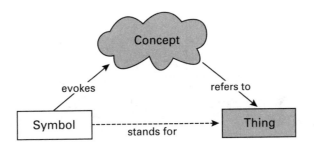

Figure 11.1
The meaning triangle.

11.2.1.2   Logics

An ontology is a general logical theory constituted by a vocabulary and a set of statements about a domain of interest in some logic language. The logical theory specifies relations between signs, and it apprehends relations with a semantics that restricts the set of possible interpretations of the signs. Thus, the ontology reduces the number of mappings from signs to things in the world that an interpreter who is committed to the ontology can perform: in the ideal case each sign from the vocabulary eventually stands for exactly one thing in the world.

Figure 11.2 depicts the overall setting for communication between human and software agents. We mainly distinguish three layers of communication: first of all, we deal with things that exist in the real world, including, in this example, human and software agents, cars, and animals. Second, we deal with symbols and syntactic structures that are exchanged. Third, we analyze models with their specific semantic structures.

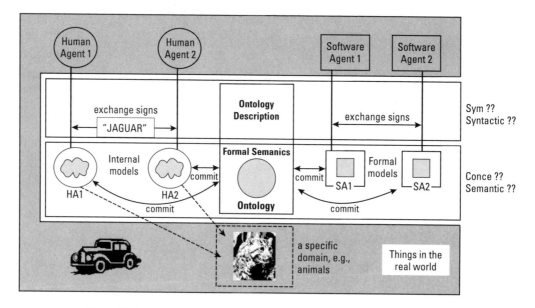

Figure 11.2
Communication between human and/or software agents.

Let us first consider the left side of figure 11.2 without assuming a commitment to any particular ontology. Two human agents HA1 and HA2 exchange a specific sign (e.g., a word like "jaguar"). Given their own internal model, each of them will associate the sign with his own concept referring to possibly two completely different existing things in the world (e.g., the animal versus the car). The same holds for software agents: they may exchange statements based on a common syntax, however, they may have different formal models that have differing interpretations of those statements.

We consider the scenario in which both human agents commit to a specific ontology that deals, for example, with a specific domain (e.g., animals). The chance that they both refer to the same thing in the world increases considerably with such a commitment. Moving now to the right side of the figure, the same holds for the software agents SA1 and SA2. They have actual knowledge, and they use an ontology to have a common semantic basis. When agent SA1 uses the term "jaguar," the other agent, SA2, may use the ontology just mentioned as background knowledge and rule out incorrect references, such as those that let "jaguar" stand for the car. Human and software agents use their concepts and their inference processes, respectively, in order to narrow down the choice of referents (e.g., because animals do not have wheels, but cars have).

11.2.1.3 *A New Model for Ontologies*

Subsequently, we define our notion of ontology. However, in contrast to that of most other research about ontology languages, it is not our purpose to invent a new logic language or to redescribe an old one. Rather, what we specify is a way of *modeling* an ontology that inherently considers the special role of signs (mostly strings, in current ontology-based systems) and references.

Our motivation is based on the conflict that arises from the fact that ontologies are for human and software agents, but logical theories are mostly for mathematicians and inference engines. Formal semantics for ontologies is a sine qua non. In fact, we build our applications on a well-understood logical framework, namely, F-logic (Kifer, Lausen, and Wu 1995). However, in addition to the benefits of logical rigor, both the user and the developer of an ontology-based system profit from ontology structures that allow possible misunderstandings to be elucidated.

For instance, one might specify in an ontology that the sign "jaguar" refers to the union of the set of all animals that are jaguars and the set of all cars that are jaguars. Alternatively, one might describe "jaguar" as a sign that may refer either to a concept "animal-jaguar" or to a concept "car-jaguar." We prefer this second method of specification. In conjunction with appropriate GUI modules (see sections 11.4ff), one may avoid presentations of "funny symbols" like "animal-jaguar" to the user while avoiding "funny inference" of the sort that may arise from artificial concepts like ('animal-jaguar' ['car-jaguar').

11.2.2 Ontology versus Knowledge Base

Concerning the general setting just sketched, the term *ontology* is defined—more or less—as some piece of formal knowledge. However, several properties of knowledge warrant making a distinction between knowledge contained in an ontology and knowledge contained in a so-called *knowledge base*. These properties are summarized in table 11.1.

An ontology constitutes a general logical theory, whereas a knowledge base describes particular circumstances pertaining to such a theory. In an

Table 11.1

Distinguishing between an ontology and a knowledge base

	Ontology	Knowledge base
Set of logic statements	Yes	Yes
Theory	General theory	Theory of particular circumstances
Statements are mostly	Intensional	Extensional
Construction	Set up once	Continuous change
Description logics	T-Box	A-Box

ontology one tries to capture the general conceptual structures of a domain of interest, whereas in a knowledge base one aims at the specification of a given state of affairs. Thus, an ontology is (mostly) constituted by *intensional* logical definitions, whereas a knowledge base comprises (mostly) the *extensional* parts. The theory in an ontology is one that is mostly developed during the setting up (and maintenance) of an ontology-based system, whereas the facts in a knowledge base may be constantly changing. In description logics, the ontology part is mostly described in the T-Box and the knowledge base in the A-Box. However, our current experience is that it is not always possible to distinguish an ontology from a knowledge base by the logical statements that are made. In section 11.9 we will touch on some of the problems that arise from this difficulty in distinguishing ontologies from knowledge bases, referring to some examples of following sections.

Certain distinctions typically made ("general" versus "specific," "intensional" versus "extensional," "set up once" versus "continuous change") indicate that for purposes of development, maintenance, and good design of a software system, it is reasonable to distinguish between ontology and knowledge base. Also, they describe a rough shape for determining where to put which parts of a logical theory constraining the intended semantic models that facilitate the referencing task for human and software agents. However, the reader should note that none of these distinctions draws a clear-cut borderline between ontology and knowledge base in general. Rather, it is typical that in a few percent of cases, whether a modeler decides to put particular entities and relations into the ontology or into the knowledge base depends on the domain being modeled and the view experience of the modeler.

Both the following definitions of ontology and knowledge base specify constraints on the way an ontology (or a knowledge base) should be modeled *in a particular logical language* like F-logic or OIL.

Definition 11.1 (Ontology)   An ontology is a sign system $O := (L, F, G, C, H, R, A)$ that consists of

- A *lexicon*. The lexicon contains a set of signs (lexical entries) for concepts, L^C, and a set of signs for relations, L^R. Their union is the lexicon $L := L^C \cup L^R$.

- Two *reference functions* F, G, with $F : 2^{Lc} \rightarrow L^C$ and $G : 2^{Lr} \rightarrow 2^R$. F and G link sets of lexical entries $\{Li\} \subset L$ to the set of concepts and relations they refer to, respectively, in the given ontology. In general, one lexical entry may refer to several concepts or relations, and one concept or relation may be refered to by several lexical entries. The inverses of F and G are F^{-1} and G^{-1}, respectively. To map easily back and forth, and because there is an n-to-m mapping between lexicon and concepts/relations, F and G are defined on sets rather than on single objects.

- A set C of *concepts*. About each concept C there exists at least one statement in the ontology, namely, its *embedding in the taxonomy*.

- A *taxonomy H*. Concepts are taxonomically related by the irreflexive, acyclic, transitive relation $H, (H \subset C * C)$. $H(C1, C2)$ means that $C1$ is a subconcept of $C2$.

- A set of *binary relations* R. R denotes a set of binary relations[1] that specify pairs of domain and ranges (D, R), with $D, R \in C$. The functions d and r applied to a binary relation Q yield the corresponding domain and range concepts D and R, respectively.

- A set of *ontology axioms*, A.

The reader may note that the structure we propose for ontologies is very similar to the WordNet model described by Miller (1995). WordNet has been conceived as a mixed linguistic/psychological model about how people associate words with their meanings. Like WordNet, we allow one word to have several meanings and one concept (synset) to be represented by several words. However, we allow for a seamless integration into logical languages like OIL or F-logic by providing very simple means of defining relations and knowledge bases.

We define a knowledge base as a collection of object descriptions that refer to a given ontology.

Definition 11.2 (Knowledge Base)   We define a knowledge base as a 7-tuple
$KB := (L, J, I, W, S, A, O)$, that consists of

- A *lexicon*. The lexicon contains a set of signs for instances, L.

- A *reference function J*, with $J : 2^L \to 2^I$. J links sets of lexical entries $\{L_i\} \subset L$ to the set of instances they correspond to. Thereby, names may be multiply used; for example, "Athens" may be used for "Athens, Georgia" or for "Athens, Greece."

- A set of *instances* I. About each $I_k \in I$, $k = 1, \ldots, l$ exists at least one statement in the knowledge base, namely, a membership for a concept C from the ontology O.

- A *membership function W*, with $W : 2^I \to 2^C$. W assigns sets of instances to the sets of concepts they are members of.

- *Instantiated relations*, S, namely, $S \subseteq \{(x, y, z) x \in I, y \in R, z \in I\}$.

- A set of knowledge base axioms, A.

- A reference to an ontology O.

Overall the decision to model some relevant part of the domain in the ontology versus in the knowledge base is often based on gradual distinctions and driven by the needs of a particular application. Concerning the technical issue it is sometimes even useful to let the lexicon of knowledge base and ontology overlap (e.g., to use a concept name to refer to a particular instance in a particular context). In fact researchers in natural language have tackled the question how the reference function J can be dynamically extended given an ontology, a context, a knowledge base, and a particular sentence.

11.3   Ontology Engineering

The conceptual backbone of our SEAL approach is the ontology. For our intranet, we had to model the concepts relevant in this setting. As SEAL has matured, we have developed a methodology for setting up ontology-based knowledge systems, which we sketch here. (An extended description of it can be found in Staab et al. 2001.) We also describe here some experiences we have had during the ontology development.

11.3.1   Methodology for Ontology Engineering

Until a few years ago ontologies were built in a rather ad hoc fashion. Lately there have been a few (but seminal) proposals for guiding the ontology development process (e.g., Uschold and Gruninger 1996; Gomez-Perez 1996; Guarino and Welty 2000). For instance Guarino and Welty (2000) give formal guidelines for constructing a consistent and reusable ontology. Another approach, the Methontology framework (Gomez-Perez 1996), includes the identification of the ontology development process and stages through which an ontology passes during its lifetime. In contrast to these methodologies, which mostly restrict their attention to within the ontology itself, our approach (see figure 11.3) focuses on the application-driven development of ontologies.

11.3.1.1   Kickoff Phase

The result of the kickoff phase is an ontology requirements specification document (ORSD) describing what an ontology should support, sketching the planned area of the ontology application, and listing, for example, valuable input sources for the gathering of the baseline taxonomy in the refinement phase. Analysis of these input sources delivers an "initial lexicon" containing relevant lexical entries. In general, the ORSD should guide an ontology engineer in deciding about inclusion and exclusion of lexical entries, their linkings to concepts/relations, and the hierarchical structure of the ontology. In this early stage one should look for already developed and potentially reusable ontologies.

11.3.1.2   Refinement Phase

The goal of the refinement phase is to produce a mature and application-oriented "target ontology" according to the specification given by the kickoff phase. This phase is divided into several subphases. First, the initial lexicon is

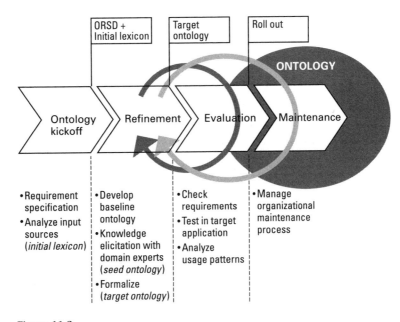

Figure 11.3
Ontology development.

linked to corresponding concepts/relations, and the concepts are ordered in a taxonomy to form a "baseline ontology." Second, knowledge is elicited from domain experts based on the initial input from the baseline ontology to develop a "seed ontology." In the seed ontology, the initial baseline ontology is modified and/or extended and axioms are added on top. Third, in a formalization subphase, the seed ontology is transferred into the target ontology, which is expressed in formal representation languages like F-logic (Kifer, Lausen, and Wu 1995), OIL (Decker et al. 2000) or Conceptual Graphs (Sowa 1992). During the formalization subphase, the ontology engineer has to draw the line between ontology and knowledge base (see section 11.2.2).

The incorporation of potentially reusable ontologies (identified during the kickoff phase) may improve the speed and quality of development during the entire refinement phase. These ontologies might, for example, give useful hints for modeling decisions.

11.3.1.3   Evaluation Phase

The evaluation phase serves as a proof for the usefulness of developed ontologies and their associated software environment. In the first step of this phase, the ontology engineer checks whether the target ontology suffices with respect to the ontology requirements specification document. In the second step, the ontology is populated by adding instances to the knowledge base and tested in the target application environment; again, requirements from the ORSD serve as a basis for evaluation. Feedback from beta users may be a valuable input for further refinement of the ontology. A valuable input may be the usage patterns of the ontology. The prototype system has to track the ways users navigate or search for concepts and relations. With such a "semantic log file" (see section 11.6.2) we may trace which areas of the ontology have been "used" often and which others have not been navigated. This phase is closely linked to the refinement phase, and an ontology engineer may need to perform several cycles until the target ontology reaches the envisaged level. The "roll out" of the target ontology finishes the evaluation phase.

11.3.1.4   Maintenance Phase

In the real world things are constantly changing—and so do the specifications for ontologies. To reflect these changes ontologies, like other parts of software, have to be maintained frequently. We stress that the maintenance of ontologies is primarily an organizational process. There must be strict rules for update-delete-insert processes within ontologies. We recommend that the ontology engineer gather changes to the ontology and initiate a switchover to a new version of the ontology only after thoroughly testing possible effects to the application, namely, by performing additional cyclic refinement and evaluation phases. As in the refinement phase, feedback from users and analysis of usage patterns may be a valuable input in the maintenance phase for identifying needed changes. Maintenance should accompany ontologies as long as they are on duty.

11.3.2   Experience with Ontology Development

The methodology outlined in the previous section describes in general how to develop ontologies. We now describe experiences we have had while performing the steps described above and include some aspects not covered in the methodology discussion.

11.3.2.1   Kickoff Phase
Setting up requirements for the AIFB ontology we had to deal mainly with modeling the topics of research done by different groups of our institute, teaching-related topics, and last but not least, personal information about members of our institute. We took ourselves as an "input source" and collected a large set of lexical entries for research topics, teaching-related topics, and personal information. The ontology developers were prevented by the sheer nature of these lexical entries from coming up with all relevant lexical entries by themselves. Rather it was necessary to go through several steps with domain experts (viz., our colleagues) in the refinement phase.

11.3.2.2   Refinement Phase
We started to develop a baseline taxonomy that contained a heterarchy of research topics identified during the kickoff phase. An important result of this beginning was our recognition that categorization was based not on an ISA taxonomy, but on a much weaker HASSUBTOPIC relationship. We then moved on to the second subphase of the refinement phase, namely, the development of the seed ontology through elicitation of knowledge from our colleagues. For that subphase, we needed three steps.

In the first step, lexical entries were collected by all members of the institute. Though we had already given them the possibility of providing a rough categorization, the categories modeled by those other than knowledge engineers were oriented not toward a model of the world, but rather toward the way people worked in their daily routine. Thus, their categorization reflected a particular rather than a shared view of the domain. A lesson learned from this was that people need an idea about the nature of ontologies to make sound modeling suggestions. It was very helpful to show existing prototypes of ontology-based systems to the domain experts.

In the second step, we worked toward a common understanding of the categorization and the derivation of implicit knowledge, such as "someone who works in logic also works in theoretical computer science," and inverseness of relations e.g., "an author has a publication" is inverse to "a publication is written by an author."

In the third step, we mapped the gathered lexical entries to concepts and relations and organized them at a middle level. Naturally, this level would involve the introduction of more generic concepts that people would usually not use when characterizing their work (such as "optimization"), but it would also include "politically desired concepts," because one own's ontology exhibits one's view of the world. Thus, an ontology may become a political issue!

Modeling during early stages of the refinement phase was done with pen and paper, but soon we took advantage of our ontology environment Onto-Edit (see figure 11.4) that supports graphical ontology engineering at an epistemological level as well as formalization of the ontology. Our underlying inference engine (see section 11.4) is based on F-logic, which we therefore chose as the representation language for the target ontology. As mentioned before, formalization is a nontrivial process in which the ontology engineer has to draw the line between ontology and knowledge base. Our final decisions in this regard were much disputed. In section 11.9 we will discuss some of the intricacies that arise using excerpts of our ontology/knowledge base, such as the ones given in section 11.5.

11.3.2.3 Evaluation Phase

We found that participation by users in the construction of the ontology was very good and met the previously defined requirements, as people were very interested in seeing their work adequately represented. Some people even took the time to learn about OntoEdit. However, we had a practical problem:

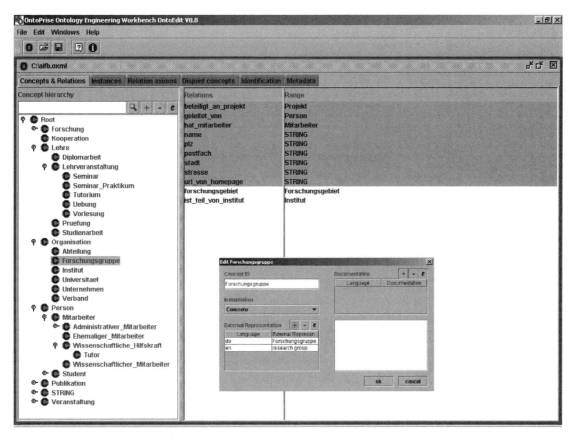

Figure 11.4
OntoEdit.

our environment does not yet support an ontology management module for cooperative ontology engineering.

We embedded version 1.0 of the ontology into our application and enabled semantic log files (see section 11.6.2) to track the usage of the ontology. On top of that we are collecting feedback from our users (basically colleagues and students from our institute). Currently we are still running version 1.0 of the ontology, but we expect maintenance to be a relevant topic soon.

11.4   SEAL Infrastructure and Core Modules

The aim of our intranet application is the presentation of information to human and software agents that takes advantage of semantic structures. In this section, we first elaborate on the general architecture for SEAL, then explain the functionalities of its core modules.

11.4.1   Architecture

The overall architecture and environment of SEAL is depicted in figure 11.5. The *backbone* of the system consists of the *knowledge warehouse* (i.e., the data repository) and the *Ontobroker* system (i.e., the principal inferencing mechanism). The latter functions as a kind of middleware run time system, possibly mediating between different information sources when the environment becomes more complex than it is now.

At the front end one may distinguish between three types of *agents*: *software agents*, *community users*, and *general users*. All three communicate with the system through the *Web server*. The three different types of agents correspond to three primary modes of interaction with the system. First, remote applications (e.g., software agents) may process information stored at the portal over the Internet. For this purpose, the *RDF Generator* presents RDF facts through the Web server. Software agents with *RDF Crawlers* may collect the facts and thus have direct access to semantic knowledge stored on the Web site.

Second, community users and general users can access information contained on the Web site. Two forms of accessing are supported: navigating through the portal by exploiting the hyperlink structure of documents and searching for information by posting queries. The hyperlink structure is partially given by the portal builder, but it may be extended with the help of the *navigation* module. The navigation module exploits inferencing capabilities of the inference engine in order to construct conceptual hyperlink structures. Searching and querying are performed via the *query* module. In addition, the user can personalise the search interface using the *semantic personalization*

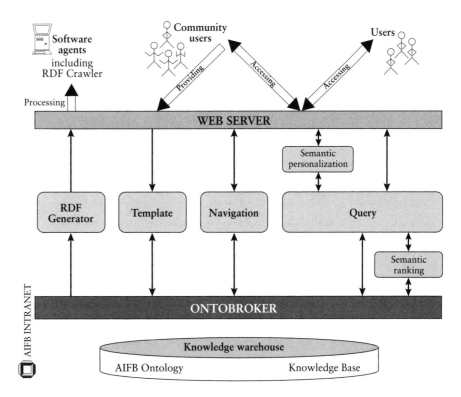

Figure 11.5
AIFB intranet: system architecture.

preprocessing module and/or rank retrieved results according to semantic similarity (done by the postprocessing module for *semantic ranking*). Queries also take advantage of Ontobroker inferencing.

Third, only community users can provide data for the ontology and knowledge base. Typical information they contribute includes personal data, information about research areas, publications, and activities, and other research information. For each type of information they contribute there is (at least) one concept in the ontology. Retrieving parts of the ontology, the *template* module may semiautomatically produce suitable HTML forms for data input. Community users fill in these forms, and the template module stores the data in the knowledge warehouse.

11.4.2   Core Modules

The core modules of SEAL have been extensively described in Staab et al. 2000. In order to give the reader a compact overview, we briefly survey their function here. In the remainder of the chapter, we delve more deeply into those aspects that have been added or considerably extended recently, namely, semantic ranking (section 11.5), semantic personalization (section 11.6), and semantic access by software agents (section 11.7).

11.4.2.1   Ontobroker

The Ontobroker system (Fensel et al. 1998) is a deductive, object-oriented database system operating either in main memory or on a relational database. It provides compilers for different languages to describe ontologies, rules, and facts. Besides other usage, in this architecture it is also used as an inference engine (server). It reads input files containing the knowledge base and the ontology, evaluates incoming queries, and returns the results derived from the interaction of ontology, knowledge base, and query.

The possibility Ontobroker offers of deriving additional factual knowledge from given facts and background knowledge considerably facilitates the life of the knowledge providers and the knowledge seekers. For instance, one may specify that if a person belongs to a research group of institute AIFB, he also belongs to AIFB. Thus, it is unnecessary to specify the person's membership both in his research group *and* in AIFB. Conversely, an information seeker does not have to deal with inconsistent assignments (e.g., those that specify membership in an AIFB research group but that have erroneously left out membership in AIFB).

11.4.2.2   Knowledge Warehouse

The knowledge warehouse (Staab et al. 2000) serves as the repository for data, represented in the form of F-logic statements. It hosts the ontology as well as the data proper. From the point of view of inferencing (Ontobroker) the difference between ontology definition and its instantiation is negligible, but from the point of view of maintaining the system the difference is useful. The knowledge warehouse is organized around a relational database, in which facts and concepts are stored in a reified format. It states relations and concepts as first-order objects, and it is therefore very flexible with regard to changes to and amendments of the ontology.

11.4.2.3 Navigation Module

In addition to the hierarchical, tree-based hyperlink structure that corresponds to hierarchical decomposition of domain, the navigation module enables complex graph-based semantic hyperlinking, based on ontological relations between concepts (nodes) in the domain. The conceptual approach to hyperlinking is based on the assumption that semantically relevant hyperlinks from a Web page correspond to conceptual relations, such as MEMBEROF or HASPART, or to attributes, like HASNAME. Thus, instances in the knowledge base may be presented by automatically generating links to all related instances. For example, personal Web pages (see figure 11.7) have hyperlinks to Web pages that describe the corresponding research groups, research areas, and project Web pages.

11.4.2.4 Query Module

The query module puts an easy-to-use interface on the query capabilities of the F-logic query interface of Ontobroker. The portal builder models Web pages that serve particular query needs, such as querying for projects or querying for people. For this purpose, selection lists that restrict query possibilities are offered to the user. The selection lists are compiled using knowledge from the ontology and/or the knowledge base. For instance, the query interface for persons allows the user to search for people according to research groups they are members of. The list of research groups is dynamically filled via an F-logic query and presented to the user for easy choice by a drop-down list (see snapshot in figure 11.6).

Even more simply, one may apprehend a hyperlink with an F-logic query that is dynamically evaluated when the link is hit. To be more complex, one may construct an ISA, a HASPART, or a HASSUBTOPIC tree, from which query events are triggered when particular nodes in the tree are navigated.

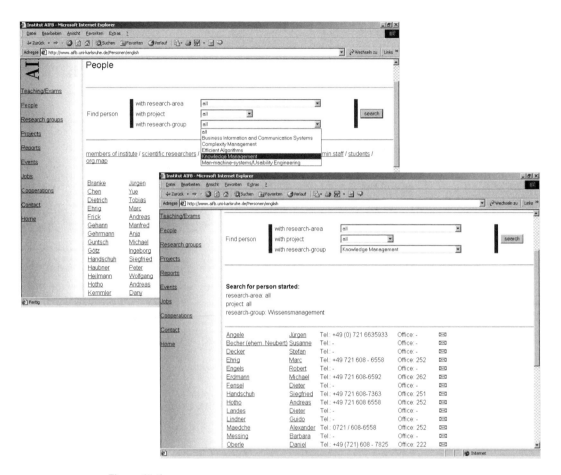

Figure 11.6
Search form based on definition of concept Person.

11.4.2.5   Template Module

To facilitate the contribution of information by community users, the template module generates an HTML form for each concept that a user may instantiate. For instance, in the AIFB intranet there is an input template (see figure 11.7, upper left) generated from the concept definition of person (see figure 11.7, lower left). The instance data are later used by the navigation module to produce the corresponding person Web page (see figure 11.7, right side).

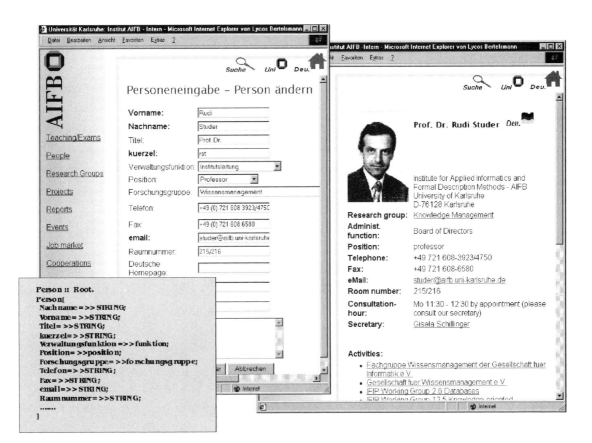

Figure 11.7
Templates generated from concept definitions.

To reduce the amount of data required for input, the portal builder specifies which attributes and relations are derived from other templates. For example, in our case the portal builder has specified that project membership is defined in the project template. The coordinator of a project enters information about which persons are participants in the project, and this information is used when generating the person Web page, taking advantage of a corresponding F-logic rule for inverse relationships. Hence, it is unnecessary to input this information in the person template.

11.4.2.6   Ontology Lexicon

The different modules described here make extensive use of the lexicon component of the ontology. The most prevalent use is the distinction between English and German (realized for presentation, though not for the template module, yet). In the future we envision that one will be able to produce more adaptive Web sites making use of the explicit lexicon. For instance, we will be able to produce short concept descriptions when the context is sufficiently narrow (e.g., when working with ambiguous acronyms like ASP[2] or SEAL.[3]

11.5   Semantic Ranking

This section describes the architecture component "semantic ranking" that has been developed in the context of our application. First, we introduce and motivate the requirement for a ranking approach with a small example we are facing. Second, we show how the problem of semantic ranking may be reduced to the comparison of two knowledge bases. Query results are reinterpreted as "query knowledge bases," and their similarity to the original knowledge base without axioms yields the basis for semantic ranking. Thereby, we reduce our notion of similarity between two knowledge bases to the similarity of concept pairs (Maedche and Staab 2000).

Let us assume the following ontology:

```
1:   Person :: Object [worksIn => Project].
2:   Project :: Object [worksIn => Topic].
3:   Person :: Object [worksIn => Topic].
```

To give an intuition of the semantic of the F-logic statements, in line 1 one finds a concept definition for a Person being an Object with a relation *worksIn*. The range of the relation for this Person is restricted to Project.

Let us further assume the following knowledge base:

```
4:   KnowledgeManagement: Topic.
5:   KnowledgeDiscovery: Topic [subtopicOf ->
     KnowledgeManagement].
```

```
6:  Gerd : Person [worksIn -> OntoWise].
7:  OntoWise : Project[hasTopic -> KnowledgeManagement].
8:  Andreas : Person[worksIn -> TelekomProject].
9:  TelekomProject : Project[hasTopic ->
    KnowledgeDiscovery].
10: FORALL X, Y, Z Z[hasTopic -> Y] <- X[subtopicOf -> Y]
    and [hasTopic -> X].
```

Definitions of instances in the knowledge base are syntactically very similar to concept definition in F-logic. In line 5 the instance KnowledgeDiscovery of the concept Topic is defined. Furthermore, the relation subtopicOf is instantiated between KnowledgeDiscovery and KnowledgeManagement. Similarly, in line 6, it is stated that Gerd is a Person working in OntoWise.

Now, an F-logic query may ask for all people who work in a knowledge management project as follows:

FORALL $Y, Z \leftarrow Y[\text{WORKSIN} \rightarrow Z]$ and

$Z : Project[\text{HASTOPIC} \rightarrow \text{KnowledgeManagement}]$,

which may result in the tuples $M_1^T := (\text{Gerd, OntoWise})$ and $M_2^T := (\text{Andreas},$ TelekomProject). Obviously, both answers are correct with regard to the given knowledge base and ontology, but the question is, what would be a plausible ranking for the correct answers? Such a ranking should be produced from any given query without assuming any user modification of the query.

11.5.1   Reinterpreting Queries

Our principal consideration in reinterpreting queries builds on the definition of semantic similarity that we first described in Maedche and Staab 2000. There we developed a measure for the similarity of two knowledge bases. Here our basic idea is to reinterpret possible query results as a "query knowledge base" and compute its similarity to the original knowledge base while abstracting from semantic inferences.

The result of an F-logic query may be reinterpreted as a *query knowledge base* (*QKB*) using the following approach. An F-logic query is of the form or can be rewritten into the form[4]

$$\text{FORALL } \bar{X} \leftarrow \bar{P}(\bar{X}, \bar{k}), \tag{11.1}$$

with X being a vector of variables $(X1, \ldots, Xn)$, k being a vector of constants, and P being a vector of conjoined predicates. The result of a query is a two-dimensional matrix M of size $m \times n$, with n being the number of result tuples and m being the length of X and, hence, the length of the result tuples. Hence, in our example above $X := (Y, Z)$, $k := (\text{"knowledge management"})$, $P := (P1, P2)$, $P1(a, b, c) := a[\text{worksIn} \rightarrow b]$, $P := (P1, P2)$, $P2(a, b, c) := b[\text{hasTopic} \rightarrow c]$ and

$$M := (M_1, M_2) = \begin{pmatrix} \text{Gerd} & \text{Andreas} \\ \text{OntoWise} & \text{TelekomProjekt} \end{pmatrix}. \tag{11.2}$$

Now, we may define the query knowledge base i (QKB_i) by

$$QKB_i := \bar{P}(M_i, \bar{k}). \tag{11.3}$$

The similarity measure between the query knowledge base and the given knowledge base may then be computed in analogy to Maedche and Staab 2000. An adaptation and simplification of the measures described there is given in the following sections, together with an example.

11.5.2 Similarity of Knowledge Bases

The similarity between two objects (concepts and/or instances) may be computed by considering their relative place in a common hierarchy *H*. *H* may, but need not, be a taxonomy *H*. For instance, in our example above we had a categorization of research topics, which is not a taxonomy! Our principal measures are based on the cotopies of the corresponding objects as defined by a given hierarchy *H* (e.g., an isA hierarchy *H*), a part-whole hierarchy, or a categorization of topics. Here, we use the *upwards cotopy* (UC), defined as follows:

$$UC(O_i, H) := \{O_j \mid H(O_i, O_j) \lor O_j = O_i\}. \tag{11.4}$$

UC is overloaded to allow for a set of objects M as input instead of only single objects, namely,

$$UC(M, H) := \bigcup_{O_i \in M} \{O_j \mid H(O_i, O_j) \lor O_j = O_i\}. \tag{11.5}$$

Based on the definition of the UC, an object match (OM) is defined by

$$OM(O_1, O_2, H) := \frac{|UC(O_1, H) \cap UC(O_2, H)|}{|UC(O_1, H) \cup UC(O_2, H)|}. \tag{11.6}$$

Basically, OM reaches 1 when two concepts coincide (the number of intersections of the respective upwards cotopies and number of unions of the respective cotopies are equal); it degrades to the extent to which the discrepancy between intersections and unions increases (an OM between concepts that do not share common superconcepts yields value 0).

We here give a small example of computing UC and OM based on a given categorization of objects H. Figure 11.8 depicts the example scenario.

Example 11.1   The upwards cotopy UC (knowledge discovery, H) is given by UC (knowledge discovery, H) = {knowledge discovery; knowledge management}. The upwards cotopy UC(optimization, H) is computed by UC(optimization, H) = {optimization}.

Computing the object match OM between KnowledgeManagement and Optimization results in 0. The object match between KnowledgeDiscovery and CSCW computes to 1/3.

The match introduced in example 11.1 may easily be generalized to relations using a relation hierarchy Hr. Thus, the predicate match (PM) for two n-ary predicates $P1$, $P2$, is defined by a mean value. Thereby, we use the geometric mean to reflect the intuition that if the similarity of one of the components approaches 0, the overall similarity between two predicates should approach 0—which need not be the case for the arithmetic mean:

A. Maedche, S. Staab, N. Stojanovic, R. Studer, and Y. Sure

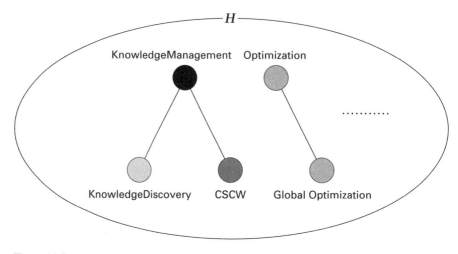

Figure 11.8
Computing UC and OM.

$$\mathrm{PM}(P_1(I_1, \ldots, I_n), P_2(J_1, \ldots, J_n))$$

$$:= \sqrt[n+1]{\mathrm{OM}(P_1, P_2, \mathcal{H}_R) \cdot \mathrm{OM}(I_1, J_1, H) \cdot \ldots \cdot \mathrm{OM}(I_n, J_n, H)}. \qquad (11.7)$$

This result may be averaged over an array of predicates. Here we simply give the formula for our actual needs, where a query knowledge base is compared against a given knowledge base *KB*:

$$Simil(QKB_i, KB) = Simil(\bar{P}(M_i, \bar{k}), KB)$$

$$:= \frac{1}{|\bar{P}|} \sum_{P_j \in \bar{P}} \max_{Q(M_i, \bar{k}) \in KB.\mathscr{S}} \mathrm{PM}(P_j(M_i, \bar{k}), Q(M_i, \bar{k})). \qquad (11.8)$$

For instance, comparing the two result tuples from our example above with the given knowledge base:

Gerd[WORKSIN ⟶ OntoWise].
OntoWise[HASTOPIC ⟶ KnowledgeManagement]. $\qquad (11.9)$

First, M1^T := (Gerd; OntoWise). Then we have the query knowledge base (QKB_1):

and its relevant counterpart predicates in the given knowledge base (*KB*) are

Gerd[WORKSIN —» OntoWise].
OntoWise[HASTOPIC —» KnowledgeManagement].   (11.10)

This is a perfect fit. Therefore *Simil*(QKB_1, *KB*) computes to 1.

Second, $M_2^T := $ (Andreas; TelekomProject). Then we have the query knowledge base (QKB_2):

Andreas[WORKSIN —» TelekomProject].
TelekomProject[HASTOPIC —» KnowledgeManagement].   (11.11)

and its relevant counterpart predicates in the given knowledge base (*KB*) are

Andreas[WORKSIN —» TelekomProject].
TelekomProject[HASTOPIC —» KnowledgeManagement].   (11.12)

Hence, the similarity of the first predicates indicates a perfect fit and evaluates to 1, but the congruency of TelekomProject[HASTOPIC → KnowledgeManagement] with TelekomProject[HASTOPIC → KnowledgeManagement] measures less than 1. The instance match of KnowledgeDiscovery and KnowledgeManagement returns $\frac{1}{2}$ in the given topic hierarchy. Therefore, the predicate match returns $(1^*1^*1/2)^\hat{}1/3 \approx 0.79$. Thus, overall ranking of the second result is based on $1/2^*(1 + 0.79) = 0.895$.

11.5.2.1 Remarks

The reader may note some basic properties of the ranking:

1. Similarity of knowledge bases is an asymmetric measure.

2. The ontology defines a conceptual structure useful for defining similarity.

3. The core concept for evaluating semantic similarity is cotopy, defined by a dedicated hierarchy.

The actual computation of similarity depends on which conceptual structures (e.g., hierarchies like taxonomy, part-whole hierarchies, or topic hierarchies) are selected for evaluating conceptual nearness. Thus, similarity of knowledge bases depends on the view selected for the similarity measure.

Ranking of semantic queries using underlying ontological structures is an important means of allowing users a more specific view of the underlying knowledge base. The method that we propose is based on a few basic principles:

- Reinterpret the combination of query and results as query knowledge bases that may be compared with the explicitly given information.
- Give a measure for comparing two knowledge bases, thus allowing rankings of query results.

Thus, we may improve the interface with the underlying structures without changing the basic architecture. Of course, the reader should be aware that our measure may produce some rankings for results that are hardly comparable. For instance, results may differ slightly because of imbalances in a given hierarchy or because of rather random differences of depth of branches. In this case, ranking may perhaps produce results that are not better than unranked ones—but the results will not be any worse, either.

11.6   Semantic Personalization

Personalization of Web sites may be enabled on different levels, such as, for example, so-called check-box personalization and preference-based personalization (see Frequently Asked Questions 2001). Both rely on the interaction between users and the underlying systems and aim at providing person-specific services and content to users. But they differ in the way systems track a user's interests to personalize Web sites.

Check-box personalization offers configuration possibilities to users, allowing them to select, from a given set of services and contents, the ones they are looking for. Content is presented based on the check boxes marked by users. Preference-based personalization keeps track of users' access patterns in log files. For example, Web usage mining tries to make sense of the Web usage data created by surfers (Srivastava et al. 2000).

Common systems rely, with respect to check-box personalization, on the selection of services and specific content areas, and for preference-based personalization, on monitoring of user activities based on the sequence of clicked URLs. Our portal differs from common systems in offering semantic access. All users who access our Web site use the underlying ontology for navigating, browsing, and querying. To address check-box personalization, users may store personalized *semantic bookmarks*. These rely on the semantic structure provided by the underlying ontology, and like common bookmarks, they facilitate access to regularly needed information.

While accessing the Semantic Web site, users leave footprints in the form of clicked hyperlinks, but they also leave a trace of concepts and relations. Every query is composed from the ontology, and (almost) every navigation follows underlying ontological structures. To enable preference-based personalization, we upgrade our log files, by including semantics, to *semantic log files*. User habits may then be semantically tracked, analyzed, and used for personalization, general optimization of the Web site, and especially, evaluation and maintenance of the ontology.

11.6.1   Semantic Bookmarks

The AIFB mainly targets students and researchers, two groups that typically have different focuses. Students tend to look for teaching-related topics, and researchers tend to look for research-related topics. To satisfy their needs, we provide links to both areas from the starting page of our Web site. But users sometimes need to have persistent pointers to specific information. Navigating and browsing through our Web site as well as posting queries relies on the underlying ontology; therefore we have introduced semantic bookmarks.

Because many navigation facilities of our Web site, such as, for example, hyperlinks and list boxes, are created on the fly by our inference engine, semantic bookmarks basically contain predefined[5] query formulas. Upon selection, bookmarks send their queries to the inference engine that reproduces the information shown to the user during his bookmarking process. Because bookmarks contain query formulas, they always produce the most recent (i.e., updated) results. Semantic bookmarks are modeled in the ontology (see Bookmark in (11.13)); their instantiations are stored in the knowledge warehouse (see Bookmark 1) in (11.13):

Bookmark[Bookmark1:Bookmark[
QUERY $\Rightarrow$ STRING;   QUERY $\rightarrow$ "FORALL X,N $\leftarrow$
                              X:Person[lastName $\rightarrow$ N].";
NAME $\Rightarrow$ STRING;   NAME $\rightarrow$ "List of all persons";   (11.13)
STYLESHEET $\Rightarrow$ PersonStylesheet;   STYLESHEET $\rightarrow$ PersonStylesheet1;
START $\Rightarrow$ BOOLEAN;   START $\rightarrow$ PALSE;
OWNER $\Rightarrow$ User].   OWNER $\rightarrow$ User1].

In addition to the QUERY formula, bookmarks contain several options for
personalization. First, users may give a specific NAME to their bookmarks to
describe their functionality. Second, they may choose a STYLESHEET from a
given set of style sheets for the presentation of results. Finally, a semantic
bookmark might be marked as a START bookmark, so that it will be executed as
soon as users enter the starting page of our Web site. This allows users to
have the quickest possible access to often-needed information. Every user
may execute, edit, and delete his own semantic bookmarks (identified by the
relation OWNER).

To deliver personalized information to users, the system needs to be able
to recognize them. We implemented a very simple ontology-based user administration, allowing users to be recognized by their user ID. Therefore our
ontology has been expanded by user-specific concepts and relations (User, ID,
NAME etc.). Our system generates for each user an identifying ID that is stored
together with all relevant user information in our knowledge warehouse. For
convenience, user IDs are also stored locally in cookies so that users are recognized automatically by the ID stored on their computer. Possible pitfalls
of such a simple approach are, for example, multiuser access from a single
computer or single-user access from multiple computers.

11.6.2 Semantic Log Files

Agents interact with our system through a Web server (see figure 11.5) that
logs every request (namely, every http request) the user makes into log files.
Queries are processed to our inference engine through embedding query for-

mulas into hyperlinks. Therefore all semantics are contained within logged hyperlinks.

Typically Web servers track the following items: Cookie, IP number, Time stamp, Request. We take advantage of the information tracked. Cookies help to identify authenticated users, and IP numbers in combination with time stamps help to distinguish nonauthenticated users from authenticated users. Finally, the request string contains all concepts and relations of the ontology that a user is interested in, because of the nature[6] of our ontology-enabled querying, navigation, and browsing.

Currently we are working on transforming these log files into appropriate formats and on applying data-mining methods and tools (like association rules). We are interested in answering, for example, the following questions:

- Does a single authenticated user have a special interest in a certain part of the ontology?

- Are there user groups that have similar interests?

- Which parts of the ontology are relevant to users, and which ones are not?

Answering these questions will help us optimize our system in iterative steps (e.g., to enable ranked index lists providing each user with personalized shortcuts). The last question in particular is important for evaluation and maintenance of the ontology (see section 11.3). To keep an ontology updated, one might want to expand highly accessed parts, shrink rarely accessed parts, and delete unaccessed parts. Research on these topics is still ongoing.

11.7   RDF Outside: From a Semantic Web Site to the Semantic Web

In the preceding sections we have described the development and the underlying techniques of the AIFB Semantic Web site. Having developed the core application, we decided that RDF-capable software agents should be able to understand the content of the application. Therefore, we have built an automatic RDF Generator that dynamically generates RDF statements on each of the static and dynamic pages of the semantic knowledge portal. Our current AIFB intranet application is "Semantic Web-ized" using RDF facts instantiated and defined according to the underlying AIFB ontology. On top of this generated and formally represented metadata, there is the RDF Crawler, a tool that gathers interconnected fragments of RDF from the Internet.

11.7.1   RDF Generator: An Example

The RDFMaker established in the Ontobroker framework (see Decker et al. 1999) was a starting point for building the RDF Generator. The idea of RDFMaker was to generate RDF statements from Ontobroker's internal database.

RDF Generator follows a similar approach and extends the principal ideas. In a first step it generates an RDF(S)-based ontology that is stored on a specific XML namespace (e.g., in our concrete application, http://ontobroker. semanticweb.org/ontologies/aifb-onto-2001-01-01.rdfs). Also, it queries the knowledge warehouse. Data (e.g., for a person) are checked for consistency and, if possible, completed by applying F-logic rules. Here we give a short example of what type of data may be generated and stored on a specific home page of a researcher:

```
<rdf:RDF
xmlns:rdf = "http://www.w3.org/1999/02/22-rdf-syntax-ns#"
xmlns:aifb = "http://ontobroker.semanticweb.org/aifb-2001-
01-01.rdfs#">
<aifb:PhDStudent rdf:ID="person:ama">
<aifb:name>Alexander Maedche</aifb:name>
<aifb:email>ama@aifb.uni-karlsruhe.de</aifb:email>
<aifb:phone>+49-(0)721-608 6558</aifb:phone>
<aifb:fax>+49-(0)721-608 6580</aifb:fax>
<aifb:homepage>http://www.aifb.uni-
karlsruhe.de/WBS/ama</aifb:homepage>
```

```
<aifb:supervisor
rdf:resource = "http://www.aifb.uni-
karlsruhe.de/Staff/studer.html#person:rst"/>
</aifb:PhDStudent>
</rdf:RDF>
```

RDF Generator is a configurable tool: in some cases one may want to use inferences to generate materialized, complete RDF descriptions on a home page, and in other cases one may want to generate only ground facts of RDF. Therefore, RDF Generator allows axioms to be switched on and off to adopt the generation of results to varying needs.

11.7.2   RDF Crawler

RDF Crawler[7] is a tool that downloads interconnected fragments of RDF from the Internet and builds a knowledge base from these data. Building an external knowledge base for the whole AIFB (its researchers, its projects, its publications ...) becomes easy using RDF Crawler and machine-processible RDF data currently defined on AIFB's Web. Here we briefly describe the underlying techniques of RDF Crawler and the process of building a knowledge base. In general, RDF data may appear in Web documents in several ways. We distinguish between pure RDF (files that have the extension ".rdf"), RDF embedded in HTML, and RDF embedded in XML. RDF Crawler uses RDF-API,[8] which can deal with the different embeddings of RDF described above.

One problem in crawling is the applied filtering mechanism: baseline crawlers are typically restricted by a given depth value. Recently new research work on so-called *focused crawling* has been published (see, e.g., Chakrabarti, van den Berg, and Dom 1999). In their approach, Chakrabarti, van den Berg, and Dom use a set of predefined documents associated with topics in a Yahoo-like taxonomy to built a focused crawler. Two hypertext-mining algorithms constitute the core of their approach. A classifier evaluates the relevance of a hypertext document with respect to the focus topics, and a distiller identifies hypertext nodes that are good access points to many relevant pages within a few links. In contrast, our approach uses ontological background knowledge to judge the relevance of each page. If a page is highly relevant, the crawler may follow the links on the particular Web site. If RDF data are available on a page, our system judges relevance with respect to the quantity and quality of available data and by the existing URIs.

We now give a brief example of an application that may be easily built using RDF metadata taken from AIFB using the RDF Crawler. The so-called *Erdoes numbers* have been a part of the folklore of mathematicians throughout the world for many years.[9]

Example 11.2 Scientific papers are frequently published with coauthors. Based on information about collaboration, one may compute the Paul Erdoes number (denoted PE(R)) for a researcher R. On the AIFB Web site, the RDF-based metadata allows estimates of the Erdoes numbers of AIFB members to be computed.

Erdoes numbers are defined recursively:

1. $PE(R) = 0$, if R is Paul Erdoes.

2. $PE(R) = \min\{PE(R1) + 1\}$ otherwise, where $R1$ varies over the set of all researchers who have collaborated with R, that is, those who have written a scientific paper together.

To put this algorithm to work, we need lists of publications annotated with RDF facts. The lists may be automatically generated by the RDF Generator. Based on the RDF facts, one may crawl relevant information into a central knowledge base and compute these numbers from the data.

11.8   Related Work

This section positions our work in the context of existing Web portals and also relates our work to other basic methods and tools that are or could be deployed for the construction of community Web portals, especially to related work in the areas of personalization and semantic ranking of query results.

11.8.1   Related Work on Knowledge Portals

One well-established portal on the web is Yahoo (http://www.yahoo.com). In contrast to our approach, Yahoo's utilizes only a very lightweight ontology that consists solely of categories arranged in a hierarchical manner. Yahoo offers keyword search (local to a selected topic or global) in addition to hierarchical navigation but is able to retrieve only complete documents; that is, it is not able to answer queries concerning the contents of documents, much less to combine facts found in different documents or to include facts that could be derived through ontological axioms. Personalization is limited to check-box personalization. Our portal avoids these shortcomings, since it is built upon a rich ontology, enabling it to give integrated answers to queries. Furthermore, our semantic personalization features provide more flexible means for adapting the portal to the specific needs of its users.

A portal that is specialized for a scientific community has been built by the Math-Net project (Dalitz, Grötschel, and Lügger 1997). At the Math-Net site (http://www.math-net.de/) is installed a portal for the (German) mathematics community that makes distributed information from several mathematical departments available. This information is accompanied by metadata according to the Dublin Core (http://www.purl.org/dc) standard (Weibel et al. 1998). The Dublin Core element "Subject" is used to classify resources as conferences, as research groups, as preprints, etc. A finer classification (e.g., via attributes) is not possible except in the case of instances of the publication category. Here the common Mathematical Subject Classification (see http://www.ams.org/msc/), which resembles a lightweight ontology of the field of mathematics, is used. Compared to our approach, Math-Net lacks a rich ontology that can enhance the quality of search results (especially via inferencing) and the smooth connection to the Semantic Web world that is provided by our RDF Generator.

The Ontobroker project (Decker et al. 1999) lays the technological foundations for the AIFB portal. The portal has been built and organizational structures for developing and maintaining it have been established on top of an Ontobroker base. Therefore, we compare our system with approaches that are similar to Ontobroker.

The approach closest to Ontobroker is SHOE (Heflin and Hendler 2000). In SHOE, HTML pages are annotated via ontologies to support information retrieval based on semantic information. Outside of the use of ontologies and the annotation of Web pages, the underlying philosophy of the two systems differs significantly: SHOE uses description logic as its basic representation formalism, but it offers only very limited inferencing capabilities. Ontobroker relies on Frame Logic and supports complex inferencing for query answering. Furthermore, the SHOE search tool provides means neither for a semantic ranking of query results nor for a semantic personalization feature.

A more detailed comparison of our system to other portal approaches and underlying methods may be found in Staab et al. 2000.

11.8.2   Related Work on Personalization

Personalization is a feature of portals that is attracting more and more interest, from a research as well as from a commercial point of view. In contrast to our semantic personalization approach, which exploits the conceptualization offered by the ontology and the inferencing capabilities provided by our Ontobroker component, preference-based personalization approaches typically rely on some notion of Web mining: exploiting the content of hypertext documents (Web content mining), analyzing the hypertext links structure (Web structure mining) or server/browser logs (web usage mining) (Kosala and Blockeel 2000). That is, the organization and presentation of a particular Web site may be optimized over time based on the analysis of the log files that result from such mining. While users are accessing Web sites, their habits are compared to previous users' behaviors to offer them personalized content such as, for example, ranked index lists (see Perkowitz and Etzioni 1999).

From a marketing point of view, customer behavior might be analyzed to relate the interaction of customers with a particular Web site to aspects that are important for customer relationship management. For example, Easyminer (Anand et al. 2000) is a Web intelligence tool that allows customer behavior to be analyzed with respect to aspects like the clicks-to-close value (i.e., how easily customers can find the information they are interested in and how this value can be improved through personalization). However, in contrast to our semantic personalization approach, the data-mining algorithms used in Easyminer analyze syntactical link structures.

11.8.3   Related Work on Semantic Similarity

Since our semantic ranking is based on the comparison of a query knowledge base with a given ontology and knowledge base, we relate our work to the comparison of ontological structures and knowledge bases (covering the same domain) and to the measurement of the degree of similarity between concepts in a hierarchy. Although there has been a long discussion in the literature about evaluating knowledge bases (Menzies 1998), we have not found any discussion about comparing two knowledge bases covering the same domain that corresponds to our semantic ranking approach. Similarity measures for ontological structures have been investigated in areas like cognitive science, databases, and knowledge engineering, as, for example, in Rada et al. 1989, Resnik 1995, Richardson, Smeaton, and Murphy 1994, and Hovy 1998. However, the approaches in all of these works are restricted to measures of similarity between lexical entries, concepts, and template slots within a single ontology, not two.

Closest to our measure of similarity is work in the NLP community, referred to as "semantic similarity" (Resnik 1995), which refers to similarity between two concepts in an isA taxonomy, such as the WordNet or CYC upper ontology. The conceptualization of similarity in our approach differs in two main aspects from this notion of similarity: first, our similarity measure is applicable to a hierarchy that may, but need not, be a taxonomy, and second, it is taking into account not only commonalities but also differences between the items being compared, expressing both in semantic-cotopy terms. This second property enables the measurement of self-similarity and subclass-relationship similarity, which are crucial for comparing results derived from the inferencing processes that are executed in the background.

Conceptually, instead of measuring similarity between isolated terms (words), which does not take into account the relationship among word senses that matters, we measure similarity between "words in context," by measuring similarity between object-attribute-value pairs in which each term corresponds to a concept in the ontology. This enables us to exploit the ontological background knowledge (axioms and relations between concepts) in measuring the similarity, which expands our approach to a methodology for comparing knowledge bases.

From our point of view, our community portal system is unique with respect to the collection of methods used and the functionality provided. We have extended our community portal approach, which provides flexible means for providing, integrating, and accessing information (Staab et al. 2000), with semantic personalization features, semantic ranking of generated answers, and a smooth integration with the evolving Semantic Web. All these methods are integrated into one uniform system environment, the SEAL framework.

11.9   Conclusion

In this chapter we have described our comprehensive approach SEAL for building semantic portals. In particular, we have focused on three issues.

First, we have considered the ontological foundation of SEAL and the methodological aspects of building ontologies for knowledge systems. We have shown through our experience that there are many big open issues that have hardly been dealt with so far. In particular, the step of formalizing an ontology raises very basic problems. The issue of where to put relevant concepts (viz., into the ontology versus into the knowledge base), is an important one that deeply affects organization and application. However, there exist so far no corresponding methodological guidelines on which to base the decision. For instance, we have given the example ontology and knowledge base in definitions 11.1 and 11.2, respectively. Using description logics terminology, we have equated the ontology with the T-Box, and we have put the topic hierarchy into the knowledge base (A-Box). An alternative method would have been to formalize the topic hierarchy as an isA hierarchy (which, however, it isn't) and put it into the T-Box. We believe that both alternatives exhibit an internal fault, namely, that the ontology should not be equated with the T-Box, but rather its scope should be independent from an actual formalization with particular logical statements. Its scope should to a large extent depend on soft issues, like "Who updates a concept?" and "How often does a concept change?" as indicated in table 11.1.

Second, we have described the general architecture of the SEAL approach, which is also used for our real-world case study, the AIFB Web site. The architecture integrates a number of components that we have also used in other applications, like Ontobroker, navigation, or query module.

Third, we have extended our semantic modules to include a larger diversity of intelligent means for accessing the Web site (viz., semantic ranking, personalization, and machine access by crawling). Thus, we have shown a comprehensive approach for meeting many of the challenges put forth in Perkowitz and Etzioni 1997.

For the future, we see a number of new, important topics appearing on the horizon. For instance, we consider approaches for ontology learning (Maedche and Staab 2001) that would enable an ontology to adapt semiautomatically to changes in the world and that would facilitate the engineering of ontologies. Currently, we are working on providing intelligent means for providing semantic information; that is, we are elaborating on a semantic annotation framework that balances manual provisioning from legacy texts (e.g., Web pages) and information extraction (Staab, Maedche, and Handschuh 2001). Given a particular conceptualization, we envision that one might want to be able to use a multitude of different inference engines, taking advantage of different inferencing capabilities (temporal, nonmonotonic, high scalability, etc.). If that is the case, however, then one needs means for changing from one representation paradigm to another (Staab, Erdmann, and Maedche 2001).

Finally, we envision that once Semantic Web sites are widely available, their automatic exploitation may be taken to new levels. Semantic Web mining considers the mining of Web site structures, Web site content, and Web site usage at a semantic rather than at a syntactic level, yielding new possibilities, for example, for intelligent navigation, personalization, or summarization, to name but a few possibilities for Semantic Web sites (Hotho and Stumme 2001).

Acknowledgments

The research presented in this chapter would not have been possible without our colleagues and students at the Institute AIFB, University of Karlsruhe, and Ontoprise GmbH. We thank Jürgen Angele, Kalvis Apsitis (now at the Riga Information Technology Institute), Nils Braeunlich, Stefan Decker (now at Stanford University), Michael Erdmann, Dieter Fensel (now at Vrige Universiteit Amsterdam), Siegfried Handschuh, Andreas Hotho, Mika Maier-Collin, Daniel Oberle, and Hans-Peter Schnurr. Research for this chapter was financed in part by Ontoprise GmbH (Karlsruhe, Germany), by the U.S. Air Force in the DARPA DAML project "OntoAgents," by the European Union in the IST-1999-10132 project "On-To-Knowledge," and by BMBF in the project "GETESS" (01IN901C0).

Notes

1. Here at the conceptual level, we do not distinguish between relations and attributes.

2. "Active server pages" versus "active service providers."

3. "SouthEast Asian Linguistics Conference" versus "Conference on Simulated Evolution and Learning" versus "Society for Evolutionary Analysis in Law" versus "Society for Effective Affective Learning" versus some other dozens of possibilities, several of which are indeed relevant in our institute.

4. Negation requires special treatment.

5. Experts might store any possible query in bookmarks by manually editing the queries.

6. Our system is based on Java servlets and uses URL-encoded queries.

7. RDF Crawler is freely available for download at http://ontobroker.semanticweb.org/rdfcrawler.

8. RDF-API is freely available for download at http://www-db.stanford.edu/~melnik/rdf/api.html.

9. The interested reader is referred to http://www.oakland.edu/~grossman/erdoshp.html for an overall project overview.

References

Anand, S. S., M. Baumgarten, A. Buechner, and M. Mulvenna. 2000. Gaining Insights into Web Customers Using Web Intelligence. In *Proceedings of the 14th European Conference on Artificial Intelligence (ECAI-2000), Berlin, Germany, 2000*, ed. V. Benjamins et al. Available from http://delicias.dia.fi.upm.es/WORKSHOP/ECAI00/8.pdf.

Angele, J., H.-P. Schnurr, S. Staab, and R. Studer. 2000. The Times They Are A-Changin': The Corporate History Analyzer. In *Proceedings of the Third International Conference on Practical Aspects of Knowledge Management, Basel, Switzerland, October 30–31, 2000*, ed. D. Mahling and U. Reimer. Available from http://www.research.swisslife.ch/pakm2000/.

Benjamins, V. R., and D. Fensel. 1998. Community Is Knowledge! (KA)2. In *Proceedings of the 11th Workshop on Knowledge Acquisition, Modeling, and Management (KAW-98), Banff, Canada, April 1998*. Available from http://ksi.cpsc.ucalgary.ca/KAW/KAW98Proc.html.

Chakrabarti, S., M. van den Berg, and B. Dom. 1999. Focused Crawling: A New Approach to Topic-Specific Web Resource Discovery. In Proceedings of the Eighth World Wide Web Conference, Toronto, Canada, May 11–14, 1999. Available from http://www8.org.

Dalitz, W., M. Grötschel, and J. Lügger. 1997. Information Services for Mathematics in the Internet (Math-Net). In *Proceedings of the 15th IMACS World Congress on Scientific Computation: Modelling and Applied Mathematics*. Vol. 4 of Artificial Intelligence and Computer Science, ed. A. Sydow (pp. 773–778). Berlin: Wissenschaft und Technik Verlag.

Decker, S., M. Erdmann, D. Fensel, and R. Studer. 1999. Ontobroker: Ontology Based Access to Distributed and Semi-Structured Information. In *Database Semantics: Semantic Issues in Multimedia Systems*, ed. R. Meersman et al. (pp. 351–369). Boston: Kluwer Academic.

Decker, S., D. Fensel, F. van Harmelen, I. Horrocks, S. Melnik, M. Klein, and J. Broekstra. 2000. Knowledge Representation on the Web. In *Proceedings of the 2000 International Workshop on Description Logics (DL-2000), Aachen, Germany, August 17–19, 2000*, ed. F. Baader and U. Sattler. Available from http://SunSITE.Informatik.RWTH-Aachen.DE/Publications/CEUR-WS/Vol-33/.

Fensel, D., S. Decker, M. Erdmann, and R. Studer. 1998. Ontobroker: The Very High Idea. In *Proceedings of the 11th International Flairs Conference (FLAIRS-98), Sanibel Island, Florida, USA, May*, ed. D. J. Cook (pp. 131–135). Menlo Park, CA: AAAI.

Gomez-Perez, A. 1996. A Framework to Verify Knowledge Sharing Technology. *Expert Systems with Application* 11(4):519–529.

Guarino, N., and C. Welty. 2000. Identity, Unity, and Individuality: Towards a Formal Toolkit for Ontological Analysis. *Proceedings of the Workshop on Applications of Ontologies and Problem-Solving Methods, 14th European Conference on Artificial Intelligence ECAI-2000, Berlin, Germany, August 20–25, 2000*, ed. V. R. Benjamins et al. Available from http://www.ladseb.pd.cnr.it/infor/ontology/Papers/OntologyPapers.html.

Heflin, J., and J. Hendler. 2000. Searching the Web with Shoe. In *Artificial Intelligence for Web Search. Papers from the AAAI Workshop* (pp. 35–40). Menlo Park, CA: AAAI.

Hotho, A., and G. Stumme, ed. 2001. Semantic Web Mining: Workshop at ECML-2001/ PKDD-2001, Freiburg, Germany, 2001. Available from http://semwebmine2001.aifb.uni-karlsruhe.de/.

Hovy, E. 1998. Combining and Standardizing Large-Scale, Practical Ontologies for Machine Translation and Other Uses. In Proceedings of the First International Conference on Language Resources and Evaluation (LREC), Granada, Spain, May 28–30, 1998, ed. A. Rubio et al. Available from http://www.lrec-conf.org/lrec98/ceres.ugr.es/_rubio/elra/program.html.

Kifer, M., G. Lausen, and J. Wu. 1995. Logical Foundations of Object-Oriented and Frame-Based Languages. *Journal of the ACM* 42:741–843.

Kosala, R., and H. Blockeel. 2000. Web Mining Reseach: A Survey. *SIGKDD Explorations* 2(1):1–15.

Maedche, A., and S. Staab. 2000. Discovering Conceptual Relations from Text. In *Proceedings of the Workshop on Applications of Ontologies and Problem-Solving Methods, 14th European Conference on Artificial Intelligence ECAI-2000, Berlin, Germany, August 20–25, 2000*, ed. V. R. Benjamins et al. Available from http://www.aifb.uni-karlsruhe.de/~sst/Research/Publications/ecai_amasst.pdf.

Maedche, A., and S. Staab. 2001. Ontology Learning for the Semantic Web. *IEEE Intelligent Systems* 16(2).

Menzies, T. J. 1998. Knowledge Maintenance: The State of the Art. *The Knowledge Engineering Review* 14(1):1–46.

Miller, G. 1995. Wordnet: A Lexical Database for English. *Communications of the ACM* 38(11):39–41.

Ogden, C. K., and I. A. Richards. 1993. *The Meaning of Meaning: A Study of the Influence of Language upon Thought and of the Science of Symbolism.* 10th ed. London: Routledge and Kegan Paul.

Perkowitz, M., and O. Etzioni. 1997. Adaptive Web Sites: An AI Challenge. In *Proceedings of the 15th International Joint Conference on AI (IJCAI-97), Nagoya, Japan, August 23–29, 1997*, ed. M. E. Pollack (pp. 16–23). San Francisco: Morgan Kaufmann.

Perkowitz, M., and O. Etzioni. 1999. Adaptive Web Sites: Conceptual Cluster Mining. In *Proceedings of the 16th International Joint Conference on AI (IJCAI-99), Stockholm, Sweden, July 31–August 6, 1999*, ed. T. Dean (pp. 264–269). San Francisco: Morgan Kaufmann.

Personalization.com. Frequently Asked Questions: Are There Different Types of Personalization? Available from http://www.personalization.com/basics/faq/faq2.asp.

Rada, R., H. Mili, E. Bicknell, and M. Blettner. 1989. Development and Application of a Metric on Semantic Nets. *IEEE Transactions on Systems, Man, and Cybernetics* 19(1):17–30.

Resnik, P. 1995. Knowledge Maintenance: The State of the Art. In *Proceedings of the Fourteenth International Joint Conference on Artificial Intelligence (IJCAI-95), Montreal, Canada, August 20–25, 1995* (pp. 448–453). San Francisco: Morgan Kaufmann.

Richardson, R., A. F. Smeaton, and J. Murphy. 1994. Using Wordnet as Knowledge Base for Measuring Semantic Similarity between Words. Technical Report CA-1294, Dublin City University, School of Computer Applications, 1994.

Sowa, J. F. 1992. *Conceptual Structures: Information Processing in Mind and Machine.* Boston: Addison-Wesley.

Srivastava, J., R. Cooley, M. Deshpande, and P. Tan. 2000. Web Usage Mining: Discovery and Applications of Usage Patterns from Web Data. *SIGKDD Explorations* 1(2):12–23.

Staab, S., J. Angele, S. Decker, M. Erdmann, A. Hotho, A. Maedche, H.-P. Schnurr, R. Studer, and Y. Sure. 2000. Semantic Community Web Portals. *Computer Networks* 33(1–6):473–491.

Staab, S., M. Erdmann, and A. Maedche. 2001. Semantic Patterns. Technical report, Institute AIFB, University of Karlsruhe, Karlsruhe, Germany.

Staab, S., and A. Maedche. 2001. Knowledge Portals: Ontologies at Work. *AI Magazine* 21(2).

Staab, S., A. Maedche, and S. Handschuh. 2001. An Annotation Framework for the Semantic Web. In *Proceedings of the First Workshop on Multimedia Annotation, Tokyo, Japan, January 30–31, 2001.* Available from http://www.sigmatics.co.jp/mma2001/.

Staab, S., H.-P. Schnurr, R. Studer, and Y. Sure. 2001. Knowledge Processes and Ontologies. *IEEE Intelligent Systems* 16(1):26–34.

Sure, Y., A. Maedche, and S. Staab. 2000. Leveraging Corporate Skill Knowledge—From ProPer to OntoProper. In *Proceedings of the Third International Conference on Practical Aspects of Knowledge Management, Basel, Switzerland, October 30–31, 2000*, ed. D. Mahling and U. Reimer. Available from http://www.research.swisslife.ch/pakm2000/.

Uschold, M., and M. Gruninger. 1996. Ontologies: Principles, Methods, and Applications. *Knowledge Engineering Review* 11(2):93–155.

Weibel, S., J. Kunze, C. Lagoze, and M. Wolf. 1998. *Dublin Core Metadata for Resource Discovery.* IETF no. 2413. Internet Society. Available from http://dublincore.org/.

III *Dynamic Aspect*

12 Semantic Gadgets: Ubiquitous Computing Meets the Semantic Web

Ora Lassila and Mark Adler

12.1   Introduction

Ubiquitous computing is an emerging paradigm of personal computing characterized by the shift from dedicated computing machinery (that requires the user's attention, e.g., PCs) to pervasive computing capabilities embedded in our everyday environments (Weiser 1991, 1993). Characteristic of ubiquitous computing are small, handheld, wireless computing devices. The pervasiveness and the wireless nature of ubiquitous computing devices require network architectures to support automatic, ad hoc configuration. An additional reason for development of automatic configuration is that ubiquitous computing technology is aimed at ordinary consumers, who are not willing or not able to configure their devices manually.

A key technology of true ad hoc networks is *service discovery*, functionality in which "services" (i.e., functions offered by various devices on an ad hoc network) can be described, advertised, and discovered by others. Several frameworks and formalisms for service discovery and capability description have already emerged. Examples of these include Sun's Jini and Microsoft's Universal Plug and Play (UPnP) (e.g., Richard 2000) as means of describing services and invoking them, as well as the W3C's Composite Capability/Preference Profile (CC/PP) (Reynolds, Woodrow, and Ohto 2000) as a means of describing device characteristics.

All of the current service discovery and capability description mechanisms are based on ad hoc representation schemes and rely heavily on standardization (i.e., on a priori identification of all those things one would want to communicate or discuss). (In addition, Jini relies on the Java object system and instance serialization, and UPnP uses XML and its own flavor of HTTP.) UPnP, for example, aims to render a user interface for some device (on another device) and facilitate the remote control by a human via the second device. In contrast, our approach aims to accomplish this task without the human in the loop. In other words, the ultimate goal is the discovery and utilization of services by other automated systems without human guidance or intervention, thus enabling the automatic formation of *device coalitions* through this mechanism. We call these devices, capable of semantic discovery and coalition formation, *semantic gadgets*.

12.2   About Representation

Various artificial intelligence technologies, particularly from the area of knowledge representation (KR) will be useful (and even necessary) for building "richer" service discovery mechanisms. Given that we are dealing with networked devices and distributed software systems, the notion of the *Semantic Web* (e.g., Fensel 2000) fits well in this context. Technically speaking, by Semantic Web, we mean the emerging knowledge representation formalism DAML (DARPA Agent Markup Language) (Hendler and McGuinness 2000) and its foundation, the W3C's RDF (Lassila 1998; Lassila and Swick 1999; Brickley and Guha 2000). In broad terms, the Semantic Web encompasses efforts to populate the Web with content that has formal semantics; thus the Semantic Web will enable automated agents to reason about Web content and produce an intelligent response to unforeseen situations. Our vision is to overlay the Semantic Web on a ubiquitous computing environment, making it possible to represent and interlink devices, their capabilities, and the functionality they offer.

RDF is the W3C's standard for metadata, but it extends the traditional notion of metadata by allowing any "resource" on the World Wide Web to be described in a unified way. Because RDF uses uniform resource identifiers (URIs) for addressing, it can even describe things that are not on the Web, as long as they have a URI. RDF serves as the foundation for DAML, an emerging, more expressive KR language suitable for building ontologies. We foresee that RDF will describe services and device functionality for the purposes of service discovery. Just as the success of the deployment of the Semantic Web will largely depend on whether useful ontologies will emerge, so will discovery services benefit from mechanisms that allow shared agreements about vocabularies for knowledge representation. This is important because sharing vocabularies and models allows automated interoperability; given a base ontology shared by two agents, each agent can extend the base ontology while achieving *partial understanding*. A base ontology is analogous to object-oriented systems, in which a base class defines "common" functionality.

To simply describe devices and functionality, frame-based representation, with its close kinship to more widely accepted technologies such as object-oriented modeling and programming, may be the right paradigm for KR (Lassila and McGuinness in press). The concept of a *frame* was proposed in the 1970s (Minsky 1975), and *frame systems* subsequently gained ground as basic tools for representing knowledge (Fikes and Kehler 1985; Karp 1992; Chaudhri et al. 1998). The idea of a frame system is simple: a frame represents an object or a concept. Attached to the frame is a collection of attributes (slots), potentially filled initially with values. When a frame is being used, the values of slots can be altered to make the frame correspond to the particular situation at hand. In the context of device description, one could think of a device as a frame and represent its characteristics as slots (this, in fact, is the approach taken by CC/PP in its use of RDF).

12.3   Scenario: Semantic Gadget in a Museum

To illustrate how a semantic gadget (SG) (e.g., a next-generation personal communicator) will work and particularly how it will integrate and interoperate with other semantic devices, we have constructed a hypothetical scenario of gadget usage in an art museum instrumented with semantic devices and services.

12.3.1 In the Car

As we approach the art museum, we check the dashboard map for parking options. Our museum membership entitles us to reduced parking fees at the two lots that are highlighted on the map. A snowstorm is predicted; knowing our dislike of cleaning snow off the car, the SG suggests parking in the garage instead of parking in the outside lot, even though parking in the garage means a longer walk to the entrance and paying a slightly higher fee. The gate lifts as we approach the garage entrance, and the dashboard map indicates an available parking spot on the third floor near the exit. We park, grab our mobile SG, and head for the stairs as our vehicle shuts off the lights and arms the security system. Our SG records the location of the car and plots our route to the nearest museum entrance.

12.3.2 In the Museum

As we enter the art museum, our SG negotiates our admission by supplying our membership number and confirming our reservation for the exhibit in the main gallery. Before we leave the lobby, the SG suggests that we check our coats, because the temperature inside the museum is too warm to wear a coat, and the SG knows how much we dislike carrying our coats. A map on the SG guides us to the coatroom. The gallery is currently near capacity, so our SG recommends a detour through other galleries to see some recent Impressionist acquisitions. A map of the museum with the suggested path appears on the touch screen. As we follow the path, a more detailed view appears, with a flashing icon for paintings that are of special interest. As we approach a painting, additional icons appear on the screen, indicating available information about the artist and the period, details about the museum's acquisition of the painting, and pointers to related art works. By clicking on the icons, we obtain the underlying information.

After a pleasant 15-minute diversion strolling through several galleries, we arrive at the main exhibition and enter without any delay. The first gallery seems crowded, but the SG suggests viewing the exhibit in reverse order because we prefer to avoid crowded viewing conditions. Using the Bluetooth-enabled headset, we listen to the museum's descriptions of the works as we stroll through the exhibit. As we make our way through the exhibit again on the way to the exit, the SG reminds us of several displays that we missed the first time we walked through.

12.3.3　In the Gift Shop

Naturally, one cannot exit the museum without passing through the gift shop. Ordinarily, we avoid this spending opportunity, but the SG flashes a message reminding us that we need a gift for our mother's birthday the following week. Based on her preference for writing notes longhand and her love of Impressionist art, the SG suggests purchasing a box of Monet stationery. The SG interacts with the cashier, obtains the member discount, charges the purchase to my credit card, and arranges to have the stationery gift-wrapped and shipped in time for Mom's birthday.

12.3.4　Exiting the Museum

As we leave the gift shop, the SG presents a list of suggested activities: it proposes (1) viewing additional art works that are highly correlated with the paintings that we spent the most time viewing, (2) attending a lecture associated with the exhibit, (3) eating at the museum restaurant, or (4) leaving the museum and going home. We choose the last, indicating our choice verbally. The SG maps our path to exit and return to our car.

12.3.5　In the Parking Garage

As we approach the car, the SG unlocks the doors. We plug in the SG to recharge, and the display switches to the dashboard screen. Our SG handles the parking fee, including our member discount, and we are on our way home.

12.4 Semantic Discovery

Semantic gadget technology begins with the discovery of functionality and services. As mentioned above, a number of mechanisms for low-level service discovery have emerged, such as Jini and UPnP; these mechanisms attack the problem at a syntactic level and rely heavily on the standardization of a pre-determined set of functionality descriptions. Standardization, unfortunately, can take us only halfway toward our goal of intelligent automated behavior vis-à-vis discovery, as it affords us only a limited ability to anticipate all possible future needs. The Semantic Web offers the possibility of elevating the mechanisms of service discovery to a "semantic" level, where a more sophisticated description of functionality is possible and the shared understanding between the consumer and the service provider can be reached via the exchange of ontologies, which provide the necessary vocabulary for a dialogue.

Semantic discovery mechanisms, once developed, will undoubtedly be layered on top of existing, lower-level services, which involve ad hoc networking technologies and other mechanisms that are beyond the scope of this chapter. It is sufficient here to state that physical devices, their functionality, and the services they offer will be abstracted as *software agents*. These agents will advertise services (if providers) and/or will query for services they need (if consumers). Both the advertisements and the queries will be abstract descriptions of functionality (in fact, there is no difference between the two, as Sycara has pointed out [Sycara et al. 1999]). Through a matchmaking process (by the provider, by the consumer, or by a third-party "matchmaker") we will be able to associate compatible advertisements with queries. The match might be *perfect* (in which case a discovered service will exactly meet the need of the consumer) or *partial* (in which case the consumer might have to combine the service with some additional functionality to meet its need; it can do this by itself, or—as we will demonstrate later—continue to discover the "missing pieces" and finally compose a service that meets its need).

The Semantic Web plays two key roles in the discovery process. First, Semantic Web techniques provide a rich mechanism for describing functionality. This is important in building and exploiting ontologies that describe the concepts and vocabulary needed to discuss functionality and services. Second, the Semantic Web provides a unifying layer of naming and distribution, that is, an addressing mechanism that can encompass virtual and physical entities and a way for various "pieces of the puzzle" to reside on various servers, devices, and so on. For example, a device description can refer to an ontology elsewhere, and this ontology in turn can be a specialization or extension of another ontology, again somewhere else. As mentioned earlier, the *polymorphic* nature of these ontologies and their extensions will allow broader interoperation through partial understanding and agreement.

12.5   Contracting for the Use of Services

Once we have discovered and identified the service (or services) that we want to use, there are several rather "bureaucratic" issues to be dealt with. These include (but are not limited to)

- assuring security, privacy, and trust.
- compensating the service provider.
- determining execution locus.

The Semantic Web promises to be extremely useful when it comes to matters of security, privacy, and trust, as these are largely issues of representation. Generally, the Semantic Web rests heavily on a framework of trust partially constructed using digital signatures and other types of cryptographic certificates. Any agent can expose its reasoning about trust using the same mechanisms by which everything else is represented on the Semantic Web. These representations of reasoning (we could call them "proofs") might themselves be exchanged between agents as a means of more "compelling" communication (e.g., for access to restricted resources or services).

We anticipate services specific to assisting agents with their security, privacy, and trust issues (e.g., there might be a service that rates the "reputation" of other services with regard to reliability, trustworthiness, or some other relevant metric). Again, these services themselves can be discovered and their use contracted.

Given a functional security and trust framework, we can introduce the notion of *payments*. Such a notion is required for the purpose of compensating providers for services rendered. Generally, we anticipate third-party services (which, again, are discoverable) to facilitate payments or other types of compensation. Note that we are not trying to imply that everything on the Semantic Web will cost something, but certainly some services will emerge that are not free. Advertising (of products and services *for humans* this time) will no longer be as viable as a revenue model once automated agents take care of a large part of the information exchange, reasoning, and service utilization. Making physical devices interoperable is an objective worth pursuing: the devices have typically already been purchased before the need arises to have them work together, and it is unlikely that a single company will be engaged in the manufacture of all the different types of devices that we anticipate will make up the Web of semantic gadgets (for example, Nokia makes cellular phones and other wireless communication devices, but it does not make thermostats; yet the consumer might benefit from a wireless device that communicates with a thermostat).

As an issue related to security, the determination of execution locus is an interesting issue. A particular service might be executed by the agent offering the service (the typical case), or such execution might involve *trusted mobile code* downloaded to the requester's computational environment, or some combination of the two. We will simply assume that this issue is resolved in some way and acknowledge that it is beyond the scope of this chapter.

12.6   Composition of Services

The discovery of services based on some description of a requirement of new functionality might result in identification of only a partial match (e.g., Sycara et al. 1999). In such cases, the requester can attempt to provide the missing parts itself or continue the discovery process and identify other services. These services can then be pieced together to form an aggregate service that fulfills the original requirement.

Composition of exact required functionality from partially matched discovered services should be viewed as a process of *goal-driven assembly*. For example, automated planning or configuration techniques could be used to achieve the assembly. In the context of ubiquitous computing and semantic gadgets, contracting for the use of services should always be viewed as a goal-driven activity because of the volatile nature of ubiquitous computing environments (not only can any of the devices and services fail or be removed from the environment at any time, but new ones can be added to it; thus *opportunistic* exploitation of services might be beneficial).

The goal-driven approach takes information system interoperability beyond what mere standardization or simple interface sharing enables, since it is based on "deeper" descriptions of service functionality and can be performed ad hoc and on demand. In fact, the dynamically composed aggregate services are the Semantic Web's virtual equivalent of real-life *value chains*: large quantities of information (i.e., "raw material") may be obtained, and at each step the value of information increases and its volume decreases.

Given that services discovered represent actual (possibly physical) functionality of devices, aggregate services might be seen as *device coalitions*. Not only can individual devices extend their functionality, but the device coalitions form a type of "superdevices."

12.7   Museum Scenario Revisited: An Analysis

There are several technologies that are required to implement the ubiquitous computing functionality illustrated in the art museum scenario:

- context awareness (including location, using global positioning systems (GPSs) outside and some analogous system inside, as well as additional sensory data that might be relevant)

- service discovery (finding available service providers in a wireless network)

- requirements/preferences (making the user's desires known to other service providers)

- user interface design (touch screen, voice input, speech output, etc.)

- the ability to match requirements to services (including planning functions to compose services to meet the user's needs)

- machine learning (to improve performance over time and adapt to better meet the user's needs).

Many of these technologies fall within the scope of this chapter. Generally, enabling all this functionality is a rich, shared, frame-based representation of the underlying information.

12.7.1   In the Car

Within the confines of the car, various gadgets can establish a network connection through Bluetooth, or a wired connection such as a recharging port, so the SG can use the dashboard display, the radio speakers, onboard computing resources, sensors, etc. Many of today's cars already have GPS sensors, maps, and wireless connectivity. In this scenario, we combine these tools with the ability to access weather reports and digital wallet features, including museum membership information, user preferences, and the ability to communicate with devices outside the bounds of the car itself, like the parking garage tollgate. Finally, recording the car's location in the garage requires some location service inside the garage, since GPS is not effective inside a building. Beyond the connectivity issues, quite a bit of information must be exchanged to provide this functionality. Location information is of course one of the keys here, but so are personal preferences and trade-offs among them, privacy of personal information, and knowledge of typical tasks, such as the steps involved in parking a car in a public garage and shutting down network connections that are severed when the SG is removed from the car's environment.

12.7.2   In the Museum

In this nonfamiliar environment, the SG must use its own user interfaces rather than rely on available peripherals. In addition, discovery of available services is of utmost importance. Here we see examples of services that include an automated box office, interactions with temperature sensors, crowd capacity services, interior location and map services, coat check services, and especially, catalogs of interrelated knowledge about art works, and again, user preferences combined with the monitoring of our progress through the exhibit. In a ubiquitous computing environment, there might be several possible implementations that could provide this functionality to the user. Privacy concerns may dictate that each person's own SG play an active role in tracking each user's progress, rather than allowing sensors in the room to capture one's position over time. The availability of required knowledge over network access is again critical to these functions.

12.7.3   In the Gift Shop

The shopping experience in the ubiquitous computing world has remarkable similarities regardless of the type of merchant or shop involved, so the fact that the gift shop in our example is in the museum is largely irrelevant to the details of the experience. Here the SG combines personal calendar information about birthdays, conventions about birthday gifts (Charniak 1972), personal preference information (in this case for others, involving trust and requiring the system to deal with privacy issues), and discovery of descriptions of available purchase inventory.

It is an interesting separate problem for the SG to determine what the appropriate context is for triggering a gift reminder, as occurred in our example. Not every shopping opportunity presents an appropriate occasion for triggering such a reminder: for example, it would seem out of place for such a reminder to appear while one was shopping for groceries.

The act of purchasing the item selected for the gift involves the digital wallet again, this time including credit card charges as well as museum membership and the availability of a member discount. The availability of the additional services of gift-wrapping and shipping (which also requires address lookup capabilities) at the time of purchase provides an example illustration of service composition.

12.7.4   Exiting the Museum

One of the interesting aspects of the scenario of leaving the museum is that of context. As we leave the gift shop, we are changing context. We have completed one scenario and are ready to proceed to the next one. It is important that the SG be able to determine these transition points as we move through our daily tasks.

At these transition points, there are multiple knowledge sources that influence the possible choices. In the example, there are additional activities at the museum, our current frame of reference, but there are opportunities outside of this context as well.

12.7.5   In the Parking Garage

Returning to the car involves a reversal of the car security features that were enacted on our arrival. Docking the SG provides a means for recharging, but it could also be a convenient way to transfer information for backup or additional planning purposes.

12.8   Conclusion

We have presented a discussion of how Semantic Web technologies can be used in the context of ubiquitous computing to enrich the capabilities of service discovery mechanisms. By abstracting device functionality as software agents, and then using Semantic Web technologies (e.g., distributed frame-based representation) to describe agent services, we can build a ''semantic'' discovery service capable of functioning beyond a priori standardization. Through the composition of partially matching (discovered) services into virtual value chains, we are able to form device coalitions that opportunistically exploit a dynamically changing ubiquitous computing environment.

References

Brickley, D., and R. V. Guha. 2000. Resource Description Framework (RDF) Schema Specification 1.0 (candidate recommendation). World Wide Web Consortium. Available from http://www.w3.org/TR/rdf-schema/.

Charniak, E. 1972. Toward a Model of Children's Story Comprehension. AI Lab Technical Report AI-TR-266, Massachusetts Institute of Technology, Cambridge, MA.

Chaudhri, V., A. Farquhar, R. Fikes, P. Karp, and J. Rice. 1998. OKBC: A Programmatic Foundation for Knowledge Base Interoperability. In *Proceedings of the Fifteenth National Conference on Artificial Intelligence and Tenth Innovative Applications of Artificial Intelligence Conference (AAAI-98), July 26–30, 1998, Madison, Wisconsin.* Menlo Park, CA/Cambridge, MA: AAAI/MIT Press.

Fensel, D. (ed.). 2000. The Semantic Web and Its Languages. *IEEE Intelligent Systems* 15(6):67–73.

Fikes, R., and T. Kehler. 1985. The Role of Frame-Based Representation in Reasoning. *Communications of the ACM* 28(9):904–920.

Hendler, J., and D. L. McGuinness. 2000. The DARPA Agent Markup Language. *IEEE Intelligent Systems* 15(6):67–73.

Karp, P. D. 1992. The Design Space of Frame Knowledge Representation Systems. Technical Report 520, SRI International AI Center, Menlo Park, CA.

Lassila, O. 1998. Web Metadata: A Matter of Semantics. *IEEE Internet Computing* 2(4):30–37.

Lassila, O., and D. L. McGuinness. 2001. The Role of Frame-Based Representation on the Semantic Web. Technical Report KSL-01–02, Stanford University, Stanford, CA.

Minsky, M. 1975. A Framework for Representing Knowledge. In *The Psychology of Computer Vision*, ed. P. H. Winston. New York: McGraw-Hill.

Reynolds, F., C. Woodrow, and H. Ohto. 2000. Composite Capability/Preference Profiles (CC/PP): Structure (working draft). World Wide Web Consortium. Available from http://www.w3.org/Mobile/CCPP/.

Richard, G. G. III. 2000. Service Advertisement and Discovery: Enabling Universal Device Cooperation. *IEEE Internet Computing* 4(5):18–26.

Sycara, K., M. Klusch, S. Widoff, and J. Lu. 1999. Dynamic Service Matchmaking among Agents in Open Information Environments. *ACM SIGMOD Record* 28(1):47–53.

Weiser, M. 1991. The Computer for the Twenty-First Century. *Scientific American* 265(3):94–104.

Weiser, M. 1993. Some Computer Science Problems in Ubiquitous Computing, *Communications of the ACM* 36(1):74–84.

13 Static and Dynamic Semantics of the Web

Christopher Fry, Mike Plusch, and Henry Lieberman

13.1 Introduction

The vast majority of the Web's early users originally perceived it as a static repository of unstructured data. This static model was adequate for browsing small sets of information by humans, but it is now breaking down as programs attempt to generate information dynamically and as human browsing is increasingly assisted by intelligent agent programs.

The next phase of the Web, as represented in this book's movement toward the Semantic Web, lies in encoding properties of and relationships between objects represented by information stored on the Web. It is envisioned that authors of Web pages will include this semantic information along with human-readable Web content, perhaps with some machine assistance in the encoding. Parsing unstructured natural language into machine-understandable concepts is not feasible in general, although some programs may be able to make partial sense out of Web content.

However, the semantics involved in this transition is primarily *declarative* semantics, semantics that changes only relatively slowly as Web pages are created, destroyed, or modified, typically by explicit, relatively coarse-grained human action. Less attention has been given to the *dynamic* semantics of the Web, which is equally important. Dynamic semantics have to do with the *creation* of content, actions that may be guided by user-initiated interface actions, time, users' personal profiles, data on a server, and other conditions.

Even less attention has been given to methods for cleanly integrating the static and dynamic aspects of the Web. In this chapter, we discuss the need for dynamic semantics and show how dynamic semantics will be enabled by and useful to the new generation of intelligent agent software that will increasingly inhabit the Web in the coming years. Though there will also be autonomous agents, the more interesting agents will cooperate interactively with humans, helping them to achieve their goals more efficiently than a user could on his own. We present here a new language, Water, that fully integrates static and dynamic semantics while remaining close to the XML framework that has made the Web successful.

Beyond that, we envision that Web end users and Web application developers will not be routinely writing code directly in Water or any other formal semantic language, but instead avail themselves of Programming by Example (Lieberman 2001) and other interactive agent interfaces that will hide the details of the formal languages. But transition to these future interfaces will be greatly aided by a foundation that can cleanly integrate static and dynamic semantics.

13.2   Static Semantics

13.2.1   The Web's Link Structure Mimics a Semantic Net

A semantic net (Woods 1975) is a network of concepts linked by relations. The Web is, of course, a network of pages, each containing text, pictures, other media types, and links to other Web pages. Though the Web has far less structure than typical artificial intelligence (AI) semantic nets, the Web pages that constitute the nodes of the Web's network often do represent concepts, and the links between them represent relations between those concepts. For example, a person's home page is the Web's representation of that person, in a sense. The links leading off her home page—to her publication list, her e-mail address, courses that she teaches, and so on—represent the relation of her to, for example, the articles she has published.

The only problem is that these relations are expressed in human-understandable natural language and human-understandable pictures. Short of full natural-language understanding, it is difficult for a computer program to extract those concepts and relations automatically in order to perform query answering, inference and other tasks.

13.2.2   Should the Semantic Web Be Static?

The Semantic Web movement, represented in the chapters in this book and in Web standards initiatives such as RDF, DAML, and OIL, is an attempt to introduce common formal languages for expressing concepts and relations in a machine-readable way. To leverage existing Web tools and emulate the Web's social success, such efforts strive to embed the descriptive information in pages similar to the way text, pictures, and conventional media are already described using HTML and XML.

However, all this is basically limited to *static* semantics. The interaction paradigm is that knowledge descriptions are authored by a developer in the same way that HTML pages are presently authored by a Web designer, then "published" on the Web to make them available in the network. Sometimes the descriptions may be automatically produced by a program from the results of user interaction in a manner similar to the way many WYSIWYG Web editors, such as Macromedia Dreamweaver or Adobe GoLive, produce HTML automatically from user editing operations.

In all of this, there is the underlying assumption that semantics

- *Is represented declaratively.* It is represented in passive data that are descriptive and can be retrieved: for example, a Web page on a Web server.

- *Changes relatively slowly.* Web publishing events happen rarely relative to actions such as browsing a page or clicking a link.

Structured static semantics are a huge advance for the Web, since they will enable software agents to find and reason about a colossal volume of information, essentially turning mere data into knowledge. But the larger and more complex the knowledge, the less complete and useful static representations become.

13.3 Dynamic Semantics

In addition to the static semantics of Web pages, links, and Web markup, there is also what we call dynamic semantics. In contrast to static semantics, dynamic semantics

▪ *Is represented procedurally.* It can be computed by programs running on the client or server side, based on immediate interactive user input. This computation can depend on the immediate *context*, including time, personal information about the user, and user-initiated actions.

▪ *Changes relatively rapidly.* A single user click can cause the semantics to be generated or to change, or it can be changed by the actions of programs continuously in real time.

As the Web matures, static semantics are being augmented and supplanted by dynamic semantics in many ways. As a simple example, some URLs are not addresses of static pages stored on Web servers, but rather act as directives to the server to initiate some computation. CGI scripts are an example of this. A question mark in a URL is a signal for the server to retrieve some named program and execute it, possibly with arguments. An Active Server Page queries a database and constructs a page on the fly. Even search engine results pages and customized ads based on cookies are examples of dynamically created Web pages. Streaming audio, video, and other media also make the Web more dynamic.

13.3.1 Transparency between Static and Dynamic Semantics

For any browser, the HTTP stream delivered by the transport procedure is identical to that which would have come from a statically stored page, so that the requester need not concern himself with the question of whether that information was stored or computed. That kind of transparency between static and dynamic data is an extremely important property for a system to have. It means that a system can always be extended by replacing some piece of formerly static data with a new, dynamically generated object, as long as the new object's behavior is compatible with that of the old. This property has long been appreciated in the communities of AI and Human-Computer Interaction (HCI) languages such as Lisp, Prolog, and Smalltalk, though it has been underappreciated in the communities of users of more conventional languages such as C and Java. In the knowledge representation community, this has long been studied under the designation *procedural attachment*. Our aim here is to extend the principle of equivalence of static and dynamic data as the Web moves toward encoding more semantics.

13.4   Sources of Dynamic Semantics

In addition to the examples of procedural Web data cited above, there are several other sources of dynamic semantics for the Web. The first is in the process of Web browsing itself.

13.4.1   Web Browsing Generates Dynamic Semantics

The process of a user navigating through Web pages might result in new objects and relations being created that need to be represented, both on the client's machine and also on the Web servers with which the client communicates. These may either be represented statically and stored explicitly or produced dynamically as a result of user action. For example, personal information about the user, such as her current interests, might be communicated from the client to the server. Now, cookies are used as a very primitive means of client-to-server communication, but they can communicate only a single piece of information. Information like the user's current interests might be represented by a complex structure with dynamic contingencies.

13.4.2   Agents Generate Dynamic Semantics

An alternative to having Web page creators explicitly author metadata is to have the metadata computed by agents from human-readable information. An active area of research involves having agents "read" Web pages containing natural-language and formatted text intended for humans and compute metadata by using machine learning to infer "wrappers" that describe the structure of the text (Kushmerick, Weld, and Doorenbos 1997). This can be done in many cases without having to completely solve the natural-language problem of formal representation. The field of information extraction uses partial parsing to perform tasks like semiautomatic topic categorization and summarization. Examples of this are price comparison shopbots that extract prices from online catalogs or filters that remove advertisements. Users may even define these wrappers dynamically (Bauer, Dengler, and Paul 2001).

13.4.3   Web Editing Generates Dynamic Semantics

Finally, the evolution of the Web itself leads to dynamic semantics. As pages are modified, new pages are added, and old ones disappear, both Web clients and Web servers might want to track and represent how pages change or maintain a history that may be dynamically accessible in different ways. Such a representation could be as simple as displaying the date of the last change to a page or highlighting the parts that have changed since the page was last visited.

13.5   Web Agents Make Use of Dynamic Semantics

A revolution is currently underway in the growing popularity of intelligent agents on the Web. Agents are programs that act as assistants to the user in the Web interface. They can track user interests, explore the Web proactively, learn through interacting with the user, provide personalized data and services, and much more. Examples of such intelligent agents are Letizia

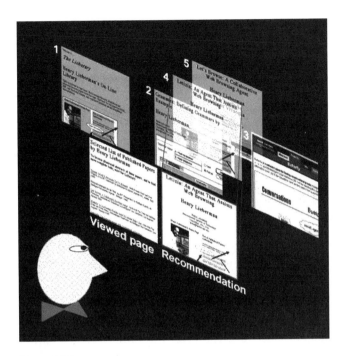

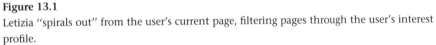

Figure 13.1
Letizia "spirals out" from the user's current page, filtering pages through the user's interest profile.

(figure 13.1) and Powerscout (Lieberman, Fry, and Weitzman in press), which act as *reconnaissance agents*, building a profile of the user's interests by watching his Web browsing and dynamically and incrementally crawling the Web or using traditional search engines as subsidiary tools to suggest related material in real time.

What sets these kinds of agents apart from more traditional tools like search engines and cookie-personalized sites is their more dynamic nature. They are computing concepts and relations dynamically from the data stored and retrieved on the Web and procedures that are attached to that data and also from the dynamic process of the user's interactive navigation through Web sites.

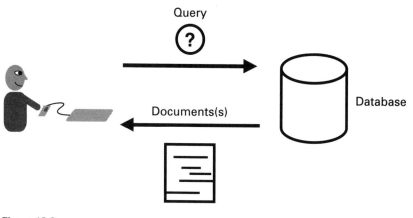

Figure 13.2
The traditional Information Retrieval paradigm.

13.6   *Information Retrieval and Theorem-Proving Perspectives*

It is instructive to consider how the advent of the Web changed the perspective of information-seeking activities from the old information retrieval (IR) model, essentially a static model, to a newer model of dynamic, continuous, and cooperative information navigation. As we embed more semantics into the Web, we need to make a similar shift in perspective from the old "theorem-proving" model of inference to a new model of dynamic and cooperative reasoning and problem solving.

Here's a characterization of what we consider the dominant paradigm in the IR field to have been prior to the advent of the Web. The old IR model (presented in figure 13.2) was that information was stored in a "database," essentially a large, static bag of "records" and "fields" that changed only slowly (via "database updates"). The user's only option for interfacing with the database was to throw a "query"—a statement of the user's interests in a formal query language like SQL—at it. The user was expected to have in mind a Platonic "ideal document" that was described by the query. The job of the database was to return one or more documents in the database ordered by how well they satisfied the query. Today's search engines are the modern manifestation of this paradigm.

This paradigm presents a number of problems as applied to the Web:

- *It is difficult for users to express queries precisely.* In the old days of IR, users were expert librarians who formulated Boolean queries in formal languages. Now, ordinary users type one or two words in the query boxes of search engines. These do not express intent precisely.

- *There may not be a "best document" in the Web.* Any query can potentially return an infinite number of documents. It is impossible to tell which is "best" from a single query alone.

- *Query-response interaction is a "batch processing" view.* It is sequential: either the user or the retrieval system is working, but not both at the same time. Except for query refinement, each query and response is essentially an independent event, and unrelated to anything else the user might be doing.

There are many other critiques of the old IR paradigm, but these will suffice for the moment.

Agent software on the Web violates all of the assumptions presented above. Agents like Letizia and Powerscout track the history of user browsing and use it as a persistent context from which to infer user interests. Rather than globally ranking documents, they present context-dependent suggestions that can improve over time. Rather than using the query-response paradigm, they are always active and deliver their recommendations in a continuous stream in real time. They essentially integrate browsing and searching into a unified process. Their goal is not to find the best document, but to make the best use of the user's time. In short, they treat browsing as a continuous, cooperative activity between one or more humans and one or more software agents.

13.6.1 The Theorem-Proving Paradigm

Adding semantics to the Web allows agents to solve problems using traditional theorem-proving techniques to process assertions and descriptions

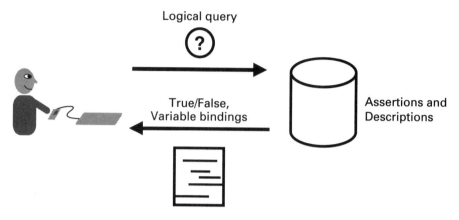

Figure 13.3
The traditional theorem-proving paradigm.

stored on the Web. Again, though, we believe that the paradigm has to change to accommodate the dynamic and fluid nature of the Web. By analogy, we present a characterization of the old theorem-proving paradigm.

The traditional theorem-proving paradigm (see figure 13.3) treated a knowledge base as a big bag of assertions and descriptions expressed in a logical language. Again, the way the user was assumed to interact with this knowledge base was to issue a logical query in the form of an assertion to be proved true or false, possibly filling in the values of logical variables contained in the assertion. This would launch an inference procedure that would find "the answer."

The theorem-proving paradigm also presents some problems when applied to the Web:

- *It is difficult for users to express logical queries precisely.* Users of Web applications are generally not mathematicians, and we cannot expect them to be. We need to have interfaces that interact with the user and help formulate queries before they are sent to an inference system.

- *There may not be a "best answer."* How much is that plane flight? Well, when are you asking? Do you have a discount? Should we ask for a price on Priceline? Buy one on Ebay? How long are you willing to wait for the answer? Can you leave a day earlier? We need the ability to put procedural hooks in the answers to queries.

▪ *Query-response interaction is a "batch processing" view.* Again, the standard view makes no provision for dynamic user input or user-agent cooperation.

Once again, the corresponding modern view should be that problem solving and inference are a cooperative venture between one or more humans and one or more computer agents. Interaction and parallelism should be available at any point in the process. After all, the expensive component is not the Internet connection, the client computer, or even the servers that store the information: it is the user's *time*. This means that the components of the future Semantic Web should be able to integrate not only text, pictures, links, and semantic descriptions, but also dynamic and procedural objects. But how should this be accomplished?

13.7   *The Semantic Web Should Not Sit on the Tower of Babel*

The approach to the Semantic Web advocated in this book via languages like DAML and OIL aims to leverage existing Web standards like XML and RDF and add new facilities that allow the expression of formal semantic information embedded in traditional HTML documents and enable inference. This approach has the advantage that encoding semantics in the Web becomes an evolutionary rather than a disruptive step in the evolution of the Web. However, procedural information has not been covered by any of the existing proposals for a language for the Semantic Web.

13.7.1   *Not My Department?*

One approach to explain the absence of procedural information is simply to say, as the current standards do, that it is out of the scope of Web standards to dictate how Web applications will be programmed. Fear of the divisiveness of arguments over programming languages in the computer science community has been motivating this abdication of responsibility for the encoding of procedures.

But a look at where such an approach has gotten us reveals why it is unworkable. Many of today's Web applications are programmed piecemeal in a bewildering array of programming languages: Javascript, Java, Perl, VBScript, and PHP, just to name a few. It is not uncommon for what appears to the end user as a single Web application to use, in total, seven or eight of these languages. The disadvantages of such multilanguage environments should be obvious:

- *The difficulty of learning multiple programming languages.* Not only does learning multiple languages duplicate the effort of learning syntax and semantics multiple times, but there is no rational relationship between the languages (e.g., Perl has nothing to do with Java). Maddeningly, despite their names and superficial similarity, Javascript and Java contain major differences in their type and object systems. Having to learn two or more to get a task done is actually more than twice as hard as learning one language, because the interface between the languages is always additional hair, usually poorly documented. Not only must one learn the two languages, one must also learn *when* to use one language or the other.

- *The difficulty of integrating Web data with multiple languages.* It is worthwhile to keep in mind that the majority of these languages were originally designed for a purpose that had nothing to do with the Web. Java was designed as a control language for small devices; Javascript, as a scripting language for Netscape; VBScript, as an extension of Basic for Microsoft desktop applications; Perl, for string manipulation via regular expressions. They were simply pasted together in manner without a guiding principle to make them "work" for the Web.

- *The necessity of conversion between different formats.* Conversion wastes computation time and storage and opens up the possibility of errors arising from mismatches in data semantics.

- *The difficulty of debugging across multiple languages and systems.* If something goes wrong with a multilanguage program, how does the programmer determine which language is at fault? None of these languages has anything approaching a decent debugger, even for programs written solely in that language, so if more than one language is involved, debugging becomes a nightmare.

Perhaps the worst problem as far as Web semantics is concerned is that the plethora of languages precludes the representation of procedural semantics in any sort of principled way. Existing Web functionality needs to be consolidated.

13.8   We Need Another Language Like a Hole in the Head

New Web languages seem to be born monthly. Rather than introducing a new language merely for implementing some specialized functionality, we recognize that sooner or later such functionality will need general-purpose utilities like conditional execution, loops, and functional abstraction. When these are added on to special-purpose languages late in the game, elegance is compromised for the sake of compatibility with the original specialized language, and we end up with a mess.

Instead, we propose, as DAML/OIL does for static Web semantics, to gently extend the semantics of the widely accepted HTML for markup and XML for static data to encode procedural semantics in Web pages. This gentle extension we are proposing is called Water.

Water is a language for the Web that embodies, in one unified language, the three primary functionalities needed for general-purpose information manipulation:

- *Markup.* Since Water is a superset of HTML, it inherits all of its capability.

- *Data.* Water permits the description of persistent structured data on the Web via XML-like syntax yet has the capability of dynamically computing values that may contain self-referential interconnections.

- *Code.* Water is a general-purpose object-oriented programming language that is, at its core, more flexible than Javascript, VBScript, and Java.

Water provides a way to define functions and call them in addition to defining and instantiating objects. The object system is a multiple-inheritance, prototype-based object system with annotations. Thus it is not merely a general-purpose procedural/object-oriented language grafted on to HTML and XML, but rather a language whose very core supports the intimate mixture of unstructured content, structured data, and active values through a highly dynamic object system.

13.9 Is Procedural Attachment Rope to Hang Oneself?

Advocates of declarative representations always get nervous when someone advocates letting the user call a procedure from any point in a declarative representation. There is the danger that the code can have unpredictable effects and that the reasoning systems cannot guarantee anything about the behavior of descriptions that contain embedded code. In this view, procedural attachment gives the user rope to hang himself.

To some extent, this is true. But we should recognize that many operations that Web applications will want to do will inevitably go beyond purely declarative representations. Input/output (I/O) operations, especially network I/O, user interface operations that interact in real time with the user, and side effects to shared data structures often have this character. If we prohibit procedures from being embedded in declarative representations, we are merely pushing the procedural information outside of the declarative representation entirely. Although this might gain some cleanliness in the declarative part, it does not alter whatever properties of unpredictability the entire system, procedures and data, has as a whole. And that, after all, is what we are really interested in.

13.9.1 Procedural Markup

A better approach than such a prohibition of procedural attachment is to allow procedures to be embedded in data, accepting the risk, but also to encourage the programmer to do what we might call *procedural markup*, analo-

gous to markup for text. Markup for text (e.g., ⟨b⟩) supplies additional declarative annotation that serves as advice to the renderer about how
to display the text. Markup for procedures involves including with an embedded procedure a declarative representation of the result of the procedure,
so that the reasoning system can operate on it. For example, a procedure that
computes the price of an airline ticket might assert that the result is a posi-
tive number in U.S. dollars.

Of course, the results of the system's reasoning will be valid only if the
markup accurately describes the result of the procedure. Although it is impossible in general to predict the result of an arbitrary program, in some
cases, automatic program verification might actually be able either to generate these assertions about results automatically or to prove that the code
actually satisfies the assertions. To enable this, it is best to keep the code
close at hand to the places where it is used. And for debugging, it is invalu-
able to have a seamless interface that integrates procedures and data so that
the programmer can see if there is a mismatch between what the program
has produced and what he is expecting.

13.10   *Water Provides a Smooth Path from Text to Code*

Like HTML, Water permits the programmer to just write a paragraph of English text and call it a Web page. Also as in HTML, in Water the programmer
can take another pass and add markup without having to rewrite his original
text. He needs only to learn the HTML tags that he needs to know to mark
up the text he wrote originally.

However, should he require dynamic behavior, with Water he need not
learn a new scripting syntax such as Javascript, or worse, a whole new programming environment such as Java. He can simply insert Water tags into
his page using the same basic syntax that his markup is in. Plain text,
markup, data, and code can be freely intermixed with no barriers between
those functionalities and no "impedance mismatches." Water tries hard to
give the user the most functionality per learning effort, emphasizing econ-
omy and elegance at the expense of hairy and rarely used features.

13.10.1   Who's the User?

The target audience for Water is the Web site author who needs more functionality than HTML can offer yet is intimidated (and rightly so) by multilanguage programs. Although Water can fulfill most of the needs of the general-purpose programmer, it is hard to convince someone who has spent years learning a difficult language like C or Java is to give up on his investment, even if he can exceed his previous productivity in a few weeks. The HTML author looking for more flexibility—and there are millions of them—is an easier sell. But the suitability of Water is not limited to toy programs. Water is not simplified at the expense of being able to accommodate complex programming tasks.

13.11   Water's Distinguishing Features

Water takes a unique approach to bridging the apparent gap between static and dynamic semantics by unifying what in other languages are objects and function calls. Yet it does not start off by throwing today's Web author in cold water, either. The following are some key features of the Water approach:

- *Minimal differences between markup, data, and code.* We discussed this point in the previous section.

- *Minimal differences between classes and instances.* Water's object system uses prototypes instead of classes (Lieberman 1986). There is no need to learn separate operations for classes and instances, since Water makes no distinction between a class and an instance. An object can be used "as an instance," and/or it can be "subclassed," with the new object inheriting any characteristics of its parent(s) that the programmer desires, whereas other characteristics are modified to differentiate the new object from its parent(s).

- *Dynamic lookup.* The language Self (Ungar and Smith 1987) had a simple and elegant prototype-based object system. Self's object system differs from that of Water in that it permitted only single inheritance and had a "copy down" semantics for inherited values rather than the "dynamic lookup" mechanism of Water. The dynamic lookup of Water makes object creation faster and uses less memory than copy down. It also preserves locality of reference for shared data, which may have additional advantages in terms of speed. But if copy down is desired, the "init" function for object creation of a given parent object can choose to copy down desired fields.

- *Minimal difference between "instance variables" and "methods."* Both are stored as values of fields in an object. A user can get the value of an instance variable or a method simply by getting the value of a named field. Methods are implemented by objects, just like everything else in the language. To call a method, the programmer uses the function-calling syntax, which looks like using an HTML tag.

- *Minimal differences between a function call and object creation.* Tag names refer to the parent object. The parameters after a tag name serve as either field initializers or function arguments, depending on the value of the tag.

- *Minimal differences between aggregate data types.* Objects, vectors, and hash tables are all represented by the same data structure. An object is a set of fields whose keys can be any object (interned strings, numbers, other objects). When an object is being treated as a vector, a mechanism permits looping over all fields whose keys are integers. A "size" field makes finding out the length of the vector quick and facilitates adding an element to the end of the vector.

- *No differences between the object system and the type system.* For example, "integer" can be thought of as a "type," but it is really just another object in the object tree that happens to be the parent object of all integers. All objects used as types can be referenced via the path syntax, just as all fields of objects can be referenced. In fact, since any object can become a parent, any object can effectively be a type.

- *Minimal differences between initialization and normal methods.* An "init" method can, in fact, return any type of object and should declare the returned type of object.

- *Minimal (but very significant) differences between local variables, fields, and subobjects for creating, setting, and referencing.*

- *Minimal differences between a field and an annotation to that field.* Water provides a way of adding information *about* a field. Say we have a field named "color" in an object named "car." We might want to add a comment about the field, such as "All colors besides black and white cost extra," or to declare that the type of the field must be integer. Annotations are the mechanism that Water uses to associate information about a field with that field. Annotations of a field "foo" are indicated by another field with a naming convention of "foo@annotation-name". A looping mechanism makes it easy to find all annotations of a given field or to ignore all annotations of an object when we want to loop through an object's field values.

- *An easy way of specifying the "evaluation kind" of each parameter in a method definition.* This controls how each argument in a call to the method is interpreted. It can be treated as code and evaluated, which is the default. It can be treated as an expression to be parsed but not evaluated, which is especially good for "delayed evaluation," in which a method takes code as an argument and can evaluate the code when it chooses. It can be treated as the string of its source code (and not even parsed) and as hypertext, which treats text within angle brackets as code to evaluate and other text just as strings (which is especially convenient for implementing HTML tags as Water objects or method calls).

- *Ability to change the parent of an object at run time.* This makes it easy for a parent to "adopt" a child, though situations requiring such a capacity are not common.

- *Optional keywords.* In HTML keywords are usually used to specify each attribute. XML requires the use of keywords. In Java and Javascript keywords cannot be used to specify any argument. Water permits the programmer to use keywords when he wants to be more explicit or pass arguments "out of order" and to pass arguments by position (without keywords) when he wants to be more concise. There is no extra overhead for declaring keywords when defining a method, as they are simply the parameter's name.

- *"Active values" on object fields.* These facilitate simple constraint systems, and along with other dynamic features, help to implement specification

Name	Water Syntax	XML 1.0
Simple, no body	`<foo/>`	same
Simple with end	`<foo></foo>`	same
Simple arg	`<foo arg1="bar"/>`	same
Optional end	`<foo></>`	`<foo></foo>`
Path and field access	`foo.bar`	`<foo><bar/></foo>` (???) `<foo arg1="bar">`
Path and method call	`foo<bar baz/> or foo.<bar baz/> or <foo <bar baz/> />`	`<foo><bar arg1="baz"/></foo>`
Simple numeric arg	`<foo arg1=123/>`	`<foo arg1="123"/>`
Optional keyword position sensitive	`<foo bar/>`	`<foo arg1="bar"/>`
Attr. Value has <>, no body	`<foo arg1=<baz> />`	`<foo><arg key="arg1"><baz></arg></foo>`
Attr. Value has <>, and had body	`<foo arg1=<baz>>testing</foo>`	`<foo><arg key="arg1"><baz></arg><content> testing</content></foo>`
Tag name has <>	`<<yak>/>`	??

Figure 13.4
Water syntax table.

changes after most of the implementation has been completed by permitting field references and setters to turn into method calls without changing the referencing and setting code at all.

Water is especially easy to write interactive programming environment tools for, because of its extensive introspection capabilities, evaluation kinds, elegant object system, uniform syntax, ultradynamic behavior, and small size. Figure 13.4 presents a summary of Water syntax, for those interested in the details. An example of Water code is given in the next section.

13.12   A Water Example

Water permits arbitrary code intermixed with HTML. Here is a snippet of ordinary HTML:

```
<font size="3">Hello World</font>
```

With Water we can place code, such as an attribute value, anywhere within this HTML:

```
<font size=1.<random 7/> > Hello World</font>
```

Water really has two syntaxes, a pure XML syntax and one that permits some shortcuts, such as "by position arguments," which make using attribute names unnecessary. Both syntaxes can be used in the same body of code.

We turn now to a more complex example, that of generating a catalog for a store. First we set up our inventory "database." This might come from another file or another method call, but here for simplicity we enter it directly as a vector of vectors:

```
<set root.inventory
  <vector
   <vector "Flannel Top Sheet" "17.95"/>
   <vector "Satin Pillow Case" "11.45"/> /> />

<set page
    <p>For our everyday unbeatable price we have
    </p> />

<set page <p>For our everyday unbeatable price we
have</p> />

root.inventory.<for_each>
     page.content.<push field_value.0/>
     page.content.<push " for the low low price of "/>
     page.content.<push field_value.1/>
     page.content.<push <br/> />
</for_each>
```

After this program has been run, the "page" variable contains our page object. We can get the string of HTML as follows:

```
page.<to_html/>
```

Here we add some variability based on the day of the month:

```
<set root.is_sale_day <date/>.day_of_month.<same 1/> />
```

Now is_sale_day is true if today is the first day of the month and false otherwise:

```
<set page <if root.is_sale_day <p>On Sale today we
have</p>
          true <p>For our everyday unbeatable price we
          have</p>
     </if> />
```

The heading of our page is now customized, so we do the same for the body:

```
root.items.<for_each>
    <set price
     field_value.1.<times <if> root.is_sale_day .75
                             true 1
                             </if>
               />
    />
    page.content.<push field_value.0/>
                        " for the low low price of "/>
                        price
                        <br/>
               />
</for_each>
```

Above, the price will be multiplied by .75 if today is the first of the month.

13.13   Comparison of Water with Java

Some of Water's features provide fixes for inconsistencies and other unnecessary complexities in Java (Lemay and Cadenhead 2001).

- All Water data types are full-fledged objects. There are no "ints" and "Integers," just "integers."

- Water has true multiple inheritance. There is no extra "interface" mechanism.

- Water supports both a prefix syntax and an infix syntax—automatically. Water does not need precedence rules or parentheses.

- The types of elements in vectors and hash tables can be declared in Water. There is no need for casting when extracting an element from a vector or a hash table.

- The types of fields and method return values need not be declared in Water. They default to the most general type of object. However, type declarations are encouraged, as they help declare the programmer's intent and can be used by programs to find inconsistencies in the programmer's intent as well as to speed up execution.

- The "init" method in Water is just like a regular method. Its body returns a value (usually but not necessarily a subobject of the called object). It is named and has a return type declaration just like a regular method.

- Instance variables in Water can be created or removed within an object at run time.

- In Water, methods can be added to a system class (or any other), extending its behavior without having to edit and recompile the original source. Water gives the programmer more flexibility in modularity so that a method for a class need not reside in the same file as the class definition if the programmer so chooses.

- Water's evaluation kinds permit the easy construction of high-level code manipulation methods that in many cases reduce the complexity of packaging up and calling advanced functionality.

- There is rarely a need in Water to create a "singleton", that is, a class with one instance object, because in Water, a "class" object can be treated just like an instance object. Its methods can be called directly using the "class" as "this." There is no need to have a distinction between static and instance variables or between static and instance methods. And each "instance" object in Water can get its own special version of a method, if the programmer so chooses, to distinguish its behavior from that of its sibling objects. "Static" is another concept that is just unnecessary in Water.

▪ Water is much more consistent with itself. For example, Java has three different syntaxes for programmatically determining the length of an array, a vector, and a string. Water has only one.

13.14 Comparison with Javascript

Water has a number of things in common with Javascript (Goodman 2000):

▪ Both can be embedded in HTML.

▪ Both are interpreted.

▪ Both have "eval," though Javascript doesn't have a "parsed but not evaled" representation for programs that manipulate code.

▪ Objects in both can have fields added dynamically, after an object is created.

But there are significant differences between them as well:

▪ Water can be "more" embedded than Javascript within HTML. Generally speaking, Javascript can be attached only to certain control attributes of Javascript tags. Water permits active code just about anywhere within HTML.

▪ Water's syntax is much more like HTML than Javascript's.

▪ The object system in Javascript is designed to be a "prototype" object system. Yet it is, at the very best, poorly documented. Water's prototype object system is easier to use.

▪ Water permits (but does not force) the declaration of types for arguments and object fields. Javascript does not permit type declarations.

▪ Water has much more flexible argument definitions that can take default values and "evaluation kinds" in addition to names and types.

▪ Water has a simple, concise syntax for referencing objects through long paths in the object hierarchy and interconnected field values.

13.15   Conclusion

We are now at a crossroads in the evolution of the Web. The Web has evolved from a relatively static collection of pages and links to a dynamic, interactive interface with semantic information. We are at the verge of being able to create the Semantic Web, in terms of declaratively representing objects that are already human-readable on the Web. The next step is to make it the Dynamic Semantic Web by encoding procedures in Web material as first-class objects.

We have presented in this chapter an argument for dynamic semantics, along with a language, Water, that integrates procedures seamlessly into Web pages, just as XML and DAML/OIL integrate descriptions. Some may think we place too much emphasis on the language. It is true that good environments can be built on top of mediocre languages, if a great deal of effort is dedicated to the task. The current Web itself may be viewed an example of such an endeavor. But great environments need a language that supports the easy construction of dynamic, interactive, and introspective tools. The difference between good environments and great environments is tens or even hundreds of percent in the speed of implementing reliable, maintainable programs. Increasing the productivity of Web applications is the ultimate goal. We can do this not just by handing current programmers more powerful tools, but by giving people who consider themselves nonprogrammers, as many of today's HTML authors do, the power to radically customize their computers.

References

Bauer, M., D. Dengler, and G. Paul. 2001. Programming by Demonstration for Information Agents. *Communications of the ACM* 43(3):98–103.

Danny Goodman's Javascript Handbook. Boston: IDG Books.

Kushmerick, N., D. S. Weld, and R. Doorenbos. 1997. Wrapper Induction for Information Extraction. *Proceedings of the 15ᵗʰ International Joint Conference on AI (IJCAI-97), Nagoya, Japan, August 23–29, 1997*, ed. M. E. Pollack (pp. 729–737). San Francisco: Morgan Kaufmann.

Lemay, L., and R. Cadenhead. 2001. *Teach Yourself Java 2 in 21 Days*. Indianapolis: Sams Press.

Lieberman, H. 1986. Using Prototypical Objects to Implement Shared Behavior in Object-Oriented Systems. *First Conference on Object-Oriented Programming Languages, Systems, and Applications [OOPSLA-86], ACM SigCHI. SIGPLAN Notices* 21(11):214–223.

Lieberman, H., ed. 2001. *Your Wish Is My Command: Programming by Example*. San Francisco: Morgan Kaufmann.

Lieberman, H., and C. Fry. 2001. Will Software Ever Work? *Communications of the ACM* 44(3):122–124.

Ungar, D., and R. B. Smith. 1987. Self: The Power of Simplicity. *Second Conference on Object-Oriented Programming Languages, Systems, and Applications [OOPSLA-87], ACM SigCHI. ACM SIGPLAN Notices* 22(12): 227–242.

Woods, W. 1975. What's in a Link: Foundations for Semantic Networks. In *Representation and Understanding*, ed. D. G. Bobrow and A. Collins. San Diego: Academic Press.

14 Semantic Annotation for Web Content Adaptation

Masahiro Hori

14.1 Introduction

Web contents are becoming accessible from a wide range of mobile devices such as cellular phones, pagers, and palmtop computers. Since these devices do not have the same rendering capabilities as desktop computers, it is necessary for Web contents to be adapted for transparent access from a variety of client agents. For example, a large, full-color image may be reduced with regard to size and color depth, removing unimportant portions of the content, when accessed by certain devices. Such content adaptation is exploited for either an individual element or a set of consecutive elements in a Web document and results in better presentation and faster delivery to the client device (Fox and Brewer 1996; Rousseau et al. 1999). Transformation of information from one form to another is often called *transcoding*, and it is particularly called *Web content transcoding* when the transformation is conducted along the Web transaction path. Web content transcoding is a way of adding value to Web contents and facilitates repurposing of Web contents. Transcoding is thus crucial for universal Web access under varying conditions that may depend on client capabilities, network connectivity, or user preferences.

Markup languages such as HTML embed annotations into documents. For example, an ⟨ol⟩ tag indicates the start of an ordered list, and a paragraph begins with a ⟨p⟩ tag. However, annotations can also be external, residing in a file separate from the original document. It seems impractical to incorporate data about Web documents, namely, Web metadata, into existing HTML documents, because of the difficulty of changing the established HTML specification to meet application-specific annotation needs. Although making annotations external to Web documents may require additional bookkeeping tasks, it has the substantial advantage of not requiring any modification of existing Web documents. More importantly, external annotation facilitates the repurposing of Web documents through the reuse of annotations that can be shared across Web documents. External annotation is thus a promising approach to facilitating Web content transcoding.

It is important to note here that the result of applying an annotation to a Web document depends on a transcoding policy. Annotations provide additional information about Web contents so that an adaptation engine can make better decisions on the content repurposing. The role of annotations is to provide explicit semantics that can be understood by a content adaptation engine. Although Web content annotation (or metadata) has a variety of potential applications (Lassila 1998), they can be categorized into three types: discovery, qualification, and adaptation of Web contents. The primary focus of this chapter is on the Web content adaptation, and the material presented herein does not necessarily address other kinds of applications, such as accurate searches of Web resources (i.e., discovery) and descriptions of users' preferences regarding privacy (i.e., qualification).

In pursuit of Web content repurposing, transcoding systems that adopt the external annotation approach are emerging (Hori, Kondoh, et al. 2000; IBM Corporation 2000; Nagao, Shirai, and Kevin in press). In the remainder of this chapter, a framework of external annotation is introduced first, and a high-level overview of annotation-based transcoding is explained, with emphasis on the idea of authoring-time transcoding. HTML page splitting is then taken up as an example of Web content adaptation, and the results of applying the transcoding module to real-life Web contents are investigated. Finally, a preliminary empirical evaluation is presented in the case of the

HTML page splitting plug-in, and the annotation-based transcoding approach is compared with related work.

14.2   External Annotation Framework

A framework of external annotation prescribes a scheme for representing annotation files and a way of associating original documents with external annotations. The role of annotation is to characterize ways of adapting content rather than to describe the contents of individual documents themselves. The basic ideas behind this annotation framework are twofold. One is that new elements and/or attributes should not be introduced into a document-type definition of documents to be annotated. The other is that annotations need to be created for arbitrary parts of annotated documents.

Annotations can be embedded in a Web document as inline annotations, which are often created as extra attributes of document elements. Most existing HTML browsers ignore unknown attributes added to HTML elements, without being hampered by proprietary inline annotations. Because of its simplicity, inline annotation has been often adopted as a way of associating annotation with HTML documents (Mea et al. 1996; Rousseau et al. 1999; Erdmann et al. 2000; Heflin and Hendler 2000). An advantage of the inline annotation approach is the ease of annotation maintenance it offers, eliminating the bookkeeping task of associating annotations with their target document. The inline approach, however, requires annotators to have document ownership, because annotated documents need to be modified whenever inline annotations are created or revised.

The external annotation approach, on the other hand, raises no issues related to document ownership. Moreover, and most important, external annotation facilitates the sharing and reuse of annotations across Web documents. Since an external annotation points to a portion of a Web document, the annotation can be shared across Web documents that have the same document fragment. Furthermore, external annotation avoids the mixing of contents and metadata, which is not desirable according to design

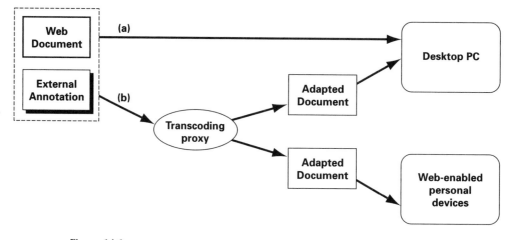

Figure 14.1
Overview of an annotation-based transcoding.

considerations that separate content from presentation (World Wide Web Consortium 2000b).

Figure 14.1 depicts paths from a Web document to different client devices. When a Web document is provided with an annotation document, a transcoding proxy may adapt the document on the basis of associated annotations upon receiving a request from a personal device (b). When a Web document can be rendered, as in the case of HTML documents, the document must be viewable in a normal browser on a desktop computer even if it is associated with an annotation document (a).

External annotation files contain metadata that address a part of a document to be annotated. XPath (World Wide Web Consortium 1999h) and XPointer (World Wide Web Consortium 2001b) are used to associate annotated portions of a document with annotating descriptions. Figure 14.2 illustrates a way of associating an external description with a portion of an existing document. An annotation file refers to portions of an annotated document. A reference may point to a single element (e.g., an IMG element) or a range of elements (e.g., an H2 element and the following paragraphs). For example, /HTML/BODY/P[3] points to the third P element of the BODY

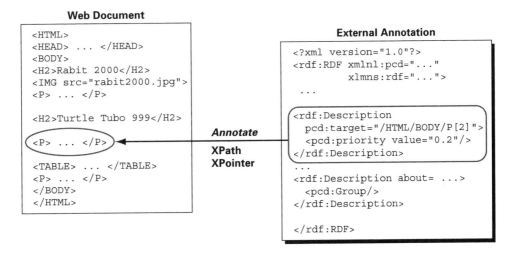

Figure 14.2
Framework of external annotation.

element of the annotated document. If a target element has an ID attribute, the attribute can be used for direct addressing without the need for a long path expression. Whereas XPath expressions basically select a node or sub-tree of a target document tree, XPointer could point to substring text contents or a range of consecutive nodes that may not necessarily constitute a subtree.

As the fundamental syntax of annotation files, RDF (World Wide Web Consortium 1999e) can be used. An annotation file, which is an XML document, therefore consists of a set of RDF descriptions. The RDF data model defines a simple model for describing relations among resources in terms of named properties and values. However, it is also necessary to deal with user preferences and device capabilities for the content adaptation. Such information profiles can be described by using the specification of Composite Capability/Preference Profiles (CC/PPs) (World Wide Web Consortium 2000a). A CC/PP specifies that client-side profiles can be delivered to a proxy server over HTTP (World Wide Web Consortium, 1999b). Furthermore, ways are currently being investigated of describing document profiles so that requirements for desired rendering can be clarified (World Wide Web Consortium, 1999g), and RDF is being employed for encoding conformance profiles. Taking account of the situations of these standardization activities, it is reasonable for annotation vocabularies to be encoded in RDF, so that comprehensive content adaptation mechanisms can be pursued in accordance with open standards.

When annotation files are stored in a repository, the appropriate annotation file for a Web document needs to be selected dynamically from the repository either implicitly, by means of a structural analysis of the subject document, or explicitly, by means of a reference contained in the subject document or some other association database. Explicit association can be made, for example, by using a ⟨link⟩ tag (World Wide Web Consortium, 1999c, 2000c). An annotation file can be associated with a single document file, but the relation is not limited to one-to-one. It is possible for multiple annotation files to be associated with a single document file, when each annotation file contains descriptions related to different portions of an annotated document. On the other hand, a single annotation file may contain an annotation description to be shared among multiple document files. This type of annotation would be useful when it is necessary to annotate common parts of Web documents, such as page headers, company logo images, and sidebar menus.

14.3 Annotation-Based Transcoding System

Since content can be adapted on a content server, a proxy, or a client terminal, an adaptation engine should not be forced to reside in any particular location. In order to resolve this potential limitation on adaptation engines, a proxy-based approach has been adopted for content adaptation (Fox and Brewer 1996; Schickler, Mazer, and Brooks 1996; Barrett and Maglio 1998; IBM Corporation 2001; Britton et al. 2001). Computational entities that reside along the Web transaction path are called intermediaries (Barrett and Maglio 1999), and existing approaches to annotation systems conform to a common abstract architecture based on intermediaries (Vasudevan and Palmer 1999).

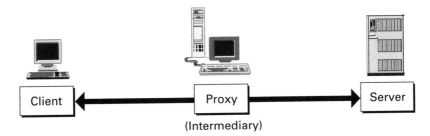

Figure 14.3
Intermediary between client and server.

14.3.1 Transcoding Architecture

As shown in figure 14.3, intermediaries are entities that reside along the path of information streams and facilitate an approach to making ordinary information streams into smart streams that enhance the quality of communication (Barrett and Maglio 1999). An intermediary processor or a transcoding proxy can operate on a document to be delivered and transform the contents with reference to associated annotation files. From a computational perspective, the use of an intermediary architecture is an approach to providing pluggable services between a Web client and server (Thompson et al. 1999). To put it another way, intermediaries provide special-purpose proxy servers for protocol extension, document caching, Web personalization, content adaptation, and so on (Barrett and Maglio 1998). The intermediary-based approach is suitable for content adaptation by means of external annotation, because the intermediary transcoding modules do not require changing the existing HTTP-based information streams.

14.3.2 Authoring-Time Transcoding

It would not be easy to create and revise annotations solely with a simple source tag editor. For example, addressing using XPath/XPointer requires following a hierarchy of document elements from the root to a focal element for the creation of an annotation, and it is also necessary for the annotator to

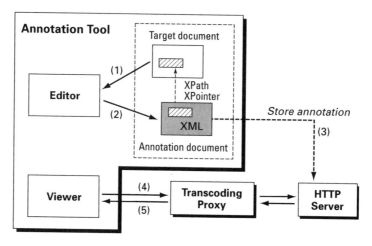

Figure 14.4
Authoring-time transcoding.

navigate from an existing annotation to a portion of an annotated document designated by a corresponding XPath/XPointer expression. Furthermore, it is substantially helpful if the results of content adaptation can be verified through a previewer. The results of adaptation are difficult to anticipate when it transforms the structure of an original document, and adaptation often has unexpected results due to inappropriate specification of the annotations. Therefore, transcoding needs to be done not only at run time, but also at design time on demand in the course of annotation authoring, so that the results of adaptation can be checked immediately.

The idea behind authoring-time transcoding is depicted in figure 14.4. An annotation tool consists of an editor for the creation and revision of annotations and a viewer to show the result of applying the annotations to a target document. The editor is employed not only to edit annotation descriptions, but also to specify a portion of a target document to be annotated. When an annotator creates an annotation file from scratch, a typical scenario of the authoring-time transcoding would be as follows. As shown in the figure, a target document is opened in the editor (1), which allows an annotator to create annotations (2). The created annotations are saved as an annotation file and then stored in an annotation repository or an HTTP server (3). When the viewer is invoked, a transcoding proxy is called over HTTP, and the corresponding annotation is applied to a target document (4). An adapted document is then sent back to the viewer for the display (5). If the adaptation results prove to be desirable in the view of the annotator, the annotation authoring can be continued to revise the annotations seamlessly in the same authoring environment.

Authoring-time transcoding is crucial when annotations are employed for content adaptation, rather than discovery or qualification of contents, because the content adaptation often changes the structure of original documents as the results of transcoding. In most annotation tools for HTML annotation, it is assumed that a target HTML document is solely displayed on an HTML browser and can never be edited (Erdmann et al. 2000; Nagao, Shirai, and Kevin in press; Sakairi and Takagi in press). On the other hand, there is an annotation tool that is fully integrated with a WYSIWYG HTML editor (Hori, Ono, et al. 2000) and allows users to annotate an HTML document as well as edit the document to be annotated.

Suitable configurations of annotation tools depend on the specifies of particular annotation situations. Browser-based annotation tools are desirable when annotators are not allowed to edit target documents without document ownership. On the other hand, an annotation tool based on a WYSIWYG editor is helpful when annotators are responsible for not only the creation of annotations but also the editing of target documents. Regardless of the variety of emerging annotation tools, a significant limitation of the current annotation tools is their lack of extensibility, which results from the fact that the existing tools were developed solely for a particular annotation vocabulary and provided with predefined views for the authoring. An annotation tool framework is currently being pursued in order to realize flexibility in the annotation tool configuration (Abe and Hori 2001).

14.4 HTML Page Splitting for Small-Screen Devices

The annotation framework mentioned above prescribes a skeletal structure of annotation, without regard to the specification of any particular annotation vocabulary and the behavior of any particular content adaptation module.

As an example of annotation-based transcoding, this section discusses an annotation vocabulary (World Wide Web Consortium 1999a) and a content adaptation module (Hori, Kondoh, et al. 2000) that splits HTML pages into smaller fragments to be displayed on small-screen devices.

14.4.1 Annotation Vocabulary

An annotation vocabulary for HTML page splitting needs to be specified to constrain the possibilities for decomposition, combination, and partial replacement of contents. The vocabulary presented here includes three types of annotation: *alternatives*, *splitting hints*, and *selection criteria*. A namespace (World Wide Web Consortium, 1999d) prefix ("pcd") is used for the transcoding vocabulary and another ("rdf") for the constructs of RDF. Further details on this annotation vocabulary can be found in (World Wide Web Consortium 1999a).

14.4.1.1 Alternatives

Alternative representations of a document or any set of its elements can be provided. For example, a color image may have a grayscale image as an alternative for clients with monochrome displays. A transcoding proxy selects the alternative that best suits the capabilities of the requested client device. Elements in the annotated document can then be altered either by replacement or by on-demand conversion.

14.4.1.2 Splitting Hints

An HTML file that can be shown as a single page on a normal desktop computer may be divided into multiple pages on clients with smaller display screens. A pcd:Group element specifies a set of elements to be considered as a logical unit and provides hints for determining appropriate page break points. For example, the annotation description in (a) in figure 14.5 indicates that the range of elements from the second occurrence of an H2 element through the first occurrence of a TABLE element is annotated as a group.

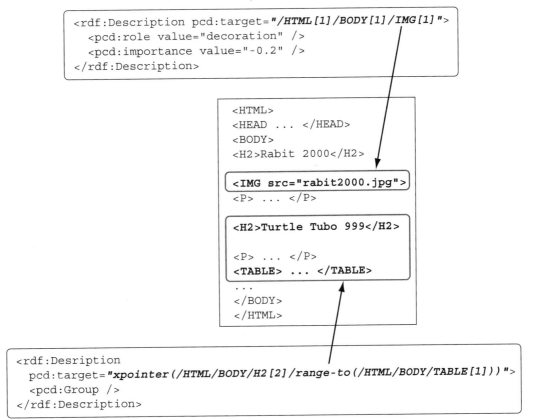

(a) Group annotation for a page-breaking point

Figure 14.5
Annotation descriptions.

14.4.1.3   Selection Criteria

An annotation may contain information to help a transcoding module select, from among several alternative representations, the one that best suits
the client device. A pcd:role element, for example, specifies the role of an
annotated element. This role element is provided with a value attribute,
which may be specified as proper content, side menu, or decoration, for example. A pcd:importance element specifies the priority of an annotated element relative to the other elements in the page. When the importance of an
element is low, for example, it may be ignored or may be displayed in a
smaller font. The importance value is a real number ranging from -1 (lowest
priority) to 1 (highest priority). The default importance value is 0. For example, when an element is designated as having a merely decorative role and is
assigned a low importance value such as -0.2, the element may not be sent
to a lightweight client. An example of such an annotation description is
given in (b) in figure 14.5.

14.4.2   Adaptation Engine

The HTML page splitting module presented here runs on an intermediary
server called WBI (IBM Corporation 2000b) that is a programmable processor
for HTTP requests and responses. It receives an HTTP request from a client
such as a Web browser and produces an HTTP response to be returned to the
client. Modules or plug-ins available at an intermediary processor control the
processing in between. A WBI plug-in is constructed from three fundamental
building blocks: monitors, editors, and generators (Barrett and Maglio 1998).
Monitors observe transactions without affecting them. *Editors* modify outgo-
ing requests or incoming documents. *Generators* produce documents in response to requests.

   An HTML page splitting module was implemented as a WBI plug-in (Hori,
Kondoh, et al. 2000). It adapts requested documents in accordance with the
capabilities of each client (figure 14.6). Hints for how a particular adaptation
should be accomplished are expressed using the annotation vocabulary dis-

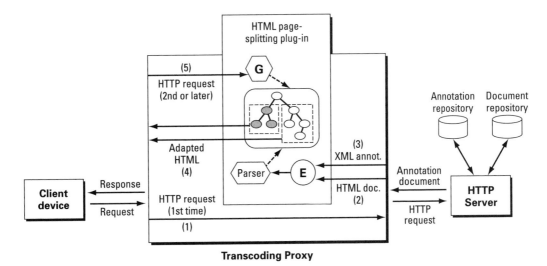

Figure 14.6
Annotation-based transcoding by a page-splitting plug-in.

cussed above and provided as external annotations. The execution sequence of the page-splitting plug-in is briefly explained below.

As shown in the figure, upon receipt of a request from a client device, an original HTML page is retrieved from a content server (1) and parsed into an internal data structure (2). The editor component of the plug-in then tries to find out the locations of the annotation files for the page. The editor component first checks whether a ⟨link⟩ tag is given in the HTML document and tries to look up a database of mappings from the URL of the HTML page to URLs of annotations. Annotation files are then retrieved from an annotation repository with reference to the URLs (3). The internal structure of the HTML page is elaborated, incorporating the retrieved annotation descriptions. Note that if no URLs of annotation files are found, the HTML page is returned as it is, and the session is terminated.

Taking into account client profile data included in the HTML request header, the generator component selects a portion of the document structure. The generator then creates and returns an adapted page that is split off as a separate page from the original page (4). When another fragment of the original page is requested, the generator component of the plug-in is activated (5). The generator examines the requested URL and determines which part of the original page is to be sent back. A split-off page is then created and returned to the client. Note here that each anchor element linking to another fragment of the same page must have an "href" attribute specified, with a special URL that is created by the page-splitting plug-in at run time. In the current implementation, such URLs include host names for the generator component and a session identifier for specifying the original page.

14.4.3   Application to Real-Life HTML Pages

This section shows the results of applying the page-splitting plug-in to real-life Web documents. The Web page used as an example is a news page from a corporate Web site (figure 14.7). Use of tables for page layout is inappropriate not only as regards making a clear distinction between style and content, but also as regards Web content accessibility. According to the W3C's accessibility guidelines (World Wide Web Consortium 1999f), content developers are encouraged to make contents navigable. In reality, however, table elements are employed for layout on a large number of HTML pages. The news page in figure 14.7 consists of three tables stacked from top to bottom, as depicted in the left panel of figure 14.8. The top and middle tables correspond respectively to a header menu and a search form. The bottom table, labeled as "Layouter (3)" in figure 14.8, is used for laying out the page.

The right panel of figure 14.8 illustrates how the news page will be fragmented in a small display. According to the header role of the top table in the original page, the same header appears in each of the split pages. The "[Side menu]" anchor in the center is created in accordance with the auxiliary role of the vertical sidebar menu in the original page. In contrast, because the importance value is "−1.0," the search form table is omitted in every split page. The main news content then starts after the "[Side menu]" anchor and allows users to access the primary content of the page directly.

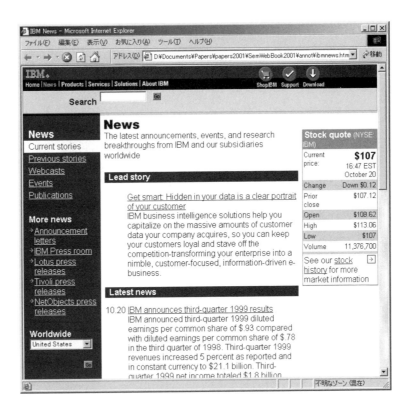

Figure 14.7
Layout of a real-life news page.

Figure 14.9 shows annotations associated with the news page discussed above. The annotation contains RDF descriptions specifying the roles of the tables. For example, the first description in the figure is about the top table, which is indicated by "Header (1)" in the left panel of figure 14.8. In accordance with the header role annotation, the page-splitting plug-in adds the table element as a header of every split page. In addition, the importance value "+1.00" indicates that this table element should not be omitted under any circumstances. The fourth description (d) in figure 14.9 concerns the left menu bar ("Side bar menu (31)" in figure 14.8). Since the role of this element is annotated as auxiliary, upon receipt of a request from a small-screen

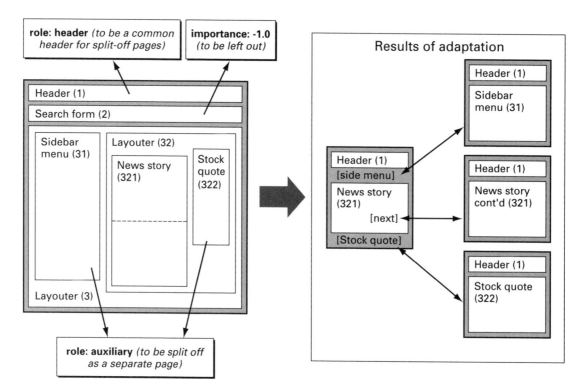

Figure 14.8
Annotation for fragmentation of the news page.

device, this portion of the news page will be presented as a separate page. On the other hand, the role of the bottom table in the news page ("Layouter (3)" in figure 14.8) is annotated as layout (c) in figure 14.9. Therefore, the bottom table will not be retained in the display for small-screen devices. The last description (f) annotates a table cell that is used solely for embedding a space for adjusting the page layout. The spacer role given to the table cell helps the page-splitting plug-in decide to remove the cell in small-screen devices. As shown in this discussion, annotations explicitly provide content semantics that may not be given in the original documents.

Figure 14.10 shows the same contents as in figure 14.7 displayed on an HTML browser in a small-screen device. The news page without content

```
<?xml version='1.0' encoding='utf-8'?>
<rdf:RDF
  xmlns:pcd="http://www.ibm.com/annot/pcd"
  xmlns:rdf="http://www.w3.org/TR/REC-rdf-syntax">

<!-- (a) Header -->
<rdf:Description pcd:target="/HTML/BODY/TABLE[1]">
  <pcd:role value="header"/>
  <pcd:importance value="+1.00"/>
</rdf:Description>

<!-- (b) Search form -->
<rdf:Description pcd:target="/HTML/BODY/TABLE[2]">
  <pcd:importance value="-1.00"/>
</rdf:Description>

<!-- (c) Layout table -->
<rdf:Description pcd:target="/HTML/BODY/TABLE[3]">
  <pcd:role value="layout"/>
</rdf:Description>

<!-- (d) Side menu -->
<rdf:Description pcd:target="/HTML/BODY/TABLE[3]/TBODY[1]/TR[1]/TD[1]">
  <pcd:role value="auxiliary" name="Side menu"/>
  <pcd:importance value="+1.00"/>
</rdf:Description>

<!-- (e) Stock quote -->
<rdf:Description pcd:target=
      "/HTML/BODY/TABLE[3]/TBODY[1]TR[1]/TD[2]/TABLE[1]/TBODY[1]/TR[1]/TD[3]">
  <pcd:role value="auxiliary" name="Stock quote"/>
  <pcd:importance value="+1.00"/>
</rdf:Description>

<!-- (f) Spacer -->
<rdf:Description pcd:target="/HTML/BODY/TABLE[3]/TBODY[1]/TR[2]/TD[2]">
  <pcd:role value="spacer:/>
</rdf:Description>

</rdf:RDF>
```

Figure 14.9
Annotations for splitting the news page.

(a) Original contents   (b) Adapted contents
without page splitting   with page splitting

Figure 14.10
Comparison of display on a small-screen device.

adaptation, presenting only the top ninth of the original content, is shown in (a). In contrast, (b) shows the result of adaptation by the page-splitting plug-in. It is important to note here that the page splitting not only reduces the content to be delivered but also places the primary content near the top of the fragmented page that is provided with navigational features. This result of adaptation follows the design guidelines for reducing scrolling during interaction with small screens: "placing navigational features (menu bars etc.) near the top of pages, placing key information at the top of pages, and reducing the amount of information on the page" (Jones et al. 1999, 58).

Small screens force users to scroll frequently, which may affect the accessibility of contents as well as the usability of devices. It has been reported that users with small screens are 50% less effective than those with large screens in completing retrieval tasks (Jones et al. 1999). Therefore, page fragmentation based on semantic annotation is more appropriate than page transformation done using solely syntactic information, such as removing white spaces, shrinking or removing images, and so on. Semantic rearrangement is one of the critical limitations of such a syntactic transformation approach. The navigational features achieved by semantic annotation are noteworthy from the perspective of Web content accessibility. The important point here is that semantic annotation helps the page-splitting plug-in make better decisions on how to adapt content appropriately for small-screen devices.

14.5   Discussion

14.5.1   Empirical Evaluation

Real-life Web documents cannot be the same for long but rather are updated and changed occasionally. Therefore, the feasibility of the external annotation approach relies on the robustness of an addressing expression annotating a portion of a target document. Such addressing expressions, which are described with XPath in this chapter, may encounter two types of problems when a target document is updated. One occurs when an addressing expression no longer points to any element of the annotated document. The other arises when an expression is forced to point to an incorrect element as the result of modification of the target document structure. The latter case would be difficult to detect, because the proper semantics of the original document are not represented explicitly in the annotation. The lack of explicit semantics is the motivation for semantic annotations. The integrity of the addressing location in problems of this second type is an important issue that requires further research and is beyond the scope of this chapter.

The first type of addressing problem is taken into account in the evaluation here. The robustness of the annotations for the news page (figure 14.9) is investigated with regard to gradual changes in the news page, considering the existence of a pointing node in the target document tree. Figure 14.11 shows a portion of the document tree of the original news page, with an indication of the nodes pointed to by the six annotation descriptions in figure 14.9. As the figure shows, the minimum depth of the annotated nodes is 2 ((a), (b), and (c)), and the maximum depth of the annotated node is 9 (e). The news page of the same URL was saved as an HTML file once a day for 60

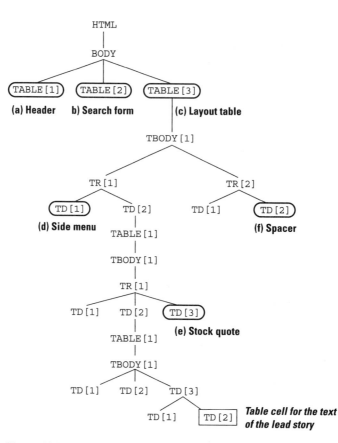

Figure 14.11
Annotated nodes in the news page.

days. The depth of the saved document trees was 22 and did not change throughout the 60 days.

Regardless of the unchanged maximum depth of the document tree, the news page itself was actually changed during the period. Figure 14.12 shows the numbers of changed nodes in each of the 60 saved pages against the original news page. Changed nodes were counted by calculating the difference between two document trees (alphaWorks 1999). The number of changed nodes was always greater than 20 after the first 10 days. The depth

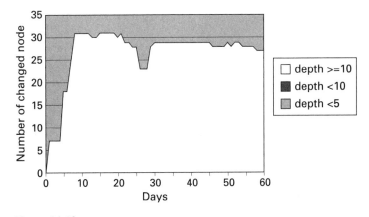

Figure 14.12
Number of changed nodes in the news page.

of the changed nodes is distinguished in figure 14.12. However, all the changes were made in nodes whose depth was greater than or equal to 10, whereas the maximum depth of the annotated nodes, as noted above, was 9. Therefore, the node changes had no effect on the locations of annotated nodes during the observed period. This statement is made merely based on the observation of a particular Web document during a limited period and can never be generalized to different situations. However, it is possible to draw from this observation an implication for tactics for making external annotations robust. The descriptions in Figure 14.9 are annotating auxiliary portions of the news page, such as the header, side menu, and stock quote table. Such auxiliary parts would not be subject to change so often as compared with the text contents of the news stories and their surrounding areas. The text of the lead story in the original news page was actually located in the table cell, whose depth was 13, as indicated at the bottom of figure 14.11. Furthermore, only one type of XPath expression was used in the annotations in figure 14.9, because that type of expression allows at most one node to be pointed at, regardless of the document structure. However, it is possible to provide other types of XPath expressions, taking account of the robustness of the addressing. This is also an important research issue that requires further investigation.

14.5.2   Comparison with Related Work

Although annotation-based transcoding is one approach to realizing content adaptation, it is possible to conceive of other approaches on the basis of the intermediary-based transcoding platform. One is to provide a custom-tailored transcoding module that runs without any external annotations. An automatic adaptation process has been proposed for device-independent access to Web contents. A heuristic planner, which searches a document transformation space, selects the most promising state that occupies the smallest display. It is reported, however, that in the worst case, the planner produces 80 versions of the document during the search process. If metadata or annotation is provided with the planner, the search space will be pruned more effectively. Note here that it is not an issue of whether metadata are embedded or external. The point is that metadata must be provided explicitly rather than implicitly in the adaptation algorithm.

Another possible approach is to use a general-purpose transformation engine such as an XSLT processor that employs externally provided transformation rules (World Wide Web Consortium 1999i). XSL Transformation Language (XSLT) rules can also be regarded as external annotations, because they can be given as a separate style sheet externally and each rule entails an XPath expression that points to target nodes to be transformed. The advantage of a general-purpose transformation engine is the broadness of its applicability, in contrast to the HTML page-splitting plug-in, for example, which is limited to the page-splitting task at hand. However, XSLT is more like a programming language than a declarative markup language. Therefore, authors of XSLT rules need to have in-depth understanding of programming using XSLT so that they can fully exploit the capability of the language.

In contrast, the advantage of a task-specific transcoding engine lies in the task-specific semantics that can be made explicit in the document definition of annotation vocabulary. To put it another way, adoption of a task-specific transcoding approach trades the scope of applicability in the general-purpose transformation approach for task-specific semantics articulated in the specification of an annotation vocabulary. In the case of the page-splitting plug-in, roles such as header, auxiliary, and spacer supplement semantics that cannot be prescribed in existing Web documents. In this sense, the importance of external annotation lies in the role of the mediating representation that articulates the semantics to be shared between human annotators and a content adaptation engine.

14.6   Conclusion

The external annotation framework presented in this chapter is applicable not only to transcoding for Web-enabled personal devices, but also to other cases in which content adaptation is desirable. For example, when HTML documents are translated into multiple target languages by means of a machine translation engine, linguistic annotations would be helpful for improving the translation accuracy (Nagao, Shirai, and Kevin in press). In other situations, content adaptation may be needed, so that user-side constraints can be taken into account.

Web content transcoding allows Web documents to be reused for purposes that are not necessarily anticipated by the original content creators. Taking account of situations of content repurposing, Web documents are not always developed with explicit semantics that are understandable by content adaptation software. The benefit of annotation as supplementary semantics is obvious for HTML documents, because they are encoded with a presentation markup, namely, HTML, for display on Web browsers. However, XML documents can also be the target of external annotation. Platform-independent markup languages have been investigated for the abstract specifications of Web applications (Gellersen and Gaedke 1999; Kitayama et al. 1999), XML user interface (Abrams et al. 1999), Web sites (Ceri, Fraternali, and Bongio 2000), and online interaction (World Wide Web Consortium 2001a). Such abstract specifications ultimately need to be specialized to become platform-dependent representations. Web content annotation is a promising approach for the specialization of abstract content, and the external annotation framework presented in this chapter is applicable to XML documents as well as HTML documents, as long as they are represented as instances of a document object model (World Wide Web Consortium 1998). Semantic annotation is thus a key to taking full advantage of Web contents, by means not only of repurposing existing, legacy contents, but also of elaborating platform-independent abstract content models for diverse needs involving content use.

Acknowledgments

This chapter has grown out of two papers: "Authoring Tool for Web Content Transcoding," by M. Hori, K. Ono, G. Kondoh, and S. Singhal, presented at Markup Technologies '99, Philadelphia, December 7–9, 1999; and "Annotation-Based Web Content Transcoding," by M. Hori, G. Kondoh, K. Ono, S. Hirose, and S. Singhal, presented at the Ninth International World Wide Web Conference, Amsterdam, May 15–19, 2000. The authors would like to thank the participants at both conferences, whose contributions have aided the development of this chapter.

References

Abe, M., and M. Hori. 2001. Visual Composition of XPath Expressions for External Metadata Authoring. Research Report RT-0406, IBM Research Laboratory, Tokyo.

Abrams, M., C. Phanouriou, A. L. Batongbacal, S. M. Williams, and J. E. Shuster. 1999. UIML: An Appliance-Independent XML User Interface Language. In *Proceedings of the 8th International World Wide Web Conference (WWW8), Toronto, Canada*, ed. A. Mendelzon (pp. 618–630). Amsterdam: Elsevier.

AlphaWorks. 1999. XML TreeDiff. IBM Corporation. Available from http://www.alphaworks.ibm.com/tech/xmltreediff.

Barrett, R., and P. P. Maglio. 1998. Intermediaries: New Places for Producing and Manipulating Web Content. In *Proceedings of the 7th International World Wide Web Conference (WWW7), Brisbane, Australia*. Available from www.dstc.edu.au/www7/.

Barrett, R., and P. P. Maglio. 1999. Intermediaries: An Approach to Manipulating Information Streams. *IBM Systems Journal* 38(4):629–641.

Britton, K. H., Y. Li, R. Case, C. Seekamp, A. Citron, B. Topol, R. Floyd, and K. Tracey. 2001. Transcoding: Extending E-Business to New Environments. *IBM Systems Journal* 40(1):153–178.

Ceri, S., P. Fraternali, and A. Bongio. 2000. Web Modeling Language (WebML): A Modeling Language for Designing Web Sites. In *Proceedings of the 9th International World Wide Web Conference (WWW9), Amsterdam*. Available from http://www9.org/.

Erdmann, M., A. Maedche, H.-P. Schnurr, and S. Staab. 2000. From Manual to Semi-automatic Semantic Annotation: About Ontology-Based Text Annotation Tools. In *Proceedings of the COLING 2000 Workshop on Semantic Annotation and Intelligent Content, Luxembourg*. Available from http://let.dfki.uni-sb.de/COLING2000/.

Fox, A., and E. A. Brewer. 1996. Reducing WWW Latency and Bandwidth Requirements by Real-time Distillation. In *Proceedings of the 5th International World Wide Web Conference (WWW5), Paris*. Available from http://www5conf.inria.fr/.

Gellersen, H.-W., and A. Gaedke. 1999. Object-Oriented Web Application Development. *IEEE Internet Computing* 3(1):60–68.

Heflin, J., and J. Hendler. 2000. Semantic Interoperability on the Web. In *Proceedings of Extreme Markup Languages, Montreal, Canada, August 13–18, 2000*. Available from http://www.gca.org/attend/2000_conferences/Extreme_2000/.

Hori, M., G. Kondoh, K. Ono, S. Hirose, and S. Singhal. 2000a. Annotation-based Web Content Transcoding. In *Proceedings of the 9th International World Wide Web Conference (WWW9), Amsterdam*. Available from http://www9.org/.

Hori, M., K. Ono, G. Kondoh, and S. Singhal. 2000b. Authoring Tool for Web Content Transcoding. *Markup Languages: Theory and Practice* 2(1):81–106.

IBM Corporation. 2000a. IBM WebSphere Transcoding Publisher Version 3.5 Developer's Guide. Available from http://www.ibm.com/.

IBM Corporation. 2000b. Web Intermediaries (WBI). Available from http://www.almaden.ibm.com/cs/wbi/.

IBM Corporation. 2001. WebSphere Transcoding Publisher. Available from http://www.ibm.com/software/webservers/transcoding/.

Jones, M., G. Marsden, N. Nasir, K. Boone, and G. Buchanam. 1999. Improving Web Interaction on Small Displays. In *Proceedings of the 8th International World Wide Web Conference (WWW8), Toronto, Canada*. Available from http://www8.org/.

Kitayama, F., S. Hirose, G. Kondho, and K. Kuse. 1999. Design of a Framework for Dynamic Content Adaptation to Web-Enabled Terminals and Enterprise Applications. In *Proceedings of the Sixth Asia Pacific Engineering Conference (APSEC '99), Takamatsu, Japan* (pp. 72–79). Los Alamitos, CA: IEEE-CS.

Lassila, O. 1998. Web Metadata: A Matter of Semantics. *IEEE Internet Computing* 2(4):30–37.

Mea, V. D., C. A. Beltrami, V. Roberto, and D. Brunato. 1996. HTML Generation and Semantic Markup for Telepathology. In *Proceedings of the 5th International World Wide Web Conference (WWW5), Paris*. Available from http://www5conf.inria.fr/.

Nagao, K., Y. Shirai, and S. Kevin. 2001. Semantic Annotation and Transcoding: Making Web Content More Accessible. *IEEE Multimedia* 8(2):69–81.

Rousseau, F., J. A. Macias, J. V. de Lima, and A. Duda. 1999. User Adaptable Multimedia Presentations for the World Wide Web. In *Proceedings of the 8th International World Wide Web Conference (WWW8), Toronto, Canada*. Available from http://www8.org/.

Sakairi, T. and H. Takagi. In press. An Annotation Editor for Non-Visual Web Access. In *Proceedings of the 9th International Conference on Human-Computer Interaction (HCI International 2001), New Orleans, LA*. Available from http://www.acm.org/sigchi/.

Schickler, M. A., M. S. Mazer, and C. Brooks. 1996. Pan-Browser Support for Annotations and Other Meta-Information on the World Wide Web. In Proceedings of the 5th International World Wide Web Conference (WWW5), Paris. Available from http://www.9.org/.

Thompson, C., P. Pazandak, V. Vasudevan, F. Manola, M. Palmer, G. Hansen, and T. Bannon. 1999. Intermediary Architecture: Interposing Middleware Object Services between Web Client and Server. *ACM Computing Surveys* 31(2).

Vasudevan, V., and M. Palmer. 1999. On Web Annotations: Promises and Pitfalls of Current Web Infrastructure. In *Proceedings of the 32nd Hawaii International Conference on Systems Sciences, Maui, Hawaii*. Available from http://www.hicss.hawaii.edu/.

World Wide Web Consortium. 1998. Document Object Model (DOM) Level 1 Specification Version 1.0 (recommendation). Available from http://www.w3.org/TR/REC-DOM-Level-1/.

World Wide Web Consortium. 1999a. Annotation of Web Content for Transcoding (note). Available from http://www.w3.org/TR/annot/.

World Wide Web Consortium. 1999b. CC/PP Exchange Protocol Based on HTTP Extension Framework (note). Available from http://www.w3.org/TR/NOTE-CCPPexchange.

World Wide Web Consortium. 1999c. HTML 4.01 Specification (recommendation). Available from http://www.w3.org/TR/html401/.

World Wide Web Consortium. 1999d. Namespaces in XML (recommendation). Available from http://www.w3.org/TR/REC-xml-names/.

World Wide Web Consortium. 1999e. Resource Description Framework (RDF) Model and Syntax Specification (recommendation). Available from http://www.w3.org/TR/REC-rdf-syntax/.

World Wide Web Consortium. 1999f. Web Content Accessibility Guidelines 1.0 (recommendation). Available from http://www.w3.org/TR/WAI-WEBCONTENT/.

World Wide Web Consortium. 1999g. XHTML Document Profile Requirements (working draft). Available from http://www.w3.org/TR/xhtml-prof-req/.

World Wide Web Consortium. 1999h. XML Path Language (XPath) Version 1.0. (recommendation). Available from http://www.w3.org/TR/xpath.

World Wide Web Consortium. 1999i. XSL Transformations (XSLT) Version 1.0. (recommendation). Available from http://www.w3.org/TR/xslt.

World Wide Web Consortium. 2000a. Composite Capabilities/Preference Profiles: Requirements and Architecture (working draft). Available from http://www.w3.org/TR/CCPP-ra/.

World Wide Web Consortium. 2000b. Style Sheets Activity Statement (user interface domain activity statement). Available from http://www.w3.org/Style/Activity.

World Wide Web Consortium. 2000c. XML Linking Language (XLink) Version 1.0 (candidate recommendation). Available from http://www.w3.org/TR/xlink/.

World Wide Web Consortium. 2001a. XForms 1.0 (working draft). Available from http://www.w3.org/TR/xforms/.

World Wide Web Consortium. 2001b]. XML Pointer Language (XPointer) Version 1.0 (working draft). Available from http://www.w3.org/TR/xptr.

15 Task-Achieving Agents on the World Wide Web

Austin Tate, Jeff Dalton, John Levine, and Alex Nixon

15.1 Introduction and Motivation

The World Wide Web currently acts as a vast electronic library, serving information and providing search facilities for accessing that information. However, given that the Web actually consists of a vast network of task-achieving agents (humans and computers), this conceptualization of the Web as a static pool of information is using only a small fraction of its real capabilities.

The idea of the Web's being a place where one can ask agents to *do* things and to *plan* activities seems intuitively attractive. However, the data models and standards developed to date for the Web mostly relate to information retrieval, rather than activity and the planning of future activity. To make the Web a place for "doing things" as well as "finding things," we need shared models and ontologies to represent the entities involved in planning and doing: activities, tasks, plans, agent capabilities, and so on.

The AI-planning and the process-modeling communities have recently started to develop standards in these areas for the purpose of working on common models and sharing information about activities and processes (Tate 1998). These common models and ontologies might form the generic core of a shared ontology to support the movement of information and data relating to activities over the World Wide Web.

This paper has two parts. In the first part, we describe work toward the creation of a common ontology and representation for plans, processes, and other information related to activity. We briefly describe the work being carried out in two areas: military planning and standards for representing activities and processes.

Our own systems are based on an underlying activity ontology called ⟨I-N-OVA⟩;[1] the chapter describes this ontology, together with the more general ⟨I-N-CA⟩ constraint-based model for representing synthesised artifacts. In both of these models, the "I" stands for *issues*, which allows us to represent synthesised artifacts that are not yet complete or that have some outstanding issues to address. The list of outstanding issues is crucial in the communication of partial results between agents, which is clearly needed in multiagent systems that work together to synthesize solutions.

In the second part of the chapter, we describe our work on producing collaborative multiagent systems consisting of human and computer agents engaging in planning and plan execution support over the World Wide Web. These applications are based on a generic interface for Web-based task-achieving agents called Open Planning Process Panels (O-P^3) (Levine, Tate, and Dalton 2000). These panels are described briefly to introduce the work that follows. Three Web-based applications are then described: the O-Plan Web demonstration, the Air Campaign Planning Process Panel (ACP^3), and a version of O-Plan that can run over the Web using a Wireless Application Protocol–enabled mobile telephone. These applications are indicative of the kind of systems that we believe will be deployed in the near future, in which the Web site acts as an interface to one or more intelligent agents and the common representation of activity-related information is crucial.

15.2 Standards for Representing Activities

There are two major stands of work in the area of creating a common ontology and representation for plans, processes, and other information related to activity. In military planning, there has already been much work in developing shared models for planning and representing plans, such as the KRSL plan representation language, Core Plan Representation (CPR), and Shared Planning and Activity Representation (SPAR).

At the same time, work in the standards community has attempted to standardize the terminology for talking about activities and processes: examples include the Process Interchange Format (PIF), NIST Process Specification Language (PSL), and work by the Workflow Management Coalition (WfMC).

Tate 1998 gives an overview and history of all these efforts and shows their relationship to SPAR, developed under the DARPA and U.S. Air Force Research Laboratory Planning Initiative (ARPI). Full references are provided in Tate 1998.

Our own systems are based on the ⟨I-N-OVA⟩[3] activity ontology; this ontology relates well to the other ontologies of activity described above, such as SPAR, and can be considered an abstract model that can underlie these. The ⟨I-N-OVA⟩ model is described in the following sections, together with the more general ⟨I-N-CA⟩ model for representing synthesised artifacts.

15.2.1 ⟨*I-N-OVA*⟩ *and* ⟨*I-N-CA*⟩

This section presents an approach to representing and manipulating plans and other synthesised artifacts in the form of a set of constraints. The ⟨I-N-OVA⟩ (Issues–Nodes–Orderings/Variables/Auxiliary) constraints model is used to characterize plans and processes. The more general ⟨I-N-CA⟩ (Issues–Nodes–Critical/Auxiliary) constraints model can be used for wider applications in design, configuration, and other tasks that can be characterized as the synthesis and maintenance of an artifact or product.

15.2.2 *Motivation*

As shown in figure 15.1, the ⟨I-N-OVA⟩ and ⟨I-N-CA⟩ constraint models are intended to support a number of different uses:

- for automatic manipulation of plans and other synthesized artifacts and to act as an ontology to underpin such use

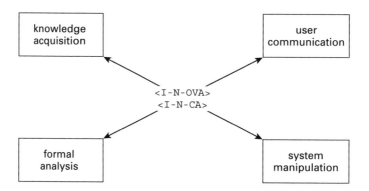

Figure 15.1
Uses of ⟨I-N-OVA⟩ and ⟨I-N-CA⟩.

- as a common basis for human communication about plans and other synthesized artifacts

- as a target for principled and reliable acquisition of plans, models, and product information

- to support formal reasoning about plans and other synthesized artifacts

These uses cover both formal and practical requirements and encompass the requirements for both human and computer-based planning and design systems.

The ⟨I-N-OVA⟩ model is a means of representing plans and activity as a set of constraints. By describing clearly the different components within plans, the model allows for plans to be manipulated and used separately from the environments in which they are generated. The underlying thesis is that activity can be represented using a set of constraints on the behaviors possible in the domain being modeled and that activity communication can take place through the interchange of such constraint information.

When first designed (Tate 1996b), ⟨I-N-OVA⟩ had to act as a bridge to improve dialogue between a number of communities working on formal planning theories, practical planning systems, and systems engineering process management methodologies. It was intended to support new work then

```
Plan Constraints
 I - Issues (Implied Constraints)
 N   - Node Constraints (on Activities)
OVA - Detailed Constraints
  O - Ordering Constraints
  V - Variable Constraints
  A - Auxiliary Constraints
    - Authority Constraints
    - Condition Constraints
    - Resource Constraints
    - Spatial Constraints
      - Miscellaneous Constraints
```

Figure 15.2
⟨I-N-OVA⟩ constraint model of activity.

emerging on automatic manipulation of plans, human communication about plans, principled and reliable acquisition of plan information, mixed-initiative planning, and formal reasoning about plans. It has since been used as the basis for a number of research efforts, practical applications, and emerging international standards for plan and process representations. (For some of the history and relationships between earlier work in AI on plan representations, work from the process and design communities and the standards bodies, and the part that ⟨I-N-OVA⟩ played in this, see Tate 1998.)

15.2.3   *Representing Plans in ⟨I-N-OVA⟩*

A plan is represented in ⟨I-N-OVA⟩ as a set of constraints (figure 15.2) that together limit the behavior that is desired when the plan is executed. The set of constraints are of three principal types, with a number of subtypes reflecting practical experience in a number of planning systems.

The node constraints (these are often of the form "include activity") in the ⟨I-N-OVA⟩ model set the space within which a plan may be further constrained. The I (issues) and OVA constraints restrict the plans within that space that are valid. Ordering (temporal) and variable constraints are distinguished from all other auxiliary constraints, since these act as *cross-constraints*,[2] which are usually involved in describing the others, such as in a resource constraint, which will often refer to plan objects/variables and to time points or ranges. In Tate 1996b, the ⟨I-N-OVA⟩ model is used to characterize the plan representation used within O-Plan (Currie and Tate 1991; Tate, Drabble, and Dalton 1994) and is related to the plan refinement planning method used in O-Plan.

We have generalized the ⟨I-N-OVA⟩ approach to design and configuration tasks with I, N, and CA components, where C represents the "critical constraints" in any particular domain, much as certain O and V constraints do in a planning domain. We believe the approach is valid in design and synthesis tasks more generally: we consider planning to be a limited type of design activity. ⟨I-N-CA⟩ is used as an underlying ontology for the I-X project.[3]

15.2.4   Rationale for the Categories of Constraints within ⟨I-N-OVA⟩

Planning is the making of planning decisions (I) that select activities to perform (N) that create, modify, or use the plan objects or products (V) at the correct time (O) within the authority, resources, and other constraints specified (A). The issues (I) constraints are the items on which selection of plan modification operators is made in agenda-based planners (see figure 15.3).

Others have recognized the special nature of the inclusion of activities in a plan compared to all the other constraints that may be described. Khambhampati and Srivastava (1996) differentiate plan modification operators into "progressive refinements," which can introduce new actions into the plan, and "nonprogressive refinements," which merely partition the search space with existing sets of actions in the plan. They call the former genuine planning refinement operators and think of the latter as providing the scheduling component.

If we consider the process of planning as a large constraint satisfaction task, we may try to model it as a constraint satisfaction problem (CSP) represented by a set of variables to which we have to give a consistent assignment of values. In this case we can note that the addition of new nodes ("include activity" constraints in ⟨I-N-OVA⟩) is the only constraint that can

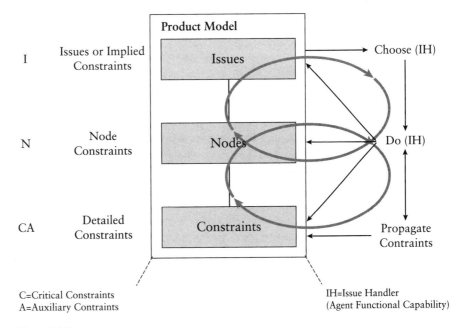

Figure 15.3
I-X: Two cycles of processing—Handle issues, respect constraints.

add variables dynamically to the CSP. The I constraints may be separated into two kinds: those that may (directly or indirectly) add nodes to the plan and those that cannot. The I constraints that can lead to the inclusion of new nodes are of a different nature in the planning process from those that cannot.

Ordering (temporal) and variable constraints are distinguished from all other auxiliary constraints, since these act as cross-constraints, which as noted above are usually involved in describing the others.

15.2.5   *Sorted First-Order Logic Base and XML*

⟨I-N-OVA⟩ and ⟨I-N-CA⟩ are meant as conceptual models that can underlie any of a range of languages that can describe activities, plans, processes, and other synthesised artifacts. For example, O-Plan is based on ⟨I-N-OVA⟩ but utilizes the Task Formalism domain description language, which has a simple keyword-introduced syntax.

It is expected that any ⟨I-N-OVA⟩ or more general ⟨I-N-CA⟩ model, in whatever language or format it is expressed, can be reduced to a conjunctive set of statements in first-order logic with strong requirements on the type of the terms involved in each statement (i.e., a sorted first-order logic). (See Polyak and Tate in press for further details and for description of a use in a planning domain modelling support system.)

⟨I-N-OVA⟩ and ⟨I-N-CA⟩ constraint sets lend themselves very well to being used in XML representations of synthesized artifacts, especially when these are still in the process of being designed or synthesized. The processes that are used to perform this synthesis and the collaborations and capabilities involved can also be described in ⟨I-N-OVA⟩ and/or ⟨I-N-CA⟩.

15.3 Web-Based Applications

15.3.1 Open Planning Process Panels

Real-world planning is a complicated business. Courses of action to meet a given situation are constructed collaboratively among teams of people using many different pieces of software. The people in the teams will have different roles, and the software will be used for different purposes, such as planning, scheduling, plan evaluation, and simulation. Alternative plans will be developed, compared, and evaluated. In general, planning is an example of a multiuser, multiagent collaboration in which different options for the synthesis of a solution to given requirements are explored.

The process of planning is itself the execution of a plan, with agents acting in parallel, sharing resources, communicating results, and so on. This planning process can be made explicit and used as a central device for workflow coordination and visualization.

We have used this idea to create O-P^3. These panels are used to coordinate the workflow between multiple agents and to visualize the development and evaluation of multiple courses of action (COAs). The generic notion of O-P^3 has been used to implement an O-Plan two-user mixed-initiative planning Web demonstration and an ACP^3. In the former, O-P^3 technology is used to enable the development and evaluation of multiple COAs by a commander, a planning staff member, and the O-Plan automated planning agent. In the latter, O-P^3 is used to build a visualization panel for a complex multiagent planning and evaluation demonstration that incorporates 11 different software components and involves several users.

O-P^3 technology could have an impact on several important research areas:

- *Automated planning.* O-P^3 shows how automated planning aids such as AI planners can be used within the context of a wider workflow involving other system agents and human users.

- *Computer-supported cooperative work.* O-P^3 uses explicit models of collaborative planning workflow to coordinate the overall effort of constructing and evaluating different courses of action. This is generalizable to other team-based synthesis tasks using activity models of the task in question (e.g., design or configuration).

- *Multiagent mixed-initiative planning.* O-P^3 facilitates the sharing of actions in the planning process among different human and system agents and allows for agents to take the initiative within the roles that they play and the authority that they have (Tate 1993).

- *Workflow support.* O-P^3 provides support for the workflow of human and system agents working together to create courses of action. The workflow and the developing artifact (i.e., the course of action) can be visualized and guided using O-P^3 technology.

We envisage O-P^3 being used in the kind of planning system in which the planning is performed by a team of people and a collection of computer-based planning agents who act together to solve a hard, real-world planning problem. Both the human and the software agents will act in given roles and will be constrained by what they are authorized to do, but they will also have the ability to work under their own initiative and volunteer results when this is appropriate. When the planning process is underway, the agents will typically be working in parallel on distinct parts of the plan synthesis. The agents will also be working in parallel to explore different possible courses of action; for example, while one COA is being evaluated, another two may be in the process of being synthesized.

This section introduces O-P^3 technology. It begins with a description of generic O-P^3 ideas, based on the central notion of an explicit shared model of the activities involved in creating a plan: the planning process.

15.3.2   Generic O-P^3 Technology

Generic O-P^3 is based on an explicit model of the planning process, which is encoded using an activity modeling language, such as ⟨I-N-OVA⟩. This represents the planning process as a partially ordered network of actions, with some actions having expansions down to a finer level of detail (i.e., to another partially ordered network).

The purpose of O-P^3 is to display the status of the steps in the planning process to the users, to allow the users to compare the products of the planning process (i.e., the courses of action) and to allow the users to control the next steps on the "workflow fringe" (i.e., what actions are possible next given the current status of the planning process). In the context of creating plans, O-P^3 is designed to allow the development of multiple courses of action and the evaluation of those courses of action using various plan evaluations.

A generic O-P^3 panel would have any of a number of "subpanels," which can be tailored to support specific users or user roles. These include

1. a course of action comparison matrix showing
• COAs versus elements of evaluation, with the plan evaluations being provided by plug-in plan evaluators or plan evaluation agents
• the steps in the planning process (from the explicit process model), the current status of those steps (the *state model*), and control by the human agent of what action to execute next

- the *issues* outstanding for a COA that is being synthesized, which must be addressed before the COA is ready to execute

2. a graphical display showing the status of the planning process as a PERT chart, which is a useful alternative view of the planning process to that given by the tabular matrix display

3. other visualisations, such as bar charts, intermediate process product descriptions, and textual description of plans.

The generic methodology for building Open Planning Process Panels consists of the following steps:

1. Consider the agents (human and system) involved in the overall process of planning. Assign roles and authorities to these agents.

2. Construct an activity model of the planning process, showing the partial ordering and decomposition of the actions and which agents can carry out which actions. This activity model can be represented using an activity-modeling language such as ⟨I-N-OVA⟩.

3. Build a model of the current state of the planning process and an activity monitor that will update this state model as actions in the planning process take place.

4. Construct appropriate O-P^3 interfaces for each of the human agents in the planning process, taking into account the role they play in the interaction. This means that each different user role will have an O-P^3 interface that is tailored to the overall nature of their task.

The O-P^3 agent interfaces then allow the human agents to play their part in the overall planning process, alongside the system agents, which will be AI planners, schedulers, plan evaluators, and so on. This is illustrated in figure 15.4.

15.4   Application 1: O-Plan on the Web

The O-Plan project (Tate, Drabble, and Dalton 1996; Tate, Dalton, and Levine 1998) was concerned with providing support for mixed-initiative planning.

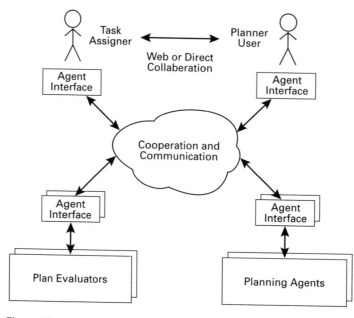

Figure 15.4
Using O-P³ interfaces.

The Web-based demonstration described here[4] shows interaction between two human agents and one software planning agent (the O-Plan plan server). The overall concept for our demonstrations of O-Plan acting in a mixed-initiative, multiagent environment is to have humans and systems working together to populate the COA matrix component of the O-P³ interface.

As shown in figure 15.5, we envisage two human agents, acting in the user roles of Task Assigner (TA) and Planner, working together to explore possible solutions to a problem and making use of automated planning aids to do this. Figure 15.6 shows how the two human agents work together to populate the COA matrix. The TA sets the requirements for a particular course of action (i.e., what top level tasks must be performed), selects appropriate evaluation criteria for the resulting plans, and decides which courses of action to prepare for briefing. The Planner works with O-Plan to explore and refine the different possible course of action for a given set of top-level require-

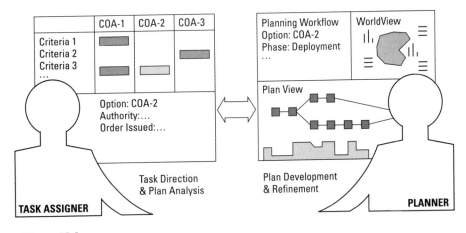

Figure 15.5
Communication between TA and Planner.

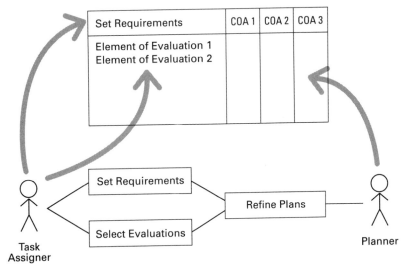

Figure 15.6
Roles of the TA and Planner.

ments. The two users can work in parallel, as is demonstrated in the example scenario (Levine, Tate, and Dalton 2000).

The overall planning task is thus shared between three agents who act in distinct user and system roles. The Task Assigner is a commander who is given a crisis to deal with and who needs to explore some options. This person will be given field reports on the developing crisis and environmental conditions. The Planner is a member of staff whose role is to provide the TA with plans that meet the specified criteria. In doing this, the Planner will make use of the O-Plan automated planning agent, whose role is to generate plans for the Planner User to examine. The Planner will typically generate a number of possible course of action using O-Plan and return only the best ones to the TA.

For our current demonstration, we are using a general-purpose logistics and crisis operations domain that is an extension of our earlier Noncombative Evacuation Operations (NEO) and logistics-related domains (Reece et al. 1993). This domain, together with the O-Plan Task Formalism implementation, is described in detail by Tate, Dalton, and Levine (1998).

The two human users are provided with individual O-P^3 panels that are implemented using a CGI-initiated HTTP server in Common Lisp and therefore run on any World Wide Web browser—the Common Lisp process returns standard HTML pages. This way of working has a number of advantages:

- The two users can be using different types of machines (Unix, PC, Mac) and running different types of Web browser (Netscape, Internet Explorer, Hotjava, etc.).

- The only requirement for running O-Plan is a World Wide Web connection and a Web browser (i.e., no additional software installation is needed).

- The two users can be geographically separate. In this case, voice communication via telephone or teleconferencing is all that is required in addition to the linked O-P^3 interfaces.

The planning process for the TA and the Planner is made explicit through the hypertext options displayed in the process parts of the O-P^3 panels.

These are either not present (not ready to run yet), active (on the workflow fringe), or inactive (completed). Further parts of the planning process are driven by issues, which O-Plan or the plan evaluation agents can raise about a plan under construction and can be handled by either or both of the human agents. Because the planning process is made explicit to the two users through these two mechanisms, other visualizations of the planning process itself are not required. However, the products of the planning process (the COAs) are complex artifacts for which multiple views are needed.

The user roles are arranged such that the TA has authority over the Planner, who in turn has authority over O-Plan. This means that the TA defines the limits of the Planner's activity (e.g., plan only to level 2), and the Planner then acts within those bounds to define what O-Plan can do (e.g., plan only to level 2 and allow user choice of schemas). Other aspects of what the two users are authorized to do are made explicit by the facilities included in their respective panels.

15.4.1   The COA Comparison Matrix

The two O-Plan panels for the TA and Planner are shown in figures 15.7 and figure 15.8. Each user has control over the plan evaluation elements that are shown to enable her to choose the critical elements of evaluation. In the example application given later, the TA is interested only in the minimum duration and effectiveness, so only these elements are selected. On the other hand, the Planner wants a variety of data to enable her to pick the best COA, so all evaluations are shown.

The role of the TA is to set up the top-level requirements for a course of action. Once this is done, the COA is passed to the Planner, whose matrix is initially blank. The Planner then explores a range of possible COAs for the specified requirements and returns the best ones to the TA. When the Planner returns a COA to the TA, the column for that COA appears in the Task Assigner's matrix. The Planner and the TA can be working in parallel, as demonstrated in the scenario.

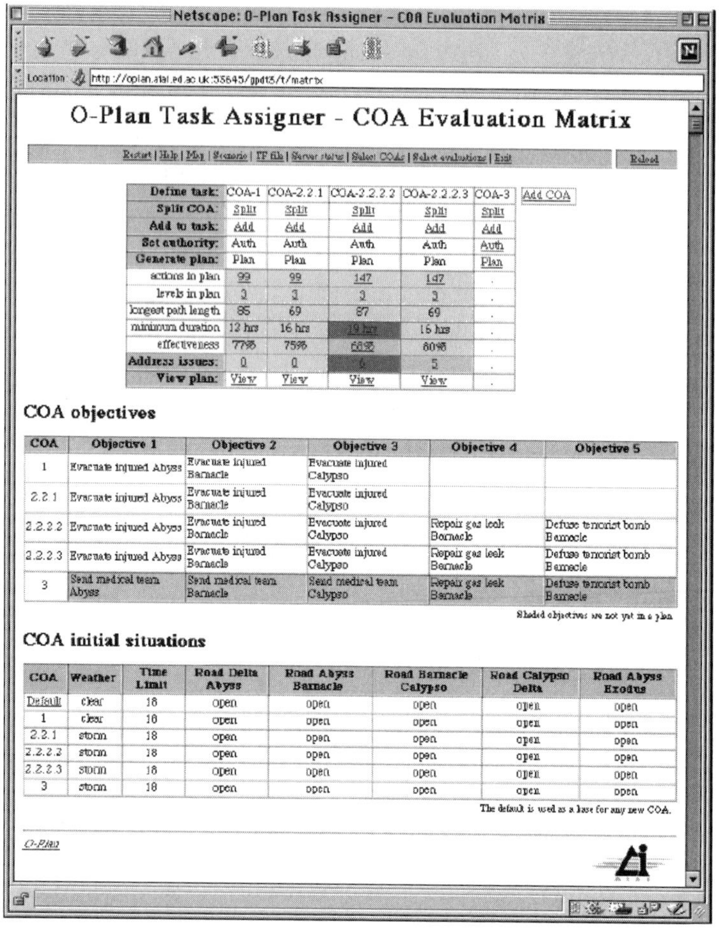

Figure 15.7
O-Plan TA's panel.

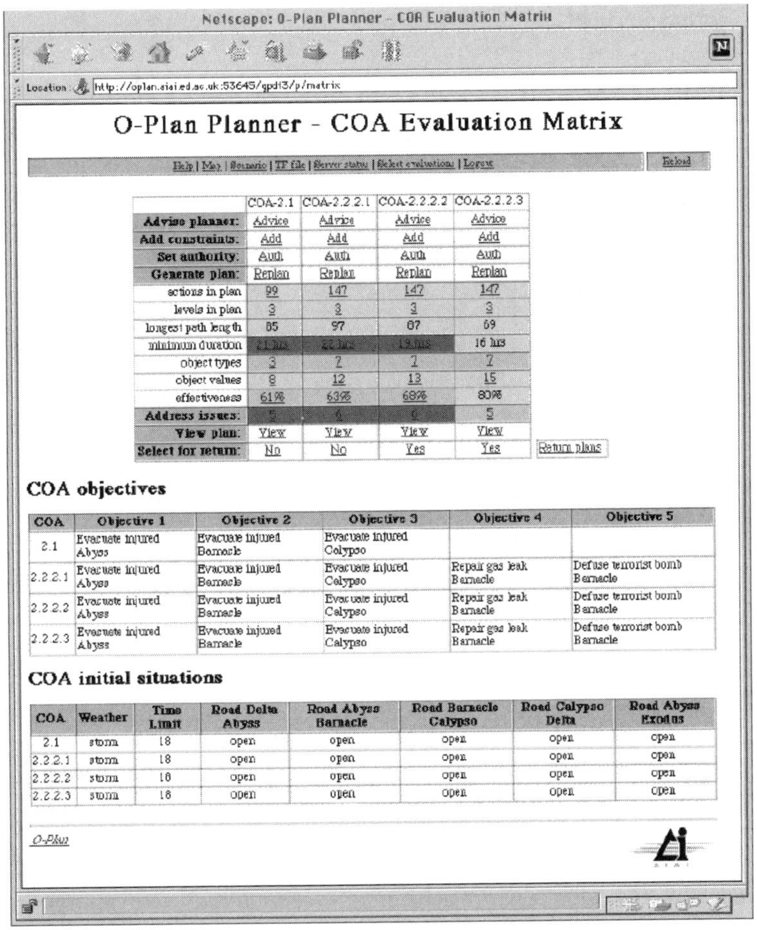

Figure 15.8
O-Plan Planner's panel.

15.5   Application 2: ACP³

One of the integrated demonstrations of O-P³ from ARPI (Tate 1996a) brings together eleven separately developed software systems for planning and plan evaluation. When the demonstration is run, these systems work together to create and evaluate multiple courses of action in the domain of air campaign planning (ACP). The systems communicate with each other by exchanging KQML messages (Finin, Labrou, and Mayfield 1997). Users could (in theory) find out what is happening at any given time by watching these KQML messages, but this was obviously less than ideal, as these messages use technological terms that are far removed from the terminology employed by the user community.

Our aim was to use O-P³ technology to build a visualization component for this demonstration that would allow the target end users to view the current state of the planning process in process terms with which they are familiar. This has resulted in the Air Campaign Planning Process Panel.

15.5.1   Modeling the Planning Process

The software components of the ARPI demonstration can be described as performing activities such as planning, scheduling, simulation, and plan evaluation. At a higher level of detail, we can talk about hierarchical task network planning and Monte Carlo simulation methods. However, end users are more likely to conceive of the processes of air campaign planning in more general, domain-related terms, such as "develop JFACC guidance" and "create support plan." The gaps in terminology and in levels of description can be bridged by building models of the planning process that are rooted in established ACP terminology. We have therefore made use of the previously elicited and verified ACP process models of Drabble, Lydiard, and Tate (1997) as our source of terminology and as the basis of our models of the planning process for the ARPI demonstration. The full models used for building ACP³ are described in Aitken and Tate 1997.

15.5.2   *Building ACP³*

The ACP³ viewer is shown in figure 15.9. The purpose of ACP³ is to track the overall planning process and display the results of this tracking to the viewers of the ARPI demonstration in a meaningful way using appropriate military process terminology. The planning process is shown in two separate sub-panels. The tabular COA comparison matrix shows COAs being developed (columns) against a tree-based view of the planning process. The graph viewer subpanel shows the planning process as a PERT network. Since the planning process consists of many nodes with expansions, the graph viewer can display only one individual graph from the planning process for one COA. Other graphs may be accessed by clicking on nodes with expansions, and the end user can choose which COA to view.

The two subpanels are required because the planning process in the ARPI demonstration is a complex artifact. It is possible to see the whole process for every COA in the COA matrix, but information about the partial ordering of the actions in a graph is lost when the graph is converted to a tree structure. The graph viewer shows the full partial ordering, but space considerations mean that only a single graph for a single COA can be shown at one time.

The ACP³ process monitor works by watching for certain KQML messages that it can relate to the status of certain nodes in the ACP process models. As the demonstration proceeds, the status of actions in the model progresses from white (not yet ready to execute) to orange (ready to execute), then to green (executing) and finally blue (complete). The final column in the COA matrix is labeled "overall" and summarizes the overall status of the COA creation and evaluation process. The panel is written entirely in Java to form the basis for future Web-based process editors and activity control panels.

15.6   *Application 3: WOPlan*

The aim of WOPlan (Nixon 2000; Nixon, Levine, and Tate 2000) was to create a mobile, limited media interface on the O-Plan system. What was envisaged was the case of a mobile human agent, equipped with a small, handheld

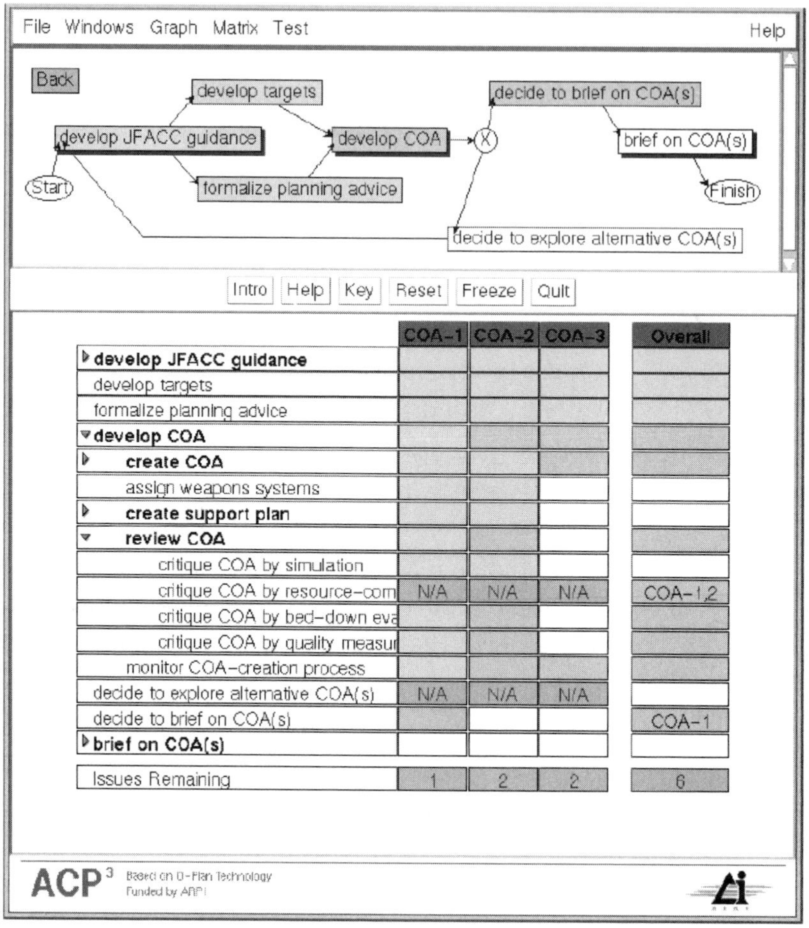

Figure 15.9
ACP[3] viewer.

wireless device, attempting to access a planning server to request some COA dependent on that user's current situation. Available Web-based demonstrations of O-Plan (Tate, Dalton, and Levine 1998; Levine, Tate, and Dalton, 2000) propose problem domains involving various military disaster relief and evacuation operations, and it was thought that a mobile telephone or personal digital assistant (PDA) could be a tool for plan delivery to mobile units in such a situation. Alternatively, a lone mobile user could access O-Plan to retrieve a plan to assist in a situation in which that user had insufficient experience. Someone who had no experience of engineering, for example, could retrieve a checklist to follow in the event of his car's breaking down. The utility of such a system would depend not only on the design of the system itself, but also on the identification of a suitable problem domain, in particular, a domain in which the users of the planner would be likely to be on the move and in need of a COA to solve an immediate task and otherwise with no access to more conventional interfaces such as PCs. The name WOPlan (for "Wireless O-Plan") was given to the system.

The design of a mobile interface for O-Plan is made more difficult by the limited screen sizes of mobile devices, especially in the case of the mobile telephone. Development of interfaces with O-Plan to date has allowed for the luxury of a full-sized terminal screen (Tate, Dalton, and Levine 1998; Levine, Tate, and Dalton 2000). Some issues of human-computer interaction that may not be critical when using a full-sized, color-terminal interface become problematic in the case of a limited-media interface. Generally users of mobile devices expect their interaction with the device to be brief, whereas users sitting down at a workstation are prepared for a more prolonged session. Browsing with a mobile device, especially with a mobile telephone, is (with current devices) slow and cumbersome; data entry is difficult and should therefore be kept to a minimum. A mobile telephone system needs only to be slightly poorly designed to be rendered unusable, especially if the system is attempting to serve long lists of data (such as delivering a plan description), as long pages increase download times and make navigation even slower and more frustrating.

WOPlan was developed as a Web application that communicates with an instance of the core O-Plan engine and delivers Wireless Markup Language (WML) to a connected client. The client may be any device that has a browser that conforms to the Wireless Application Protocol (WAP), such as a WAP-enabled mobile telephone (see http://www.wapforum.org/). The WOPlan Web application is a Java servlet. In development and testing the Nokia WAP Toolkit WML browser emulator (see http://www.forum.nokia.com/wapforum/) was used in place of a physical WAP device, and the servlet was hosted within the Tomcat Jakarta Web server (see http://jakarta.apache.org/tomcat/). The client initiates a session by connecting to WOPlan, which connects to the O-Plan server and initializes the service and provides the user (on the WAP device) with a list of available problem domains. The user is prompted to choose a planning *domain* (defined as a *Task Formalism* file), then to choose a *task* within that domain, and then to view, execute, or evaluate the resulting *plan* or to get a different plan that accomplishes the same specified task.

The architecture of the WOPlan system is shown in figure 15.10. The *WAP Client* is the component with which the WOPlan user interacts. The user activates WOPlan by initiating an Internet session on the WAP Client and navigating to the Internet address of the second component, the WOPlan servlet. The WAP client can be any device with a WAP-enabled browser and Internet connectivity, although WOPlan has been tested only in use with

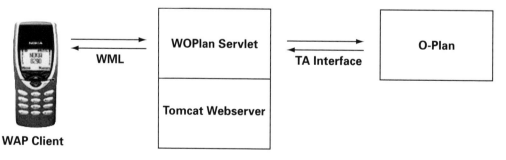

Figure 15.10
Architecture of WOPlan.

WAP emulator browsers running on a workstation. Noteworthy features are the very limited screen size (only four lines of text) and the user interface objects. Directly below the screen are two arrow buttons (used for scrolling up and down a WML page), between which is a single SELECT button (used for selecting whatever item is currently highlighted in the WML page). Below and to the left of the screen is the OPTIONS button, which, when available and selected, should display a context-sensitive list of options. Below and to the right of the screen is the BACK button, which, when available and selected, should navigate the user to the previous screen.

The *WOPlan servlet* sits between the WAP Client and the core O-Plan system. It accepts WAP requests from the client (or from multiple clients simultaneously) and communicates with O-Plan, initially connecting to O-Plan as required and sending and receiving messages through the the standard O-Plan Task Assignment interface.[5] The development work for the WOPlan system has focused on the WOPlan servlet; it is in this component that the logic specific to this implementation resides. The servlet dynamically creates WML pages, depending on the responses it is receiving from O-Plan, which are then sent to the WAP Client for browsing. These WML pages may themselves contain logic, such as navigational directives or actions to perform after a certain length of time has passed. Although these directives are executed by the WAP Client, their source is the servlet. The *O-Plan Server* sits in the bottom tier of the architecture, responding to requests from the WOPlan servlet.

In user trials (Nixon 2000), it was found that WOPlan provides reasonably stable, scalable, and usable access to the O-Plan system through a mobile telephone. Although it does not provide all of the functionality that O-Plan, and in particular the standard Task Assignment interface, has to offer, it does provide a useful subset of this functionality and has addressed the core issues of plan review and execution through the narrative and execution facilities (shown in figures 15.11 and 15.12, respectively).

Investigation of the possible use of properties specific to mobile devices was a secondary aim of the WOPlan project. Two such properties that have

Figure 15.11
WOPlan narrative display.

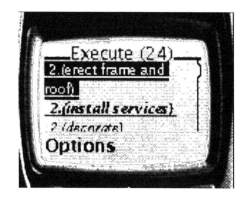

Figure 15.12
WOPlan execution display.

been discussed are voice technology and mobile positioning technology. No provision for voice or location integration exists in currently available WAP devices, although such capabilities will certainly become available in the near future. One possibility for the former would involve the use of VoiceXML, an XML variant intended to make Internet content and information accessible via voice and phone. VoiceXML has the backing of industry giants IBM, AT&T and Motorola. Motorola's *Mobile ADK* (see http://www.motorola.com/ spin/mix/faqs.html) is a development environment for integrating Voice-

XML and WML services. The provision of *location services* (LCS) as a standard for mobile devices is still currently at the design stage. It is likely that some kind of service based on GPS technology will be available to GSM (Global System for Mobile Communications, the current European standard) telephones in the near future.

The execution facility provided with this version of WOPlan is little more than a prototype, but it offers interesting possibilities for further development and research. It could certainly be improved, augmented, and made more usable within the context of the WOPlan system. Perhaps more importantly, however, its simple, ordered, one-dimensional format, with action items emphasized according to what may be done with those items, could provide a basic template for any system with a mobile limited media interface that is attempting to deliver COAs to human agents on the move.

15.7   Conclusion

In this chapter, we have argued that the World Wide Web should be seen as a place for "doing things" as well as "finding things." To make such a view of the Web possible, we need shared models and ontologies to represent plans, processes, activities, tasks, and issues. We have described work toward this aim, concentrating on the ⟨I-N-OVA⟩ constraint model of activity and the ⟨I-N-CA⟩ constraint model of synthesized artifacts. These models are designed to combine strengths from a number of different communities: the AI-planning community, with both its theoretical and practical system-building interests; the issue-based design community, those interested in formal ontologies for processes and products; the standards community; those concerned with new opportunities in task-achieving agents on the World Wide Web; and others. We have described three Web-based applications that use these models and have been implemented to "do things" on the Web: the O-Plan Web demonstration, the Air Campaign Planning Process Panel, and O-Plan use via a WAP phone (WOPlan). In the future, we envisage many more such applications, with the possibility that the individual planning applications can communicate with each other using the ⟨I-N-OVA⟩ issue-based and constraint-based models of activity described in this chapter.

Acknowledgments

The O-Plan and I-X projects are sponsored by the Defense Advanced Research Projects Agency (DARPA) and Air Force Research Laboratory Command and Control Directorate under grant number F30602-99-1-0024 and the U.K. Defence Evaluation Research Agency (DERA). The U.S. government, DERA, and the University of Edinburgh are authorized to reproduce and distribute reprints of this chapter for their purposes notwithstanding any copyright annotation hereon. The views and conclusions contained herein are those of the authors and should not be interpreted as necessarily representing official policies or endorsements, either express or implied, of DARPA, the Air Force Research Laboratory, the U.S. government, DERA, or the University of Edinburgh.

Notes

1. ⟨I-N-OVA⟩ is pronounced with a long "a" sound, as in the first six letters of "innovate."

2. Temporal (or spatiotemporal) and object constraints are cross-constraints specific to the planning task. The cross-constraints in other domains may be other types of constraints.

3. I-X is the successor project to O-Plan; see http://www.aiai.ed.ac.uk/project/ix/.

4. The reader can try this demonstration out for herself at http://www.aiai.ed.ac.uk/project/oplan/.

5. This is the standard API provided for external programs to communicate with O-Plan.

References

Aitken, S., and A. Tate. 1997. Process Modeling of the TIE 97-1 Demonstration: Modeling Complex Techniques Using ACP Terminology. ISAT Technical Report ISAT-AIAI/TR/6, Version 1. Available from http://www.aiai.ed.ac.uk/~arpi/.

Currie, K. W., and A. Tate. 1991. O-Plan: The Open Planning Architecture. *Artificial Intelligence* 51(1):49–86.

Drabble, B., T. Lydiard, and A. Tate. 1997. Process Steps, Process Product and System Capabilities. ISAT Technical Report ISAT-AIAI/TR/4, Version 2. Available from http://www.aiai.ed.ac.uk.

Finin, T., Y. Labrou, and J. Mayfield. 1997. KQML as an Agent Communication Language. In *Software Agents*, ed. J. Bradshaw (pp. 291–316). Cambridge, MA: MIT Press.

Khambhampati, S. and Srivastava, B. 1996. Unifying Classical Planning Approaches. ASU CSE TR 96-006, Arizona State University, Tempe.

Levine, J., A. Tate, and J. Dalton. 2000. O-P^3: Supporting the Planning Process Using Open Planning Process Panels. *IEEE Intelligent Systems* 15(5):56–62.

Nixon, A. 2000. Limited Media Interface for AI Planning System. M.Sc. Project dissertation, Division of Informatics, University of Edinburgh.

Nixon, A., J. Levine, and A. Tate. 2000. Limited Media Interface for AI Planning System. In *Proceedings of the 19th Workshop of the UK Planning and Scheduling Special Interest Group (PLANSIG 2000), Open University, Milton Keynes, United Kingdom*. Available from http://mcs.open.ac.uk/plansig2000/Papers.htm.

Polyak, S., and A. Tate. 1998. A Common Process Ontology for Process-Centred Organisations. Earlier version published as Department of Artificial Intelligence Research Paper 930, University of Edinburgh.

Reece, G. A., A. Tate, D. Brown, and M. Hoffman. 1993. The PRECiS Environment. Paper presented at the ARPA-RL Planning Initiative Workshop at AAAI-93, Washington D.C.

Tate, A. 1993. Authority Management: Coordination between Planning, Scheduling and Control. Paper presented at Workshop on Knowledge-based Production Planning, Scheduling and Control at the International Joint Conference on Artificial Intelligence (IJCAI-93), Chambery, France.

Tate, A., ed. 1996a. *Advanced Planning Technology: Technological Achievements of the ARPA/Rome Laboratory Planning Initiative (ARPI)*. Menlo Park, CA: AAAI.

Tate, A. 1996b. Representing Plans as a Set of Constraints: The ⟨I-N-OVA⟩ Model. In *Proceedings of the Third International Conference on Artificial Intelligence Planning Systems (AIPS-96)* (pp. 221–228). Menlo Park, CA: AAAI.

Tate, A. 1998. Roots of SPAR: Shared Planning and Activity Representation. *Knowledge Engineering Review* 13(1). Also available from http://www.aiai.ed.ac.uk/project/spar/.

Tate, A., J. Dalton, and J. Levine. 1998. Generation of Multiple Qualitatively Different Plan Options. In *Proceedings of Fourth International Conference on AI Planning Systems (AIPS-98), Pittsburgh, Pennsylvania* (pp. 27–34). Menlo Park, CA: AAAI.

Tate, A., B. Drabble, and J. Dalton. 1994. Reasoning with Constraints within O-Plan2. In *Proceedings of the ARPA/Rome Laboratory Planning Initiative Workshop, Tucson, Arizona*. Palo Alto: Morgan Kaufmann.

Tate, A., B. Drabble, and J. Dalton. 1996. O-Plan: A Knowledge-Based Planner and Its Application to Logistics. In Advanced Planning Technology: Technological Achievements of the ARPA/Rome Laboratory Planning Initiative (ARPI), ed. A. Tate (pp. 259–266). Menlo Park, CA: AAAI.

Contributors

Mark Adler
Nokia Research Center
Burlington, Massachusetts
USA
⟨mark.adler@nokia.com⟩
⟨http://www.alumni.caltech.edu/
∼madler/⟩

Richard Benjamins
Isoco
Madrid, Spain
⟨richard@isoco.com⟩
⟨http://www.swi.psy.uva.nl/usr/
richard/home.html⟩

Jeen Broekstra
Vrije Universiteit Amsterdam
Amsterdam, The Netherlands
⟨jbroeks@cs.vu.nl⟩
⟨http://www.cs.vu.nl/∼jbroeks/⟩

Monica Crubézy
Stanford University
Stanford, California
USA
⟨crubezy@SMI.Stanford.edu⟩

Jeff Dalton
University of Edinburgh
Edinburgh, Scotland
UK
⟨j.dalton@ed.ac.uk⟩
⟨http://www.aiai.ed.ac.uk/project/
ix/⟩

Ying Ding
Leopold-Franzens-Universitaet
Innsbruck
Innsbruck, Austria
⟨ying.ding@deri.org⟩
⟨http://www.deri.org⟩

Dieter Fensel
Leopold-Franzens-Universitaet
Innsbruck
Innsbruck, Austria
⟨dieter.fensel@deri.org⟩
⟨http://www.deri.org⟩
National University of Ireland
Galway, Ireland
⟨dieter.fensel@deri.org⟩
⟨http://www.deri.org⟩

Richard Fikes
Stanford University
Stanford, California
USA
⟨fikes@ksl.stanford.edu⟩
⟨http://www-ksl.stanford.edu/
people/bio/fikes.html⟩

Christopher Fry
Clear Methods, Inc.
Lynnfield, Massachusetts
USA

Yolanda Gil
University of Southern California
Marina del Rey, California
USA
⟨gil@isi.edu⟩
⟨http://www.isi.edu/~gil/⟩

Frank van Harmelen
Vrije Universiteit Amsterdam
Amsterdam, The Netherlands
⟨Frank.van.Harmelen@cs.vu.nl⟩
⟨http://www.cs.vu.nl/~frankh/⟩

Jeff Heflin
Lehigh University
Bethlehem, Pennsylvania
USA
⟨heflin@cse.lehigh.edu⟩
⟨http://www.cse.lehigh.edu/
~heflin/⟩

James Hendler
University of Maryland
College Park, Maryland
USA
⟨hendler@cs.umd.edu⟩
⟨http://www.cs.umd.edu/
~hendler/⟩

Masahiro Hori
IBM Tokyo Research Laboratory
Kanagawa, Japan
⟨horim@jp.ibm.com⟩

Ian Horrocks
University of Manchester
Manchester, England
UK
⟨horrocks@cs.man.ac.uk⟩
⟨http://www.cs.man.ac.uk/
~horrocks/⟩

Rob Jasper
Seattle University
Seattle, Washington
USA
⟨jasperr@seattleu.edu⟩
⟨http://fac-staff.seattleu.edu/
jasperr/⟩

Arjohn Kampman
Aidministrator Nederland bv
Amersfoort, The Netherlands
⟨arjohn.kampman@aidministrator.
nl⟩

Michel Klein
Vrije Universiteit Amsterdam
Amsterdam, The Netherlands
⟨mcaklein@cs.vu.nl⟩
⟨http://www.cs.vu.nl/~mcaklein/⟩

Ora Lassila
Nokia Research Center
Burlington, Massachusetts
USA
⟨ora.lassila@nokia.com⟩
⟨http://www.lassila.org/⟩

John Levine
University of Edinburgh
Edinburgh, Scotland
UK
⟨j.levine@ed.ac.uk⟩
⟨http://www.aiai.ed.ac.uk/project/
ix/⟩

Henry Lieberman
MIT Media Laboratory
Cambridge, Massachusetts
USA
⟨lieber@media.mit.edu⟩
⟨http://lieber.www.media.mit.edu/
people/lieber/⟩

Sean Luke
George Mason University
Fairfax, Virginia
USA
⟨sean@cs.gmu.edu⟩
⟨http://www.cs.gmu.edu/~sean/⟩

Alexander Maedche
Forschungszentrum Informatik
Karlsruhe, Germany
⟨Maedche@fzi.de⟩
⟨http://www.fzi.de/wim/people/
maedche/maedche.html⟩

Deborah L. McGuinness
Stanford University
Stanford, California
USA
⟨dlm@ksl.stanford.edu⟩
⟨http://www.ksl.stanford.edu/
people/dlm/⟩

Enrico Motta
Open University
Milton Keynes, England
UK
⟨E.Motta@open.ac.uk⟩
⟨http://www.kmi.open.ac.uk/
people/motta/⟩

Mark Musen
Stanford University
Stanford, California
USA
⟨musen@smi.stanford.edu⟩
⟨http://smi-web.stanford.edu/
people/musen/⟩

Alex Nixon
University of Edinburgh
Edinburgh, Scotland
UK
⟨http://www.aiai.ed.ac.uk/project/
ix/⟩

Borys Omelayenko
Vrije Universiteit Amsterdam
Amsterdam, The Netherlands
⟨borys@cs.vu.nl⟩
⟨http://www.cs.vu.nl/~borys/⟩

Shuchi Patel
University of Georgia
Athens, Georgia
USA
⟨shuchi@cs.uga.edu⟩
⟨http://www.cs.uga.edu/~shuchi/⟩

Mike Plusch
Clear Methods, Inc.
Wellesley, Massachusetts
USA

Amit Sheth
University of Georgia
Athens, Georgia
USA
⟨amit@cs.uga.edu⟩
⟨http://www.cs.uga.edu/~amit/⟩

Steffen Staab
University of Karlsruhe
Karlsruhe, Germany
⟨Steffen.Staab@ontoprise.de⟩
⟨http://www.aifb.uni-karlsruhe.de/
~sst/⟩

Lynn Andrea Stein
Franklin W. Olin College of
Engineering
Needham, Massachusetts
USA
⟨las@olin.edu⟩
⟨http://www.ai.mit.edu/people/las/⟩

Nenad Stojanovic
University of Karlsruhe
Karlsruhe, Germany
⟨nst@aifb.uni-karlsruhe.de⟩
⟨http://www.aifb.uni-karlsruhe.de/
WBS/nst/⟩

Rudi Studer
University of Karlsruhe
Karlsruhe, Germany
⟨studer@aifb.uni-karlsruhe.de⟩
⟨http://www.aifb.uni-karlsruhe.de/
Staff/studer.eng.html/⟩

York Sure
University of Karlsruhe
Karlsruhe, Germany
⟨sure@aifb.uni-karlsruhe.de⟩
⟨http://www.aifb.uni-karlsruhe.de/
WBS/ysu/⟩

Austin Tate
University of Edinburgh
Edinburgh, Scotland
UK
⟨a.tate@ed.ac.uk⟩
⟨http://www.aiai.ed.ac.uk/project/
ix/⟩

Sanjeev Thacker
University of Georgia
Athens, Georgia
USA
⟨sanjeev@cs.uga.edu⟩
⟨http://www.cs.uga.edu/~sanjeev/⟩

Mike Uschold
The Boeing Company
Seattle, Washington
USA
⟨michael.f.uschold@boeing.com⟩

Wolfgang Wahlster
German Research Center for AI
Saarbrücken, Germany
⟨wahlster@dfki.de⟩
⟨http://www.dfki.de~wahlster/⟩

Bob Wielinga
University of Amsterdam
Amsterdam, The Netherlands
⟨wielinga@swi.psy.uva.nl⟩
⟨http://www.swi.psy.uva.nl/usr/
wielinga/home.html/⟩

Index